SN-1541-1524

CONTEMPORARY
Hispanic
Biography

Profiles from the International Hispanic Community

Volume 4

Ashyia N. Henderson, Ralph G. Zerbonia, Project Editors

GALE®

THOMSON

GALE

Detroit • New York • San Diego • San Francisco • Cleveland • New Haven, Conn. • Waterville, Maine • London • Munich

Contemporary Hispanic Biography, Volume 4

Project Editors
Ashyia N. Henderson, Ralph G. Zerbonia

Editorial
Jennifer M. York

Permissions
Ken Breen, Margaret Chamberlain

Manufacturing
Dorothy Maki, Stacy Melson

Composition and Prepress
Mary Beth Trimper, Gary Leach

Imaging and Multimedia Content
Barbara Yarrow, Robyn V. Young, Leitha Etheridge-Sims, David G. Oblender, Lezlie Light, Randy Bassett, Robert Duncan, Dan Newell

ISBN 0-7876-7151-7
ISSN 1541-1524

Contemporary Hispanic Biography
Advisory Board

Lemuel Berry, Jr.
President
National Association of Hispanic and Latino Studies

Alan Nichter
Selection Services
Hillsborough County Public Library System, Tampa, Florida

Shirlene Soto
Author, professor, Department of Chicano(a) Studies
California State University, Northridge

David Unger
U.S. Representative
Guadalajara International Book Fair

Contents

Introduction ix

Photo Credits xi

Cumulative Nationality Index 227

Cumulative Occupation Index 229

Cumulative Subject Index 235

Cumulative Name Index 243

Acosta, Carlos 1
Vibrant ballet dancer

Alvariño, Angeles 4
Respected marine biologist

Arenas, Reinaldo 8
Revolutionary Cuban writer

Arrarás, María Celeste 12
Popular television journalist

Baca-Barragán, Polly 15
Colorado's first Hispanic woman state
senator

Baird, Lourdes G. 18
High-profile Circuit Court judge

Benitez, Elsa 21
Stunning super model

Big Punisher 23
First Latin-American Hip-Hop star

Brito, Maria 26
Acclaimed painter and sculptor

Bustamante, Cruz M. 29
Hard-working Californian politician

Cantinflas 33
Comedic Mexican actor

Carter, Lynda 36
Talented television actress

Cavazos, Richard E. 40
First Hispanic four star general

Cepeda, Orlando 43
Hall of Fame baseball player

Chavez, Linda 48
Passionate civil rights advocate

Chávez, Nick 53
Successful hair stylist

Cisneros, Marc 56
Multi-faceted army general

De Varona, Donna 58
Dedicated sports activist

Díaz-Oliver, Remedios 62
Unwavering entrepreneur

Dunbar, Huey 65
Ground-breaking salsa singer

Estés, Clarissa Pinkola 68
Self-discovering author

Estrada, Erik 73
Notable television actor

Favaloro, Rene 77
Devoted heart surgeon

Fernández, Emilio "El Indio" 80
Father of Mexican cinema

Francisco, Don 83
Beloved television host

García, Héctor Pérez 86
Legendary veteran's rights advocate

Gaviño, Juan Bosch 90
Prominent politician and author

González Márquez, Felipe 95
Progressive Spanish Prime Minister

Gurulé, Jimmy 98
First Hispanic assistant attorney general

Gutierrez, Carlos M. 102
Driven Kellogg executive

Guzmán, Alejandra 106
Bad girl of Latin pop

Hidalgo, Edward 109
First Hispanic U.S. Secretary of the Navy

Infante, Pedro 112
Mexican silver screen idol

Juan Carlos de Borbón y Borbón 115
King of Spain

Lagos, Ricardo..118
Outspoken Chilean president

Lamarque, Libertad 122
Prolific Argentinean actor and singer

Leal, Luis 125
*Founder of Chicano/Chicana literary
studies*

Lucero-Schayes, Wendy......................................129
Impressive Olympic diver

Mares, Michael A. 132
World's foremost desert life expert

Marin, Cheech 135
Versatile actor

Mármol, Miguel...139
Persevering union activist

Martinez, Arthur C. 143
Innovative business executive

Moneo, Rafael 147
Exceptional Spanish architect

Montoya, José 150
Chicano cultural movement leader

Ocampo, Adriana C. 154
Distinguished planetary geologist

Orlando, Tony 158
Entertaining singer and actor

Ortega, Daniel 162
Controversial Nicaraguan president

Ortega, Katherine D..166
Trailblazing U.S. Secretary of the Treasury

Pérez Esquivel, Adolfo 170
Nobel Prize winning activist and artist

Quiñones, John 173
Award winning television journalist

Ramirez, Tina..177
Ballet Hispanico founder

Richardson, Bill..180
Diplomatic politician

Rodriguez, Carlos Manuel 184
Beatified religious educator

Roman, Phil 187
Brilliant animator and director

Ros-Lehtinen, Ileana..191
First Hispanic congresswoman

Rubio, Paulina 194
"Golden Girl" of pop rock

Sabatini, Gabriela..198
Victorious tennis player

Santaella, Irma Vidal 201
*First Puerto Rican New York Supreme
Court judge*

Eligio Sardiñas 203
World champion Cuban boxer

Serrano, Lupe..205
Inspirational ballerina

Sheen, Charlie..209
Prodigal son of Hollywood

Soto, Gary..213
Exceptional children's author and poet

Tápies, Antoni 216
Spain's greatest living artist

Valenzuela, Alfred A...219
Prominent military officer

Wilcox, Mary Rose Garrido 222
Tireless Arizona county official

Introduction

Contemporary Hispanic Biography provides informative biographical profiles of the important and influential persons of Latino heritage who form the international Hispanic community: men and women who have changed today's world and are shaping tomorrow's. *Contemporary Hispanic Biography* covers persons of various nationalities in a wide variety of fields, including architecture, art, business, dance, education, fashion, film, industry, journalism, law, literature, medicine, music, politics and government, publishing, religion, science and technology, social issues, sports, television, theater, and others. In addition to in-depth coverage of names found in today's headlines, *Contemporary Hispanic Biography* provides coverage of selected individuals from earlier in this century whose influence continues to impact on contemporary life. *Contemporary Hispanic Biography* also provides coverage of important and influential persons who are not yet household names and are therefore likely to be ignored by other biographical reference series.

Designed for Quick Research and Interesting Reading

- *Attractive page design* incorporates textual subheads, making it easy to find the information you're looking for.

- *Easy-to-locate data sections* provide quick access to vital personal statistics, career information, major awards, and mailing addresses, when available.

- *Informative biographical essays* trace the subject's personal and professional life with the kind of in-depth analysis you need.

- *To further enhance your appreciation* of the subject, most entries include photographic portraits.

- *Sources for additional information* direct the user to selected books, magazines, and newspapers where more information on the individuals can be obtained.

Helpful Indexes Make It Easy to Find the Information You Need

Contemporary Hispanic Biography includes cumulative Nationality, Occupation, Subject, and Name indexes that make it easy to locate entries in a variety of useful ways.

Available in Electronic Formats

On-line. *Contemporary Hispanic Biography* is available on-line through Gale Group's Biography Resource Center. For more information, call (800) 877-GALE.

Disclaimer

Contemporary Hispanic Biography uses and lists websites as sources and these websites may become obsolete.

We Welcome Your Suggestions

The editors welcome your comments and suggestions for enhancing and improving *Contemporary Hispanic Biography.* If you would like to suggest persons for inclusion in the series, please submit these names to the editors. Mail comments or suggestions to:

The Editor
Contemporary Hispanic Biography
Gale Group
27500 Drake Rd.
Farmington Hills, MI 48331-3535
Phone: (800) 347-4253

Photo Credits

PHOTOGRAPHS AND ILLUSTRATIONS APPEARING IN *CONTEMPORARY HISPANIC BIOGRAPHY,* VOLUME 4, WERE RECEIVED FROM THE FOLLOWING SOURCES:

All Reproduced by Permission: **Acosta, Carlos**, photograph by Drew Donovan. Houston Ballet. **Alvariño, Angeles**, photograph. Arte Publico Press Archives, University of Houston. **Arenas, Reinaldo**, photograph. Liaison Agency. **Arrarás María Celeste**, photograph. Courtesy of María Celeste Arrarás, **Baca-Barragán, Polly**, photograph. AP/Wide World Photos. **Baird, Lourdes G.**, photograph. AP/Wide World. **Benitez, Elsa**, photograph by Jennifer Greylock. AP/Wide World Photos. **Brito, Maria**, photograph. Courtesy of Maria Brito. **Bustamante, Cruz M.**, photograph. Courtesy of Lt. Governor Cruz M. Bustamente. **Cantinflas**, photograph. Getty Images. **Carlos, Juan I**, photograph. The Library of Congress. **Carter, Lynda**, photograph. AP/Wide World Photos. **Cavazos, Richard E**, photograph. Courtesy of the U.S. Department of Defense. **Cepeda, Orlando**, photograph. Corbis-Bettmann. **Chavez, Linda**, photograph. AP/Wide World Photos. **Chávez, Nick**, photograph by Carrie Pike. Courtesy of Nick Chávez. **de Varona, Donna**, photograph. Bettmann/Corbis. **Dunbar, Huey**, photograph by J. Pat Carter. AP/Wide World Photos. **Estrada Erik**, photograph. Arte Publico Press Archives, University of Houston. **Favaloro, Rene**, photograph by Tony Gomez. AP/Wide World Photos. **Fernández, Emilio**, photograph. AP/Wide World Photos. **García, Héctor Pérez**, photograph by Larry Rubenstein. Corbis. **González Márquez, Felipe**, photograph. AP/Wide World Photos. **Gurulé, Jimmy**, photograph. Courtesy of Jimmy Gurulé, **Gutierrez, Carlos M.**, photograph. AP/Wide World Photos. **Guzmán, Alejandra**, photograph by Reed Saxon. AP/Wide World Photos. **Hidalgo, Edward**, photograph. AP/Wide World Photos. **Kreutzberger, Mario**, photograph. AP/Wide World Photos. **Lagos, Ricardo**, photograph by Roberto Candia. AP/Wide World Photos. **Lamarque, Libertad**, photograph. Reuters New Media Inc./Corbis. **Leal, Luis**, photograph. Courtesy of Luis Leal. **Lucero-Schayes, Wendy**, photograph. Courtesy of Wendy Lucero-Schayes. **Mares, Michael, A.**, photograph. Courtesy of Michael A. Mares. **Marin, Richard "Cheech"**, photograph. AP/Wide World Photos. **Mármol, Miguel**, photograph. AP/Wide World Photos. **Martinez, Arthur C.**, photograph by John Zich. AP/Wide World Photos. **Moneo, Rafael**, photograph. AP/Wide World Photos. **Montoya, José**, photograph by Szabo Photography. Courtesy of José Montoya. **Ocampo, Adriana C.**, photograph. Courtesy of Adriana C. Ocampo. **Orlando, Tony**, photograph. AP/Wide World Photos. **Ortega, Daniel**, photograph. Getty Images. **Ortega, Katherine D.**, photograph. The Library of Congress. **Pérez Esquivel, Adolfo**, photograph. Corbis-Bettmann/UPI. **Quiñones, John**, photograph by Rose Prouser. Reuters New Media Inc/Corbis. **Ramirez, Tina**, photograph by David Bazemore Photo. Courtesy of Tina Ramirez. **Rios, Christopher "Big Punisher"**, photograph by Tibor Bozi. Bozi/Corbis. **Rodriguez, Carlos Manuel**, photograph by Gabriel Bouys. AFP/Corbis. **Roman, Phil**, photograph by Robert Mora. Getty Images. **Ros-Lehtinen, Ileana**, photograph. AP/Wide World Photos. **Rubio, Paulina**, photograph by Chris Pizzello. AP/Wide World Photos. **Sabatini, Gabriela**, photograph. AP/Wide World Photos. **Sardinas, Eligio "Kid Chocolate,"** photograph. Arte Publico Press Archives, University of Houston. **Serrano, Lupe**, photograph. AP/Wide World Photos. **Sheen, Charlie**, photograph. Getty Images. **Soto, Gary**, photograph by M. L. Marinelli. Courtesy of Chronicle Books. **Tápies, Antoni**, photograph. Artists Rights Society, New York/ADAGP, Paris. **Wilcox, Mary Rose Garrido**, photograph. Courtesy of Mary Rose Garrido Wilcox.

Carlos Acosta

1973—

Dancer

In one of the last, largely un-integrated bastions of high culture, Carlos Acosta has been hailed as ballet's next major star. The Cuban-born dancer, of mixed Spanish and African heritage, came to prominence in the early 1990s while still in his teens, and esteemed dance companies in both North America and Europe began offering him lead romantic roles over the next decade. After a stint in Houston, Acosta joined England's Royal Ballet in 1998. With his fabled grace and athleticism, he has earned comparisons to Mikhail Baryshnikov or Rudolf Nureyev. A writer for London's *Independent* newspaper described Acosta as "a dancer who slashes across space faster than anyone else, who lacerates the air with shapes so clear and sharp they seem to throw off sparks."

Born in 1973, Acosta was the eleventh and last child in an impoverished Havana family whose home was in one of the rougher quarters of that city. His father was a truck driver, and his mother often suffered from health problems. The island nation of Cuba had become a socialist state after the 1959 victory by Marxist guerrilla leader Fidel Castro, but remained overwhelmingly poor. Acosta grew up with no toys, sometimes went shoeless, and did not even have a birthday cake until he turned 23. The streets of his neighborhood provided plenty of entertainment, however, and he spent his time playing soccer, break-dancing, and raiding nearby mango groves with his friends. He was an overly energetic child, and Pedros Acosta, his father, felt that his youngest son would soon land in serious trouble. Dance training at one of the state-funded schools, his father decided, would teach the boy discipline and provide him with a free lunch every day.

Had Early Troubles With Ballet Image

At the age of nine Acosta entered a school that served as a feeder for Cuba's National Ballet School. He had to wake at five a.m., then take three buses to get to after-school ballet class; sometimes he fell asleep on the bus, however, and missed his stop. Moreover, he found the ballet training very dull compared to Havana's lively streets, and worried what his friends would think. He began to skip classes outright, recalling that "I started to have problems because I thought ballet was sissy," Acosta told a writer for London's *Independent* newspaper. When his father learned of this, he punished him harshly. "He beat me with a belt, one time with a

At a Glance . . .

Born in 1973, in Havana, Cuba; son of Pedro Acosta (a truck driver) and Maria Quesada. *Education:* Attended ballet school at Pinar del Río, Cuba, and the National Ballet School of Cuba, Havana.

Career: English National Ballet, principal dancer, 1991-92; National Ballet of Cuba, principal dancer, 1992-93; Houston Ballet, principal dancer, 1993-98; Royal Ballet of England, principal dancer, 1998–; American Ballet Theater, New York City, guest dancer, 2002; guest dancer with companies in Munich, Stuttgart, St. Petersburg, and Athens, 2000s.

Awards: Prix de Lausanne, 1990.

Address: *Office*—Royal Ballet, The Royal Opera House, Covent Garden, London WC2E 9DD, England.

machete, another time with a cable," Acosta recalled in an interview with *Dance* writer Margaret Putnam. "Man, I was scared. I wanted to quit, but my father wouldn't listen. One time I told him, 'I want to be a normal person.' He took me to the balcony of our apartment and pointed to the people on the street below. 'You want to be like them, with no future?'"

Acosta was finally ejected from the school at age 13, but his teachers suggested another place that might take him; when he and his father arrived in the city of Villa Clara, there had been a mistake, and there was no chance of enrollment in its school. He and his father were forced to sleep in the bus station for two nights while waiting for the next bus home. Still determined, Acosta's father found a ballet school in Pinar del Río that would take his son, and it was a boarding school as well—which would make it harder for him to miss class. Moreover, some of his siblings lived in the city, so he could stay with them on the weekends. Teachers at the Pinar del Río school gave him a one-month tryout, and in those first weeks alongside other students, Acosta suddenly realized that he had a natural affinity for ballet. He began working much harder than he had before, and teachers were pleased with his steady progress.

The school also took a field trip to see a performance of the National Ballet of Cuba, and Acosta was surprised at how athletic the dancers were. "I realized I could touch people with ballet," he told *New York Times* journalist Anna Kisselgoff. "That's when I started to like it." He gained entrance into the prestigious National School of Ballet when he was 14, and quickly emerged as one of its most promising students. The school was considered, even on an international

level, an excellent training ground, for many of its teachers had benefited from rigorous Russian schooling—a legacy of the cultural ties between the former Soviet Union and Cuba. Acosta was able to travel outside of Cuba for the first time, taking part in an exchange program in Italy at the age of 16, and winning the 1990 Prix de Lausanne in Switzerland, one of ballet's most coveted honors.

Rose to Fame in Ballet World

In 1991 Acosta was offered a slot with the English National Ballet, but a bone spur injury in his ankle hampered his performance time in London. After surgery in Cuba, he joined the National Ballet of Cuba for its 1992-93 season. While on a tour of Spain, Acosta was approached by Ben Stevenson, director and choreographer of the Houston Ballet, and Stevenson offered Acosta—just twenty years old—to join what was one of leading companies in the United States. Acosta made his debut in Houston in November of 1993. Stevenson became an important mentor to Acosta, working with him to develop his repertoire in several lead roles, and the novice dancer thrived under the tutelage and came into his prime. He appeared in *Don Quixote, Dracula,* and *The Nutcracker,* and traveled to Europe for special guest performances.

Invited for a stint as principal dancer in fall of 1997 season with London's Royal Ballet, Acosta was slightly disappointed that he did not dance as much as he had hoped. After appearing in just eleven performances in one three-month span, he reflected in an interview with *Houston Chronicle* writer Molly Glentzer that the London scene was a far different one from the nurturing corps de ballet environment in Houston under Stevenson. "Who said ballet is easy?" Acosta reflected. "And sometimes it's not fair. You find there's a lot of politics. They don't give you the right part sometimes. But you keep pushing. You just have to show the right attitude." Still, Acosta did make enough of an impression on international balletomanes that some began deeming him the next Baryshnikov or Nureyev, perhaps the best known male ballet dancers of the twentieth century. In a 1997 article, *Dance* writer Putnam asserted that Acosta "has polish, power, and ease when launching himself into the air with apparently no preparation, tossing off yet-to-be-named steps that leave audiences dazzled. His turns are marvels, both for their number of revolutions and their control: After speeding up at will, he often slows the ending in an insolent display of cool."

As his repertoire widened, Acosta also won praise for his acting abilities. A fellow dancer, Paloma Herrera, told *WWD*'s Robert Haskell that Acosta's "presence is unbelievable when he goes onstage. He has a very powerful personality, but at the same time his dancing is clean and pure, so there's a wonderful contrast. As a ballerina, you feel very secure with him." Acosta has said that his biggest fear is dropping a ballerina during one of their lifts, and reportedly does a thousand push-ups daily in order to maintain the necessary upper-body strength.

Surprised by Success

In 1998 Acosta joined the Royal Ballet permanently, after an emotional farewell performance in Houston. He toured Japan and China with the Royal Ballet, appeared in Brazil, and still danced with the National Ballet of Cuba on occasion. The source of financial support for his family back in Cuba, Acosta once bought himself a new German luxury automobile—but realized that it cost more than his parents' Havana home and traded it in for a used one. He remains grateful that his father pushed him so hard, as he told Putnam in the *Dance* interview, "He means everything to me." Acosta declared, "He never gave up on me."

In June of 2002 Acosta delighted New York City audiences with an appearance with the American Ballet Theater in a run of *Le Corsaire.* He has started to write his autobiography, and will premiere a new dance project, *Tocororo (A Cuban Tale)* in London in the summer of 2003. "It's about a woman who separates two gangs, and tells them that we don't learn from the past if we make war," Acosta explained to the *New York Times*'s Kisselgoff. "Tocororo is the national Cuban bird, and the music has drums and salsa: Cuban rhythms." He remains an ardent salsa dancer himself, and still owns the first trophy he ever won—at age nine, for break-dancing. "I never thought I was going to get this far," Acosta told the *Houston Chronicle's* Glentzer. "If somebody had told me, 'Five years from now, you'll be doing this or that,' I would have said, 'Nah.' Everything happened so fast." Modestly, he dismissed comparisons to the other great male dancers before him, but did concede in the *Houston Chronicle* article that with "Baryshnikov and all the biggest stars … it's not about one thing," Glentzer quoted him as saying. "It's about everything…. When I think of Baryshnikov, I don't think how many pirouettes he can do or how high he jumps. It's the charisma: how he does it. You really have to enjoy dancing. Every time I perform, I have fun."

Sources

Books

Newsmakers 1997, Issue 4, Gale, 1997.

Periodicals

Back Stage, June 14, 2002, p. 11.
Dance, March 1998, p. 92; June 1999, p. 78; September 2001, p. 14.
Houston Chronicle, September 6, 1998, p. 15; September 5, 1999, p. 11.
Independent (London, England), December 26, 1998, p. 8.
New York Times, June 13, 2002, p. E1; June 19, 2002, p. E5.
People, March 31, 1997, p. 85.
Time International, August 13, 2001, p. 59.
WWD, May 31, 2002, p. 4.

—Carol Brennan

Angeles Alvariño

1916—

Marine biologist, oceanographer

Dr. Angeles Alvariño, also known by her married name of Angeles Alvariño de Leira, is an expert on marine zooplankton. These are non-photosynthetic, primarily microscopic organisms that drift in the upper layers of salt water and form the base of the marine food chain. Much of Alvariño's research has focused on the zooplankton of fish spawning grounds. Over a career spanning more than 50 years, Alvariño has discovered 22 new marine species. Since her retirement from the Southwest Fisheries Science Center (SWFSC) in La Jolla, California, as an emeritus scientist, Alvariño has been researching the biological collections made by early marine expeditions.

Angeles Alvariño was born on October 3, 1916, in El Ferrol, Spain. Her parents, Antonio Alvariño Grimaldos and Maria del Carmen Gonzáles Díaz-Saavedra de Alvariño, encouraged her early interest in natural history. From a very young age, she read the volumes on zoology in her father's library. Alvariño studied piano throughout her childhood until she entered the university; but from the age of four, she was determined to become a physician like her father. However, her father vehemently opposed this choice because he did not want her to experience the pain and suffering associated with patients whose conditions were untreatable.

Dreamed of Becoming a Doctor

As an undergraduate Alvariño attended the Lycee Concepcion Arenal in El Ferrol. There she studied the natural sciences, physics, chemistry, and mathematics, as well as languages, world literature, history, geography, philosophy, psychology, logic, and art history. In 1933 Alvariño received her baccalaureate degree, summa cum laude, from the University of Santiago de Compostela in Spain, after passing her final examinations and submitting dissertations in both sciences and letters—on social insects, bees, and ants, and on the women in *Don Quixote.*

Although her ambition to study medicine remained strong, Alvariño's father continued to object. Therefore she entered the University of Madrid (now University Complutense) in 1934 to study the natural sciences, a curriculum that shared several subjects with the medical course. However, the university closed in 1936 and remained closed for the duration of the Spanish Civil War. During this period Alvariño improved her French and began studying English. When the university reopened in 1939, she resumed her studies, earning a master's degree with honors in natural sciences in 1941. During her years at the University of Madrid,

At a Glance . . .

Born Angeles Alvariño on October 3, 1916, in El Ferrol, Spain; daughter of Antonio Alvariño Grimaldos and Maria del Carmen Gonzáles Díaz-Saavedra de Alvariño; married Sir Eugenio Leira Manso, 1940; children: Angeles Leira Alvariño. *Education:* University of Santiago de Compostela (Spain), baccalaureate degree, 1933; University of Madrid (now University Complutense), MS, 1941, doctoral certificate, 1951, DSc, 1967.

Career: El Ferrol (Spain), instructor, biology, zoology, botany, geology, 1941-48; Department of Sea Fisheries (Spain), fishery research biologist, 1948-52; Superior Council of Scientific Research, histologist, 1948-52; Spanish Institute of Oceanography, biologist-oceanographer, 1952-57; Marine Biological Laboratory, Plymouth, England, British Council fellow, 1953-54; Woods Hole Oceanographic Institute, Fulbright fellow, 1956-57; Scripps Institution of Oceanography, University of California, La Jolla, biologist, 1958-69; SWFSC, National Marine Fisheries Service, NOAA, fishery research biologist, 1970-87, emeritus scientist, 1987–; National Autonomous University of Mexico, associate professor, 1976; San Diego State University, associate professor, 1979-82; Federal University of Paraná (Brazil), visiting professor, 1982; University of San Diego, associate professor, 1982-84; National Polytechnic Institute of Mexico, visiting professor, 1982-86.

Memberships: Emeritus fellow, American Institute of Fishery Research Biologists; fellow, San Diego Society of Natural History; Association of Natural History Societies; Biological Society of Washington; Hispano-American Association of Researchers on Marine Sciences.

Awards: Great Silver Medal of Galicia, 1993.

Address: *Home*—7535 Cabrillo Ave., La Jolla, CA 92037-5206.

Alvariño lived in the Women's Residence of University Students, under the directorship of Dr. Maria de Maeztu. There she immersed herself in an international intellectual environment that included students from around the world who had come to study Spanish art and literature. In 1940 Alvariño married Sir Eugenio Leira Manso, an officer in the Royal Navy of Spain and a Knight of the Royal and Military Order of Saint Hermenegild.

After earning her degree Alvariño taught biology, zoology, botany, and geology at various colleges in El Ferrol until 1948, when she moved to Madrid with her husband and daughter. There she joined the Department of Sea Fisheries, as a fishery research biologist. Between 1948 and 1952 she also worked as a histologist at the Superior Council of Scientific Research.

Alvariño wanted to continue her studies at the Spanish Institute of Oceanography in Madrid. However, women were officially barred from the institute because research in marine biology was conducted on vessels belonging to the Spanish Royal Navy and a law, dating back to Charles III, prohibited women from staying on navy ships. Nevertheless, based on her academic qualifications, Alvariño was admitted to the institute's courses in biological, physical, and chemical oceanography and she was allowed to begin conducting research there. Simultaneously pursuing her studies at the University of Madrid, Alvariño earned her doctoral certificate in chemistry in 1951 with three separate dissertations: a study of personality for a thesis in experimental psychology, a study of phosphates in the ocean for a chemistry thesis, and a study of the distribution, uses, and commerce of seaweeds for a plant ecology dissertation. In 1952, as a result of a competitive examination, Alvariño won an appointment as a biologist and oceanographer at the Spanish Institute of Oceanography. Since the institute was a part of the Spanish navy, Alvariño was given an honorary military rank of captain.

Became Zooplankton Expert

The following year Alvariño was awarded a British Council Fellowship to study zooplankton at the Marine Biological Laboratory in Plymouth, England. There she worked with the prominent English marine biologist, Dr. Sir Frederick Stratten Russell, an expert on zooplankton, particularly the medusae or jellyfish. Thus Alvariño began her lifelong study of the Chaetognatha, Siphonophora, medusae, and fish larvae. Very little was known about these animals in the 1950s. Chaetognaths, a phylum of about 50 species of marine plankton, also called arrowworms, are abundant, tiny carnivores that feed on other zooplankton. Their responses to small chemical and physical characteristics of sea water make them important biological indicators of water type. Siphonophores and other hydrozoans are colonial, swimming or floating animals of the phylum Cnidaria (coelenterates), including *Physalia*, the Portuguese man-of-war. These organisms are made up of zooids, colonial cells that are specialized for floating, sensing, feeding, or reproduction. The gastrovascular canals of all of the zooids in a colony are contiguous. New colonies bud from the stem of the siphonophore.

Siphonophores, like the chaetognaths, are predators that feed on other plankton, including fish larvae and krill (small shrimp-like crustaceans). Medusae are the free-swimming forms of the hydrozoan cnidarians.

Alvariño studied all of the zooplankton groups that were found in collections from the Bay of Viscay and the English Channel. She discovered *Sagitta friderici* in plankton samples of the chaetognatha. This is a species normally found in the shallow, warm or temperate waters of the eastern Atlantic coast. She also found abundant eggs and larvae of *Sardina pilchardus* in samples from herring fishery areas. Her discovery of these organisms off the British coast indicated the abnormal northward movement of warm water that was displacing the herring fisheries.

Returning to Spain in 1954, Alvariño began designing and manufacturing plankton nets, which she gave to Spanish fishing boats and research ships for collecting samples. This enabled her to study zooplankton collected from the Iberian Atlantic, the Mediterranean Sea, and the Grand Banks of Newfoundland. In 1956 Alvariño was awarded a Fulbright Fellowship to work with Dr. Mary Sears at the Woods Hole Oceanographic Institute in Massachusetts. Sears, a well-known expert on zooplankton, especially the Siphonophora, and chair of the First International Congress on Oceanography, was so impressed with Alvariño's research and the breadth of her knowledge, that she recommended her to Dr. Roger Revelle, director of the Scripps Institution of Oceanography at the University of California in La Jolla. From 1958 until the end of 1969, Alvariño worked as a biologist at Scripps, examining the chaetognaths, siphonophores, and medusae in plankton collected off the coast of California and from the Atlantic, Pacific, and Indian Oceans. During those years she was a grantee of the U. S. Office of the Navy and the California Cooperative Oceanic Fisheries Investigations. Between 1961 and 1969 she also held grants from the U. S. National Science Foundation. Alvariño also became a United States citizen in 1966.

An expert on taxonomy and zoogeography, Alvariño's discoveries included 12 new species of Chaetognatha, nine new species of Siphonophora, and a new medusa. She also established the worldwide three-dimensional distribution of various species of chaetognaths and siphonophores. Alvariño's research at Scripps earned her a doctor of sciences degree summa cum laude in 1967 from the University of Madrid.

Joined the SWFSC

In 1970 Alvariño accepted a position as a fishery research biologist at the Southwest Fisheries Science Center (SWFSC), a division of the newly formed National Marine Fisheries Service, a branch of the National Oceanic and Atmospheric Agency (NOAA). Alvariño's research focused on the geographic distribution and ecology of zooplankton, especially the distribution of chaeognath and siphonophore species in the Pacific and Antarctic Oceans and on the relationships between zooplankton and the ocean environment. She examined the effects of plankton predation on fish larvae survival and the impact on fisheries and the biotic environment of fish spawning grounds. She identified zooplankton that are indicator species, based on their associations with specific ocean currents and other forms of ocean dynamics or with other types of organisms, such as spawning fish, eggs, and larvae. She also studied the artificial transport of plankton into new areas of the ocean, via pollution and ship bilge tanks, and the effects of these exotic organisms on the biotic environment.

Between 1977 and 1979 Alvariño coordinated oceanic research for Hispano-American countries. She held Antarctic research grants between 1979 and 1982 and grants from the Food and Agriculture Organization of the United Nations and from the United Nations Educational, Scientific and Cultural Organization (UNESCO). Alvariño directed doctoral theses candidates at various universities in the western hemisphere and served on thesis committees in the United States and abroad. Her concurrent university appointments included associate professorships at the National Autonomous University of Mexico in 1976, San Diego State University between 1979 and 1982, and at the University of San Diego between 1982 and 1984. She held visiting professorships at the Federal University of Paraná in Brazil in 1982 and at the National Polytechnic Institute of Mexico between 1982 and 1986.

Alvariño has published more than 100 original scientific books, book chapters, and journal articles. On July 23, 1993, King Juan Carlos I and Queen Sophia of Spain awarded her the Great Silver Medal of Galicia. She is an emeritus fellow of the American Institute of Fishery Research Biologists and a fellow of the San Diego Society of Natural History. She is a member of the Biological Society of Washington and the Hispano-American Association of Researchers on Marine Sciences. In addition to Spanish and English, Alvariño is fluent in French and Portuguese and speaks some German. A lover of art, classical music, and literature, Alvariño and her husband, a retired naval captain, have one daughter, Angeles Leira Alvariño, who is an architect and city planner.

Angeles Alvariño has continued her scientific work on plankton and other subjects since her official retirement from the SWFSC as an emeritus scientist in 1987. The first woman scientist to work on a British research vessel, she has continued to participate in expeditions on the research vessels of various countries. In recent years Alvariño has conducted historical research focusing on early oceanography, including the explorations of Spanish navigators who discovered the oceans of the world and the main oceanic currents and the First Scientific Oceanic Expedition that sailed the western Atlantic Ocean and all of the Pacific Ocean between 1789 and 1794. In 2000 she published an account of this expedition. A second edition of this work, with additional illustrations in full color, is forthcoming. She also has prepared English and Spanish manuscripts on the scientific study of 100 species of animals, including plankton, mollusks, turtles, fish, and birds, that were collected from the western South Atlantic and Pacific Oceans, and illustrated in color, during the expedition.

Selected writings

Books and reports

Distributional Atlas of Chaetognatha in the California Current Region During the CALCOFI Monthly Cruises of 1954 and 1958, California Cooperative Oceanic Fisheries Investigations, 1965.

The Chaetognatha of the NAGA Expedition (1959-1961) in the South China Sea and the Gulf of Thailand, Scripps Institution of Oceanography, 1967.

Atlantic Chaetognatha. Distribution and Essential Notes of Systematics, Travaux Spanish Institute of Oceanography, 1969.

Siphonophores of the Pacific with a Revision of the World Distribution, University of California Press, 1971.

The Relation Between the Distribution of Zooplankton Predators and Engraulis Mordax Larvae (Anchovy), California Cooperative Oceanic Fisheries Investigations Reports, 1980.

(With S. C. Hosmer and R. F. Ford) *Antarctic Chaetognatha: United States Antarctic Research Program, ELTANIN Cruises 8-28,* American Geophysical Union, 1983.

(With D. F. Verfaillie and R. F. Ford) *Antarctic Chaetognatha: United States Antarctic Research Program, ELTANIN Cruises 10-23, 25 and 27,* American Geophysical Union, 1983.

(With Joan M. Wojtan and M. Rachel Martinez) *Antarctic Siphonophores from the Plankton Samples of the United States Antarctic Research Program, ELTANIN Cruises from Spring, Summer, Fall and Winter (Cruises 3-4, 6-23, 25-28, 30, 35 and 38),* American Geophysical Union, 1990.

Spain and the First Scientific Oceanic Expedition (1789-1794). Malaspina and Bustamante with the Corvettes DESCUBIERTA and ATREVIDA, (in Spanish) 2000.

Book chapters

"Chaetognatha," in *Oceanography and Marine Biology: Annual Review,* George Allen and Unwin Ltd., 1965.

"Chaetognatha. Oogenesis, Ovoposition, and Oosorption," in *Reproductive Biology of Invertebrates,* Vol. 1, John Wiley & Sons Ltd., 1983.

"Chaetognatha. Spermatogenesis and Sperm Function," in *Reproductive Biology of Invertebrates,* Vol. 2, John Wiley & Sons Ltd., 1983.

"Fertilization, Development and Parental Care in Chaetognatha," in *Reproductive Biology of Invertebrates,* Vol. 4, Oxford & IBH Publishing, 1990.

"Sexual Differentiation and Behavior in Chaetognatha. Hermaphroditism," in *Reproductive Biology of Invertebrates,* Vol. 5, Oxford & IBH Publishing, 1990.

"Asexual Propagation and Reproductive Strategies in Chaetognatha," in *Reproductive Biology of Invertebrates,* Vol. 6, Oxford & IBH Publishing, 1991.

Periodicals

"Two New Pacific Chaetognaths: Their Distribution and Relationship to Allied Species," *Bulletin of the Scripps Institution of Oceanography,* 1962.

"Egg Pouches and Other Reproductive Structures in Pelagic Chaetognatha," *Pacific Science,* 1968.

"Distribution of Siphonophores in the Regions Adjacent to the Suez and Panama Canals," *U.S. Fishery Bulletin,* 1974.

"The Importance of the Indian Ocean as Origin of Species and Biological Link Uniting the Pacific and Atlantic Oceans," *Journal of the Marine Biological Association of India,* 1974.

"The Depth Distribution, Relative Abundance and Structure of the Population of the Chaetognatha *Sagitta scrippsae* Alvariño 1962, in the California Current off California and Baja California," *Anales Indtituto Ciencias del Mar y Limnologia,* 1983.

"*Pandea cybeles* a New Medusa from the Sargasso Sea," *Proceedings of the Biological Society of Washington,* 1987.

"Abundance of Zooplankton Species, Females and Males, Eggs and Larvae of Holoplanktonic Species. Zooplankton Assemblages and Changes in the Zooplankton Communities Related to *Engraulis mordax* Spawning and Survival of the Larvae," *Memoirs III Encontro Brasileiro de Plancton,* 1989.

"Hydromedusae: Daylight and Night and Seasonal Bathymetric Abundance off California and Baja California, and Study of the Species in the Eastern Pacific and Other Regions," *Revista de Biología Marina y Oceanografía,* 1999.

Sources

On-line

"From Johah To NOAA: Women in the Fisheries Profession," *Women in Natural Resources Magazine,* www.womentechworld.org/bios/fisheries/articles/women.htm (May 13, 2003).

Other

Information for this profile was obtained through personal communications between Dr. Alvariño and *Contemporary Hispanic Biography* in February, 2003.

—Margaret Alic

Reinaldo Arenas

1943-1990

Cuban writer

Viciously oppressed in his native Cuba for both his literary attacks on Fidel Castro's revolution and his open homosexuality, Reinaldo Arenas became a literary star by smuggling his books overseas. His extraordinary novels, flush with magical realism and sensual detail, won several prestigious awards abroad. *Interview* magazine wrote, "[Arenas's] writing is so exquisitely evocative and truthful and free it's as though his words have wings that could take him—artistically, sexually, and even politically—anywhere on a physical or emotional level." Yet, under the totalitarian regime of Communist Cuba, Arenas couldn't travel anywhere. For twenty years he endured harassment, surveillance, and imprisonment. Arenas finally escaped to New York in 1980.

By the time of his death in 1990, Arenas had completed nine novels, an autobiography, scores of poems, plays, and short stories, as well as dozens of political and literary essays. However, he had long-since gone out of literary favor. As he noted in his autobiography, *Before Night Falls,* "Ironically, while I was in jail and could not leave Cuba, my chances of being published were better because I was not allowed to speak out." As an exile in the United States, he was much less

compelling. He died in relative obscurity; barely a dozen people attended his funeral. Yet, a writer often finds immortality through his words, and Arenas, whose work resonated with viscerally wrenching imagery, was no exception. Following his death *Before Night Falls* was published to critical acclaim and turned into a 2000 film of the same name. The film brought Arenas's work to a wider audience and helped prompt his posthumous rise to take his place as "one of the truly great writers to come out of Latin America" according to the *Chicago Tribune.* His work is currently widely available and is required reading in several university programs. However, in Cuba it remains banned.

Escaped Poverty Through Stories

Reinaldo Arenas was born in rural Cuba on July 16, 1943. Abandoned by his father, Arenas was raised by his mother on her parents' farm. At the time Cuba was ruled by the dictator Fulgencio Batista and Arenas recalled to the *St. Louis Post-Dispatch,* "The situation under Batista in the countryside was terrible." Poverty was ever-present and hunger a constant companion.

At a Glance . . .

Born on July 16, 1943, in the Oriente province of Cuba; died on December 7, 1990, in New York, NY; son of Oneida Fuentes. *Education:* La Pantoja, Cuba, studied agricultural accounting, 1959; University of Havana, Cuba, studied economic planning, 1966-68; attended Columbia University, 1980s.

Career: Accountant, early 1960s; National Library of Cuba, assistant, 1963-68; writer, 1967-90; Cuban Book Institute, editor, 1967-68; *La Gaceta de Cuba,* journalist and editor, 1968-74; International University of Florida, visiting professor of Cuban literature, 1981; Center for Inter-American Relations, visiting prof, 1982; Cornell University, visiting prof, 1985; guest lecturer at Princeton University, Georgetown University, Washington University of St. Louis, University of Stockholm, Sweden, University of Kansas, University of Miami, and University of Puerto Rico.

Awards: First place for best novel, *Singing From the Well,* Cuban Writers Union, 1965; Prix Medici for best foreign novel, *Singing From the Well,* France, 1969; Best Foreign Novel, *Hallucinations, Le Monde,* France, 1969; Cintas Foundation, fellow, 1980; Guggenheim Foundation, fellow, 1982; Wilson Center Foundation, fellow, 1987; *The New York Time's* top ten books of the year, *Before Night Falls,* 1993.

Arenas often ate dirt just to have something in his stomach. His only solace was nature. "I think the splendor of my childhood was unique because it was absolute poverty but also absolute freedom; out in the open, surrounded by trees, animals ...," he wrote in *Before Night Falls.* It was there that he began his literary career, composing songs and stories to keep himself company. "I would perform them in those lonely fields as if they were theater pieces," he wrote.

By the time Arenas reached his teens, his family had sold their farm and moved to the dreary town of Holguín. About this time Arenas took a job at a guava paste factory, working 12 hour shifts for one peso a day. The work was mind-numbingly boring and Arenas began channeling that boredom into stories he churned out on a small typewriter. Eventually the boredom of Holguín, as well as the continued hardships under Batista, convinced the 14 year-old Arenas to join Fidel Castro's rebel forces. However, his youth—and more importantly his lack of a rifle—kept him from fighting. Nevertheless, when Castro took control of the island in

1959 Arenas was swept up in the revolutionary fervor. "I believed, or wanted to believe, that the Revolution was something noble and beautiful," he wrote. However, he soon began to notice that the new government was wrought with hypocrisy. It would not be long before he would come to believe that he had helped overthrow one dictator only to replace him with another.

Arenas received a scholarship to study agricultural accounting and was assigned to work on a government chicken farm after graduation. It was a tedious job and Arenas leapt at the chance to move to Havana when he was offered a scholarship to study economic planning at the University of Havana in 1961. Not long after arriving in Havana Arenas began to immerse himself in the then-thriving gay subculture of the city. He had realized he was homosexual when he was still a child, but during his years in school he hid his feelings because of the persecution that gays were subjected to by the government. Many were fired from their jobs, kicked out of school, or sent to concentration camps to be rehabilitated. One of Arenas's earliest boyfriends was taken to such a camp. "I never saw him again, nor have I heard of him since my exile," he wrote in *Before Night Falls.*

In Havana Arenas entered a storytelling contest sponsored by the National Library and won. However, the judges were less interested in his storytelling ability than in the story he had told. Rather than read a well-known tale, he had written his own. The library directors, impressed with his literary skill, immediately offered Arenas a job at the library. "My transfer there was decisive for my literary education. My job consisted in looking for the books people requested, but there was always time to read," he wrote in *Before Night Falls.* There was also time to write, and his first book, *Singing from the Well,* was written in the library. The story of a mentally-impaired child growing up in rural Cuba won an award from the Cuban Writers and Artists Union (UNEAC) in 1965 and became the only one of Arenas's books to be published in Cuba. According to an article in the *Village Voice* Mexican novelist Carlos Fuentes called the book, "One of the most beautiful novels ever written about childhood, adolescence, and life in Cuba." Arenas's next book was *Hallucinations: Being an Account of the Life and Adventures of Friar Servando Teresa de Meir.* It was a fantastical rewriting of the autobiography of a revolutionary Mexican friar who defied the Spanish conquest of his country and was mercilessly persecuted for it. It was also an almost eerie foreshadowing of the fate that was to befall Arenas.

Imprisoned For His Books

Though *Hallucinations* also won an award from UNEAC, it was banned by the government for its anti-revolutionary tone. The following year, with the help of French friends, Arenas smuggled *Hallucinations* out of the country. It was published to acclaim in Mexico and Spain; in France it was named the best foreign novel of 1969. "If I had been living in the free world, this would have served me well," he wrote in *Before Night Falls.* Instead, "in Cuba, the official impact ... was for me absolutely negative." For publishing abroad, without the consent of the government, Arenas was labeled a counterrevolutionary. "By the year 1969 I was already being subjected to persistent harassment by State Security, and feared for the manuscripts I was continually producing."

In 1970 Arenas—along with many other young intellectuals—was sent to work on a sugarcane plantation. "Unless you have lived through it, you could not possibly understand what it means to be in a Cuban sugar plantation under the noon sun, and to live in barracks like slaves," he wrote in *Before Night Falls.* It inspired his long poem *El central,* which was smuggled out and published in Spain. Meanwhile Arenas was working on *Farewell to the Sea,* one of five novels to make up his *Pentagon* series detailing the history of Cuba. Set at a beach resort, the novel reveals the inner thoughts of a Cuban couple and the way Castro's revolutionary government damaged their lives. That the book was written is a testament to Arena's determination. The original manuscript was lost when he placed it in hiding with friends. He rewrote the book, only to have it confiscated by the police. Finally, he was able to smuggle his third rewrite of the book to France in 1980. Other books in the *Pentagon* included *Singing From the Well; The Palace of the White Skunks,* which was also smuggled to France; *The Color of Summer;* and *The Assault.* The latter two were written in the United States.

In 1973, after an altercation on a beach, Arenas was arrested and charged with "ideological deviation." While out on bail he made a daring escape and eluded police for several months. During that time he attempted to leave the country several times. When that failed, he tried to commit suicide by slicing his wrists with a broken bottle. When that also failed, he resorted to his oldest companion—writing. He wrote an open letter to international agencies and free governments. "I wanted to report all the persecution I was being subjected to," he wrote in *Before Night Falls.* The letter was smuggled out by a French friend and was published in France and Mexico. When Arenas was finally captured he was sent to El Morro prison—coincidentally the same prison where Friar Servando had been incarcerated. The prison was loud, hot, and overcrowded. Excrement piled in corners, urine flowed like rancid rivers, bugs were everywhere. Murder was common and vicious. Food was scarce and barely edible. In addition, Arenas was subjected to intense interrogation. The government wanted him to confess to being a counterrevolutionary and a homosexual and to vow to change. Arenas eventually gave in. It was a bitter, demoralizing defeat for him. "Before my confession I had a great companion, my pride," he wrote in *Before Night Falls.* "After the confession I had nothing; I had lost my dignity and my rebellious spirit."

Though Arenas was released from prison in 1976, he continued to live in fear. He was regularly visited by the police and his room was occasionally ransacked. He had to write in secret and could trust no one. "That was my life in early 1980; surrounded by spies and seeing my youth vanish without ever having been a free person," he wrote in *Before Night Falls.* In 1980 Arenas decided he had had enough and, after doctoring his identity card, joined the over 130,000 Cubans who were allowed to leave the island during the Castro-sanctioned Mariel Boat Lift. On May 4, at one in the morning, Arenas boarded a boat for Key West. "When officials in the government realized I was gone, I discovered later, they sent a boat after me, but it was too late," he told the *St. Louis Post-Dispatch.* By the end of the year Arenas was living in New York City, 37 years old, and free for the first time in his life.

Wrote Furiously in Freedom

In New York Arenas entered a creative frenzy. He completed the *Pentagon* series and wrote *Journey to Havana, Mona and Other Tales,* and *The Doorman.* He also completed *Before Night Falls* which he had begun during his days as a fugitive hiding from the police. When it was published three years after his death it made *The New York Time's* top ten list. Along with other exiled Cuban writers he founded the short-lived literary magazine *Mariel.* When not writing, he taught Cuban poetry and lectured at universities including Cornell, Princeton, and Georgetown. In 1982 Arenas won a Guggenheim Fellowship and in 1987 a Woodrow Wilson Center Fellowship. In addition he relished his new freedom, traveling throughout Europe and road tripping across the United States. He wrote of his travels in *Before Night Falls:* "for the first time we were able to enjoy the sense of freedom and the thrill of adventure without feeling persecuted; in short, the pleasure of being alive."

Despite his hard-won freedom, Arenas continued to suffer. His foreign publishers either refused to pay him for his books or paid him a pittance after much hassle. "None of this surprised me: I already knew that the capitalist system was also sordid and money-hungry," Arenas wrote in *Before Night Falls.* He continued, "In one of my first statements after leaving Cuba I had declared that 'the difference between the communist and capitalist systems is that, although both give you a kick in the ass, in the communist system you have to applaud, while in the capitalist system you can scream. And I came here to scream.'" His screaming did not win him a lot of friends. The intellectual left tended to side with Castro without really knowing what the Cuban people suffered. Other exiled Cubans were busy building wealthy new lives. It was suggested that Arenas forget his past and go on. "But after twenty years of repression, how could I keep silent about those crimes?" he asked in *Before Night Falls*. At the same time he longed for Cuba and loathed his exiled state. He wrote, "I ceased to exist when I went into exile."

In 1987 Arenas was diagnosed with AIDS. He rapidly deteriorated and was hospitalized several times. Each time he recovered, crediting his works for his returns to health. "Writing those books kept me alive," he told the author of *A Sadness as Deep as the Sea*. "Especially the autobiography. I didn't want to die until I had put the final touches. It's my revenge." On December 7, 1990, not long after completing the manuscript, wholly debilitated from the disease, Arenas took an overdose of pills. In his suicide note, reprinted in *Before Night Falls*, he wrote, "Due to my delicate state of health and to the terrible emotional depression it causes me not to be able to continue writing and struggling for the freedom of Cuba, I am ending my life." He went on to blame Castro for his life's sufferings and concluded with the type of defiant hope that had allowed him to create brilliant art despite the darkest oppression: "Cuba will be free. I already am."

Selected writings

Celestino antes del alba, Cuba, 1967, translated as *Singing from the Well,* Viking, NY, 1987.
El mundo alucinante, France, 1969, translated as *Hallucinations: Being an Account of the Life and Adventures of Friar Servando Teresa de Mier,* Harper, NY, 1971.
El palacio de las blanquisimas mofetas, France, 1975, translated as *The Palace of the White Skunks,* Viking, NY, 1990.
El Central, Spain, 1981, translated as *El Central: A Cuban Sugar Mill,* Avon, NY, 1984.

Otra vez el mar, 1982, translated as *Farewell to the Sea,* Viking, NY, 1986.
El portero, 1988, translated as *The Doorman,* Grove Press, NY, 1991.
El asalto, 1990, translated as *The Assault,* Viking, NY, 1994.
El color del verano, 1991, translated as *The Color of Summer,* Viking NY, 2000.
Antes que anochezca, 1992, translated as *Before Night Falls: A Memoir,* Viking, NY, 1993.
Mona and Other Tales, Vintage, 2001.

Sources

Books

Arenas, Reinaldo, *Before Night Falls: A Memoir,* Viking, NY, 1993.

Periodicals

Interview, January-April 2001, p. 46.
St. Louis Post-Dispatch, February 23, 2001, p. E1.

On-line

"A Sadness as Deep as the Sea," *Eminent Maricones,* www.actupny.org/diva/CBmanrique.html (May 20, 2003).
"The Revival of Reinaldo Arenas: After Night Falls," *Village Voice,* www.villagevoice.com/issues/0049/manrique.php (May 22, 2003).

—Candace LaBalle

María Celeste Arrarás

1960—

Journalist

The defection of María Celeste Arrarás from Univision, North America's largest Spanish-language network, to the rival Telemundo broadcasting group in 2002 roused industry attention and was heralded as the start of a new era for Hispanic media. Arrarás was given a plum spot at Telemundo, and her arrival coincided with news that the National Broadcasting Company (NBC)'s $2.7 billion acquisition of the Spanish-language news and entertainment provider had just won U.S. government approval. Arrarás, an attractive and admired media celebrity in the Latino world, was to host her own Telemundo show, but would also file English-language reports for *Dateline,* NBC's top-rated prime-time newsmagazine. Arrarás's hire—and the Telemundo/NBC venture—was seen as a sign of an increased Hispanic presence in mainstream media news organizations, and *New York Times* journalist Mirta Ojito called the new, lucrative contract for this popular journalist "NBC's first coup in the Latino media."

Arrarás was born in 1960 in the city of Mayaguez, Puerto Rico, but spent most of her youth in the country's capital, San Juan. Her father was a university chancellor who became a politician, serving as Puerto Rico's housing secretary and minority leader in the

House of Representatives. Arrarás recalled in an interview with Knight Ridder/Tribune News Service reporter Judy Hevrdejs that she and her family were well-known in Puerto Rico because of her father's career. "I hated it. ... whatever we would do, we would get interruptions constantly." She told Hevrdejs that as a child she vowed to lead a quieter life, one out of the public eye.

Found Career in Television Journalism

Arrarás grew up in an achievement-oriented family, and earned good grades. She was also a talented swimmer, and at the age of eleven took a gold medal at the 1971 Central American Games in Cuba. After qualifying for a spot on Puerto Rico's Olympic team for the 1976 Summer Games in Montreal, the teenaged Arrarás was forced to quit when she was diagnosed with mononucleosis. Sensing a need for a new challenge for his daughter, Arrarás's father suggested that she begin writing a column for a newspaper he owned. She was pleasantly surprised to realize she liked journalism. "It was like 'click,'" she told Ojito in the *New York Times.* "A light went on."

Fluent in English, Arrarás attended Loyola University in New Orleans, where she earned her 1982 honors

At a Glance . . .

Born on September 27, 1960, in Mayaguez, Puerto Rico; daughter of Jose Enrique (a university chancellor, politician, and newspaper publisher); married Guillermo (divorced); married Manny Arevesu; three children. *Education:* Loyola University of New Orleans, BA, 1982.

Career: Univision television network, news anchor, 1986, Los Angeles bureau chief, 1987-1990s, Miami weekend newscaster, 1987-1990s, co-anchor of *Noticias y Mas,* 1990s, host of *Primer Impacto,* 1993-2001; writer, 1997–; actress, 1997–; Telemundo television network, host and managing editor of *Al Rojo Vivo con María Celeste,* 2002–.

Memberships: People for the Ethical Treatment of Animals (PETA), spokesperson.

Awards: Genesis Award, National Ark Trust Fund.

Address: *Office*—Telemundo Communications Group, Inc., 2290 West 8th Ave., Hialeah, FL 33010.

degree in communications, and began her career in broadcast journalism with an all-news station in San Juan as an anchor and reporter in 1986. Soon, Univision's New York City affiliate hired her as its news anchor, and the WXTV job in Manhattan was considered a career-making post. Yet Arrarás was forced to give up the job when station executives deemed her not glamorous enough. It was a tough lesson, she remembered during a *New York Times* interview. "He said, 'I've handed you a bag of lemons. You can either get sour or make lemonade.' I chose to stay and make lemonade." Arrarás went on to other slots at the network, serving as Univision's bureau chief in Los Angeles and anchor of the weekend newscast in Miami. In time she was given a co-anchor spot with a well-known Univision personality, Myrka Dellanos, on the show *Noticias y Mas.* That news and feature-story show eventually became the hugely successful *Primer Impacto,* which would launch Arrarás's career in earnest.

Airing in several U.S. markets and in 15 Latin American countries, with a total viewership of 100 million, *Primer Impacto* offered news and entertainment stories and even an astrology report. Arrarás was the host and reported on special events, such as the U.S. presidential conventions and the Olympics; she also interviewed top political leaders of the Latin world. The

show's impressive ratings brought in lucrative advertising dollars for Univision, and one prime-time special edition of the show earned the second-highest rating—ever—in the Nielsen Hispanic Index. For many, though, Arrarás was the draw, and she seemed to hit her stride on the show. She loosened up her wardrobe and her hairstyles, and began making jokes. "For the first time, I could smile on the air," she recalled in an interview with Ojito. "It was refreshing and different, and it suited my personality better." She was also becoming a well-known figure in the South Florida Hispanic community, and found that she was a news story herself: every detail of her personal life was avidly chronicled by the local press. By this time she had wed a Miami attorney and had three children. The larger national Hispanic media in the United States also liked to run stories about her, and she became a popular cover personality. Deemed a role model for working mothers, Arrarás returned after one maternity leave to *Primer Impacto* and the show pulled in a record number of viewers.

During her tenure at *Primer Impacto,* Arrarás attained an important coup when she landed an exclusive interview with Yolanda Saldivar, the woman convicted of slaying Tejano singing star Selena in 1995. Saldivar had been a business associate of the star's family, and founder of the Selena fan club. Arrarás interviewed her from prison, and Saldivar hinted that there was a "secret" behind the tragic slaying. Arrarás pursued the story further and wrote a book, *Selena's Secret: The Revealing Story Behind Her Tragic Death,* that was published in 1997 in Spanish and English editions. The resulting press helped land Arrarás on *People* magazine's annual "Most Intriguing People of 1997" list.

Left Univision for Telemundo and NBC

In 2001, when Arrarás's contract with Univision expired, she chose not to renegotiate. Instead, she jumped ship to rival network Telemundo, and her decampment was made public the same week that the Federal Communications Commission (FCC) announced its approval of NBC's bid to acquire Telemundo. Arrarás's bold move was considered such a coup for Telemundo that her hire was announced at a press conference in April of 2002 by NBC president Andrew Lack and Telemundo president Jim McNamara. NBC announced its intention to give her a show as well as reporting assignments for NBC news shows like *Dateline* and the *Today Show.* Arrarás, Lack told Ojito in the *New York Times,* "is a star, along the lines of talent like Diane Sawyer and Jane Pauley. I have confidence that she will bring her enormous talent to some of our programs in NBC."

Arrarás's new show was slated to debut that spring as well. The name *Al Rojo Vivo con María Celeste* was concocted by her best friend, she explained to Hevrdejs in the Knight Ridder/Tribune News Service report, and meant loosely "red hot"; it was also a pun on her middle name, Celeste, or "sky blue" in Spanish. "You can say, 'Oh my God! That interview was al rojo vivo.'" she told Hevrdejs. "Why? Because that person spoke out. They said everything. A confession." As both host and managing editor, Arrarás wanted *Al Rojo Vivo* to serve as a kind of "'paella noticias,' like a news paella," as she told Hevrdejs. "You have chicken, you have fish, you have sausage, you have rice and vegetables. And what happens is, in one hour, you have news from everything that is going on in the afternoon."

Al Rojo Vivo was a ratings success for Telemundo right from the start, but Arrarás's debut on *Dateline* was, again, a news story in itself. In August of 2002 she filed a report on ten-month-old conjoined twins from Guatemala who came to the United States for surgery that would separate them. "Wearing a blue sanitary paper hat and a matching UCLA Medical Center gown," noted *Los Angeles Times* writer Dana Calvo, "the glamorous María Celeste Arrarás made her NBC debut on *Dateline* and in the process made herself into the most prominent player in a blossoming media experiment." The *Los Angeles Times* article noted that Arrarás and other journalists who file stories for both networks would need to be extremely fluent in both languages. NBC president Lack, it was reported, had been a bit nervous about Arrarás's *Dateline* debut and her bilingual skills, but Lack told Calvo that Arrarás "was credible, so I didn't think viewers were sitting around thinking, 'Why is this Spanish-accented person doing this story?' I think they thought, 'This person knows the place, knows the story, and it's important and authoritative.' She's a serious, smart journalist."

News Star for Twenty-First Century

A *Los Angeles Times* article discussed the inherent differences in the Telemundo and NBC networks, from how a breaking news story is written to the amount and style of accessories its female journalists are allowed to wear on the air. But after just a few months on the job, Arrarás herself was surprised at how little a difference there was between the Spanish-language broadcasting stalwarts and a well-established, deep-pocketed news source like NBC. She said that as a Univision reporter, she and her colleagues had often dreamed of working in the "majors," as she called them. "We had this big myth that it would be a different ballgame—that it would be awesome, bigger and better," Arrarás told Calvo. "But, to my surprise, it was very similar. The only difference is there were more resources. You can pre-plan and take things at a more normal pace. In Spanish TV, we have less resources, so we are more aggressive. We are hungrier."

Despite the tremendous attention given to her debut Arrarás was frank about her talents. "I'm not the greatest anchor in the world," she told Ojito in the *New York Times,* "but what I lack in talent I make up with honesty." Arrarás is the first Latina celebrity spokesperson for PETA, People for the Ethical Treatment of Animals, and is working to ban circuses in Puerto Rico that use animals. Her high-profile job landed her on *People en Espanol*'s "10 Most Intriguing People of the Year" in 2002. With her own agent at entertainment-industry powerhouse William Morris, Arrarás was, in the end, still surprised by her choice of career—given the fact that she often disliked being in the public eye as a youngster. "I said I'll never do that," she said in the Knight Ridder/Tribune News Service interview, "and little did I know—I ended up doing the same thing."

Selected works

Books

Selena's Secret: The Revealing Story Behind Her Tragic Death, Simon & Schuster, 1997.

Films

Contact, 1997.

Sources

Books

Notable Hispanic American Women, Book 2, Gale, 1998.

Periodicals

Broadcasting & Cable, April 15, 2002, p. 51.
Cincinnati Post April 12, 2002, p. 16C.
Electronic Media, April 15, 2002, p. 22.
Houston Chronicle, April 26, 2002, p. 10; July 26, 2002, p. 1.
Knight Ridder/Tribune Business News, April 10, 2002.
Knight Ridder/Tribune News Service, February 26, 2002; April 11, 2002; April 19, 2002.
Library Journal, July 1997, p. 67.
Los Angeles Business Journal, April 15, 2002, p. 16.
Los Angeles Times, November 24, 2002, p. E35.
Multichannel News, April 15, 2002, p. 14.
New York Times, May 5, 2002, p. 1.
Publishers Weekly, January 27, 1997, p. 90.
Star-Ledger (Newark, NJ), April 12, 2002, p. 64.

—Carol Brennan

Polly Baca-Barragán

1941—

Politician, media relations specialist

Polly Baca-Barragán (known also as Polly Baca) was the first Hispanic woman to win a state senate election in Colorado. She was elected to the state house of representatives in 1974 and the state senate in 1984. Baca's life has been marked by a passion for public service. As a young woman she worked as an editor for trade journals; she combined this experience with her passion for politics and activism throughout her career. Although much of her focus has been Hispanic issues, her strong belief in the value of multiculturalism has been a key element of her life inside and outside politics.

The oldest of four children, Polly Baca was born in 1941 (some sources say 1943) in Greeley, Colorado. Her parents, Jose Manuel and Leda Sierra Baca, were migrant farmers who worked hard to support their family. Baca remembered in particular that her mother instilled a deep sense of pride in her—pride in her heritage and in her ability to succeed.

Showed Early Interest in Politics

As a teen-ager, Baca became an orphan; her father was killed in an accident and her mother died not long afterward. She was suddenly faced with the responsibility of caring for her three younger brothers—but she was determined to stay in high school and finish her studies. A bright student, she won a scholarship to Colorado State University and planned to major in physics, even though she was more interested in political science and had aspirations of becoming a politician. Part of her decision to major in physics came from a science teacher who told her that a science career would be better for her because as a Hispanic and a woman her chances of success in public life were twice as slim. This was something that Baca would remember throughout her career. Knowing that as a Hispanic and a woman she would have a harder time achieving success was hardly a detriment; actually it gave her the impetus to try harder. It was perhaps not surprising that although she did enter college as a physics major, before long she had switched to political science.

While in college Baca became active in campus politics, serving as freshman class secretary. She also became active in her campus chapter of Young Democrats (a group she had been involved with in high school), becoming vice-president and then president. She did volunteer work for the Democratic Party and helped with the campaigns of local candidates; she was also active in the Viva Kennedy clubs that promoted John F. Kennedy to the Hispanic electorate.

At a Glance . . .

Born in 1941 (some sources say 1943), in Greeley, CO; married Miguel Barragán, 1968 (divorced); children: Monica, Michael. *Education:* Colorado State University, BA, political science, 1962; American University, graduate courses, 1966-67.

Career: International Brotherhood of Pulp, Sulfite, and Paper Mill Workers, AFL-CIO, editorial assistant, 1962-65; Brotherhood of Railway and Airline Clerks, AFL-CIO, editor and assistant director of research and education, 1966-67; White House Cabinet Committee on Opportunities for the Spanish Speaking, public information officer, 1964-68; Robert F. Kennedy presidential campaign, Hispanic division, deputy director, 1968; National Council of La Raza, director of research services, 1969-70; Democratic National Committee, Spanish speaking affairs, director, 1971-72; Colorado Committee on Mass Media and the Spanish Surnamed, director, 1972-73; Colorado state House of Representatives, 1975-78; Colorado state senator, 1979-86; Sierra Baca Systems, president, 1985-89, CEO, 1999–; Colorado Hispanic Institute, executive director, 1989-94; General Services Administration, Rocky Mountain Division, regional administrator, 1994-99.

Memberships: InSites; Latin American Research and Service Agency (LARASA).

Awards: National Hispanic Hall of Fame, 1988; Colorado Women's Hall of Fame; honorary doctor of laws, Wartburg College, Waverly, IA; honorary doctor of humane letters, University of Northern Colorado, Greeley, CO.

Address: *Home*—1777 Larimer, Unit 510, Denver, CO 80202.

Upon graduation in 1962, Baca moved to Washington, D.C., where she worked on the editorial staff of two trade unions (both branches of the AFL-CIO) that represented paper mill workers and rail and air employees. In addition to giving her valuable experience in writing and editing, these jobs also gave her the chance to see how public policy was made both within the union and the federal government.

Began Political Career

In 1967 Baca landed a job in the White House, working as a public information officer in the Cabinet Committee on Opportunities for the Spanish Speaking. This job involved research and speechwriting, but it also required her to help coordinate events and speeches that were brought to Hispanic communities. A year later, she became national deputy director of the Hispanic division of Robert F. Kennedy's presidential campaign. Kennedy's assassination that summer left Baca and so many of his supporters feeling shocked and lost. Baca took a two-month tour through Latin America, and when she returned she resumed her career, this time as research and information director for the National Council of La Raza in its Phoenix office. She was married briefly to Miguel Barragán, a Chicano activist and former priest. The couple had a son and a daughter. In 1970 she moved back to Colorado and opened up a small public relations business in Denver, Bronze Publications, which she operated for the next 14 years in addition to her many other commitments. Bronze specialized in publicity materials—everything from brochures to press materials to annual reports. Among the organizations she worked with were the National Institute of Mental Health, the Chicano Mobile Institute, the Colorado State University Chicano Studies Program, the National Institute of Education, and VISTA.

Those commitments were drawing her closer to a run for public office. From 1971 to 1972 she served as director of Spanish speaking affairs for the Democratic National Committee. In 1974, the state representative seat in her district (Adams County, Colorado) became vacant, and Baca decided to take a chance and seek the nomination. She won the nomination and was elected that November.

Baca's experience with both politics and communication served her well during her tenure as a state representative. In her first year there, she introduced nine house bills and brought six senate bills into the house. This was a surprise to the legislators; usually laws were introduced by members with more seniority. Baca felt that as a public servant she had a greater obligation to her constituents than to political tradition. Of the nine house and six senate bills she brought before the legislators, five were passed by both houses and signed into law. During her term in the house, Baca served as chair of the house Democratic Caucus (the first woman to hold the position), and she sat on a special joint study committee on school finance.

In 1978 Baca made a bid for a seat in the state senate and won, making her the state's first Hispanic senator. As senator, she was responsible for numerous pieces of legislation, including a 1985 bill to allow the state district courts to enforce subpoenas, a 1985 bill regulating the operation of non-state post-secondary schools, and a 1986 bill to protect deposits of public money held by state and national banks. In 1985 Baca was elected chair of the senate Democratic Caucus. She was the first Hispanic woman to hold that position in the state. In fact, she was the first Hispanic woman in the United States to hold a leadership position in a state senate.

During her state senate tenure, Baca also interacted with the international community. She was one of eight state legislators chosen by the American Council of Young Political Leaders to visit the Soviet Union for a study tour. In 1981 the German Marshall Fund selected Baca and 14 other Americans to participate in a "Successor Generation" seminar in Brussels.

Created Strong Ties as Politician

Part of Baca's success as a politician was her visibility among her constituents and throughout her state. Another element was her good relationship with the Democratic party leadership in Washington, D.C. Her years in Washington, coupled with her hard work and her expertise in public relations and communication, made her one of the best connected Democratic politicians in Colorado. From 1981 to 1989 she served as vice chair of the Democratic National Committee, and she was co-chair of the 1980 and 1984 Democratic National Conventions. The *Denver Post* went so far as to suggest that Baca had more influence in Washington than then-governor Richard Lamm.

In 1986 Baca decided it was time to try for the U.S. Congress. She fought a hard battle and was defeated despite her popularity and track record. She decided to retire from politics and devote her time to Sierra Baca, a management consulting firm she had begun in 1985. Sierra Baca focused on many of the same issues that Baca had tackled while in politics: education reform, the role of women and minorities in society, understanding public policy. She ran the company until 1989 when she accepted a position as executive director of the Colorado Hispanic American Institute. The Institute's mission was to develop multicultural leadership and develop programs that would benefit Hispanics and other minorities. One of the projects she worked on during her five years at the Institute was the

direction of Visiones, a leadership development program that brought community leaders from different racial and ethnic groups together and helped them to understand one another's cultures more completely.

In February of 1994 Baca was back in Washington briefly. This time she was a special assistant to President Bill Clinton and director of the Office of Consumer Affairs. As part of her duties, she chaired the U.S. delegation to the Organization for Economic Cooperation and Development (OECD) Committee on Consumer Policy conference.

From November of 1994 to May of 1999, Baca was regional administrator for the Rocky Mountain Region of the U.S. General Services Administration (GSA). In that capacity she oversaw GSA activities for an area covering six states and 48,000 government employees working in 43 government agencies. In 1999 she went back to her consulting business, Sierra Baca. Her civic activities include serving as executive director of the Latin American Research and Service Agency (LARASA), an advocacy group for the Hispanic community; and InSites, a nonprofit organization that conducts research and evaluation programs for educational organizations.

Sources

Books

Meier, Matt S., *Mexican American Biographies: A Historical Dictionary, 1836-1987,* Greenwood Press, 1988.

Periodicals

Denver Post, October 21, 1979.
Vista, February 4, 1992.

On-line

"Polly B. Baca" *9 News,* www.9news.com/latino/baca _resume_long.htm (June 4, 2003).

—George A. Milite

Lourdes G. Baird

1935—

Judge

Lourdes G. Baird became one of the highest-ranking Hispanic women in the U.S. Justice Department when she was appointed U.S. attorney for the Central District of California in 1990. The post involved supervising cases in a jurisdiction that was the largest in the United States at the time, comprised of seven counties with more than 12 million citizens. During her time in office, Baird played a role in the Justice Department's civil trial against the Los Angeles police officers who assaulted Rodney King. In 1992 she left the job for a federal judgeship with the Ninth U.S. Circuit Court, where she has continued her involvement in high-profile legal challenges in the Los Angeles area.

Baird was born on May 12, 1935, in Quito, Ecuador. Her father moved the family of seven children to Los Angeles a year later, where she attended Roman Catholic parochial schools in the city not far from the family home on Van Ness Avenue. She remembered her female-only high school, Immaculate Heart, as a particularly encouraging environment. "There's something in retrospect that was great about going to an all-girls high school," she told Henry Weinstein in a *Los Angeles Times* interview years later. Weinstein noted

that the school "was run by a highly independent order of nuns, who later clashed with the Los Angeles Archdiocese," and Baird affirmed this. "Those nuns were so independent, even in the 1950s," she told the newspaper.

Appointed U.S. Attorney by Republicans

Baird attended secretarial school for a time before marrying William T. Baird, a businessman, at age 21. They couple had three children, and Baird was a homemaker living in the Hancock Park neighborhood of Los Angeles when she decided to return to school. She began taking classes at Los Angeles City College on a part-time basis, and it took her five years to earn an associate of arts degree. From there she transferred to the University of California at Los Angeles (UCLA), and earned her sociology degree in 1973. She applied to and was accepted at UCLA's law school, and did well despite the hardship of a 1975 divorce. After graduating a year later, she took the state bar exam and passed it.

Baird began her career as an attorney at the age of 41. Her first job was as a prosecutor in the United States

At a Glance . . .

Born on May 12, 1935, in Quito, Ecuador; daughter of James C. Gillespie and Josefina Delgado; married William T. Baird (a businessman), 1956 (divorced, 1975); children: William Jr., Maria, and John. *Education:* Attended secretarial school in Los Angeles, c. 1954; Los Angeles City College, associate of arts degree; University of California at Los Angeles, BA, 1973, JD, 1976. *Politics:* Democrat.

Career: United States Attorney's Office, Los Angeles, CA, prosecutor, 1977-83; Baird, Munger and Myers, partner, 1983-86; East Los Angeles Municipal Court, judge, 1986-87; Los Angeles Municipal Court, judge, 1987; Los Angeles Superior Court, Juvenile Court division, judge, 1988; California's Central District, U.S. attorney, 1990-92, district court judge, 1992–.

Member: UCLA School of Law Alumni Association, president, 1981-84; Ninth Circuit Court of Appeals, advisory committee, 1983-86; California Women Lawyers Association; Mexican American Bar Association; Latino Judges Association; National Association of Women Judges.

Address: *Office*—Edward R. Roybal Federal Building and Courthouse, 255 E. Temple St., Los Angeles, CA 90012.

attorney's office in Los Angeles. Six years later, in 1983, she went into private practice as partner in Baird, Munger and Myers. In 1986 she accepted an appointment as a municipal court judge in Los Angeles, and two years later became a juvenile-court judge in Los Angeles County Superior Court. Baird's legal acumen attracted the attention of U.S. Senator Pete Wilson, a Republican, and he proposed her name for a soon-to-be vacant U.S. attorney post in the Los Angeles area; the nomination was somewhat unusual because of Baird's Democratic political affiliation. Her name was seconded by U.S. President George H. W. Bush, and her appointment was confirmed a few months later by Senate vote. When she was sworn into office in July of 1990, Baird became one of a few U.S. attorneys in history to be appointed during a political administration not of his or her own political affiliation. "Baird will become one of only five female U.S. attorneys in the country and one of the few who speaks Spanish fluently," wrote Weinstein of the *Los Angeles*

Times at the time. "She also is the first grandmother ever selected for the post."

Baird's role as U.S. attorney in Los Angeles was an important one. As Weinstein noted, the former judge "assumes her post at a time when the area is considered one of the major national centers of drug crime, money laundering, savings and loan scams and defense contracting fraud, four principal areas of concern to federal prosecutors," the *Los Angeles Times* article noted. When she took over, there was even a federal grand jury investigation at her office of Los Angeles mayor Tom Bradley for his possible links to a banking scandal.

Confronted With Variety of High Profile Cases

In 1991 Baird's office became involved in the Rodney King case. In March of that year, King, an African-American motorist, was stopped by Los Angeles police officers; a subsequent beating was filmed surreptitiously from a nearby apartment building, and released to the media. The tape ignited a firestorm of controversy, and a criminal case against the officers ended in their acquittal. The announcement of that verdict caused Los Angeles's black community to erupt in anger, and several days of rioting ensued in April of 1992. The federal courthouse that housed Baird's office was even targeted. Noting her importance as "the top Justice Department official in town," *Los Angeles Times* writer Jim Newton went on to describe the scene. "The federal courthouse had come under attack during the early hours of the rioting, and when Baird and other lawyers showed up for work on Thursday morning, the smell of smoke from torched palm trees hung in the elegant entryway, and broken glass carpeted much of the building's first floor." By then Baird was part of another investigation into the King incident, after Justice Department officials in Washington launched a probe into whether or not King's civil rights were violated. "Amid the uproar, Baird moved calmly to choose the attorneys who would represent her office in the case," Newton wrote. The trial ended with guilty verdicts for the officers, with a jury agreeing that they violated King's constitutional right to be free from the intentional use of unreasonable force.

By that time, however, Baird had moved on to a seat on the bench of the Central District of California's District Court in September of 1992. There she went on to play a role in several other important cases, including a 1996 lawsuit filed by U.S. Immigration and Naturalization Service (INS) agent Jorge Guzman, who claimed that he had been unduly harassed at his job because of his Hispanic heritage. Some two dozen internal investigations of him had taken place, but he was never reprimanded, nor did they hinder his subsequent promotions. Guzman "alleged the existence of pervasive anti-Latino sentiments in the inspector general's office and the INS, especially among old-line officers in high positions," explained *Los Angeles Times* writer Patrick J. McDonnell. "As a senior supervisory agent, Guzman is one of the highest-ranking Latinos in the INS' Los Angeles district." The final straw was a raid on his home by plainclothes officers with weapons, who frightened the nanny for Guzman's daughter and his sister, and allegedly made sexual advances toward one of the women; they became co-plaintiffs in his suit. After a trial presided over by Baird, the Justice Department agreed to pay Guzman $400,000 in damages.

Baird also put an end to a legal challenge to block California's controversial Proposition 227, approved by voters in June of 1998. It ended three decades of bilingual-education programs in the California public school system, specifying that all classes be taught "overwhelmingly" in English. Supporters of bilingual education asked Baird's court to block it just before it was set to go into effect, but she refused. The following year, she heard sides in a case against three banks in Mexico suspected of money-laundering by the U.S. Customs Service. She also agreed with plaintiffs in 1999 that the use of a special restraining chair by sheriffs' authorities in Ventura County violated the constitutional rights of detainees. In 2000 she reversed a record $143 million award given to a British computer-chip maker for lost pets called Trovan. The suit was brought against pharmaceutical giant Pfizer, who made and marketed an antibiotic also called "Trovan" that was linked to liver failure in animals. Pfizer lost the first round, and was ordered to pay the $143 million—the largest trademark infringement verdict in U.S. history at the time—but then allegations surfaced that the lawyers for Trovan had falsified evidence, including spurious letters by pet-owners confused about the news about the antibiotic and its dangers.

In 2003 Baird decided in favor of a group of farm laborers from Mexico, who had come to Ventura County at the invitation of a labor contractor under the provisions of a federal guest-worker program known as H-2A. The workers helped harvest the county's lemon crop during a farm-labor shortage, but alleged that they were not paid in full, nor allowed proper breaks and lunch periods as specified by law. The defendant moved to have the case transferred to federal court, since the guest-worker program was a federal one, but Baird disagreed and returned the case to the Ventura County Superior Court. In her written ruling, she pointed out that the workers from Mexico were still protected under California statutes. "In creating a new system for the admission of H-2A workers … there is no evidence that Congress intended to eliminate these workers' state law remedies," she was quoted as saying in her decision by *Los Angeles Times* journalist Fred Alvarez.

Baird has numerous professional ties to the legal community in Southern California and beyond. She belongs to the California Women Lawyers Association, the Mexican American Bar Association, the Latino Judges Association, and the National Association of Women Judges.

Sources

Books

Dictionary of Hispanic Biography, Gale, 1996.

Periodicals

Buffalo News, August 1, 1998, p. A2.
Los Angeles Times, July 19, 1990; June 27, 1993; September 24, 1996; January 21, 1999; March 31, 1999, p. 2; November 23, 1999, p. B1; December 22, 1999, p. B3; July 21, 2001, p. B5; January 24, 2003.
Wall Street Journal, May 24, 2000, p. B2.

—Carol Brennan

Elsa Benitez

1977—

Model

Mexican-born model Elsa Benitez graced the cover of *Sports Illustrated*'s famous swimsuit issue in 2001. Her career seemed off to a promising start, but she took a break from the fast-paced fashion world to study acting and become a mother. She and her husband, former Miami Heat player Rony Seikaly, became parents to daughter Mila in 2003.

Born in 1977, Benitez is a native of Hermosillo, capital city of the northwest Mexican state of Sonora, about an hour's drive from the Gulf of California. Hermosillo, which lies on the Sonora River, is home to a Ford Motor Company manufacturing plant where the Escort model was once made, and is a thriving agricultural center as well. Growing up, Benitez idolized one of the top models of the 1980s, Linda Evangelista. As a young woman, she reached five feet, ten inches in height, and won a model-search contest in Costa Rica in 1995. She soon began finding work in Latin America, and then signed with Elite Model Management, the agency founded by John Casablancas and later run by Evangelista's husband, Gerald Marie.

Benitez first came to international attention modeling in Europe, and her nascent career was boosted im-

mensely when influential photographer Steven Meisel began working with her. In 1996 she appeared on three covers of Italian *Vogue*. She also became a favorite of Italian designers Dolce e Gabbana, and appeared in their spring/summer collections shown in Milan in October of 1996. Stefano Gabbana told a writer for London's *Observer* newspaper, Roger Tredre, that he and Domenico Dolce felt that Benitez "embodies the Mediterranean woman," Gabbana enthused. "Her beauty reminds us of the actresses of the neo-realist Italian cinema, like Anna Magnani." At the time of the interview, Benitez still spoke just rudimentary English.

Benitez went on to work for designers Oscar de la Renta, Valentino, and Rena Lange; she has appeared in ad campaigns for Episode, J. Crew, and Nine West. Her biggest career coup, however, came early in 2001 when she appeared on the cover of *Sports Illustrated*'s annual swimsuit issue. Under the heading "Goddesses of the Mediterranean," the model's sultry photo was captioned, "Elsa Benitez Heats Up Tunisia." The issue—a February tradition—is centered around an immense promotional blitz, and sales ordinarily hit the $50-million mark. Some of the world's top models had

At a Glance . . .

Born in 1977, in Hermosillo, Sonora, Mexico; married Rony Seikaly (a professional athlete), 1999; children: Mila Seikaly.

Career: Won modeling contest in Costa Rica, 1995; signed with Elite Model Management; appeared in runway shows and ad campaigns for Dolce e Gabbana, Oscar de la Renta, Valentino, and Rena Lange; appeared in ad campaigns for Episode, J. Crew, Victoria's Secret, and Nine West; appeared on the February 2001 cover of *Sports Illustrated*'s annual swimsuit issue.

Address: *Home*—Miami, FL. *Office*—c/o Elite Model Management, 111 E. 22nd St., Fl. 2, New York, NY 10010-5400.

graced the *SI* cover before Benitez, among them Heidi Klum, Tyra Banks, Elle MacPherson, Christie Brinkley, and Cheryl Tiegs. Launched in 1964 as a way to lure readers during a slow sports-story month, the swimsuit issue grew racier over the years, and the exotic locales of its shoots are usually kept top-secret. "No matter where the magazine drapes its models, though, the issue manages to do one thing no other feature can: it gathers sports fans of every stripe beneath a single umbrella," noted a *Financial Times* report. "With the swimsuit issue in hand, no one complains that baseball lacks action, that hockey is too violent, that football is for those too fat or too dumb to play hockey."

Benitez's career for the rest of the year seemed promising: she became the spokesperson for Budweiser and Bud Light, and also appeared in ads for the Taco Bell fast-food chain and its new stuffed burrito menu item. One television commercial for the product featured a dream sequence of her walking past two men, who are enamored of the burrito she is carrying, not her. "Agency creatives said the Mexican-born Benitez will help the product earn quick recognition with fickle fast-food customers," wrote Justin M. Norton in *ADWEEK Western Edition*. A representative of the San Francisco-based advertising agency involved, Tom O'Keefe, told the trade journal that Benitez "is the ideal spokesperson, because she perfectly embodies the essence of the product."

Benitez appeared again in the 2002 *SI* swimsuit issue. The *New York Post* reported in March of 2002 that *Sports Illustrated* had struck a deal with the Playboy magazine empire to publish some of the other photos from the shoot in the German edition of *Playboy*. Some of the models—Klum and Eva Herzigova among them—objected to the deal, claiming that the models had not been consulted, and had not signed waivers allowing the publication of outtakes from the shoot in which they were nude in some cases.

Benitez seemed to drop out of the public eye afterward, however. She wed Rony Seikaly, whom she had met in 1997, and was dividing her time between their homes in Miami and New York City. The basketball player, who retired from the New Jersey Nets in 2000, was the first Lebanese player in NBA history, and stands at an impressive six feet, eleven inches. Seikaly was nonplussed by the attention his wife usually received in public. "I've always said I'm the luckiest guy in the world, not because she's beautiful on the outside, but because she's beautiful on the inside, too," Seikaly once told the *New York Post*. Benitez gave birth to daughter Mila in February of 2003. She has begun taking acting lessons and harbors an ambition for a film career, in both Spanish- and English-language productions.

Sources

Periodicals

ADWEEK Western Edition, April 30, 2001.
Daily Record (Glasgow, Scotland), May 9, 2002, p. 30.
Financial Times, March 16, 2002, p. 24.
Hispanic, April 2003.
Independent (London, England), December 2, 1999, p. 13.
National Petroleum News, June 2001, p, 58.
New York Post, February 21, 2001, p. 22; February 22, 2001, p. 79; March 5, 2002, p. 10.
Observer (London, England), November 3, 1996, p. 25.
Olympian (Olympia, WA), February 24, 2001, p. B3.

On-line

"Model of the Week," *Ask Men,* www.askmen.com/women/models/20_elsa_benitez.html (July 3, 2003).

—Carol Brennan

Big Punisher

1971-2000

Rapper

Puerto Rican rapper Big Punisher, also known as Big Pun, was the first Latin-American hip-hop star. He brought Latino rap—popular before only in his South Bronx neighborhood—into the hip-hop mainstream, which has typically been dominated by African-American artists. His first hit single, "I'm Not a Player," set the stage for the release of his immensely successful 1998 full-length debut, *Capital Punishment*. The album was the first by a Latin rapper to earn double-platinum status for record sales. Big Pun sealed his place in history by becoming the first Latin rapper to be nominated for a Grammy award. The rapper's name referred to his great size; many MCs rapped about "living large," but Big Pun was medically obese—he weighed in at nearly 700 pounds at the time of his death from heart failure, in 2000.

Big Pun was born Christopher Rios on November 10, 1971, in the South Bronx neighborhood of New York City. He was raised in a strict household by his mother and militaristic stepfather, and was in good shape as a teen. He enjoyed boxing and basketball. Conflicts with his parents caused him to leave home at age 15. He dropped out of high school after just one year, but Big

Pun read encyclopedias on his own to expand his knowledge and vocabulary. Within a few years, he was an expectant father with bills to pay, and worked odd jobs until collecting on a long-standing legal claim. He received an estimated half-million dollars from an accident that took place in a public park when he was a child. He began over-eating to cope with stress and, with his slow metabolism, began to pack on the pounds. In 1990 he married his junior high school sweetheart, Liza. The two had three children together: Christopher, Vanessa, and Amanda.

Discovered by Fat Joe

In 1989 Big Pun, who then went by the moniker Big Moon Dog, formed the Full-A-Clips Crew with fellow Latin rappers Triple Seis and Cuban Link. Popular Bronx producer and fellow Puerto Rican rapper Joseph Cartagena, a.k.a. Fat Joe, singled Big Pun out in 1995, after hearing the hefty rapper rhyme. "I knew he was one of the great ones," Fat Joe told Aliza Valdes-Rodriguez of the *Los Angeles Times*. "I was totally impressed by his rapping, the delivery with the tongue-twisting metaphors."

At a Glance . . .

Born Christopher Rios on November 10, 1971, in Bronx, NY; died on February 7, 2000, in White Plains, NY; married Liza; three children.

Career: Rap singer, 1989-2000.

Big Pun and Fat Joe developed a close relationship; Big Pun would later refer to Fat Joe, who weighed in at 300 pounds himself, as his "twin." The two would later become heroes of New York's Puerto Rican community; they each rode their own floats in the 1998 and 1999 Puerto Rican Day parades in New York City. Fat Joe immediately recognized Pun's extraordinary rhyming and lyrical skills, and invited him to record a cameo on Fat Joe's song "Watch Out." Renamed Big Punisher, the rapper became part of the Terror Squad, a crew made up of the Latin rappers associated with Fat Joe. Soon after his recording debut, Fat Joe negotiated Pun's contract with New York's Loud Records. Pun was one of the few newcomers included on *The Mix Tape Vol. 1,* a compilation put together by influential New York DJ Funkmaster Flex.

Pun released the single "I'm Not a Player" in the winter of 1997, and his debut full-length album, *Capital Punishment,* followed a few months later. The album featured cameos by some of the hottest names in hip hop at the time: Wyclef Jean on the reggae-flavored song "Caribbean Connection," Black Thought from the Roots on "Super Lyrical," and Wu-Tang Clan's Inspectah Deck and Prodigy from Mobb Deep on "Tres Leches." Big Pun laments mistreatment from an ex-lover in the ballad "Punish Me" and, on the album's closer, "Parental Discretion," featuring Busta Rhymes, Pun let loose one of the tongue-twisting, run-on rhymes he was famous for: "I recollect when I was just a boy eating Chips Ahoy/wasn't allowed to raise my voice/now I'm making noise." The single "Still Not a Player" pushed the album to platinum status within a few months of its release.

Pun was known for his remarkable breath control and ability to squeeze out a seemingly endless stream of rhymes in one breath. He also was known for his lyrical humor and ability to string together complex and tongue-twisting rhymes. "Big Pun possessed a lyrical gift of incessant breath control and a knockout punch with the rhymes," according to his biography on the *Loud Records'* website. While other rappers strung together rhymes about flashy riches, disrespecting women, and the violence and crime of ghetto street life, Big Pun described his style as "sophisticated hardcore," according to Jon Pareles of the *New York Times.* "I'm talking about everyday life," Big Pun said in an MTV interview, "losing your job, losing a loved one, stress, happiness, whatever." The rapper was hardly relating the struggles of the average working man, however. His "lyrical stance fitted the late 1990s sexual braggadocio and drugs and gun culture which attracted teenage America to the hip-hop world," according to Pierre Perrone in the London *Independent.*

Weight Gain Lead to Early Death

Pun's rise in hip-hop was fast and steady, and so was his weight gain. When *Capital Punishment* was released in 1998, he weighed in at 400 pounds. By the time of his death, just two years later, he weighed 698 pounds, and could no longer tie his own shoelaces. "He was so big and he knew his weight was causing a health problem," Fat Joe is quoted as saying at *Rolling Stone* online. "For a long time, even though he was a big guy, he could do whatever he wanted. He'd play sports with us and everything. But as time went on, his health got worse." Encouragement from friends and family led Pun to enter a diet program at Duke University during the summer of 1999, but he quickly regained the weight he lost there. "He really wanted to lose weight," Fat Joe told *Rolling Stone* online. "It was just overwhelming."

Known for his remarkable live performances, Big Pun was less and less able to get around because of his weight. "Given his size, Pun's performance is filled with suspense," critic Rob Marriot wrote in the *Village Voice.* The hot lights and physical activity on stage clearly tested the rapper's stamina, and audience members often wondered if he would make it through a set. Still, Marriot continued, "Big Pun even outshone the headliners." He and Fat Joe rapped together on Jennifer Lopez's hit "Feelin' So Good," and were scheduled to appear with her on *Saturday Night Live* on February 5, 2000, but Big Pun was unable to make it.

Big Pun, his wife, and their children were staying in a hotel in suburban White Plains, New York, in early 2000 while their Bronx home was being renovated. On February 7, he had trouble breathing and collapsed. Paramedics arrived on the scene but could not revive him, and he was pronounced dead on arrival at a local hospital. Heart failure was later determined as the cause of death.

Fame Continued After Death

If Big Pun was considered a hero of the Latin community during his short lifetime, his fans tried to elevate him to legendary status after his death. The professional mural company TATS Cru, made up of graffiti artists, painted a 35-foot-mural in the Bronx memorializing the rapper days after his death. A campaign was launched to rename a stretch of 163rd Street in the South Bronx, Big Pun Avenue. "He was a ghetto rapper; he didn't forget his people," one South Bronx grandmother told the *Washington Post.* "Other rappers tend to forget where they're from, but not Big Pun. With all the money that he had and everything, he still lived around here, his home was here. He's legend. This guy is going to be a legend for us."

The rapper's death was mourned by hip-hop fans and artists alike. Fans called in to radio stations and wept openly on air. "I lost a brother," Fat Joe told the *Los Angeles Times.* He added that hip hop "lost a great personality, a great guy who really cared about everybody. One of the best, man. Another one of us gone. Thank God it ain't no violence. But he's gone."

Big Pun's last album, *Yeeeah Baby,* was released a few weeks after his death, and debuted at number three on the charts. The rapper "is at his habanero hottest" on the album, wrote Matt Diehl on the *Rolling Stone* website, "when representing his Latino pride" on songs like "100 Percent." Hip hop and pop stars Lil' Kim, Puff Daddy, and Jennifer Lopez appeared together as a tribute to the rapper in the video for the album's first single, "It's So Hard."

Unlike Tupac Shakur, another deceased rapper, Big Pun left few recordings unreleased before his death. Nonetheless, his record label, Loud, was able to put together a handful of Big Pun performances to release on *Endangered Species* in 2001. The album included songs from *Capital Punishment,* guest appearances, and previously unreleased material. "How We Roll," the album's first single, is built around Janet Jackson's hit ballad "Let's Wait Awhile." The Beatnuts' "Off the Books" is included, featuring Big Pun's classic cameo. Songs by Kool G. Rap, Brandy, Fat Joe, and Ricky Martin appeared on *Endangered Species,* as well, all of them featuring the late rapper's voice. "What's most striking about *Endangered Species* is that it shows Pun's rejection of musical limits," critic Rashuan Hall wrote in *Billboard.*

Selected discography

(with Fat Joe) "Fire Water," 1996.
(with Fat Joe) "Watch Out," 1996.
(with the Beatnuts) "Off the Books," 1997.
(Contributor) *Soul in the Hole,* 1997.
Capital Punishment, Relativity, 1998.
Yeeeah Baby, Loud, 2000.
Endangered Species, Relativity, 2001.

Sources

Periodicals

Billboard, April 7, 2002, p. 18.
Independent (London, England), February 10, 2000, p. 6.
Los Angeles Times, February 9, 2000, p. A16.
New York Times, February 8, 2000, p. B9; February 9, 2000, p. B10; May 2, 2001, p. B3.
Orange County Register (Santa Ana, California), June 5, 1998, p. F56.
Rolling Stone, May 28, 1998, p. 192.
Village Voice, June 9, 1998, p. 69.
Washington Post, February 9, 2000, p. B6; February 11, 2000, p. C1.

On-line

"Big Punisher," *All Music Guide,* www.allmusic.com (April 7, 2003).
"Big Punisher," *Loud Records,* www.loud.com/bigpun/right_bio.html (April 7, 2003).
"Big Punisher," *Rolling Stone,* www.rollingstone.com/bigpun (April 7, 2003).
"Big Punisher," *Sing 365,* www.sing365.com (April 7, 2003).

—Brenna Sanchez

Maria Brito

1947—

Painter, sculptor

A member of "The Miami Generation" of Cuban-born artists who relocated to the United States after Cuba's communist revolution, Maria Brito has won acclaim for paintings and sculptures that evoke themes of displacement, loss, and the search for identity. Her work, praised for its intuitive appeal and its densely symbolic qualities, has earned national attention and is included in several permanent collections, including the Smithsonian American Art Museum.

Born in Havana, Cuba, in 1947, Brito was sent to the United States with her younger brother in 1961 through Operation Pedro Pan, a sort of "underground railroad" that allowed children to leave the communist island. Brito, only thirteen years old at the time, traveled alone with her brother to Miami, Florida, where her family soon joined them. There Brito grew up amid a vibrant Cuban immigrant community that had established firm roots. The city remains her home.

Brito earned degrees in studio art and art education at Florida International University, and also did graduate study at the University of Miami. A course in ceramics sparked her interest in exploring what was to become

her most characteristic avenue of expression, mixed media. The work that she did for her MFA, which she received from the University of Miami in 1979, already showed her growing fascination with the creative possibilities of found objects and mixed media installations.

Her inspiration, Brito told *Miami Herald* writer Helen Kohen, often comes from a suggestive word, or from objects that Brito picks up at flea markets. Everyday objects such as faucets and pipes, electrical cords, books, and household furniture are common elements in her installations. In her large installation "Merely a Player," for example, which was part of the "Transcending the Border of Memory" exhibit at the Norton Gallery in West Palm Beach Florida in 1995, Brito creates a living-room set that contains a comfortable-looking sofa and books. Though the set "appears inviting," according to *Art in America* writer Anne Barclay Morgan, "a narrow, salmon-colored passage quickly led the viewer into a labyrinth of tiny, claustrophobic rooms, evoking an agonized search for self-discovery and emancipation."

"The Patio of My House," part of the "Arte Latino: Treasures from the Smithsonian American Art Mu-

At a Glance . . .

Born in 1947, in Havana, Cuba; two children. *Education:* University of Miami, BA, art education, 1969, MFA, 1979; Florida International University, BFA, 1997, MS, art education, 1997.

Career: Painter and sculptor, 1979–; Barry University, Miami, Florida, adjunct professor of art, 1990s–.

Awards: Two National Endowment fellowships; Cintas Fellowships, 1981, 1985; Florida Department of State grant; Pollack Krasner Foundation Grant.

Address: *Office*—Barry University, School of Arts and Sciences, Department of Fine Arts, 11300 NE Second Ave., Miami, FL 33161-6695.

seum" exhibit, also evoked a domestic room. *Los Angeles Times* writer Scarlet Cheng described the piece as showing a "cutaway of a cramped kitchenette" on one side and "on the other side a crib, from which rises a stylized tree whose roots are cut into." The installation, critic Katherine Hough observed to Cheng, suggests the movement from innocence to maturity.

As Thomas D. Boswell and James R. Curtis acknowledged in their book *The Cuban-American Experience,* Brito is a leading artist among a new generation: "The Cuban spirit, tinted by recollections of the past, circumstances of the present, and visions of the future has been captured by a new generation of painters who have been able to live through the circumstances." These artists, according to Boswell and Curtis, "blend Cuban and American artistic traditions, yet in a highly individualistic fashion. Likewise, their subjects are frequently drawn from both cultures, as well as a mixture of the two." Guillermo Martinez in a *Miami Herald* article described both "touches of Cuba" as well as elements from Miami-Cuban culture in the work of Brito and other "Miami Generation" artists.

By the early 1980s Brito was showing her art in major venues and receiving significant national and international recognition. In 1988 she received a commission to create a sculpture for the Olympic Sculpture Park in Seoul, South Korea. Her work was included in "The Decade Show" in 1990, "Cuba Twentieth Century: Modernism and Syncretism," a show that traveled around Europe, and the Iberoamerican Biennal in Lima, Peru. Brito has received numerous awards, including two fellowships from the National Endowment for the Arts, two Cintas fellowships, a grant from the Florida Department of State, and a Pollack Krasner Foundation grant.

In 1998 Brito had her first solo museum show in South Florida, "Maria Brito: Rites of Passage." The exhibition included sculptures, paintings, and installations created over a ten-year period. Critics noted the themes of entrapment, repression, and death that pervaded the pieces. "This exhibition," commented curator Jorge Santis in a critique posted by *Traditional Fine Art Online,* "exemplifies the sadness that many who left Cuba still feel as well as the struggle of trying to enculturate in a new country."

Critics have often noted the autobiographical elements in Brito's work. Many pieces recall the experience of displacement, entrapment, and physical suffering. In "The Traveler (Homage to B.G.)," another piece from "Transcending the Borders of Memory," Brito surrounded a portrait of herself with images associated with Christian martyrdom, such as the spiked wheel on which St. Catherine was murdered. A work completed in 2001, "Self-Portrait as a Swan," shows an image of a white swan with wings outspread. A much larger human hand holds the swan's right foot between thumb and index finger as the swan, with twisted body and neck, apparently tries to escape. In the background is a dark shape that suggests a box with a narrow opening. The piece conveys physical pain and captivity. "Feed," another piece from 2001, presents a doll-like image of a girl who lies flat on a shelf apparently suspended in mid-air. Above her hangs an intravenous bottle with a tube that apparently connects with the female figure behind her dress. The work, which creates an eerie tension by employing flat cutout forms, suggests themes of helplessness and exposure as well as external menace.

Brito was among several artists in 2001 invited to ceremonies with First Lady Laura Bush when the "Arte Latino: Treasures from the Smithsonian American Art Museum" exhibit traveled to the Terra Museum of American Art in Chicago. The exhibit featured works from 200 years of Latino art in the United States. When Brito is not on the road with her art, she is an adjunct professor of art at Barry University in Miami. She has two sons.

Sources

Books

Boswell, Thomas D., and James R. Curtis, *The Cuban-American Experience: Culture, Images, and Perspectives,* Allanheld & Osmun, 1984.
Notable Hispanic American Women, Book 1, Gale (Detroit, MI), 1993.

Periodicals

Art in America, May 1995, p. 124.
Los Angeles Times, May 5, 2002.
Miami Herald, June 15, 1984, p. 25A.
US Newswire, September 4, 2001.

On-line

"Maria Brito," *Bernice Steinbaum Gallery,* www. bernicesteinbaumgallery.com/ (March 29, 2003).

"Maria Brito: Rites of Passage," *Fort Lauderdale Museum of Art,* www.tfaoi.com (March 29, 2003).

"Oral History Interview with Maria Brito," *Smithsonian Archive of American Art,* www.archivesof americanart.si.edu/oralhist/brito97.htm (June 4, 2003).

—Elizabeth Shostak

Cruz M. Bustamante

1953—

Lieutenant governor, politician

Cruz M. Bustamante is a Democrat who became the first Latino to hold a statewide office in California in over 100 years when he was elected lieutenant governor in 1998. Prior to that position, Bustamante served as a California assemblyman and he was the first Latino speaker of the state assembly. Throughout his career Bustamante has supported the agricultural and immigrant communities of California, particularly in his home district of Fresno. He has promoted better education, environmental responsibility, and racial tolerance and diversity during his two terms as lieutenant governor. He is a low-profile politician who has earned a reputation as someone who works hard and who is not afraid to address controversial issues.

Childhood Filled With Work and Values

Cruz M. Bustamante was born on January 4, 1953, in Dinuba, California, the first of six children born to Cruz and Dominga Bustamante. He grew up in San Joaquin living near both sets of grandparents who came to the United States from Chihuahua and Zacatecas, Mexico.

Spanish was spoken in the home and it was Bustamante's first language. He only began learning English when he started attending kindergarten.

Bustamante's father worked primarily as a barber and his mother was a homemaker. "My mother made sure we understood how to behave and my father taught us the value of hard work as he held down two jobs, sometimes three, to keep us clothed, fed, and in school," Bustamante said on the California lieutenant governor's official website in 2003. Bustamante learned the value of serving other people from his parents, both of whom were actively involved in community service organizations. The senior Cruz Bustamante was also elected city councilperson and he unsuccessfully ran for the position of county supervisor.

Bustamante attended Tranquility High School, and when he was not in school, he worked in the fields of San Joaquin. "A barber's son who grew up working mostly in the fields of the country's largest agricultural region, where the class division between farm workers and farm owners is as clear as night and day, he shared the feelings of self-doubt and lowered expectations that

At a Glance . . .

Born Cruz M. Bustamante on January 4, 1953, in Dinuba, CA; son of Cruz and Dominga Bustamante; married to Arcelia De La Pena, 1977; children: Leticia, Sonia, and Marisa. *Education:* Fresno City College, 1972-73; Fresno State University, 1973-77.

Career: Congressman B.F. Sisk, Washington, D.C., intern, 1972; Fresno Summer Youth Employment Program, director, 1977-83; Congressman Rick Lehman, district representative, 1983-87; Assemblyman Bruce Bronzan, district representative, 1988-92; California State Assembly, assemblyman, 1993-95, speaker of the assembly, 1996-98; California, lieutenant governor, 1998–.

Memberships: Association of Mexican American Educators; University of California Alumni Association.

Awards: National Legislative Award, League of United Latin American Citizens, 2003; Coastal Hero Award, California CoastKeeper Alliance, 2002; Legislator of the Year, Faculty Association of Community Colleges; True American Role Model, Mexican American Political Association; Lifetime Award, Golden State Mobilehome Owners League; Friend of Labor Award, Mexican American Political Association.

Address: *Office*—State Capitol, Room 1114, Sacramento, CA 95814.

so many children of his social stature experienced," wrote Fernando Quintero of *LatinoLink*. As a child Bustamante did not imagine becoming one of the most influential leaders in California when he grew up. After high school he went to Fresno City College to learn butchery. It was a short-lived career choice because Bustamante's entry into politics came when he was just 19 years old.

In 1972 Bustamante's father found an internship opportunity for his son in Washington, D.C., working for Congressman B.F. Sisk, who was the chairperson of the Rules and Means committee. It was an eye-opening experience for the working class rural Californian to be exposed to Washington's fast-paced political scene and elegant social life. Bustamante was assigned to read and answer the congressman's letters from his constituents. He enjoyed the task of helping people and he decided to pursue a career in government instead of

butchery.

Bustamante returned to California after his internship and transferred to Fresno State University to study public administration. He stayed at Fresno State until 1977 when he married Arcelia De La Pena and began having children. Soon after, he was offered a part-time job as a fundraiser for local assemblyman Rick Lehman. Bustamante knew that the part-time job was an excellent way to break into California politics, but he also knew that he needed a full-time job to better support his family. Bustamante passed up the opportunity and instead went to work as the director of the Fresno Summer Youth Employment Program. Five years later, in 1983, Assemblyman Lehman became a U.S. representative and he again offered Bustamante a job, this time in a full-time capacity as a district representative. Bustamante quickly jumped at the chance to reenter politics and worked for Lehman for the next five years.

In 1988 Bustamante became a district representative for Assemblyman Bruce Bronzan. Bronzan was up for reelection as assemblyman in 1992 when he decided to take a job at the University of California, San Francisco, just eight days before the November elections. A special election was held in 1993 to fill Bronzan's vacant seat and Bustamante, a Democrat, easily won the election.

Moderate Politics Lead to Lieutenant Governorship

Bustamante was not a high-profile politician early in his career, but he was also not afraid to speak out about important issues. He was especially vocal about the agricultural industry and the immigrant labor force, which were both central to his district. In 1994 Bustamante took a stand against California Governor Pete Wilson's immigration policies. "I take it real personal when immigrants are made out to be the root of all evil," Bustamante told the *California Journal Weekly* in July of 1994. "They're saying that my grandparents, who worked for themselves and succeeded without being dependent on any social programs, had no merit."

In 1994 Bustamante was reelected as assemblyman of the 31st District. Two years later he became the first Latino speaker of the state assembly. Although Bustamante won 90 percent of the Latino vote in the 1996 election and he had been a strong proponent of immigrants' rights and issues, Bustamante was not a militant Latino who pushed an ethnic agenda. He was a self-described moderate or centrist, which he attributed to his upbringing. Bustamante recalled the tensions between white and Latino children in school and he learned as a child that it was best for him to tread in the middle of the two extremes. "I am built moderate. That's who I am," Bustamante was quoted from a speech by Peter Maass of *U.S. News & World Report* in March of 1997.

Bustamante has repeatedly explained that he has an American political agenda, not an ethnic agenda. Since his days in the California Assembly, this agenda has consisted of promoting good schools, safe neighborhoods, decent jobs, and opportunities for personal achievement. This straightforward platform won Bustamante the 1998 election for California's lieutenant governor, a constitutional officer who is elected separately from the governor. With this victory Bustamante became the first Latino to be elected to a statewide office in California since 1878. This historic event was celebrated by numerous high ranking political officials, including the vice president of the United States at that time, Al Gore. When Bustamante was sworn into office, he vowed to create more jobs for Californians. "I will work to breathe life into the dreams of entrepreneurs and to eliminate the needless regulation that strangles innovation," Bustamante said to the *San Francisco Chronicle* in January of 1999.

Laid Groundwork During First Term

California's lieutenant governor is second in command in the state. The lieutenant governor assumes the role of governor if the governor is unable to perform his or her duties. The lieutenant governor also serves as the president of the state senate, regent of the University of California, and trustee of the California State University System. While some politicians describe the lieutenant governor's position as a thankless job that is constantly overshadowed by the governor, Bustamante has aimed to make the most of his position. He has not been content to just sit on state boards and commissions. Instead he has launched his own statewide initiatives, in addition to attending to his regular duties.

Among Bustamante's many accomplishments as lieutenant governor, he has worked to improve education in the state. In particular, he established the Schiff-Bustamante Standards-Based Instructional Materials Program to provide proper textbooks for school children. Bustamante also worked for equal access to higher education and promoted educational incentives for college students. He was also involved in the development of a new University of California campus in Merced in the Central Valley, an area of California that had been underserved in the area of education.

Bustamante was in office during California's highly publicized and very expensive energy crisis at the turn of the century and he quickly stepped up to address the problem. In May of 2001 Bustamante filed a civil law suit in the Los Angeles Superior Court against five energy generators for overcharging California residents for electricity. He also sponsored legislation that would permit the criminal prosecution of companies that manipulated the energy market. Additionally, Bustamante appeared in statewide public service announcements to encourage Californians to conserve energy.

One of Bustamante's original initiatives as lieutenant governor was the creation of the Commission for One California to promote racial tolerance and diversity. The committee held hearings on the topics of racial profiling by law enforcement, diversity in the media, and tolerance in schools. Bustamante also led the government outreach effort to Sikh and Arab-American communities after the September 11, 2001, terrorist attacks on the United States that left these communities vulnerable to ethnic and religious discrimination and violence. Most notably, Bustamante took a stand against Proposition 187, a 1994 ballot measure to cut social services for illegal immigrants which was approved by 60 percent of California voters. This controversial and politically contentious issue put Bustamante at odds with Governor Gray Davis, but Bustamante stood firm on his position. "This is a matter of principle to me," Bustamante told Robert B. Gunnison of the *San Francisco Chronicle* in April of 1999. "I am not going to back off this issue until it's resolved."

Continued to Push For Ethnic Education

In 2002 Bustamante ran for reelection as lieutenant governor of California. "I want to continue working on the things we've started. I want to be able to help people," Bustamante explained to Gregg Jones of the *Los Angeles Times* in October of 2002. Bustamante won the election against Republican State Senator Bruce McPherson of Santa Cruz. The theme for his 2003 inaugural address was "Celebrating One California." In his inaugural speech he declared, "I plan to roll up my sleeves and work closely with county, state, and federal leaders from both sides of the aisle to strengthen California.... It will be up to all Californians to do their fair share to make our state strong again."

In his second term as lieutenant governor, Bustamante has continued the initiatives he started during his first term. In particular he has promoted the Cal Grant Outreach Program to inform disadvantaged students about funding opportunities for college. He has also remained committed to cultural diversity and understanding. In 2003 he unveiled an educational book aimed at teaching children about the Sikh culture and community and he distributed educational kits about the internment of Japanese Americans during World War II to schools and libraries throughout the state. Bustamante has also worked to promote international trade and development, improve health care for all Californians, and respond to the issues of Native Americans.

Bustamante has been a low-profile California politician who has made a name for himself by speaking out on controversial issues, particularly immigration. Since becoming lieutenant governor in 1998 he has worked to expand the scope of the lieutenant governor's office to pursue important initiatives. In the past 120 years only two sitting lieutenant governors in California have been elected to governor. It is likely that Bustamante, in announcing his candidacy in the recall election, will try to be the third person to accomplish this feat in the California gubernatorial elections in late 2003. Bustamante has managed to create a successful political career coming from a very modest upbringing and therefore he sees himself as a role model for other Latinos. He encourages them to believe in themselves and to pursue their dreams. As he told the *San Francisco Chronicle,* "If a short, overweight, balding guy from Fresno can do it, you [students] can do it too."

Sources

Books

The Complete Marquis Who's Who, Marquis Who's Who, 2003.

Periodicals

California Journal Weekly, July 4, 1994.
Jet, March 5, 2001, p. 8.
Knight Ridder/Tribune Business News, August 7, 2003.

Los Angeles Times, October 16, 2002, p. 6.
Sacramento Bee, January 5, 1999.
San Diego Union-Tribune, July 1, 2001, p. G5.
San Francisco Chronicle, January 5, 1999, p. A11; April 22, 1999, p. A23; February 14, 2001, p. A3.
U.S. News & World Report, March 17, 1997, p. 28.

On-line

"California Lt. Gov. Cruz Bustamante: The Making of a Latino Leader," *LatinoLink,* www.americanpatrol. com/MECHA/makingofbustamante991030.html (May 23, 2003).
"CSEA Endorses Cruz Bustamante for Lt. Governor," *The California State Employees Association,* www. calcsea.org/politics/20020830-cruz-4-lt-gov.asp (May 23, 2003).
"Election 2002," *KTVU News,* http://netelection.org /ktvu/Candidates/Lt_Governor/Cruz_ Bustamante.asp (May 23, 2003).
Lieutenant Governor of California Official Website, www.ltg.ca.gov (May 23, 2003).
"Statewide Offices — Lieutenant Governor," *California Voter Foundation,* www.calvoter.org/officers/ ltgovernor.html (May 23, 2003).

—Janet P. Stamatel

Cantinflas

1911-1993

Actor, comedian

The comedic Mexican actor Cantinflas was one of Latin-America's most popular cinematic figures. Using both physical and verbal comedy, Cantinflas embodied the everyday Mexican. His half-century career included 49 films, including the American films *Around the World in Eighty Days* and *Pepe*. His comedic journey began in 1930 as a performer in the carpas (travelling, vaudevillian tent shows showcasing a variety of performers). In the carpas, and later in his film career, the young performer created and polished his character, the disheveled underdog known to the world as Cantinflas. Through this character and the use of nonsensical verbal comedy, he lanced the privileged and wealthy classes of Mexican culture.

Came From Humble Beginnings

Cantinflas was born Mario Moreno Reyes on August 12, 1911, in Mexico City, Mexico. Moreno was the sixth of twelve sons and three daughters born to Jose and Maria (Guizar) Moreno. Although he grew up in a poor section of Mexico City, Cantinflas was privileged enough to attend good schools, like the Bartolome de las Casas School. More interested in the street life than in his books, Cantinflas often cut class to watch street performers and eventually performed himself. It was here that he found the skills that he would later need in a career of entertaining audiences.

As a child in the streets, Cantinflas learned how to play to the crowds. He won several contests with the valero, a ball-and-stick toy, and made small change as a child by singing and dancing. More importantly, he became closely familiar with the effects of destitution and the ravages of poverty. Both lessons would influence his work as a performer.

At fifteen, he entered the national agricultural school at Chapingo, but soon was tempted back to performing. He ran away from the school to join a carpa as a dance performer. In the carpas, Cantinflas found the excitement he desired. Colorful characters, loud, raucous audiences, and the reward of a clapping hand held the young performer captive for the rest of his life. He attempted to return home, but soon ran away again and joined the Campania Novel in Tacambara as a dancer.

At a Glance . . .

Born Mario Moreno Reyes on August 12, 1911, in Mexico City, Mexico; died on April 20, 1993, in Mexico City, Mexico; married Valentina Subareff, 1937 (died 1966); children: one son.

Career: Stage and screen actor, 1935-93.

Awards: Special Prize, Ariel Awards, Mexico, for "work on behalf of the Mexican cinema," 1950-51; Golden Globe for Best Actor, for *Around the World in Eighty Days,* 1956; Special Award, Golden Globe, 1960; Special Prize, Mexican Silver Goddesses, 1969; named "symbol of peace and happiness of the Americas," by the Organization of American States, 1983; Diploma of Honor, Inter-American Council of Music, 1983; honored for lifelong contribution to Mexican cinema, by the Mexican Academy of Cinemagraphic Arts and Sciences, 1988.

Became the Master of Bumbling Speech

As a dancer in the carpas, Cantinflas performed in front of audiences that included soldiers, laborers, and peasants that expected to be entertained with feats of acrobatics, scenes of drama, and skits of comedy. In this environment Cantinflas learned how to control larger crowds of people through comedy and honed the skill of dealing with heckling audience members. On one night, Cantinflas was forced to be a substitute for a sick master of ceremonies. Upon centering himself on the stage, stage fright caused the stand-in to forget what he was supposed to say. Cantinflas recounted, in *Americas* magazine, the launch of his trademark verbal comedy; "I just started talking nonsense. The audience began to laugh, so I continued ..." When the audience returned the next night they booed the official announcer.

The reign of the nonsense speech that would become Cantinflas' signature had begun. Krebs, in the *New York Times*, defined Cantinflas' routine as a "combination of gibberish, double-talk, mispronunciation, wild exaggeration and pantomime." However, others see the routine as a way in which Cantinflas used the language proscribed to the lower classes when addressing a member of a higher class as a way to lampoon those higher classes. In 1935 Cantinflas joined the Follies Bergere Theater and soon became a popular figure on the theater scene of Mexico. In 1936 he appeared in his first cinematic comic role in *No te Enganes Corazon*. However, this appearance did not

cause his film career to take off. Then, in 1937, Cantinflas married Valentina Subareff, the daughter of a Russian-born carpa owner.

Under constant urging by Valentina, Cantinflas began to appear in a series of short films. These short films were basically commercials advertising everything from trucks to beer. The reaction to Cantinflas on the screen was so overwhelming that theater owners began to request more film commercials featuring him. The director of the film commercials, Santiago Reachi, was impressed by the response to his commercials and produced two full-length films featuring Cantinflas. *Ahi Esta el Detalle* in 1940 and *Ni Sangre Ni Adrena* in 1941 shattered all previously-held Mexican and Latin American film records and outgrossed Charlie Chaplin's *The Dictator* in the Mexican box office, which was out at the same time. The two films also skyrocketed Cantinflas into cinematic stardom in his native Mexico. This was the first time, according to the *New York Times*, that Mexican "men and women stood in the rain, waiting for admission to a show."

Mexico's Answer to Charlie Chaplin

From the beginning of his film career, Cantinflas was tempted by Hollywood. As stated in the *New York Times,* after the release of *Ni Sangre Ni Arena*, his studio, Posa Films, sent him to Hollywood "to see how things are done there." Cantinflas most often found himself compared to the famous American film comedian Charlie Chaplin. Chaplin, upon seeing *Ni Sangre Ni Arena,* declared Cantinflas to be the greatest comedian alive. Although Cantinflas was most often compared to Chaplin, he was also compared to the comedic likes of W.C. Fields, Buster Keaton, Bob Hope, and Will Rogers.

While early American films inspired the young boy who grew to become Cantinflas, the character of Cantinflas was truly a Mexican offspring. Dressed in drooping pants, a rope belt, and rumpled cap over his always-mussed hair and sporting a tiny mustache on the corners of his lips, Cantinflas entertained and amused scores of Mexican and American moviegoers. So popular were his films in Mexico and theaters in Spanish-speaking American markets like Texas, Arizona, and California, that by the time Cantinflas appeared in his first American film, he was already a millionaire 25 times over.

Becoming a millionaire, while arguably diminishing the social commentary of his films, did not diminish the social responsibility of Cantinflas. Starting in 1952 the actor began his crusade against poverty. In this year he set up an aid fund to help, according to the *New York Times,* "solve the problems of the poor." He donated money, matched by the government, to help build hospitals, maternity clinics, housing and restaurants for the sole use of the poor. To promote his aid program, Cantinflas, in a partnership with the afternoon newspaper *Ultimas Noticias,* began printing the estimated earnings and pictures of over a dozen known Mexican millionaires in order to pressure them into giving to the fund. He gained the support of the country's president, who donated both personal and public funds to the program.

Resolved to Help More

In 1966 Cantinflas' wife was fighting cancer. President Lyndon Johnson, personal friend of the comic actor, sent a U.S. government plane to Mexico City to rush Valentina to a Houston hospital for treatment. The cancer, however, was too strong and even with treatment, Valentina died that same year. The death of his wife only furthered the resolve of Cantinflas to continue his plight for the poor. At his home in Mexico City, droves of people formed a line to his front door. He gave over $175,000 out of his own pocket annually to these people. At one time, he was the sole supporter of more than 250 destitute families in the Mexico City slum of Granjas. He later built 64 apartment houses in Granjas and then sold the apartments to poor families for a fraction of their worth.

Cantinflas also raised money for charities by performing. He appeared at dozens of these charitable benefits every year. The performances that were the most popular and raised the most money were the ones in which he performed as a comedic bullfighter. Annually Cantinflas would fill the 46,000 seat Plaza Mexico in Mexico City and climb into the bullring to perform a comedy routine with a bull. A similar performance can be seen in *Around the World in 80 Days.*

Towards the end of his career his movie appearances dwindled, yet Cantinflas remained involved in acting through his charitable performances. However, one of the actor's most memorable movies came late in his career. His first role in an American film, as Passepartout the valet in the film *Around the World in 80 Days* garnered him an Oscar nomination. His second and last American film, *Pepe,* highlighted the much beloved actor in the title role. Although the cast of this movie included scores of Hollywood elites, like Edward G. Robinson, Debbie Reynolds, and Frank Sinatra, it was essentially a box office flop. In 1978 *Patrol Car 777* acted as a theatrical book end to the career which had spanned five decades. In 1985, the sixth decade of his career, Cantinflas appeared in his last acting role on a made-for-television movie.

Cantinflas' success as both an entertainer and a philanthropist is best noted by the droves of people who attended his wake. Lines of people filled the streets of Mexico City for days mourning the comedian after his death on April 20, 1993. He is an indelible feature of Mexican culture that is proven by his appearance in the half-block long Diego Rivera mural that depicts heroes of Mexican history. His influence has spread beyond the silver screen the halls of academe. Spanish linguists now recognize the noun cantinflada as a long-winded, meaningless speech, and the verb cantinflear as meaning to talk too much but say too little. By the wealth of his charity and the appeal of his comedy, it is clear that no one can cantinflear about Cantinflas.

Selected filmography

No te Enganes Corazon, 1936.
Águila o sol, 1938.
Siempre listo en las tinieblas, 1939.
Ahi Esta el Detalle, 1940.
Ni Sangre Ni Adrena, 1941.
Los Tres Mosqueteros, 1942.
Romeo y Julieta, 1943.
Gran Hotel, 1944.
Dia con el Diablo, 1945.
Soy un prófugo, 1946.
A volar joven, 1947.
El Supersabio, 1948.
El Mago, 1949.
El Portero, 1950.
Si you fuera diputado, 1952.
Caballero a la medida, 1954.
Around the World in Eighty Days, 1956.
Sube y baja, 1959.
Pepe, 1960.
Por mis pistolas, 1968.
The Great Sex War,, 1969.
Conserge en condomino, 1973.
El Barrendero, 1981.

Sources

Books

Dictionary of Hispanic Biography, Gale Research, 1996.

Periodicals

Los Angeles Times, April 11, 2001, pp. A1.
New York Times, June 15, 1941, p. X3; June 23, 1952, p. 3; December 22, 1960, p. 18; April 22, 1993, p. D26; April 23, 1993, p. A4.

On-line

"Cantinflas" *Biography Resource Center,* www.gale net.com/servlet/BioRC (March 10, 2003).

—Adam R. Hazlett

Lynda Carter

1951—

Actress

Lynda Carter became famous in the 1970s for her starring role in the television series *Wonder Woman.* The five-foot-nine-inch Carter won thousands of fans as the super-powered Wonder Woman, dressed in her shiny red boots, star-spangled hot pants, golden breastplate, headband, and bracelets, completed with a golden lasso that, when wrapped around evildoers, forced them to tell the truth. The three-year series was her biggest break and her most difficult burden. In the years that followed, Carter struggled for public and critical acceptance as a talented actress, dancer, and singer. She had a productive career as a regular in made-for-television movies, as well as successfully staging variety shows both in Las Vegas and on television.

Won Miss USA

Carter was born on July 24, 1951, in Phoenix, Arizona, as Linda Jean Cordoba Carter, the youngest of three children born to Colby and Jean Carter. Her parents divorced when she was ten years old, and her mother, who is of Spanish and Mexican descent, found work at a Motorola factory to support the family. Lynda admired her mother, telling *People Weekly,* "She taught me more than anything to survive in a dignified, honorable, gracious way." Lynda, who changed the spelling of her first name during grade school, was exceptionally tall during her youth, leading kids to call her "Olive Oyl," referring to Popeye's lanky girlfriend. "I was taller than all the boys except the tackles on the football team," she told *TV Guide.* "And all my girl friends seemed to be 5-foot-3-inch blonds. I even was rejected as a pompon girl because I towered over everyone else." Always athletic, Carter competed in swimming and volleyball.

Although she had few dates during her days at Arcadia High School, Carter found a release for her teenage angst in music. At the age of 15 she began singing professionally, performing at a pizza parlor in Tempe for $25 a week. By the time she turned 17, she was making $400 a week singing in lounges in Reno and Las Vegas. After graduating from high school she sang for two different groups, traveling about the country. Tired of constantly being on the road, she quit singing after two years on tour. Carter then attended Arizona State University in Tempe for a time. Carter, now considered tall and beautiful rather than lanky and

At a Glance . . .

Born on July 24, 1951, in Phoenix, AZ; daughter of Colby and Jean Carter; married Ron Samuels, 1977 (divorced, 1982); married Robert A. Altman, January 29, 1984; children: (second marriage) James Clifford, Jessica Carter.

Career: Actress, 1975–.

Awards: Miss USA, 1973; Jill Ireland Award for Volunteerism; Unihealth's Pinnacle Award.

Addresses: *Agent*—William Morris Agency, 151 El Camino Drive, Los Angeles, CA 90212. *Manager*—Baumgarten Prophet Entertainment, 1640 S. Sepulveda Blvd., Suite 218, Los Angeles, CA 90025.

awkward, entered the Miss Arizona contest in 1972 on a whim. She quit school after being named Miss USA in 1973. Although she failed to secure the Miss World title, she did represent the United States at the international pageant.

After a year of fulfilling her duties as Miss USA, Carter moved to Los Angeles to begin acting lessons, training for the stage with Stella Adler, Lieux Dressler, and Charles Conrad. Within months she was getting bit parts on television, including a small guest shot on NBC's short-lived series *Nakia*. In 1976 she appeared as Bobbie Jo in the forgettable film *Bobbie Jo and the Outlaw.* She also continued to work on her music, releasing her only album, *Portrait,* in May of 1978. Her big break came when her agent urged her to audition for the lead role of Sharon Fields in the movie version of Irving Wallace's novel *The Fan Club.* Although Larry Gordon, the film's producer liked Carter, he felt she was wrong for the part. He did, however, call his friend Douglas Cramer of Warner Bros., who was in the midst of casting a second pilot based on the Wonder Woman comic strip, to be known as *The New Original Wonder Woman.*

Became Wonder Woman

The *Wonder Woman* series was based on the 1942 comic strip by Charles Moulton, who had decided that little girls needed a superhero because little boys already had Superman, Batman, and Captain Marvel. Diana Prince, the comic's main character, comes from the uncharted Paradise Island, which she and fellow Amazons fled to around 200 B.C. to escape the male-dominated society of the ancient Greeks and Romans. When needed, the character, Diana Prince,

could whirl into her brief and sexy Wonder Woman costume, complete with star-spangled hot pants and a golden breastplate. Her golden belt gave her superhuman strength, her bracelets deflected bullets, and her golden lasso ensnared evildoers, forcing them to tell only the truth.

The first *Wonder Woman* pilot, which had starred Kathy Lee Crosby, was a flop, and, among the hundreds of Wonder Woman-hopefuls, Garner thought Carter had the perfect look for the revamped version of the comic heroine. Thus, at the age of 25, Carter stepped into her role as Diana Prince. The ABC pilot aired on November 7, 1975, and did very well in the ratings. Despite the good showing, the future of the show was uncertain. ABC, which already had a female-based comic strip show *The Bionic Woman* in its fall 1976 lineup, ordered two more one-hour episodes that ran in the spring of 1976. When those airings proved equally popular, ABC committed to the *Wonder Woman* series.

Carter worked hard on her new leading role. She followed a strict diet (mostly vegetarian) and exercise program to keep in shape, and she did most of her own stunts. Carter understood the limitations in portraying a comic book character realistically. "I think that being convincing in a part like mine takes a lot of acting," Carter told *Ladies' Home Journal* in 1978. "I've never stopped trying to stay true to the character, hoping to make her believable. I doubt that anyone but me could play that part *and* pull it off." Although the series was very popular, Carter earned few accolades from critics for her acting skills. Following the debut of the pilot *TV Guide* noted, "[Carter's] acting is rudimentary, but it doesn't matter. Just as in the comic strip all she has to do is stand up real straight and say lines like the following to Major Trevor, played by Lyle Waggoner: 'Follow me, Major. I'll teach those dirty Nazi agents a thing or two about democracy.'"

Carter starred in *The New Original Wonder Woman* on ABC for one season. In this version, the show was set in the 1940s, during World War II, true to the comic strip. The following season CBS purchased the show and introduced a revamped version with a contemporary setting, titled *The New Adventures of Wonder Woman,* which aired for two more seasons. Carter's career was managed by her husband, Ron Samuels, a talent agent, whom she married in 1977. Samuels also managed the careers of Jaclyn Smith of *Charlie's Angel* and Lindsay Wagner of *The Bionic Woman.* Samuels helped Carter reap financial benefits from her success as Wonder Woman. During her first season, she was paid $3,500 per episode. By the final season, she was making over $1 million for the season, a record amount at the time for a woman in a television series.

Samuels was involved in every aspect of Carter's career, from sponsorships to photo shoots. Carter seemed to have foretold her future in a 1980 interview with *Money* when she said, "If money became the preoccupation, we would have no business being married." In the same interview, Samuels noted, "We make decisions jointly. But if it comes down to a final decision, Lynda will defer to what I have to say as the man of the house." By 1982 Carter was done deferring and filed for divorce.

Life after Wonder Woman Career

Although *Wonder Woman* was still pulling in decent ratings, CBS let the series go after the 1979 season. The series left Carter financially secure, but with a comic book character monkey on her back. For the next several years she worked hard to shed the image of Wonder Woman and be accepted as a serious talent. Pouring $200,000 of her own money into the project, Carter produced her own Las Vegas variety show staged at Caesars Palace, which was based around her singing and dancing. To the surprise of some, the show was a popular and financial success. Carter followed up her career in television with several variety show specials airing on CBS in the early 1980s, including *Lynda Carter: Encore, Lynda Carter's Special, Lynda Carter's Celebration,* and *Lynda Carter: Street Lights.* Although *People Weekly* panned it, her last special, *Lynda Carter: Body and Soul,* received an Emmy nomination.

Carter's first starring role in a made-for-television movie came in 1980 in CBS's *The Last Song.* She followed that with *Born to Be Sold,* which aired on NBC in 1981. In 1983 Carter stretched her acting skills by portraying Rita Hayworth in CBS's *Rita Hayworth: The Love Goddess.* "I knew I'd be subject to a lot of criticism for the part," Carter told *People Weekly* in 1983. "But I really, really wanted the challenge. … We both had Hispanic backgrounds. We were both in show business at an early age. We both sing and dance. We were both married to our managers." Around the time of the filming of the Hayworth movie, Carter's life was changing. Raised Catholic, she was led by her sister to religious renewal that filled a spiritual void in her life. She also met her next husband, Robert Altman, a Washington, D.C., lawyer. The two were married on January 29, 1984; they have two children: James, born in early 1988, and Jessica, born in late 1989.

In 1984 Carter appeared in her second—albeit short-lived—television series, *Partners in Crime,* costarring Loni Anderson. Carter and Anderson portray ex-wives of a recently deceased private detective who left his agency and posh San Francisco house to both of them. The two, armed only with their charms and designer wardrobes, set off to solve crimes and corral bad guys. Even though the series was quickly cancelled, Carter remained very busy, including a long-standing relationship as a spokesperson for Maybelline. She and Alt-

man, who was the president of First American Bank, built a 20,000-square-foot home in Potomac, Maryland, and Carter loved to play hostess to many well-known financiers with whom her husband associated. She continued to appear in television movies, including *Stillwatch, Mike Hammer: Murder Takes All, Danielle Steel's Daddy,* and *Posing: Inspired by Three Real Stories.*

Late Career Plagued by Bank Scandal

Carter's picture-perfect world came to an abrupt halt in 1992 when unscrupulous business practices were alleged between First American and Pakistani banker Agha Hasan Abedi, the founder of the scandal-ridden Bank of Credit and Commerce International (BCCI). When Altman was indicted for bank fraud in relation to his dealings with BCCI, Carter was outraged and defended her husband vehemently in the press. After a year, Altman was cleared of any wrongdoing. However, fighting the charges had cost Carter and Altman $10 million in legal fees.

In 1994 Carter appeared in her third television series, the syndicated adventure series *Hawkeye.* In the show Carter starred as a beautiful and brave frontierswoman Elizabeth Shields. The series lasted for two seasons before being discontinued. During the 1990s Carter continued to live in the Washington, D.C., area, traveling back to Hollywood to take on parts in television movies. In the late 1990s her made-for-television appearances included *A Secret Between Friends, Shadow Zone: The Undead Express, She Woke Up Pregnant, A Prayer in the Dark, Someone to Love Me,* and *Family Blessings.*

Although Carter has scaled back her acting engagements, she continues to work occasionally. In 2002 she had a bit part as the governor in the raunchy police parody *Super Troopers,* which was panned by critics but developed something of a cult following. In 2003 she appeared opposite Parker Stevenson in a PAX Network production titled *Terror Peak.* Even though her role as Wonder Woman lasted just three years, she has never completely broken away from her most famous character. Carter told *Entertainment Weekly* in 1994: "Pretty soon people will look at me and say, 'That old woman was Wonder Woman?'" Continuing, she added, "But it's kind of fun to be regarded as a cult figure. I could resent it and be miserable. Or not. What am I going to fight it for?"

Selected works

Films

Bobbie Jo and the Outlaw, American International Pictures, 1976
The Shape of Things to Come, Film Ventures, 1979
Super Troopers, Fox Searchlight Pictures, 2002.

Television movies

The Last Song CBS, 1980.
Born to Be Sold, NBC, 1981.
Rita Hayworth: The Love Goddess, CBS, 1983.
Stillwatch, CBS, 1987.
Mike Hammer: Murder Takes All, CBS, 1989.
Danielle Steel's Daddy, NBC, 1991.
Posing: Inspired by Three Real Stories, CBS, 1991.
A Secret Between Friends, NBC, 1996.
Shadow Zone: The Undead Express, 1996.
She Woke Up Pregnant, ABC, 1996.
Somone to Love Me, 1998.
Family Blessings, CBS, 1999.
Terror Peak, PAX Network, 2003.

Television series

Wonder Woman, ABC, 1976-77.
The New Adventures of Wonder Woman, CBS, 1977-79.
Partners in Crime, NBC, 1984.
Hawkeye, syndicated, 1994-95.

Television specials

Lynda Carter: Encore, CBS, 1980.
Lynda Carter's Special, CBS, 1980.
Lynda Carter's Celebration, CBS, 1981.
Lynda Carter: Street Lights, CBS, 1982.
Lynda Carter: Body and Soul, CBS, 1984.

Sources

Books

Contemporary Theatre, Film and Television, Vol. 31. Farmington Hills, MI: Gale Group, 2000.
Dictionary of Hispanic Biography, Farmington Hills, MI: Gale Research, 1996.

Periodicals

Entertainment Weekly, September 16, 1994; August 9, 2002.
Ladies' Home Journal, July 1978.
Money, January 1980.
People Weekly, November 7, 1983; March 19, 1984; October 15, 1984; September 2, 1991; September 12, 1994; July 17, 1995.
Saturday Evening Post, May-June 1983.
Time, January 25, 1988.
TV Guide, January 29, 1977; October 24, 1981.

On-line

The Wonder Woman Pages, www.wonderwoman-online.com (June 4, 2003).

—Kari Bethel

Richard E. Cavazos

1929—

U.S. Army general

In 1976 Mexican American Richard E. Cavazos made military history by becoming the first Hispanic to attain the rank of brigadier general in the United States Army. Less than 20 years later, the native Texan would again make history by being appointed the Army's first Hispanic four-star general. It was a long way from Cavazos' days as a lieutenant with the 65th Infantry Regiment during the Korean War. The 65th, comprised mostly of soldiers from Puerto Rico, was a minority unit similar to the African-American Tuskegee Airman of World War II. Though praised by General MacArthur who said of the 65th, "They are a credit to Puerto Rico and I am proud to have them in my command," according to a speech given by the Secretary of the Army Louis Caldera in 2000, the unit—called "The Borinqueneers" after an indigenous Puerto Rican Indian tribe—suffered racism and segregation away from the frontlines. According to Caldera, this took a "toll on the 65th, leaving scars that have yet to heal for so many of the regiment's proud and courageous soldiers." However, Cavazos rose above this racism, going on to become one of the most respected generals—Hispanic or otherwise—in the military. He also worked with military luminaries such as General Colin Powell and General H. Norman Schwarzkopf, the latter of whom wrote in his autobiography, *It Doesn't Take a Hero,* that Cavazos was one of the finest division commanders he ever worked for.

Cavazos was born on January 31, 1929, in Kingsville, Texas, and raised on a ranch. He attended Texas Technological University, graduating with a bachelor's degree in geology in 1951. During college he was an active member of the ROTC program and through it received an officer's commission as a second lieutenant in the United States Army on June 15, 1951. He topped off his degree with officer basic training at Fort Benning in Georgia and then completed Airborne School before heading off to Korea with the 65th Infantry. He joined Company E as a platoon leader and eventually became a company commander. Cavazos proved to be a fearless soldier. On February 25, 1953, Cavazos' platoon was attacked by a large enemy force. A fierce battle ensued, yet Company E managed to overcome the enemy. According to *Frontiernet*, as the battle was winding down, "By the light of a flare, Lieutenant Cavazos observed an enemy soldier lying wounded not far to the front of his position. He requested and obtained permission to lead a small force to secure the prisoner.

At a Glance . . .

Born on January 31, 1929, in Kingsville, TX; married with four children. *Education:* Texas Technological University, BS, geology, 1951; U.S. Army Command and General Staff College, 1961; British Army Staff Coll, 1962; Armed Forces Staff Coll, 1965; United States Army War Coll, 1969. *Military Service:* US Army, four-star general ,1951-84.

Career: Career Army officer: Company E, 65th Infantry, Korean War, platoon leader and company commander, 1953; 1st Armored Division, executive officer, 1954; Texas Technological Univ, ROTC instructor, 1957; US Army Europe, West Germany, operations officer, 1960s; 1st Battalion, 18th Infantry, Vietnam War, commander, 1967; Concept Studies, U.S. Army Combat Developments Command Institute, director, 1969-70; Offense Section, Dept of Division Operations, Army Command and General Staff Coll, chief, 1970-71; Pentagon, defense attaché, Mexico, assistant deputy dir of operations, 1970s; Inter-American Region, Office of the Assistant Secretary of Defense for International Security Affairs, dir, 1970s; 2nd Armored Division, asst div leader, 1976; 2nd Brigade, 1st Infantry Div, commander, 1976; 9th Infantry Div, commander, 1977-80; III Corps, commander, 1980-82; US Army Forces Command, commander, 1982-84.

Awards: Two Distinguished Service Crosses; two Legion of Merit awards; five Bronze Stars for Valor; Purple Heart; Combat Infantry Badge; Parachutist Badge; honorary lifetime member, National Guard Association of Texas; inductee, Fort Leavenworth Hall of Fame; inductee, Hall of Fame, Ranger Regiment Association; Doughboy Award, National Infantry Association, 1991.

Addresses: *Home*—San Antonio, TX.

guished Service Cross for another battle fought on June 14, 1953.

Became U.S. Army's First Hispanic General

Following the Korean War, Cavazos joined the 1st Armored Division as an executive officer. In 1957 he returned to his alma mater, Texas Technological University, where he worked as an ROTC instructor. His next post was in West Germany as an operations officer at the U.S. Army's European headquarters. Meanwhile Cavazos continued his military training. He attended the U.S. Army Command and General Staff College, the British Army Staff College, and the United States Armed Forces Staff College where he graduated in 1965. By this time the Vietnam War was underway and in February of 1967, Cavazos—who had since achieved the rank of lieutenant colonel—was appointed commander of the 1st Battalion of the 18th Infantry Division. In September and October of that year, Cavazos' unit engaged in heavy sporadic fighting near the border of Cambodia culminating in a ferocious two-day assault—now known as the Battle of Loc Ninh—during which the 1st Battalion lost five soldiers. In contrast, the enemy troops suffered over 100 deaths. For his personal actions during these battles Cavazos received his second Distinguished Service Cross.

With his tour of duty in Vietnam complete, Cavazos returned stateside and resumed his peace time career path with fervor. He became the director of concept studies at the U.S. Army Combat Developments Command Institute and in 1969 completed additional military training at the Army's famed War College. His next post was from 1970 to 1971 at Kansas's Fort Leavenworth where he served as the chief of the Offense Section in the Department of Division Operations at the Army Command and General Staff College. In the early 1970s Cavazos held several positions including assistant deputy director of operations at the Pentagon, defense attaché in Mexico, and director of the Inter-American Region, Office of the Assistant Secretary of Defense for International Security Affairs. In 1976, 25 years after receiving his military commission, Cavazos was promoted to the rank of brigadier general and pinned one gleaming star on his uniform lapel. In doing so, he became the first Hispanic general in the Army and a role model for the thousands of minority recruits who join the military each year.

Cavazos' first post after becoming a general was as assistant division commander of the 2nd Armored Division. He then assumed a larger leadership role as commander of the 2nd Brigade in the 1st Infantry Division. In 1977 he took over the top spot of the 9th Infantry Division. One of the officers in this division at that time was H. Norman Schwarzkopf who was appointed to brigadier general under Cavazos.

Intense enemy mortar and small arms fire completely blanketed the route to be covered. Nevertheless, Lieutenant Cavazos, with complete disregard for his personal safety, continued alone through the enemy fire to capture and return with the enemy soldier." For his actions Cavazos received a Silver Star, one of the military's highest honors. He later received the Distin-

Schwarzkopf later went on to military fame as the commander of U.S. forces in Desert Shield and Desert Storm in Iraq. Meanwhile Cavazos continued moving up in rank and by 1978 he was promoted to major general. In 1980 he became the commander of III Corps based in Fort Lewis, Washington. Cavazos' final military post was overseeing the U.S. Army Forces Command (FORSCOM). He assumed this role in 1982, the same year that he received his fourth star, becoming a full general. According to the website of the Fort Leavenworth Hall of Fame, at FORSCOM Cavazos' "early support for the National Training Center and his involvement in the development of the Battle Command Training Program enormously influenced the war fighting capabilities of the U.S. Army." Under his command at FORSCOM, combat troops were deployed to Grenada, West Indies, in 1983. On June 17, 1984, after a brilliant military career that spanned three decades, Cavazos retired with his wife and four children to Texas.

Repeatedly Recognized for His Military Achievements

Throughout his long and distinguished career, Cavazos has received many awards. In addition to the two Distinguished Service Crosses he received in the Korean and Vietnam Wars, he has received two Legion of Merit awards, five Bronze Stars for Valor, a Purple Heart, a Combat Infantry Badge, and a Parachutist Badge. Recognition of his achievements did not stop with his retirement. The National Guard Association of Texas made him an honorary lifetime member. He was also inducted into the Fort Leavenworth Hall of Fame, which, according to their website, honors those "who after being stationed at Fort Leavenworth significantly contributed to the history, heritage and traditions of the Army." The Ranger Regiment Association also inducted Cavazos into their hall of fame which honors outstanding former U.S. rangers. In 1991 the National Infantry Association bestowed its highest award on Cavazos, the Doughboy Award. Presented annually to an Infantryman who has made an outstanding contribution to the U.S. Army Infantry, the Doughboy is a

highly prestigious honor presented on behalf of all Infantrymen, past and present.

In his retirement Cavazos remained busy. In 1985 he was appointed by President Ronald Reagan to serve on the eight-member Chemical Warfare Review Commission. Back in Texas, he served on the board of regents of Texas Technological University. He also regularly advised the Army on leadership, serving as a mentor to younger generals. The *Killeen Daily Herald,* a mostly military paper based out of Fort Hood, Texas, described one such program that Cavazos participated in: "To help train its leaders, the Army reaches into its past by pairing each general with a senior retired general.... [Passing] along the special experiences of the retired generals to their successors." One of the planners of this training session noted, "General Cavazos comes here with a reputation that inspires everyone who sees him." Well into 2003, that reputation persisted as Cavazos continued to lend his military expertise to the U.S. Army—and as a result, the United States.

Sources

"1967—35 Years Ago—2002," *18th Infantry Regiment Association Newsletter,* www.18inf.org/newsletter0402.html (April 29, 2003).

"Battles generated by computers are challenging for III Corps troops," *Killeen Daily Herald,* www.kdhnews.com/military_battlepc.html (April 29, 2003).

"General Richard E. Cavazos," *Hispanos Famosos,* http://coloquio.com/famosos/cavazos.html (April 28, 2003).

"In Honor of Veterans of the 65th Infantry Regiment, Remarks by the Secretary of the Army, Arlington Cemetery," *Frontiernet,* www.frontiernet.net/~john/arlingtoncemetery.html (April 28, 2003).

"Puerto Rico's 65th Infantry Regiment," *Frontiernet,* www.frontiernet.net/~john/1st.Lt.RICHARDE.CAVAZOS.html (April 28, 2003).

"Richard Cavazos, General, USA," *Fort Leavenworth Hall of Fame,* http://cgsc.leavenworth.army.mil/carl/resources/ftlvn/postww.asp (April 29, 2003).

—Candace LaBalle

Orlando Cepeda

1937—

Baseball player

The life of Orlando Cepeda was played out in two very different places. One was on the baseball field where he demolished the competition, hitting a career average .297 consisting of 2,351 hits. He racked up 417 doubles, 27 triples, and 379 home runs all contributing to an outstanding 1,131 runs and 1,365 Runs Batted In (RBI). He was known to many as "Cha Cha" and "Baby Bull" and was legendary for being the spirit of the St. Louis Cardinals during their championship run in 1967. His life on the baseball field was one of glory and of honor. His second life, off the baseball field, was filled with turmoil and rejection. In 1975, a year after leaving the game as an immortalized player, Cepeda found himself standing before a judge on drug trafficking charges that lead to a five-year jail sentence in 1978. While Cepeda only served ten months of the sentence, the event tarnished his entire baseball career and effectively barred him from obtaining the holy grail of baseball, a spot in the Baseball Hall of Fame, for over 15 years. But Cepeda fought back into the hearts of baseball fans and worked to rebuild his image throughout the 1980s and 1990s. Finally, in 1999, Cepeda was granted his long awaited spot in the Baseball Hall of Fame by the Veterans Committee, but it was his change in personality and spirit that Cepeda was especially proud of. He told *Sports Illustrated*, "The biggest victories come over yourself, when you control your mind and your destiny. My life has been a drama of inner change."

Followed in Father's Footsteps

Orlando Manuel Cepeda was born on September 17, 1937, in the seaport city of Ponce, Puerto Rico. Like many Puerto Ricans during this time period, Cepeda lived with few physical possessions and had little formal education. Yet his life was filled with hope and inspiration, much of it stemming from his father, Perucho Cepeda. Perucho was a baseball player who excelled in the Caribbean leagues, playing on Dominican club teams alongside Negro League greats Satchel Paige, James "Cool Papa" Bell, and Josh Gibson. He was nicknameded the "Bull" and because he was a power hitter was known as "the Babe Ruth of Puerto Rico." But the Caribbean leagues were difficult for even the best players and as Perucho began to get older, he found himself moving around from team to team, often living in destitution away from his family, and what money he did not send back to his wife and children, he gambled away.

At a Glance . . .

Born Orlando Manuel Cepeda on September 17, 1937, in Ponce, Puerto Rico; son of Perucho Cepeda; married Annie (divorced 1973); married Nydia, 1975 (divorced 1984); married Marian Ortiz, 1985; children: Orlando Jr., Malcolm, Ali Manuel, Hector.

Career: Baseball player: San Francisco Giants, 1st baseman, 1958-66; St. Louis Cardinals, 1966-68; Atlanta Braves, 1969-72; Oakland Athletics, 1972; Boston Red Sox, 1973; Kansas City Royals, 1974; San Francisco Giants Organization, community representative and scout, 1990–.

Awards: Rookie of the Year, 1958; Comeback Player of the Year, 1967; National League Most Valuable Player, 1967; Designated Hitter of the Year, 1973; Puerto Rican Sports Hall of Fame, inductee, 1993; Baseball Hall of Fame, inductee, 1999.

Address: *Office*—San Francisco Giants, Three Com Park, San Francisco, CA 94124.

Perucho passed on his love of baseball to Cepeda at an early age and whenever he was not off chasing a job on a Caribbean league team, he was teaching Cepeda how to hit, field, and even pitch. Cepeda saw the prestige and honor that his father received from playing baseball, and commented to the *San Francisco Chronicle,* "When I was a kid, I wanted to be like my father. He was such a well-known person. In the morning, we used to go shopping. Every second, people stopped to say hello. I wanted to be a ballplayer just like him." Cepeda worked hard to make that dream become a reality, even going so far as to move to the United States, knowing little English and few people, to join a minor league team in Virginia. Shortly after Cepeda had moved to Virginia, Perucho came down with malaria and quickly deteriorated. He flew back to Puerto Rico when he heard the news, but found his father in a coma by the time he arrived. Perucho died on April 16, 1955, sinking Cepeda into a deep depression, one so great it almost prevented him from returning to the minor leagues. Cepeda's mother, however, would not let that happen. He told *The Sporting News,* "My mother said, 'You made a commitment to your father. Too, we have no money.' I was making $175 a month. So I flew back to Virginia."

From Virginia Cepeda moved on to play for a minor league team in Minneapolis. It was here that Giants scout Tom Sheehan first saw Cepeda play first base. As Jim Davenport, one of Cepeda's former teammates in both the minor and major leagues, told the *San Francisco Chronicle,* " Tom went back to the Giants and said, 'I don't know about this Davenport kid, but you've got a first baseman down there who's going to make it to the Hall of Fame someday.'" Cepeda was soon courted by the Giants, and by 1958 he had signed a contract to play in San Francisco.

Won Rookie of the Year

Cepeda's rookie season was spectacular, starting with his first Major League game with the Giants against the Dodgers. At only his second-at-bat, he hit a homerun that scored the winning run for the Giants. He would go on to belt out 24 more homers that season, bring in 96 runs, and bat an impressive .312. These numbers along with his amazing fielding skills garnered Cepeda the Rookie of the Year award and thrust him into the limelight for Giants fans as well as baseball fans across the country.

Cepeda would not disappoint his fans in the coming seasons, continuing to excel and craft his game. In 1961 Cepeda had one of the most outstanding years of his career, leading the entire Major League with 46 homeruns and 142 RBIs. This performance allowed Cepeda to outshine many players that season, including teammate and veteran Willie Mays, who many still felt was the best player on the Giants during that time period. Giants manager Bill Rigney called Cepeda on the *Latino Legends in Sports* website, "The best young right-handed power hitter I've ever seen."

Unfortunately for Cepeda, the Giants went through a rotating succession of managers, not all of whom were as excited about Cepeda's skills as Rigney. First there was Alvin Dark, who served as Giant's general manager in the early 1960s, and he made statements often of how he felt that black and Latino players were inferior to white players. Following him was Herman Franks, a man many people feel crippled Cepeda's career in San Francisco by moving him from first base to the outfield where Cepeda began to have knee problems from an injury that he sustained by diving for a ball. This knee injury would bench Cepeda for all but 33 games in the 1965 season and was ultimately the reason he was traded to the St. Louis Cardinals in 1966 even though he was still hitting close to, if not over, a .300 batting average per season.

Helped Cardinals Win Championship

For the next three years, Cepeda succeeded greatly with the St. Louis Cardinals, helping the team to win the World Series in 1967. Although he hit well during the regular season, boasting a .325 batting average and hitting 111 RBIs, he went three for 29 at the plate during the seven games of the World Series. But as many teammates and fans knew, Cepeda was the heart and soul of the St. Louis team. According to the *Sporting News,* "After nearly every victory, Cepeda, climbs onto a truck or table and leads his teammates in cheers or cranks up Latin music on a record player. Says teammate Dal Maxvill: 'Even if he's gone 0-for-4, and we win, he gets on the trunk and leads the cheers.'" Because of his amazing play during the regular season as well as his spirit that held his "El Birdos"—Cepeda's nickname for the Cardinals—he was easily elected as the National League MVP, the first unanimous selection for the award ever made. He helped them to return in 1968, but after gaining three games on the Detroit Tigers, they lost the final three games of the series.

In 1969 the Cardinals owner Gussie Busch decided to restructure the team, immediately sending Cepeda to the Atlanta Braves. Many Cardinals fans were distraught at the thought of "Cha-Cha" playing for another team, and many blamed this move for the reason that the club was not able to even compete for a pennant for close to 13 years. In Atlanta Cepeda performed well at the plate, but his knees continued to give him problems. He was also beginning to become one of the older players on the field and training camps and constant traveling were beginning to take a toll on him. Between 1972 and 1974 he was traded three times, first from Atlanta to Oakland, then to Boston, and finally to Kansas City where he finished out the 1974 before declaring that he was going to retire. By the time he retired, Cepeda had played in seven All-Star games, sported a World Series ring, and had been dubbed the best Latino player since Hall of Famer Roberto Clemente, who had died in a 1972 plane crash.

Then, on December 12, 1975, everything changed for Cepeda. Cepeda arrived at the San Juan airport after attending a baseball clinic in Colombia. When he went to retrieve two packages he had sent with his luggage, San Juan police confiscated the packages and found 170 pounds of marijuana in them. Cepeda was arrested for smuggling marijuana with the intent to distribute and was immediately put in jail. The trial dragged out in Puerto Rico over the next two years, but finally, in late 1977, a judge found Cepeda guilty of the trafficking charge and sentenced him to five years in jail.

Lost Respect of Fans and Baseball Community

To many fans, the guilty verdict shattered the image of the fun-loving and honorable Cepeda that they had known on the baseball field. Many could not understand why he had done it. But as Cepeda said to *Sports Illustrated,* "When you play baseball, you have a name and money and you feel like you're bulletproof. You forget who you are. Especially in a Latin country, they make you feel like you are God." The damage to

Cepeda's image was swift and harsh. Many Puerto Ricans took his crime as a personal slight against the country. As Mariano Diaz, one of Cepeda's closest friends told *Sports Illustrated,* "So Orlando was judged. He no longer walked with Clemente. To the people, it was like Roberto was pointing down at Orlando and saying, 'Bad boy! You sinned, and you disgraced your people.'"

Cepeda only spent ten months in jail during 1978 and was released on good behavior, but even though he had served his time to the government, his penance to the baseball community had just begun. As he told *Sports Illustrated,* "I learned that one mistake, in two seconds, can make a disaster that seems to last forever." Cepeda had lost everything by going to jail, including his car, his land in Puerto Rico, and his wife as well after being hit with a paternity suit over a child he had fathered out of wedlock. Cepeda sunk into a deep depression and found that work was scarce for a baseball player who was out of public favor.

Another low point for Cepeda came in 1984 when he was kicked out of Dodger Stadium while watching batting practice and catching up with some of the players. According to the Dodgers security, the team did not want to be associated with Cepeda in any form and that included anyone seeing him in the stadium when he wasn't a paying customer. Cepeda has admitted in interviews that it was at this moment that he almost gave into his despair and ended his life, but thoughts of his son, Orlando Jr., whom he had custody of, saved him. He told *Sports Illustrated,* "I lay in bed and thought, He depends on me. I'm the only one he has." From that point on, Cepeda began to look for a way to turn his life around.

Buddhism and Wife Changed Outlook

Between 1984 and 1987, Orlando found two very important things. The first was the Buddhist sect Nichiren Shosu, which taught him to deal with the bitterness and anger that he was feeling. The second was his third wife, Mirian Ortiz, a Puerto Rican native he had met while in New York. It was she who first suggested that they move to San Francisco to return to a place where Cepeda had shone as a player. Cepeda, of course was reluctant to go, figuring he would receive the same reaction from fans in San Francisco that he had received in every other part of the country. It wasn't until *Giants Magazine* publisher Laurence Hyman visited Cepeda in 1986 and invited him to attend a game at Candlestick Park that Cepeda was convinced that he could win back fans. Cepeda attended the game and was received by fans wanting autographs, to shake his hand, and looking to get pictures with him. Shortly after, Cepeda and his wife boxed up their things and moved permanently to San Francisco.

In 1987 the Giants organization hired Cepeda to work for their community relations staff. He worked in the community encouraging students to stick to school and sports and not take the paths of drug use and gang membership. The next year, he worked as a scout for the Giants and began to develop young players. By the 1990s, he was not only scouting for the Giants, but he represented the organization around the United States and internationally as well. He was especially effective in Puerto Rico where he rebuilt his image as a public speaker and a goodwill ambassador for the Giants. Cepeda credited his success with these endeavors directly to "the fans and the Giants who stood by me," according to the *Sporting News*.

Made Hall of Fame Run

It seemed as if the community of fans had come to reaccept and respect Cepeda, but the baseball community was a good deal slower. Even thought the Giants had opened their doors to him, many people in Major League Baseball (MLB) felt that Cepeda could never regain his former status as a man of character, integrity, and good sportsmanship. Because of this, Cepeda was often not invited to play in games with former All-Stars or other MLB events. And most importantly, Cepeda was denied the highest honor the MLB can award, entry into the Baseball Hall of Fame. Eligible since 1979, Cepeda was on the ballot of possible entrants since that time and for many years got very few votes from those in the baseball community.

But Cepeda began to sway those naysayers as well, and his vote totals began to rise. Needing 75 % of the votes to gain induction to the hall, fans of Cepeda began to campaign for his entrance to the hall in the 1990s. His work for the community of San Francisco as well as his work to promote sports as a way to stay away from bad influences began to outweigh his past transgressions. Year after year, Cepeda would receive more and more votes, but he could never seem to get quite near enough to the magic number of 318. The Hall rules state that once a player has been on the ballot for 15 years, he must be taken out of consideration, and as 1993—his fifteenth year—approached, many of Cepeda's fans became fearful that the silent ban on the once great baseball player would keep Cepeda out of the hall forever. When all of the votes were counted in 1993, Cepeda—who earlier that year had been inducted into the Puerto Rico Sports Hall of Fame—found himself seven votes short of the 318 votes.

Cepeda was disappointed by the fact that he was not included, saying to the *San Francisco Chronicle*, "In fact, I was very negative about the Hall of Fame. When they used to mention it to me I would say, 'I don't need the Hall of Fame. Everything is politics,' even though deep inside I knew I wanted to be there." But there was still hope. After a three-year waiting period, a Veterans Committee was allowed to induct any player who could no longer be voted in, and Cepeda's name was added to the list in 1996. Many fans and baseball critics alike felt that Cepeda would never be inducted to the Hall since the list was extremely long and many people in the community would never be able to reconcile with his actions.

All of these critics were silenced in 1999 when Cepeda learned that he had been selected by the Veterans Committee for entrance to the Hall of Fame. As he said to the *Latino Legends in Sports* website, "It's hard to explain the feeling when they told me I was selected to the Hall of Fame. I've been ready for this for 17 years. I've been through good things, bad things, but I was blessed to be born with the talent to play baseball." When Cepeda went to the Hall of Fame to be inducted, he found that his picture would be hanging with many other great players of ethnicity in the Hall, including his father Perucho Cepeda.

Cepeda currently lives in San Francisco and continues to work with new players and as a representative for the San Francisco Giants. He has written a book about his life, entitled *Baby Bull: From Hardball to Hard Times and Back*, that he hopes will help many people to look at his life as a whole and see not only the mistakes he made, but how people can reform from the traps that they fall into. He also continues to stress the importance of family and heritage, and how everything is relative to those strong backgrounds. According to the *Latino Legends in Sports* website, he said in his acceptance speech at the Baseball Hall of Fame, "I'm proud to be a Puerto Rican and I will be a role model to the people of my country."

Selected works

(with Herb Fagen) *Baby Bull: From Hardball to Hard Times and Back,* Taylor, 1999.

Sources

Books

The Complete Marquis Who's Who, Marquis Who's Who, 2003.

Periodicals

Library Journal, February 1, 1999, p. 95.
San Francisco Chronicle, July 23, 1999.
Sports Illustrated, June 14, 1990, p. 14; July 26 1999, pp. 74-77.
Sporting News, January 10, 1994, pp. 33-34; January 31, 1994, p. 7; March 1, 1999, p. 63; July 26, 1999, pp. 26-29.

On-line

"Cepeda, Orlando M.," *Hickok Sports,* www.hickoksports.com/biograph/cepedaor.shtml (June 27, 2003).
"Orlando Cepeda," *Baseball Library,* www.baseballlibrary.com/baseballlibrary/ballplayers/C/Cepeda_Orlando.stm (June 27, 2003).

"Orlando Cepeda," *Baseball-Reference,* www.baseball-reference.com/c/cepedor01.shtml (June 27, 2003).

"Orlando Manuel Cepeda," *Biography Resource Center,* www.galenet.com/servlet/BioRC (June 27, 2003).

"Orlando Manuel Cepeda," *Latino Legends in Sports,* www.latinosportslegends.com/cepeda.htm (June 27, 2003).

—Adam R. Hazlett

Linda Chavez

1947—

Civil rights advocate, columnist, commentator

Bowed but far from broken by the 2001 derailment of her nomination to serve as labor secretary in the administration of George W. Bush, Linda Chavez remains as outspoken as ever in support of the conservative ideals she champions. At one time almost as passionate about liberal causes, Chavez—like thousands of other political converts—today is even more zealous in her advocacy of right-leaning doctrine than many life-long conservatives. Although Chavez is fiercely proud of her Mexican-American roots, her conservative political stance, particularly her opposition to affirmative action and bilingual education, has put her at odds with many in the Hispanic community. So estranged has Chavez become from the majority of her fellow Hispanics that in 1992 *Hispanic* magazine referred to her as "the most hated Hispanic in America." Never one to be cowed by vocal opposition to the ideals she espouses, Chavez remains steadfast in her beliefs. As she told an interviewer, "I believe fervently that it is important for Hispanics, as other groups have before them, to learn English, improve their education, and climb the economic ladder.... I am proud of my Hispanic roots. But I am even prouder of being an American and to have benefited from the freedom and opportunity that al-

lowed someone of my humble roots to aspire to the highest reaches of government and public life."

For more than three decades, Chavez has worked both behind the scenes and within the government itself to advance the political causes in which she believes. In the early 1970s, shortly after moving to the nation's capital, Chavez went to work for U.S. Representative Don Edwards, a Democratic congressman from San Jose, California. She also spent time working for the Democratic National Committee and the House Judiciary Committee. During the Carter administration, she served as a consultant to the Office of Management and Budget's reorganization project. A strong believer in the need for educational reform, Chavez worked, in turn, with the National Education Association (NEA), the country's largest teachers' union, and the American Federation of Teachers (AFT), the NEA's biggest rival. Increasingly disillusioned with prevailing liberal attitudes about the position of minorities, particularly within the academic world, she began to form strong views in opposition to the notion that students should be advanced solely on the basis of their race with little regard for their merits. Still a registered Democrat but espousing increasingly

At a Glance . . .

Born Linda Chavez on June 17, 1947, in Albuquer-que, NM; married Christopher Gersten, 1967; children: David, Pablo, and Rudy. *Education:* University of Colorado, BA, 1970; undergraduate studies at University of California, Los Angeles, 1970-72. *Religion:* Roman Catholic. *Politics:* Republican Party.

Career: House Judiciary Committee, Subcommittee on Civil and Constitutional Rights, staff member, 1972-74; Office of Management and Budget, consultant to civil rights division, 1977; *American Educator,* editor, 1977-83; U.S. Commission on Civil Rights, director, 1983-85; White House Office of Public Liaison, director, 1985-86; unsuccessful candidate for U.S. Senate from Maryland, 1986; U.S. English, president, 1987-88; WJL-TV, Baltimore, reporter and commentator, 1988–; United Nations Subcommittee on Human Rights, consultant, 1992-96; Center for Equal Opportunity, founder and president, 1995–.

Addresses: *Office*—c/o Center for Equal Opportunity, 14 Pidgeon Hill Dr., Ste. 500, Sterling, VA 20165.

conservative views on several key issues, Chavez in 1981 was invited to serve the administration of Ronald Reagan as a consultant. Two years later Reagan named her as director of the nonpartisan U.S. Commission on Civil Rights. In the face of growing liberal and Hispanic opposition to her attitudes on civil rights, Chavez in 1985 officially ended her affiliation with the Democratic Party and signed on as a Republican.

Difficult Childhood Lead to Early Action

Chavez's childhood was not an easy one. Born into a working class family in Albuquerque, New Mexico, on June 17, 1947, she was raised in Albuquerque and Denver, where her family moved when she was nine years old. Her father, Rudy, a Hispanic descended from 17th- and 18th-century Spanish and Mexican settlers who had come to Mexico as merchants and wool traders, worked in his family's real estate business and later launched his own contracting business. However, all of Rudy's businesses were compromised by his problem drinking, which grew progressively worse over time. Chavez's mother, Velma, of English and Irish descent, worked for the U.S. Post Office when Linda was younger but later become involved in retail sales. Although Chavez encountered little discrimination dur-

ing her early years in Albuquerque, she began to experience some of the prejudice practiced against Hispanics after the family moved to Denver.

Chavez experienced great personal tragedy during her childhood, losing three of her four siblings by the time she was 12. When she was only five, her half-sister, Pamela, was put up for adoption. Dickie, an older half-brother, was killed in a car accident, and her younger sister, Wendy, succumbed to kidney disease. Adding to the tumult of her childhood, Chavez was entrusted to the care of relatives frequently when her parents were unable to care for her. As a result, she had attended six schools in two states by the time she reached third grade. This childhood upheaval, Chavez said in an interview posted on the *Stop Union Political Abuse (SUPA)* website, "gave me what has been described as my 'cool,' 'tough' demeanor. But that emotional reserve and toughness also enabled me to face crises in public as well as my private life."

Chavez's exposure to such prejudice galvanized her into action, and she soon became involved in civil rights campaigns to secure the rights of Hispanics and other minorities, including African Americans and women. While still in her teens, Chavez picketed a segregated department store in downtown Denver. The realization that many of her fellow citizens considered minority members intellectually inferior motivated Chavez to excel academically to prove such prejudiced assumptions groundless. After graduating from high school, she enrolled at the University of Colorado in nearby Boulder, working her way through college to a bachelor's degree in education in 1970. It was during her undergraduate studies at Boulder that Chavez first began to develop misgivings about the government's affirmative action policies. She helped launch a program to tutor Mexican-American students who had been admitted to the school under affirmative action. According to a *SUPA* website interview, what she witnessed was disillusioning: "Instead of giving students the remedial help they needed in order to succeed, the activists who ran the programs spent their time indoctrinating students in the politics of racial grievance. No one benefited. Not the kids, many of whom dropped out or barely made it through, often by taking ethnic studies courses that ill-prepared them to earn a living afterwards. Nor the schools, which lowered standards to admit the affirmative action students and then offered watered-down curricula to keep them there."

Deemed "Not Minority Enough"

A major factor in Chavez's decision to attend the University of Colorado was a young Jewish man named Christopher Gersten, whom she'd begun dating shortly after high school. Also an ardent supporter of the civil rights movement, Gersten persuaded her to join him as a student in Boulder. The couple were married in a Jewish synagogue in 1967. Although Chavez has said she still considers herself a Catholic, reports persist that she converted to Judaism before her marriage to Gersten. Chavez and Gersten, who heads the Institute for Religious Values, live on a nine-acre farm in Loudon County, Virginia, not far from the nation's capital. They have three children—David, Pablo, and Rudy— and two grandchildren.

Chavez developed further misgivings about affirmative action in 1970 when she applied for a Ford Foundation graduate fellowship for Mexican-American students. She was flown to New York to be vetted by an evaluation panel but later recalled that the interview went badly almost from the start. In introducing herself to the interviewers, Chavez told how she'd grown up in a working class family, worked her way through college, and helped launch an affirmative action program for Hispanic students at Boulder. After she'd concluded her remarks, one of the interviewers commented on how well she spoke English. In an interview posted at the *SUPA* website, she recalled "He seemed surprised, despite the fact I was about to begin graduate work in English literature! One of the other interviewers then began speaking to me in Spanish, which I don't speak. But the worst part was their reaction to my Graduate Record Exam scores, which they seemed to believe were too high to qualify me as a bona fide minority worthy of their help."

Although she failed in her bid to win the Ford Foundation fellowship, Chavez went ahead with her plans to pursue a graduate degree in English literature, enrolling at the University of California, Los Angeles (UCLA). Once again, she became involved in a program to tutor affirmative action students from the Hispanic community. Assigned to teach a course on Chicano literature, Chavez initially resisted, protesting the lack of available published material. When she was pressured to go ahead with the course, she put together the most appropriate reading list she could but then met resistance from students, many of whom refused to read the assigned books and otherwise disrupted her classes. The situation hit a low point when her home was vandalized by a handful of students she had failed in the course. In 1972 she and her husband, who had also abandoned a short-lived career as a teacher, moved to Washington, D.C.

Experienced Political Transformation

Despite her growing disillusionment with prevailing liberal philosophy, Chavez still considered herself a Democrat. She also remained deeply committed to educational issues. She worked briefly for the Democratic National Committee shortly after she arrived in Washington. Not long thereafter, she went to work on Capitol Hill for Don Edwards, a Democratic congressman from California and chairman of the House Judiciary Committee's Subcommittee on Civil and Constitutional Rights. She also worked briefly for the

National Education Association (NEA), the nation's largest teacher's union, but left when she found herself increasingly at odds with some of the NEA's policies. In 1977 she signed on as editor of *American Educator,* the official magazine of the American Federation of Teachers (AFT), the second largest U.S. teachers' union and a rival of the NEA.

During her tenure as editor of *American Educator,* which continued until 1983, Chavez also served in 1977 as a consultant to the civil rights division of the Office of Management and Budget during the presidential administration of Democrat Jimmy Carter. In her position as editor, Chavez won growing popularity among conservatives for her support of a return to traditional values in the public schools as well as for her opposition to affirmative action. Shortly after the 1981 inauguration of Republican President Ronald Reagan, she was hired as a consultant to the White House, and in 1983, at the urging of William Bennett, who then chaired the National Endowment for the Humanities, Chavez was named director of the U.S. Commission on Civil Rights.

In the spring of 1985 Chavez became the highest-ranking woman on Reagan's White House staff when she was named director of the White House Office of Public Liaisons. With her appointment to that post, the time had finally come for her to officially switch her party allegiance from Democratic to Republican. One of her primary duties in that post was to lobby Congress in support of administration policies. She grew disillusioned with the job when she found that her influence over public policy was minimal and in February of 1986 resigned to seek the Republican Party's nomination as its candidate for a U.S. Senate seat from Maryland. Although she cleared the first hurdle, winning the GOP nod as candidate, Chavez was soundly defeated in the November election by Democrat Barbara Mikulski, who had served five terms in the House of Representatives.

Advanced Conservative Causes

After her failed bid for a Senate seat, Chavez turned her attention to another of her pet conservative causes: the formalization of English as the official language of the United States. In 1987 she agreed to serve as president of U.S. English, a nonprofit lobbying organization founded in 1983 by conservative John Tanton. She resigned the following year after learning of Tanton's alleged prejudices against Roman Catholics and Hispanics. To help ensure that the conservative viewpoint was properly showcased in the media, Chavez in 1988 began working as a reporter and commentator for Baltimore TV station WJL-TV. As she gradually developed a reputation as a conservative policy spokesperson, Chavez was invited to appear on a number of news talk shows, many of them broadcast nationally. Chavez also began writing a syndicated column, distributed by Creators Syndicate, and was a frequent contributor to such publications as the *Wall Street Jour-*

nal, *USA Today, Reader's Digest, Washington Post, Commentary,* and *New Republic.*

In 1991 Chavez published *Out of the Barrio: Toward a New Politics of Hispanic Assimilation,* in which she argued that it was not racism holding back Hispanics but rather misguided public policies such as affirmative action and bilingual education. The following year she joined the conservative think tank Manhattan Institute and served as director of its Center for the New American Community. Chavez also began work as a consultant to the United Nations Subcommittee on Human Rights, in which capacity she served until 1996.

Chavez founded the Center for Equal Opportunity (CEO) in 1995, a "think tank devoted exclusively to the promotion of colorblind equal opportunity and racial harmony," according to the mission statement on CEO's website. CEO, which Chavez continues to lead as president, focused primarily on the three interrelated issues of affirmative action, immigration and assimilation, and bilingual education. In announcing the formation of CEO, Chavez said: "We're very concerned that many of our public policies do more to set people apart than bring them together. We need to have a truly colorblind set of laws." In the late 1990s Chavez served as an adviser to Silicon Valley millionaire Ron Unz, who helped to finance the successful campaign for California's Proposition 227 that dismantled the bilingual education system in that state.

Cabinet Nomination Derailed

Through the late 1990s and into the new millennium, Chavez's stature as a conservative spokesperson grew significantly. When President-elect George W. Bush nominated her to be his labor secretary on January 2, 2001, conservatives were delighted. Just as predictably, liberal and labor forces were quick to voice their vigorous opposition to her nomination. It was clear from the outset that her nomination would be a tough sell on Capitol Hill. In the end, however, Chavez was undone by the revelation that she had once knowingly harbored Marta Mercado, an illegal immigrant from Guatemala, within her household in the early 1990s. She was also charged with paying Mercado less than the minimum wage to do household chores, an allegation Chavez denied. The ensuing furor proved too much to withstand. On January 9, 2001, she withdrew her name from consideration. At a news conference posted on the *About Conservatives: U.S.* website, Chavez stated, "I have decided that I am becoming a distraction and therefore, I have asked President Bush to withdraw my name as secretary of labor." She added, "I do this with some regret because I think that it is a very, very bad signal to all of those good people out there who want to serve their government and want to serve the people of the United States."

Liberals who thought the nomination debacle would in any way muzzle Chavez were soon disabused of such notions. In her memoir, *An Unlikely Conservative: The Transformation of an Ex-Liberal,* published in October of 2002, Chavez once again spoke out forcefully against the liberal public policies she had spent the previous two decades battling. Although she conceded that she had been wrong not to have disclosed the Mercado experience to the Bush transition team, Chavez argued that her alleged offense was not something that should have disqualified her from serving as labor secretary. In his review of the book for *American Enterprise,* Eric Cox noted the absence of any defense from Chavez. "Instead, she blames a hostile press and political foes who would have used any excuse to sabotage her confirmation. She is undoubtedly right on both counts. But her refusal to refute the merits of the case against her suggests that she believes there are none, which is either a slight aimed at her conservative critics or a remarkable display of political naivete."

Selected writing

Out of the Barrio: Toward a New Politics of Hispanic Assimilation, Basic Books, 1991.
An Unlikely Conservative: The Transformation of an Ex-Liberal, Basic Books, 2002.

Sources

Books

Complete Marquis Who's Who, Marquis Who's Who, 2003.
Dictionary of Hispanic Biography, Gale Research, 1996.
Encyclopedia of World Biography, 2nd ed., 17 vols., Gale Research, 1998.
Newsmakers 1999, Issue 3, Gale Group, 1999.

Periodicals

American Enterprise, January-February 2003.
Commentary, March 1998; November 2002.
Insight on the News, July 21, 1997; February 12, 2001.
National Review, February 5, 2001.
PR Newswire, February 21, 1995.

On-line

"Chavez Withdraws as Labor Sec.-Designate," *About Conservative Politics: US,* http://usconservatives .about.com/bln0109chavez.htm (July 15, 2003).
"Linda Chavez," *Barber & Associates,* www.barber usa.com/diversity/chavez_linda_bio.html. (July 15, 2003).
"Linda Chavez," *Biography Resource Center,* www. gale net.com/servlet/BioRC (July 15, 2003).
"Linda Chavez," *Dads Against the Divorce Industry,* www.dadi.org/lc_eng1.htm (July 15, 2003).

"Linda Chavez," *Eagles Talent Connection, Inc.,* www.eaglestalent.com/talent/chavez.html (July 15, 2003).

"Linda Chavez," *Harry Walker Agency,* www.harry walker.com/ speakers_template_printer.cfm?Spea_ID=74&Sub catID=152 (July 15, 2003).

"Linda Chavez; A Favorite of Conservatives," *ABC-NEWS.com,* http://abcnews.go.com/sections/poli tics/DailyNews/chavez_profile010201.html (July 15, 2003).

"Linda Chavez - An Unlikely Conservative: The Transformation of an Ex-Liberal," *SUPA: Stop Union Political Abuse* http://128.121.183.34/lindacha vez/interview.htm (July 15, 2003).

"Linda Chavez Biography," *Republican Issues Campaign,* http://republicanissues.com/biography.asp (July 15, 2003).

—Don Amerman

Nick Chávez

19(?)(?)—

Hair designer, model, entrepreneur

Growing up among the dusty desert ranchlands of the Southwest, Nick Chávez developed an early obsession with animals—horses in particular. As a youngster Chávez filled his days trimming and grooming his horses to perfection, earning piles of awards when he presented them at horse shows. Most people thought Chávez would grow up to be a horse trainer. Instead, Chávez turned his infatuation with grooming into a professional career as a hair stylist and became one of the hottest hair gurus in Beverly Hills, California. The Nick Chávez Salon attracts clients like comedienne Caroline Rhea, Maria Shriver, Ivana Trump, and Queen Noor of Jordan. To complement his salon, Chávez created his own line of hair-care products called Perfect Plus, which hair-conscious consumers seize at a rate of up to $1 million worth of products sold per hour on the QVC home shopping network.

Got Start Grooming Horses

Chávez's path from farm boy to hair guru has taken many twists and turns. He was a December baby, born and raised in the desert terrain of Yuma, Arizona, where his father worked on a ranch. Chávez was the second of seven children born to Kathryn and Juan Chávez and counts among his relatives political activist Cesar Chávez, who was a third cousin. Chávez's bloodline can be traced back to Chihuahua, Mexico, the city his great-grandfather left behind when he came to the United States. He also carries some Yaqui and Quechuan Indian blood.

Chávez's fascination with horses began around the age of ten. To earn money to keep and show his own horses, Chávez spent a fair amount of time grooming and taking care of other people's horses. He also belonged to the 4-H Club and Future Farmers of America. Chávez raised his own lambs and cattle. Whenever the county fair rolled around, he trimmed and brushed their coats to perfection so that they would fetch a first-place ribbon for showmanship.

In his book, *Perfect Hair Every Day,* Chávez joked about his early start in the hair-styling business. "I guess this means my hairdressing career actually began with those animals.... The great thing about the animals was that they let me do my thing, and they never talked back. Boy, was I surprised when I came to Beverly Hills and started to do hair!" After perfecting his shearing skills on the animals, Chávez began trimming the locks of his cousins. By high school, he had a large local clientele.

At a Glance . . .

Born in Yuma, AZ; son of Kathryn and Juan Chávez.

Career: Model for Yvez St. Laurent, Thierry Mugler, Jean Paul Gaultier, Gianfranco Ferre, and Valentino, 1980s-90s; actor, 1990s; Perfect Plus hair care products, creator and promoter, 1994–; Nick Chávez Salon, Beverly Hills, CA, owner and head stylist, 1997–.

Address: *Salon*—9032 Burton Way, Beverly Hills, CA, 90210.

Chávez is quick to credit his parents for his success in life. Growing up, Chávez said, his parents did not make many demands on him; they let him be his own person. His father's only request was that each child finish high school. Chávez's mother took care of him and his brothers and sisters and "was always home to make the tortillas," Chávez recalled to *Contemporary Hispanic Biography (CHB)*. She became a driving force in his life. "My family instilled in me lots of love," he told *CHB.* "Even though we didn't have anything, we always had each other. When you come from that kind of background, you know you can do anything."

After graduating from Yuma Union High School, Chávez headed to Los Angeles. "I had big dreams and aspirations of becoming rich and famous," he recounted to *CHB.* After arriving in Los Angeles, Chávez, just 19, took a job at a salon on Hollywood's famed Sunset Boulevard. His duties: cleaning up. Chávez spent his days sweeping up mounds of hair instead of styling it. He cleaned the salon bathrooms and washed the floors, having faith that his moment would come. As Chávez told *Hispanic* magazine, "Even if you are cleaning toilets, I've always believed that if you're the best you can be, you will always go forward."

He also earned money in nightclubs with a dance revue. As disco became popular during this time, he joined The Rhythm Co. dance troupe. One year he and his dance partner, Sarah Miles, placed in the top ten at the Playboy National Disco Championships. By 1977 Chávez was working in a well-known Beverly Hills salon as an apprentice while trying to get licensed to do hair. An early riser, Chávez walked into the salon early each morning and had the coffee brewing by 8 a.m. Most of the salon's hairdressers did not start work until mid-morning, so customers began asking Chávez to do their hair because he was available so early. His list of clients began to grow. Chávez soon landed up-and-coming stars like Margaux Hemingway, Dana Plato of *Diff'rent Strokes,* and Mindy Cohn and Kim Fields, both of the 1980s NBC hit *The Facts of Life.*

Became Runway Model

In his late twenties Chávez put his hair dressing career on hold and headed to Paris to become a model. "I told myself that I was going to go over there and get an agent," he recalled to *CHB.* "I was always talking to myself, telling myself what I was going to do, telling myself this is my plan. If you have a plan, an idea, just do it," Chávez continued.

In Paris, Chávez had no trouble signing with a modeling agency. His only decision was which one. On his first day with an agency, Chávez went on an interview and landed a job, beating out 200 other models who were vying for the slot. "I had a look," he told *CHB,* which he described as exotic. "There's something for everybody. That day they were looking for my look." At six feet three inches tall, the dark-haired, dark-eyed Latino Chávez certainly stood out in Paris. Soon, Chávez was a jet-setting model, working in Paris, Milan, and Switzerland. He was a runway model for the menswear collections of Yves St. Laurent, Thierry Mugler, Jean Paul Gaultier, Gianfranco Ferre, and Valentino. He appeared on the pages of *Vogue, GQ, Elle,* and *Esquire.* Swatch and Piaget used him in their campaigns. He also appeared on a 100-foot billboard in New York City's Times Square in a Jeff Hamilton advertisement. Chávez was also the pitchman for Valvoline oil, Mazda Miata cars, and Taco Bell and appeared in several other TV commercials.

Chávez told *CHB* that while growing up he suffered relentless teasing. Because he was so wiry, kids called him "the human spring." They also called him "Roadrunner" because he moved quickly and had a large Adam's apple that resembled the cartoon character. Kids followed him around shouting taunts of "beep, beep." This made the validation he received from modeling very therapeutic for Chávez. He commented to *CHB,* "I finally realized that if people were spending thousands, millions of dollars on the campaigns I was featured in—and it was working—then I must look OK. The validation helped me realize that I must look OK." Chávez modeled for about five or six years. Then, his steamy good looks landed him a role on *The Young and The Restless.* He played a character named Steve for about a year, and also appeared on the show *Hollywood Detectives.*

Developed Own Hair-Care Products

Still drawn to hair, Chávez returned to hair styling and Beverly Hills. The more he worked with the various hair-care products on the market, the more dissatisfied he became. Unable to find a full hair-care product line he liked, Chávez took matters into his own hands. He pulled together all of the products he liked and delivered them to a chemist, asking for the ingredients. As Chávez created new products, he tested them on clients to be sure they worked. Instead of rushing his products to the market, Chávez took the time to create products that worked well on all types of hair. In 1994, after two years of experimentation, his "Perfect Plus" line hit the market.

In August of 1994 Chávez appeared on QVC and sold 1,200 hair kits in two minutes. Chávez recalled the moment in his book, "I could hardly believe it, and the look on my face must have been one of pure shock. Moments later, when it hit me, I ran to the phone to call my mom and dad and just started crying. What an amazing feeling that was, and I'll never forget it as long as I live." Chávez still appears on QVC in its U.S., British, and German outlets, as well as on Canada's The Shopping Channel. The products are also an e-commerce hit on QVC's website. He credited the product's success to his perfectionism in taking the time to test and create a perfect product.

In May of 1997, Chávez opened his own salon, called The Nick Chávez Salon. Chávez told CHB that he enjoyed hair styling because it allows him to listen to lots of people and soak up their advice, giving him an education money cannot buy. He also loves the creative side of the business and delights in the immediate gratification both he and his clients get from his services. Chávez is not one to keep his secrets to himself. In 2000 he published Perfect Hair Everyday, aimed at helping people get that stylish salon look in their own homes. The book is packed with step-by-step instructions—including pictures and illustrations—for shampooing and styling every type of hair, from straight to wavy and curly to kinky hair.

Chávez is still interested in horses and owns more than 50. They live at his Yuma, Arizona, ranch, which is complete with an indoor, air-conditioned training facility. His pride and joy is a stallion named José Bueno Chex, who won the United States Equestrian Team Futures Competition silver medal in June of 2002.

With all of his success, Chávez has never forgotten his roots. He used his profits to help with various charities, including the Race to Erase M.S.; the Carousel of Hope Ball for diabetes, held annually in Beverly Hills; the Crenshaw Christian Center of Los Angeles; and Best Buddies International, an organization that helps people with intellectual disabilities. He also gives scholarships to adults going back to school to earn their high school diploma or GED. "As a Latino, I can be a great role model," he told CHB. "By being my best, I can inspire and let others know they have a chance. I'm blessed to have the name Chávez, which I honor and respect by being the best I can be."

Selected Writings

Perfect Hair Every Day, QVC Publishing, Inc., 2000

Sources

Books

Chávez, Nick, Perfect Hair Every Day, QVC Publishing, Inc., 2000

Periodicals

Atlanta Journal and Constitution, April 15, 2001, p. 8M.
Hispanic Magazine, June 2002.

On-line

"Making It With Style," Hispanic Magazine www.hispanicmagazine.com/2001/jun/Features/nickchavez.html (June 9, 2003).

Other

Additional information for this profile was obtained through a personal interview with Contemporary Hispanic Biography on May 30, 2003.

—Lisa Frick

Marc Cisneros

1939—

Army general, college president, chief executive officer

Over the course of his lifetime, Marc Cisneros has navigated a lot of terrain. Cisneros began life among the cowhands in the dusty ranchlands of South Texas, knuckled his way through the jungles of Vietnam, became an Army general, and ended up establishing policy among the halls of academia. His accomplishments have made Cisneros a favorite South Texas son. On the outskirts of his hometown of Premont, Texas, a sign proudly announces that it is the home of retired three-star Lieutenant General Marc Cisneros. His success reminds South Texans—Hispanics in particular—of their unlimited potential. "He has made a positive impact," Premont middle school principal Luis A. Canales told the *San Antonio Express-News*. "He is Mexicano, and that affects all of South Texas."

A tenth generation South Texan, Marc Anthony Cisneros was born April 5, 1939, in Brownsville, Texas, to Antonio and Herlinda (Canales) Cisneros. He was raised in the cattle country of Premont, Texas, not far from the Mexican border. Cisneros comes from a family with a history of public service. His great uncle, J.T. Canales, was a leading Texas Mexican-American political leader, who helped found the League of United Latin American Citizens. Growing up, Cisneros learned to speak both English and Spanish. Like many Texan boys, Cisneros was involved with ranching and was active with the Future Farmers of America. He graduated from San Antonio's Central Catholic High School and entered St. Mary's University, also in San Antonio, as a member of the Army's Reserve Officer Training Corps (ROTC). In 1961, Cisneros received a bachelor's degree in business administration and

planned to attend law school. Instead, the Army commissioned him a second lieutenant and he spent the next 30 years in uniform.

Helped Orchestrate Numerous Army Offensive Strikes

From 1963 to 1965, Cisneros served as battery commander of the U.S. Army forces in Europe, stationed in Babenhausen, Germany. Cisneros's first combat experience came during the Vietnam war. In 1968, Cisneros worked as a senior operations advisor during the Tet offensive. The Tet offensive was a campaign launched in 1968 by the Viet Cong from the north in an effort to overtake South Vietnam. While the Viet Cong did not win the offensive militarily, they proved themselves to be a formidable force and Cisneros and his comrades worked hard to maintain their ground. Later, between 1971 and 1973, Cisneros served as a regional adviser trying to keep the South Vietnamese army from caving in.

From 1975 to 1977, Cisneros was a battalion commander at Fort Hood, Texas, and an artillery commander from 1984 to 1986. By the late 1980s, he was serving in Panama and worked his way up the ranks to become a general. Cisneros is most remembered for his role in the 1989 Panama invasion, in which he helped orchestrate the invasion and capture of then-dictator General Manuel Noriega, accused of drug trafficking and other crimes. During "Operation Just Cause," as the offensive was named, Cisneros served

At a Glance . . .

Born Marc Anthony Cisneros on April 5, 1939, in Brownsville, TX; married Eddy Virginia Durham on November 3, 1964; children: Marc Jr., Kenric, Kara. *Education:* St. Mary's University, San Antonio, TX, BA, 1961; Shippensburg State University, Shippensburg, PA, MA, 1968; U.S. Army War College, Carlisle, PA, graduate, 1978. *Military Service:* U.S. Army.

Career: U.S. Army, second lieutenant, 1961; U.S. Army in Europe, Babenhausen, Germany, battery commander, 1963-65; U.S. Army, Fort Hood, TX, battalion commander, 1975-77; U.S. Army, artillery commander, 1984-86; stationed in Panama, late 1980s; U.S. Army South, Panama, commander, 1989-90; Investigations and Oversight in the Office of the Secretary of the Army, deputy inspector general 1992-94; Fifth U.S. Army at Fort Sam Houston, TX, commanding general, 1994-96; Texas A&M-Kingsville, president, 1998-01; John G. and Marie Stella Kenedy Memorial Foundation, Corpus Christi, TX, CEO, 2001–.

Awards: Received two Distinguished Service Medals, Legion of Merit, Bronze Star; named one of "100 Most Influential Hispanics," *Hispanic Business Magazine,* 1997.

Address: *Home*—PO Box 1292, Premont, TX, 78375.

as commander of the U.S. Army South, making him the highest-ranking Latino in the U.S. Army. While the U.S. military planned to use force, Cisneros reminded his comrades that the enemy would probably crumble without an extreme use of force. According to the *St. Petersburg Times,* Cisneros told his commanding officers, "Listen, most of these people are not going to fight. Give them a chance to surrender and they will. You don't have to blow everything to kingdom come." Cisneros wanted to win the campaign, but he wanted to minimize the devastation to the country's cities and homes.

On the day after the invasion, Cisneros discovered that one of Noriega's captains, Amadis Jimenez, had been captured. Fluent in Spanish, Cisneros persuaded Jimenez to call his comrades and urge them to surrender. By working the phone lines, Cisneros and Jimenez got all nine of Noriega's provincial commanders to surrender their collective 5,000 troops—75 percent of the forces. "People describe Marc as having won the war

with a telephone," General Fred Woerner told the *St. Petersburg Times.* "He saw a way to accomplish the mission, and at the same time minimize the loss of life and destruction. He was the glue in Just Cause." Cisneros did not give himself much credit for his role in minimizing the loss of life in Panama. According to *U.S. News & World Report,* when a friend asked him how he wanted to be remembered, Cisneros said, "Just say, 'He was a hell of a soldier.'" Cisneros was also the one who calmed the fears of Panamanians by going into their villages and speaking to them in Spanish.

Took Command of Texas A&M-Kingsville

Following his service in Panama, Cisneros worked his way up the ranks. From 1992 to 1994, he served as the deputy inspector general for Investigations and Oversight in the Army's Office of the Secretary and in February of 1994 became commanding general of the Fifth U.S. Army at Fort Sam Houston, Texas. He retired in August of 1996 after earning two Distinguished Service Medals. Next, Cisneros worked as a general manager of government services for Fluor Daniel Inc., a large engineering and construction contractor.

On September 1, 1998, Cisneros made history when he became the 15th president of Texas A&M-Kingsville. He was the first non-educator to be hired in that post, and faculty at first were leery of having a general take over the school. However, during his three-year tenure Cisneros covered a lot of ground. Raised among the cowhands, Cisneros never forgot his roots and even after becoming a general remained down to earth and approachable, comfortable around everyone from students to senators to presidents. "I have walked among the most humble and most egotistical," Cisneros told the *San Antonio Express-News.* "My troops always used to say, 'You don't act like a general.'" As president, Cisneros remained approachable to students and under his leadership, enrollment stabilized. He also worked to increase student retention. Freshman student retention stood at 56 percent when Cisneros came and rose to 61 percent. Cisneros also helped found an extension campus in San Antonio as well as implement a pharmacy school at the Kingsville campus, the first professional school south of San Antonio.

Because of his military background, Cisneros was offered a chance to work in Washington, D.C. Following the November of 2000 presidential election, vice president Dick Cheney asked Cisneros to join the Bush cabinet and become Secretary of Veterans Affairs. Cisneros, however, said he had a job to finish at the university.

Cisneros completed his vision and left the university in August of 2001. However, he did not stray far from his

South Texas roots. Cisneros became chief executive officer of the multimillion-dollar Corpus Christi, Texas-based John G. and Marie Stella Kenedy Memorial Foundation, a foundation that supports Catholic activities across the state. In this capacity, Cisneros has continued to positively influence the lives of young Texans. Cisneros has said his mission is to use foundation funds to promote family life and reach the poor in their homes. Cisneros also wanted to increase parental involvement in children's lives, believing this will help children become more successful and eventually lead to economic stability for South Texas.

Along the way Cisneros married Eddy Virginia Durham on November 3, 1964. They have three children. When he is not busy, Cisneros spends his free time with his grandchildren. He also has a pilot's license and likes to fly his own plane. Cisneros believes that the element of risk in flying keeps his senses sharp.

Sources

Periodicals

Corpus Christi (Texas) Caller-Times, June 12, 2001, p. A1.
La Prensa de San Antonio, June 6, 2001, p. 1.
San Antonio (Texas) Express-News, January 16, 2000, p. 1B.
St. Petersburg (Florida) Times, December 20, 1999, p. 1A.
U.S. News & World Report, July 30, 1990, p.32.

On-line

"Marc Cisneros Take Over Command as President of Texas A&M University-Kingsville" *Texas A&M University-Kingsville,* www.tamuk.edu/news/archive/arch98/september/presidente.html (June 9, 2003).

—Lisa Frick

Donna de Varona

1947—

Olympic swimmer, sportscaster, activist

Olympic swimmer Donna de Varona has had a rich and varied career. She won two gold medals in the 1964 Olympics, and was one of the first women hired as a sports reporter for a major television network. A dedicated activist on behalf of women in sports, de Varona helped found the Women's Sports Foundation and has testified before Congress on issues related to women in sports. She has held advisory positions to five U.S. presidents since 1966.

Donna de Varona was born in April of 1947 in San Diego, California. Her father, David de Varona, was a Hall-of-Fame rower and an All-American football player for the University of California. As her first swimming coach, he encouraged de Varona to develop her swimming ability, and made sure that she attended meets. De Varona's mother, Martha, was also warm and supportive of her interests.

Won Two Gold Medals Before Twenty

Initially, de Varona wanted to play Little League baseball, like her beloved older brother David. She loved the game so much that in elementary school, she chose the desk closest to the door so she could be the first one out on the field when the bell rang to signal the end of class.

However, because she was a girl, and Little League was only open to boys at the time, she was barred from any position other than "bat girl." She quickly became bored with spending her time at every game on the sidelines. As she told Marty Benson in the *NCAA News*, "Being that close and not being able to play hurt too much." When David injured a knee and switched to swimming, she followed him to a new sport.

de Varona's ability in the pool was readily apparent, since even as a young child, she had always been a strong swimmer. She entered her first meet when she was nine, and soon outgrew her father's coaching, becoming a protege of some of California's best coaches. She specialized in the difficult 400-meter medley, in which competitors swim four laps, each in a different stroke: freestyle, butterfly, breast stroke, and back stroke. In 1960, when she was 13, she qualified for the U.S. Olympic team in that event. She was the youngest member of the American team that year, and loved the excitement of traveling to Rome with the other athletes. Unfortunately, her event was canceled and she did not compete.

During high school, de Varona trained up to six hours a day, but managed to maintain a B average in her studies. In 1964 she qualified for the Olympic team

At a Glance . . .

Born Donna de Varona in April of 1947, in San Diego, California; daughter of David and Martha de Varona; married John Pinto (a lawyer and investment banker); children: John David, Joanna. *Education:* University of California-Los Angeles, BA, political science, 1986.

Career: Swimmer, 1960-64; ABC, *Wide World of Sports,* Olympics broadcaster, 1968, 1972, 1976; NBC, *Sports World, Today Show,* broadcaster, 1978-83; commentator, consultant, writer, coproducer, contributor: *Wide World of Sports, ABC News, Good Morning America,* ESPN, ABC radio, 1984; Roone Arledge, president of ABC News and Sports, ABC, assistant, 1983-86; NBC, Olympics, broadcaster, 1996, 2000; Sporting News Radio, radio sports commentator, 1998–; *Sporting News,* Olympics reporter, 2002.

Selected awards: Winner of 37 U.S. swimming championships, 1960-64; gold medals in swimming, Pan-American Games 1963; gold medals, 400-meter medley and 400-meter freestyle relay, Olympic Games, 1964; Associated Press and United Press International Most Outstanding Female Athlete, 1965; Emmy Award, 1991; Gracie Award from American Women in Radio and Television, 2000, 2001; Susan B. Anthony "Trailblazer" Award, 2001; inductee: International Swimming Hall of Fame; U.S. Olympic Hall of Fame; Women's Sports Hall of Fame.

Address: *Office*—Sporting News Radio, P.O. Box 509, Techny, IL 60082.

again, and won a gold medal in the 400-meter medley. As a member of the 400-meter freestyle relay team, she then won another gold medal.

After setting 18 world swimming records, de Varona retired from competitive swimming in 1965. She retired largely because she was now in college at the University of California-Los Angeles, and the school, like most other universities at the time, had no athletic programs for women. With bills to pay de Varona had to spend her spare time working, and she began looking around for work that would use her interest in and knowledge of sports. Undeterred by the fact that at the time, all the sportscasters on the major television

networks were male, she used her Olympic experience to her advantage, and became the first female broadcaster on the ABC network's *Wide World of Sports.* After graduating from college, she decided to make a career in broadcasting.

Became a Reporter and Activist

Despite her early success with ABC, it was difficult for de Varona to find work in her male-dominated field. She traveled all over the United States, filling in temporarily when regular anchormen became ill or went on vacation. Eventually, she found permanent work as an Olympic reporter with NBC and ABC.

During the 1970s, de Varona also became involved in activism for the cause of women's sports. She was a founding member of the Women's Sports Foundation, and in 1975 she served on President Ford's Commission on Olympic Sports. She also testified on behalf of Title IX legislation in front of both the House of Representatives and the Senate. Title IX legislation ultimately ensured that girls and women received the same opportunities and federal funding in sports education that boys and men did. According to an article in *Great Women in Sports,* de Varona told a *Women's Sports and Fitness* writer, "I will always be an activist. That is a lifetime commitment."

De Varona began covering the Olympics in 1972, and would report on the 1976 and 1984 Olympic Games for ABC. According to *Great Women in Sports,* she told a *Women's Sports and Fitness* reporter that the 1984 Olympics in Sarajevo, Yugoslavia were the most difficult for her: "I was there by myself, no producer, no assignments. I hustled everything myself. I just went out, grabbed a crew, did spots and wrote stories. That was my test because I was just back at ABC and we were in a crisis situation with the problems of scheduling and snow."

Clashed With ABC

Though de Varona received critical acclaim for her coverage of the 1984 Summer Olympics, choice assignments were few and far between. She told Sally Jenkins in *Sports Illustrated,* "I don't feel the rewards [I should have gotten] came after that. You do good work, and then wait and wait for another good assignment." However, she also noted that despite the widespread discrimination against women in sportscasting, "It's too easy to play the victim. We're making progress. It's coming. It's just taking longer than I ever thought it would."

In 1988 de Varona continued her Olympic coverage when she reported from Calgary. She also expanded her career by working for Turner Network Television and Sporting News Radio. In 1991 de Varona won an Emmy award for her reporting of a story about a Special Olympics athlete.

In 1998 ABC let de Varona's contract lapse and, according to de Varona, encouraged her to leave. In *People,* de Varona told a reporter that the network was trying to attract more of the [age] "18-to-39 male market" and that network executives believed that she was too old to hold this audience's interest. In 2000 she filed an age-discrimination suit against ABC, arousing controversy in the sports broadcasting world. Of her decision to take legal action against ABC, she told *People* magazine, "It would have been much easier to walk away, but I felt I had to do it." The case was later settled out of court, and de Varona resumed working at ABC.

Declaring her candidacy for the presidency of the U.S. Olympic Committee in 2002, de Verona withdrew from the race after six days. According to Mer-Jo Borzilleri in an article provided by the Knight Ridder/ Tribune News Service, de Varona said that "time and resources" did not allow her to give the job the attention it would require. In addition, she noted that it would probably create a conflict of interest for her to report on the Olympics at the same time that she was serving as president of the Olympic committee, and she did not want to stop reporting. However, she also said that she would reconsider running for the position in 2004. In 2003 de Varona was selected to receive the NCAA's highest honor, the Theodore Roosevelt Award. The award, also known as the "Teddy," is given to a distinguished citizen who is a former college student-athlete and who shows a continuing interest in physical fitness and sport.

Controversy Over Title IX

Later in 2003 de Varona took a controversial position regarding the Title IX legislation she had been instrumental in creating during the 1970s. President George Bush had asked Education Secretary Rod Paige to establish a commission to determine whether the legislation should be altered. The commission recommended making certain controversial changes to the legislation; according to *Women's E-News* the Save Title IX campaign, which opposed the changes, said they would cost high school girls 305,000 opportunities to participate in sports; college women would miss 50,000 participation opportunities as well as $122 million in athletic scholarships.

Opposed to the changes, de Varona, who served on the commission, and another commission member, Julie Foudy, refused to sign the commission's list of propositions for change. As a result, Secretary Paige subsequently announced that he would only consider recommendations for change that won unanimous support from the commission.

In addition to her political work on behalf of women's sports, de Varona continues to work as a broadcaster for Sporting News Radio. On the radio network's website, a press release noted, "Each week [de Varona's] commentary explores and highlights the positive stories of athletes, coaches and the people who support them. She brings to light the behind-the-scenes achievements that often go unnoticed." Summing up her goals in life, de Varona told Marty Benson in the *NCAA News,* "My passion is to see as many opportunities as possible for as many people as possible, all the way from the grass-roots level to the colleges."

Sources

Books

Great Women in Sports, Visible Ink Press, 1996.

Periodicals

Broadcasting and Cable, April 17, 2000, p. 69.
Knight Ridder/Tribune News Service, July 19, 2002, p. K7770; February 25, 2003, p. K2941.
People, May 15, 2000, p. 89.
Sports Illustrated, June 17, 1991, p. 78.
Women's E-News, March 11, 2003, p. 0.

On-line

"Donna de Varona," *NCAA News,* www.ncaa.org (May 7, 2003).
"Donna de Varona," *Sporting News Radio,* http://radio.sportingnews.com/experts/donna_de_varona/index.html (May 15, 2003).
"Sporting News Radio's Donna de Varona wins second-consecutive Gracie Allen Award," *Sporting News Radio,* http://radio.sportingnews.com/about/pres/20010426_donna.html (June 4, 2003).

—Kelly Winters

Remedios Díaz-Oliver

1938—

Entrepreneur

As a well-educated young adult in Cuba, Remedios Díaz-Oliver hoped to become a college professor, but Fidel Castro and his communist regime undercut her plans and caused her and her new family to go into exile in the United States. In southern Florida, Díaz-Oliver stumbled upon a greater use of her talents: international sales and entrepreneurial executive positions. She would succeed in business despite her gender and ethnic background, as well as retain respect as one of the most prominent Hispanic businesswomen even as she battled years of litigation.

Found Opportunity in United States

Born in Cuba on August 22, 1938, Díaz-Oliver experienced business dealings firsthand as a child. Her father owned a hotel and also distributed hotel supplies throughout Cuba. She often accompanied him on business trips to the United States and Spain. This exposure to international business would later be beneficial to her. An excellent student, Díaz-Oliver graduated from high school a year early. She matriculated at business colleges before earning a Ph.D. in education from the University of Havana. Fluent in English, French, and Italian, Díaz-Oliver's worked for Havana Business Academy and Havana Business College, which had exchange programs with U.S. business-people and close ties to the U.S. Embassy, and had plans to become a full-time educator when political upheaval sidetracked her course.

One day when she was pregnant with her first child, Díaz-Oliver and her husband, Fausto, encountered Fidel Castro, whom her father had known in the early days of the revolution. As she recalled to Paul Miller for the *Dictionary of Hispanic Biography,* "'Nenita (which my father used to call me) how are you?' he said. I looked at him and I said, 'Surprised you didn't keep your promises!' he didn't throw me in jail right then and there probably because I was pregnant, but I was in jail a year later." Both she and her husband were jailed nine days during the Bay of Pigs invasion, ostensibly for protesting against government imposed mail inspections. Shortly after their release, the American Red Cross assisted Remedios, Fausto, and baby Rosa, along with others, to immigrate to the United States. Díaz-Oliver's family arrived in Florida on May 11, 1961.

Although the wages were low, the couple found work to support their family: Fausto at a yacht company; Díaz-Oliver in the accounting department of Richford Industries, a container distributor. Soon Díaz-Oliver familiarized herself with the company's products and became the company's Spanish-speaking employee who communicated with clients in Cuba and other Latin American countries. The woman who had never sold anything before coming to America proved to be an excellent merchandiser. Within a year she was in charge of the newly created International Division of a company that had never exported products before and, furthermore, had generated so many sales that the company ranked first among companies exporting containers to Central America. President Lyndon Johnson recognized her accomplishment in 1968 by awarding her the "E" Award (Excellence in Export); she was the award's first woman recipient. Combating what Miller termed "double-barrelled stereotypes," Díaz-Oliver guided the International Division's (not to the mention the United States's) expansion of market share in a region previously dominated by exporting container companies from France and Italy.

Success Marred by Legal Troubles

Díaz-Oliver credited her Spanish mother with her determination. In her conversation with Miller, she recalled her mother teaching her that "the only way you can succeed in life is by working hard." In 1976, when Richford Industries was sold to a division of Alco Standard Corp., she left and founded American International Container (AIC) with her husband, Fausto, and glass manufacturer, Frank H. Wheaton, Jr.; she be-

came the new company's president. Wheaton gave her $50,000 to launch AIC and verbally agreed on a 50-50 partnership. Wheaton Industries was Richford's top supplier of bottles and containers. "I could have started the distributorship on my own, but with Frank I thought I would have national connections—really worldwide connections. Many times Frank was called Mr. Glass," Díaz-Oliver told *Miami Herald* reporters Mimi Whitefield and Barbara DeLollis. AIC's rapid growth bore out her abilities as an executive. The company grew from $800,000 in sales its first year to an astounding $90 million in revenues in 1991. In that year *South Florida Business Journal* placed AIC 33rd on its list of top privately owned companies. Díaz-Oliver's abilities also caught the attention of other companies, which enlisted her for their supervisory boards. At one time she was the only Florida woman to be a board member of three Fortune 500 companies simultaneously: Avon Products, Inc., U.S. West Inc., and Barnett Banks (Bank of America). Furthermore, she took part in elite events. She chaired a ball honoring *Dynasty*'s Joan Collins for the American Cancer Society in 1983; represented former President George Bush at South American inaugurations; was in a group that met with former British Prime Minister Margaret Thatcher in 1989; attended a dinner aboard the royal yacht for Queen Elizabeth II and Prince Philip in 1991; and was recognized by *Hispanic Business* magazine as one of the nation's most influential Hispanics, and her family, with a net worth of $25 million, as one of the wealthiest Hispanic families in America, in 1997.

However, in 1991 Díaz-Oliver may have thought a hex had been put on her charmed life. Unhappy with the performance of Wheaton Industries, some of Frank Wheaton, Jr.'s relatives started investigating his handling of company operations. What they found out caused them to oust him, and later Díaz-Oliver. Their investigation revealed that, contrary to what Díaz-Oliver had been claiming for years, she did not own American International, nor did she even own half the company, because she never signed a written contract with Wheaton. Moreover, the investigation revealed business irregularities, including more than $1 million off the books, the use of company money to pay for personal expenses and contributions to charitable and political causes, and shell companies. Díaz-Oliver provided explanations for all the irregularities. She said it was common practice for Wheaton executives to use company money and resources for personal expenses instead of drawing a large salary; her 1991 salary was only $75,000. As for claiming full ownership of AIC and setting up shell companies, she did that because some companies wouldn't do business with a Wheaton subsidiary.

Explanations not withstanding, AIC's new management charged Díaz-Oliver and her family and friends with embezzling $3.5 million while she ran the company. She and her husband countered by suing Wheaton Industries and ten of its executives for $50 million for slander. The legal wrangling caught the attention of federal investigators, who uncovered fraudulent bank accounts and records believed to have been set up to avoid paying customs duties and taxes. At the heart of the investigation was the now-defunct Spanish Foods Inc., whose minority shareholders were Díaz-Oliver's son and a longtime friend. The scheme involved claiming phony business expenses to hide some revenues from the IRS and the submitting of phony invoices to U.S. Customs to deflate the true value of goods being imported from Spain. The probe resulted in an 18-count felony indictment against Díaz-Oliver, as well as charges against her husband and others.

Determined to continue in a business she knew thoroughly, Díaz-Oliver, her husband, and two children formed All American Containers, Inc. (AAC) in 1991. Under her guidance as president and CEO, AAC secured accounts with McCormick, Schering, Pepsi-Cola, Coca-Cola, and other large companies and set up a marketing network reaching into Central and South America, the Caribbean, Europe, Asia, Africa, Australia, and New Zealand. Today, the company sells more than five thousand different types of glass, plastic, and metal containers and caps to manufacturers.

As she built AAC, Díaz-Oliver lured many AIC employees back into her fold and engaged in years of litigation. In 1995 she dropped her slander suit against Wheaton in return for being able to buy AIC for $3.7 million. At the time it was valued at more than $11 million. After the settlement Díaz-Oliver started selling Wheaton bottles again. Son Fausto is president of AIC, which remains a separate company that competes with AAC. In 1999 another of Díaz-Oliver's legal problems was settled when federal prosecutors dropped their 18-count indictment against her and allowed her to plead guilty to two misdemeanors. She received three years probation for her part in customs fraud and tax evasion in connection with Spanish Foods. Her plea, however, unexpectedly garnered national attention and embarrassed the presidential campaign of Texas Governor George W. Bush when reporters revealed she was the host of a fund-raiser in Florida.

Continued to Help Others

In their *Miami Herald* article, Whitefield and DeLollis described Díaz-Oliver as not only a prominent businesswoman but also as "an untiring worker for charitable causes, a champion of women in business, a symbol of Hispanic success and a friend of political leaders." No matter her tribulations, she remains actively involved in civic, business, and charitable organizations. She is the national president of the American Cancer Society's Hispanic Development Center and is on the boards of Infants in Need, Hispanic Heritage, and the Public Health Trust. She served several years on the presidential Advisory Committee of U.S. Trade Policy and Negotiations. In the 1980s she worked for both Republicans and Democrats, and even served as national co-chair of Hispanics for George Bush during the 1988 presidential election. She has received accolades from Presidents Lyndon Johnson, Ronald Reagan, and George Bush, the state of Florida, the City of Miami, and Metropolitan Dade County, as well as numerous awards from organizations.

Díaz-Oliver believes she has been supported during her difficulties because she often has helped others. "It was a different and difficult world for women when I started. I think I was a pioneer in my own city and I haven't turned my back on women on the way up. That's why I think a lot of people are here for me now," she explained to Whitefield and DeLollis.

Sources

Periodicals

Florida Trend, January 1995.
Miami Herald, July 5, 1999; November 3, 1999.
South Florida Business Journal, September 23, 1991.

On-line

"Remedios Diaz-Oliver," *Biography Resource Center,* www.galenet.com/servlet/BioRC (May 20, 2003).

—Doris Morris Maxfield

Huey Dunbar

1974—

Singer

Hailed by many critics as the future of salsa music, Huey Dunbar helped to revitalize the genre and introduce it to a new generation during his stint as the lead singer of Dark Latin Groove (DLG). The group's three albums gained DLG a large following not only among salsa music fans but listeners across the musical spectrum as well. After winning two *Billboard* Latin Music Awards, DLG amicably split up in 2000 and Dunbar began a promising solo career. His first album, *Yo Si Me Enamore,* was released in 2001 and earned a gold record for selling over a half-million copies. With an English-language album in the works in 2003, Dunbar looked forward to branching out into new musical styles. As he told an interviewer with the *Salsa Wild* website, "I always planned on going in different directions. I always think it's necessary for me to not stay on doing the same thing over because I don't want to get pigeonholed. I don't want anyone to think that Huey's only good for one kind of music."

Huey Dunbar was born on May 15, 1974, and grew up in New York City, although he also spent time in Puerto Rico. His mother, an immigrant from Puerto Rico, was an aspiring opera singer who passed on her love of music to her son. His father, a native of Jamaica who enjoyed playing the conga drums, died during Dunbar's youth. Dunbar's unlikely introduction to a career in music occurred while he was a student at Bayside High School in the borough of Queens in New York City. After seeing a flyer posted for a talent contest, Dunbar decided to enter by singing the song "Lately," a hit by the R & B group Jodeci. Dunbar's rendition of the song impressed one of the judges, Latin music producer Sergio George. When George asked Dunbar whether he sang in Spanish, however, Dunbar encountered his first setback. Not having spoken much Spanish while he was growing up, Dunbar decided to throw himself into learning the language so that he could pursue his contact with George. He also began a lengthy romantic relationship with a high-school classmate that produced two children before the couple broke up several years later.

Entered Salsa Scene With DLG

The connection with George proved to be a vital stepping stone in the young singer's career. Like Dunbar, George was a New York City native who had

At a Glance . . .

Born on May 15, 1974, in New York, NY; two children.

Career: Singer, 1995–.

Awards: *Billboard* Latin Music Award, Album of the Year, Tropical/Salsa Group, *Swing On,* 1998; *Billboard* Latin Music Award, Album of the Year, Tropical/Salsa Group, *Gotcha,* 2000.

Addresses: *Record company*—Sony Discos, 605 Lincoln Road, Miami Beach, FL, 33139; Phone: (305) 695-3494; *Record company website*—www.sonydiscos.com. *Official artist website*—www.hueyonline.com.

an all-encompassing love of music, especially salsa. In the early 1990s George began producing records for the leading salsa label in North America, RMM Records, in New York City. Adding contemporary urban sounds to traditional Latin salsa to produce a hybrid genre, George's productions appealed to younger Hispanic listeners who had previously turned away from Latin music in favor of rap and hip-hop. By the time he formed Sir George Productions in 1995, George was the undisputed leader of the Latin music scene in New York City. With George's help, Dunbar began appearing as a backup vocalist on tracks by Latin music stars India, Yolandita Monge, and Victor Manuelle in 1994 and 1995.

As one of the first acts signed to his management company, George put together Dark Latin Groove (DLG), which immediately signed a recording contract with the Sony Discos label. DLG embodied George's vision of a Latin music act that incorporated the sounds of traditional salsa, contemporary hip-hop and rap, and classic R & B. Dunbar, its lead singer, had a sweet and soulful voice that immediately drew comparisons to Michael Jackson. James (Da Barba) de Jesus, the group's resident expert in rap and reggae, had grown up in Spanish Harlem in New York City but added elements of Jamaican dance hall "toasting," or rapping, to DLG's tracks. Rounding out the trio, Wilfredo (Frangancia) Crispin was also an experienced reggae-style rapper and energetic live performer. "DLG's music is about inclusion," Dunbar said of the group's philosophy in a *Musica Virtual* website profile, "It's like an open door, not being closed to the daily influences of multiple styles of music."

DLG's first album, *Dark Latin Groove,* was released in early 1996 and became an immediate critical and commercial success. In a *New York Times* review, Peter Watrous called the release "the most radical salsa album made in the last decade," adding that "*Dark Latin Groove* is completely aware of tradition and hell-bent on modernizing it." The album entered the top forty on *Billboard's* Top Latin Albums chart and the top ten on the magazine's Tropical/Salsa albums list. Capping off the successful debut, the group earned a Grammy Award nomination for Best Tropical Latin performance and a nomination as Best New Tropical and Salsa Artist for the *Premio Lo Nuestro* award. With international tours throughout Latin America, DLG's popularity indeed spread far beyond the United States.

DLG's sophomore release, *Swing On,* was released in 1997 to even greater commercial and critical acclaim. The album peaked at number two on *Billboard's* Tropical/Salsa chart and number fourteen on its Top Latin Albums chart. Regarded as the group's best album, it made DLG's members into Latin music superstars or, as *The Rough Guide's World Music* volume called them, "the three coolest dudes in Latin New York." It also won DLG the *Billboard* Latin Music Award for Album of the Year by a tropical or salsa group. The group repeated that feat with its third release, *Gotcha,* which was released in 1999 and quickly entered the top ten on the *Billboard* top Latin Albums chart. The album also earned DLG another Grammy Award nomination for Best Tropical Latin performance.

Launched Solo Career

By the time DLG earned its second *Billboard* Latin Music Award, the group had already disbanded so that Dunbar could pursue a solo career. The split was amicable and Dunbar immediately went back into the studio with George, who was producing his debut solo effort. The result, *Yo Si Me Enamore,* took nine months to make, in part because Dunbar was intent on forging ahead with new sounds, just as he had with DLG. "The reason why I left DLG and broke up the group is because I couldn't grow anymore within the confines of that style and I was desiring to do more things," he explained in an interview with the *Salsa Wild* website. The album reflected this outlook, with a *Billboard* review noting of its eclectic style, "Dunbar sings ballads, salsa, and even pop in what's probably a ploy to straddle all radio formats. In the end, the results are good enough to work." Dunbar also transformed his image for his solo debut, going from his formerly multicolored hair styles and streetwise attire—which earned him comparisons to Dennis Rodman—to a much more sophisticated and suave look for his new album's cover.

Released in 2001, *Yo Si Me Enamore* hit number one on *Billboard's* Tropical/Salsa chart and earned a gold record for Dunbar by selling over a half-million copies. Dunbar also had the biggest hit single of his career to date, with the ballad "Con Cada Beso" hitting the top five on the Hot Latin Tracks chart in *Billboard*. Following on the heels of *Yo Se Me Enamore,* Dunbar announced plans for an English-language album. He hoped that the release would broaden the fan base of Latin music beyond its traditional confines of Spanish-language listeners. As he explained in an interview with the *Salsa Wild* website, "The next step is to take it to the next level and take it to the rest of the world. Take our music to the rest of the people in a way that they can understand it and appreciate it even more.... It's not the American public's responsibility to learn Spanish to listen to my music. It's my job to go out there and offer my perspective of Latin music to the American markets and that's what I want to do."

Discography

(with DLG) *Dark Latin Groove,* 1996.
(with DLG) *Swing On,* 1997.
(with DLG) *Gotcha,* 1999.
(with DLG) *Greatest Hits,* 2000.
(solo) *Yo Si Me Enamore,* 2001.

Sources

Books

Broughton, Simon, and Mark Ellingham, eds., *World Music: The Rough Guide Volume 2,* Rough Guides, 2000.

Periodicals

Billboard, September 27, 1997, p. 8; November 1, 1997, p. 1; April 29, 2000, p. LM-8; March 10, 2001, p. 32.
Latinia, August 2000, p. 78.
New York Times, May 28, 1996, p. C11; February 8, 1998, p. E1.

On-line

"DLG," *All Music Guide,* www.allmusic.com/cg/amg.dll (March 29, 2003).
"DLG: 'Gotcha'," *MusicaVirtual,* www.musicavirtual.com/dlg.html (April 2, 2003).
"Huey Dunbar," *All Music Guide,* www.allmusic.com/cg/amg.dll (March 29, 2003).
"Huey Dunbar," *Recording Industry Association of America,* www.riaa.com (April 1, 2003).
"Huey Dunbar," *Sony Discos,* www.sonydiscos.com/discos/content.nsf/bio/20010314045826_79?Open&language=english (March 29, 2003).
"Huey Dunbar, Un innovador de la Salsa," *America Salsa,* www.americasalsa.com/entrevistamx/huey_dunbar.html (April 1, 2003).
"Interview: Huey Dunbar," *Salsawild,* www.salsawild.com/salseros-report/interviews/huey-interview.htm (April 2, 2003).

—Timothy Borden

Clarissa Pinkola Estés

1943—

Writer, psychologist

When Clarissa Pinkola Estés went on a journey of self-discovery, she never intended to make a living telling the stories that made up her personal identity as woman and an individual. Yet with the publication of *Women Who Run with the Wolves: Myths and Stories of the Wild Woman Archetype,* Estés directed the field of women's studies toward the study of the self through storytelling, both in reciting individual unique stories as well as putting the individual self into myths and tales to decipher how the concept of self and womanhood has been constructed by society. Estés, who worked her way up from poverty into the realm of academia, breaks down large issues of social psychology into simple stories that all women can relate to, and many readers use her books to answer questions about themselves they had yet to even consider.

Childhood Embraced by Storytelling

Clarissa Pinkola Estés was born on January 27, 1943, in Indiana. The date of her birth has become somewhat less clear in recent years. Initially, her year of birth was listed as 1943, but in later interviews, she changed her year of birth to 1946 and later still to 1949; however, the most commonly cited date is 1943. When asked in interviews about her age, Estés declined to reveal how old she is, and so the differences in dates of birth may be her attempt to muddy the dates and create some mystery about her age. Estés is equally reluctant to provide biographical information. In the 1994 *Marquis Who's Who,* her entry consisted of about 150 words. In later editions of this book, the entry is reduced to ten

words, presumably at her request. Thus her past, except for whatever information she chooses to tell in her books, remained less well known than that of other best-selling authors.

Yet much is still known about Estés' early years. She was born to Cepción Ixtiz and Emilio Maria Reyés, who were mestizos—Mexicans of Spanish and Indian descent. At the time of her birth, her parents were Mexican laborers, who worked near the Michigan-Indiana border. From her parents, Estés learned to speak Spanish, but for reasons that Estés has never explained, she was given up for adoption when she was a small child. She was adopted when she was four years old by Maruska Hornyak and Joszef Pinkola, immigrant Hungarians, who were uneducated, and who, like her biological parents, could not read or write.

As a child, Estés was surrounded by people from many different traditions, most of whom were first generation Americans, immigrants who were not educated but who were the repositories of much knowledge, which they passed on through the stories that they had learned. In her household, the oral traditions of the European storyteller were an important part of everyday life. She was told stories and was expected to remember and retell the stories that she heard. Her family bought their first television when she was 12 or 13 years old, but this object did not replace the family's storytelling tradition. How strongly Estés felt about both the oral tradition of storytelling and the intrusion of the television as a replacement for this tradition was made clear in a 1997 speech before the Catholic Press Association's national convention. Estés told her listen-

At a Glance . . .

Born on January 27, 1943, in Indiana; three children. *Education:* Loretto Heights College, BA, 1976; The Union Institute, Cincinnati, OH, PhD 1981; The Inter-Regional Society of Jungian Analysts, Zurich, Switzerland, post-doctoral diploma, 1984.

Career: Psychologist, 1971–; "Writing as Liberation of the Spirit" developer and teacher, 1971–; Women in Transition Safe House, Denver, co-coordinator, 1973-75; writer, 1992–.

Memberships: C. G. Jung Center for Education and Research, executive director; Colorado Authors for Gay and Lesbian Equal Rights, co-founder and co-director; C.P. Estés Guadalupe Foundation in Colorado, founder.

Selected awards: Las Primeras Award, National Latina Foundation in Washington DC, MANA, 1992; Book of the Year Honor Award, American Booksellers Association, 1993; Colorado Authors League Award, 1993; The President's Medal for social justice, The Union Institute, 1994; Joseph Campbell Keepers of the Lore Award, Joseph Campbell Festival of Myth, Folklore, and Story, 1994; Associated Catholic Church Press award for Writing, 1994; The Gradiva Award from the National Association for the Advancement of Psychoanalysis, New York, 1995.

Address: *Agent*—Ned Leavitt Agency, 70 Wooster St., Suite 4-F, New York, NY 10012.

ers that the television has turned "into a hole in the wall in our houses that pours sewage into our homes." The promise that it once held as a storyteller has emerged instead to contribute to a picture of society that is akin to a river "overflowing with filth and garbage set afire." Instead of television, Estés found that her family's stories and her own love of books, which grew from a gift of books when she was 14, have led to a lifelong love of books, poetry, and writers.

Self Exploration Lead to Nature and Education

In the introduction to her first book, *Women Who Run with the Wolves: Myths and Stories of the Wild Woman Archetype* (1992), Estés related that when she was a small child, she "was an aesthete rather than an athlete, and my only wish was to be an ecstatic wanderer." A love of art and of nature led her toward a different life. Rather than remaining indoors, she preferred "the ground, trees, and caves for in those places I felt I could lean against the cheek of God." Estés described her childhood as one of having "been brought up in nature." She learned about nature and about the history of the land by exploring and even digging in the dirt. She learned compassion for all things by observing animals and the necessity of death for the ill and old. In *Women Who Run with the Wolves: Myths and Stories of the Wild Woman Archetype*, she discussed her childhood and the joys of living in a rural, wooded location. Estés' first book also provided an opportunity to tell stories about her childhood. She especially loved winter in Michigan and the snow that it brought, "for these meant the time of flower blossoms on the river was coming." She also related that it was on a trip that she and her family took to Big Bass Lake in Michigan, that she first learned of the unity and love that women can find in the telling of stories. She says of this trip that she was about twelve years old, and after breakfast, she was playing near where the women were sunning themselves on chaise lounges. She heard riotous laughter, as they laughed at something one was reading. Later she came to understand that the women's shared laughter was a gift, a way to strengthen their lives. These women had been widowed by war, but although she understood that "none of us can entirely escape our history," she also understood that stories were a way to move toward healing.

After she completed high school, Estés began an odyssey that would lead her both to a career and to her future as a storyteller. In the 1960s she left Michigan and moved west, eventually settling in Colorado. She was looking for a place that was thick with trees, and that was densely populated with the animals that she had loved in the forests of Michigan, the fox, bear, eagle, and wolf. The wolf was being exterminated in much of the United States, and so Estés headed to the southwest in search of wolves. What she found, instead, were stories, especially stories about wolves, which occupy the opening chapter of her first book.

Estés, however, would not become a writer or a storyteller for many years. She married for the first time in 1967 and was divorced by 1974. Estés came out of the divorce in the custody of her three daughters and minimal child support, thrusting her into poverty. To make ends meet, Estés baked bread early every morning and took on other menial jobs. It was not long, however, before she realized that the best future for her family rested on her continuing her education. Estés enrolled at Loretto Heights College, a small Catholic college in Denver that has since been purchased by a group of Japanese businessmen and been renamed Teikyo Loretto Heights University. At Loretto Heights College, Estés earned a bachelor of arts with distinction in psychotherapeutics in 1976.

After graduating from Loretto Heights and securing schooling for her daughters, Estés traveled to Mexico to meet her birth family, where she found herself an accepted member of a second family. Like her Hungarian family, her birth family also had a strong tradition of storytelling. The stories that Estés learned were more than just entertainment or the passing down of oral traditions. Both her adopted and her biological cultures viewed such stories as a path to healing. There were lessons to be learned and paths suggested in both the telling and the listening that led to personal recovery. In her travels, she visited many communities in the American Midwest and Southwest, and in Central America, where she heard many more stories. Her love of both stories and of the diversity of culture led Estés to enroll in graduate school, and in 1981, she completed a doctorate in ethno-clinical psychology at The Union Institute in Cincinnati, Ohio. Estés' field of study included both clinical psychology and ethnology, the psychology of groups, especially tribes. While studying psychology, she studied the amplification of motifs in music, archetypal symbology, world mythology, ancient and popular visual motifs, ethnology, world religions, and fairy-tale interpretation. After she completed her Ph.D., she also completed a post-doctoral diploma in 1984, as a certified Jungian analyst from the Inter-Regional Society of Jungian Analysts in Zurich, Switzerland. Jung used storytelling as a way to study the archetypal patterns of the human unconscious, and so his approach fit well with Estés' own experience and interests. After completing her education, Estés became a Jungian analyst, but she remained a collector of myths, legends, and fairytales, in her a search for the female archetype.

Career in Storytelling Emerged

Estés was 25 when she began to write, although it would take nearly another 25 years before her first work would be published. Estés disciplined herself to write every day. She wrote down the stories that she heard, but she also wrote down other things, such as poetry that interested her. Over the many years that she was writing, she was also sending sections of the manuscript to publishers, but all she received in return were rejection letters. Then, when she was 45 years old, things took a turn for the better both privately and professionally. She met and married her second husband, a master sergeant in the Air Force. Shortly after, in 1989, Estés spoke about Carl Jung to a radio audience in Denver. Her approach on the radio was particularly engaging and popular. Very quickly her ease of speaking led to a contract with Sounds True Recordings to create audio tapes of her writings. Estés recorded a new tape every few months, and within a few months, Estés' tapes were the company's best selling product. Estés would eventually combine these tapes into a six-volume set called the *Jungian Storyteller,* and much like the individual tapes the series was financially successful.

Publishers began to hear about her success in selling audio tapes, and within a few months, at least six publishers were bidding on the rights to publish her book. With her audio tapes, Estés had a built-in audience for her book, but before it could be published, there was a lot of work to be completed. Estés had to revise and trim the first section of the more than 2500 pages that she had written into a more manageable length. It took her six months to get the book ready for publication. Estés' first book, *Women Who Run With the Wolves: Myths and Stories of the Wild Woman Archetype,* was not an instant best seller, but within a few months, through word of mouth and excellent reviews, Estés' book was selling beyond anyone's initial anticipation. It held a place on *The New York Times* best-seller list for more than 70 weeks.

Because she was not able to attend college until she was in her twenties, Estés' writing style is a unique meld of influences, reflecting both her upbringing in an uneducated working class home and her later extensive university education. The result is an easy-to-grasp prose style that appeals to readers. She wrote as she spoke, in a relaxed first person narrative that combines the language of scholarship with the relaxed narrative style of a storyteller, which is how Estés most often identified herself. *Women Who Run With the Wolves* is made up of stories that she had heard and collected over several decades. Estés re-reads these stories from a woman's perspective. She looks for the hidden meanings in the story and not the conventional meanings assigned by the stories' much earlier male readers. Especially interesting are the stories that she now reads without the overlay of religious convention, such as the myth of Bluebeard. Without the overlay of Christianity, the pagan story of women's strength becomes an inspiring myth for women and not a story that denigrates women. Estés quite simply stripped away the interpretations that clouded the stories.

In a 1993 review of *Women Who Run With the Wolves,* written for the *Montreal Gazette,* Linda Helser reported that some readers were using the book in discussion meetings, in which they read a section from the book and then told something from their own lives that the reading recalled. Estés engagement with her readers has not gone unnoticed by the academic community. In "Covenants, Liminality, and Transformations: The Communicative Import of Four Narratives," a lengthy 2002 article that examined the works of several authors, including Estés, authors Marc D. Rich and Karen Rasmussen suggested that Estés' short story, "Guadalupe: The Path of the Broken Heart," is the kind of work that created "a covenant between the narrator and reader." The covenant is created when the reader takes an active role in the text. This is what has happened to *Women Who Run With the Wolves*; women readers created discussion and study groups and then related their personal experiences to Estés' narrative.

However, not all women embraced the book. Some feminists were apparently disappointed that Estés seemed not to embrace their cause more completely. In a 1993 review written for *The Vancouver Sun*, Marke Andrews addressed this issue and noted that, "The fact that she hasn't come out and called for matriarchy to replace patriarchy has put her at odds with some feminists." Estés responded to this complaint by suggesting that matriarchy is not the answer to all the problems that women faced. Andrews quoted her as saying that, "A culture of decency that has regard for humans, regardless of gender and regardless of ethnicity—that is more the idea to move toward. Rather than an idea of gender. Because there are women who have as much meanness as any man, and there can be men as nurturing as any woman."

Estés continued to write following the success of *Women Who Run With the Wolves*. *The Gift of Story: A Wise Tale about What Is Enough* is a rewriting of the O Henry story, *The Gift of the Magi*, now set in Hungary during World War II. A third book, *The Faithful Gardener: A Wise Tale about That Which Can Never Die*, included stories she had heard as a child from her Hungarian uncle, a World War II slave camp survivor. These stories also center on the burning of European forests during the war.

Continued to Respond in Storytelling

Estés sees herself as participating in the storyteller legacy. In her first book she related that "In my traditions there is a storyteller legacy, wherein one storyteller hands down his or her stories to a group of 'seeds.' 'Seeds' are storytellers who the master hopes will carry on the tradition as they learned it." Estés thought that stories and storytellers grow within the person. "The story is most successful if it changes the life of the teller."

Estés also saw stories as a medicine that have the power to repair or reclaim that part of the individual that has been lost to the pain of living. Estés does not abandon organized religion in favor of storytelling. Instead, she sees a compatibility of the two to co-exist, but she also is also careful to avoid controversy whenever she can. In 1997 she was the object of controversy when she was asked to speak at the Catholic Press Association national meeting. Stories about Estés' sympathy for lesbian and gay groups caught the attention of the media and a debate ensued over her suitability to speak at a Catholic function. When these questions were put to her, Estés refused to engage in any kind of theological debate, and when pressed on the issue, she told Pamela Schaeffer, a writer for the *National Catholic Reporter*, that, "Your faith is something you can spend lots of time debating or you can live it as best you can. That's not to demean in any way the agonies or the opinions of others. I understand faith to be a struggle, not a cake that's baked."

In spite of the controversy about her choice as speaker, no reference at the meeting was made to Estés' championing of gay and lesbian causes. Gay and lesbian issues are an important focus in her professional life. In addition to her work as an author and Jungian analyst, Estés is also the founder of the C.P. Estés Guadalupe Foundation in Colorado, which funds programs on lesbian and gay issues, in addition to its use of shortwave radio to broadcast programming to the people in oppressed countries worldwide.

Estés also found the need to respond to the issue of terrorism and the threat of psychological insecurity that terrorism created. In an essay written after the attack on the United States on September 11, 2001, Estés offered some advice to help people cope with the many fears that terrorism had left in its wake and that had caused its victims to become frightened of the future and of life. She suggested that people "dwell on what strengthens you," and "refuse to dwell on what psychically depletes you of hope, contentment and ease." She also suggested such common sense approaches as eating well and getting sufficient rest. But perhaps her most important advice was that people should refuse to think that they are less able to cope than they were before the attack. Estés suggested that one way for any individual to heal is in the telling of his or her own story. She also suggested that people should remember that "each person telling their story over and over is the way to heal." This advice certainly is in keeping with Estés' function as a storyteller and her belief that storytelling is a medicine that heals the soul. Estés currently lives in northern Colorado and in Cheyenne, Wyoming.

Selected writings

Women Who Run with the Wolves: Myths and Stories of the Wild Woman Archetype, Ballantine, 1992, revised edition, 1995.
The Gift of Story: A Wise Tale about What Is Enough, Ballantine, 1993.
The Faithful Gardener: A Wise Tale about That Which Can Never Die, Harper, 1995.
"Guadalupe: The Path of the broken Heart," published in *Goddess of the Americas / La Diosa de las Americas: Writings on the Virgin of Guadalupe*, edited by Ana Castillo, Riverhead, 1996, pp. 34-45.
"Healing From Terrorism Sickness," originally posted at *The Shalom Center*, www.shalomctr.org/html/peace57.html, 2001.

Sources

Books

Estés, Clarissa Pinkola, *Women Who Run with the Wolves: Myths and Stories of the Wild Woman Archetype*, Ballantine, 1992, revised edition, 1995.

Periodicals

American Communications Journal, Fall 2002, pp. 1-2.
Gazette (Montreal), December 13, 1993, p. F3.
National Catholic Reporter, May 16, 1997, pp. 3, 8.
Vancouver Sun, June 23, 1993, p. C4

On-line

"Healing From Terrorism Sickness," *The Shalom Center,* www.shalomctr.org/html/peace57.html (May 21, 2003).

—Sheri Elaine Metzger and Ralph Zerbonia

Erik Estrada

1949—

Actor

Erik Estrada, the star of one of American television's biggest hits in the late 1970s and early 1980s, traded in Hollywood stardom in the early 1990s for a brand new career as the leading man in Latin TV's highest-rated telenovela (soap opera). Estrada, a native of Spanish Harlem in New York City, made his professional film debut as a gang member in *The Cross and the Switchblade,* released in 1970. This was followed by a handful of television and motion picture roles, leading eventually to his breakthrough role as California Highway Patrol motorcycle cop Frank "Ponch" Poncherello on NBC's hit series, *CHiPs.* The series, which spotlighted the exploits of Ponch and his partner Jon Baker, played by Larry Wilcox, premiered on September 15, 1977, and ran on NBC until July 17, 1983. The role of Ponch, originally conceived by scriptwriters as sort of a second banana to Wilcox's lead role as Jon Baker, soon had to be expanded in response to the immense popularity of Estrada among the show's viewers. For much of their time together, the relationship between Estrada and his co-star was strained, to say the least.

After *CHiPs* was cancelled by NBC in 1983, Estrada returned to his acting roots in New York City, starring in a successful limited engagement in the off-Broadway production of *True West* at Greenwich Village's Cherry Lane Theater. Although he stayed busy throughout the 1980s and into the early 1990s, none of the scores of roles he played on television and in motion pictures during this period managed to click with audiences as he had with his portrayal of Ponch on *CHiPs.* He next hit pay dirt south of the border when in 1993 he accepted a leading role in Mexican television's hit soap opera *Dos Mujeres, Un Camino.* Although produced by Mexican television, the show was a huge hit with Latino audiences throughout the Americas and won Estrada a new wave of popularity among Spanish-speaking televiewers. Estrada, who is of Puerto Rican descent and grew up in Spanish Harlem, didn't speak Spanish well enough to take on the role, so he took lessons to increase his fluency in the language.

Grew Up in Spanish Harlem

Estrada was born Henry Enrique Estrada on March 16, 1949, in New York City, the son of Renildo and Carmen Estrada. Estrada's parents divorced when he

At a Glance . . .

Born Henry Enrique Estrada on March 16, 1949, in New York, NY; son of Renildo and Carmen Estrada; married Joyce Miller (divorced); married Peggy Rowe (divorced); married Nanette Mirkovich; children: (from second marriage), Anthony Eric, Brandon Michael-Paul, (from third marriage) Francesca Natalia. *Religion:* Roman Catholic.

Career: Actor, 1972– ; author, 1997–.

Addresses: *Office*—11288 Ventura Blvd., Studio City, CA 91604. *Official website*—www.erikestrada.com.

was only two years old, and for most of the first decade of his life, he, his mother, and brother and sister lived with his grandfather in the Spanish-speaking ghetto of East Harlem. Although he saw his biological father only sporadically, Estrada as a boy discovered by accident that the older Estrada was hooked on drugs. As he wrote in his autobiography, *My Road from Harlem to Hollywood,* "I accidentally opened the bathroom door and saw him sitting on the toilet. He had his belt around his arm and a spoon on the counter. I can still smell the burned match and see the anger mixed with shame in his eyes." He credited his mother with keeping him out of trouble and teaching him important lessons about self-respect, faith in God, morals, and perseverance. As a single mother, she was forced to dance in strip clubs to earn the money she needed to keep her family together. In her absence, young Erik spent a great deal of time with his grandfather and at the age of ten felt a deep sense of loss when this important father-figure died.

As a pre-teen, Estrada seriously considered a career as a policeman but turned instead to acting after joining the drama club at Brandeis High School on Manhattan's Upper East Side. Although he had joined the group mostly to impress a female classmate in whom he'd become interested, Estrada soon found himself playing the lead role in a play the club was staging. In his biography, he wrote of the transformation that followed: "I was hooked on acting from that time on. I experienced emotions I had never felt before. I still don't understand it all—I only know that I need to perform. It must be my way of giving to others and giving to myself at the same time."

After high school Estrada worked at a variety of jobs while continuing to pursue his interest in acting. For a while he worked overtime in a neighborhood laundromat to earn tuition money for his studies at New York's American Musical and Dramatic Academy (AMDA). He also worked briefly as a security guard and in 1968

joined an AMDA dance troupe that paid him only $38 a week but provided him with free lunches and, more importantly, free tuition. On his own, Estrada sought out jobs as a gofer/interpreter for film companies working in his Spanish Harlem neighborhood. Estrada's first big break came when he managed to win the pivotal role of Nicky in the film production of *The Cross and the Switchblade.* The aspiring actor managed to convince director/screenwriter Don Murray and lead actor Pat Boone that he was right for the role by ad-libbing his audition while convincingly wielding a prop knife.

Won Leading Role in CHiPs

Next up for Estrada was a key role in the 1972 film production of Joseph Wambaugh's *The New Centurions,* in which he played rookie cop Sergio Duran. Key roles in *Airport 1975, Midway,* and *Trackdown* followed, but Estrada's biggest break came in 1977 when he was cast as California Highway Patrol motorcycle cop Frank "Ponch" Poncherello in NBC's weekly cop drama *CHiPs.* Although the role was a key one from the start, the audience response to Estrada was so positive that his role was significantly expanded not long after the series debuted on September 15, 1977. In short order, Estrada's popularity had eclipsed that of Larry Wilcox, who played motorcycle patrolman Jon Baker and was originally seen as the star of the series. Not surprisingly, this contributed to tension between Estrada and Wilcox and transformed the show's set into something of a battleground. As Estrada recalled in his autobiography, "The set was divided into two camps, Larry's people and my people. The factions tried to get the best of each other. As soon as the director called 'cut,' we'd head off in different directions without saying another word to each other."

Although Estrada was now far from the streets of Spanish Harlem, he retained the tough exterior he had been forced to develop to survive as a boy. Determined to see that his interests were stoutly defended against the predations of both agents and studio executives, Estrada developed a reputation as a difficult actor and a stubborn negotiator. Involved in a bitter salary dispute, the actor was missing from a number of the *CHiPs* episodes in the fall of 1981, replaced temporarily by gold medal-winning Olympian and aspiring actor Bruce Jenner. When the salary dispute was eventually resolved, Estrada returned to the show and Jenner disappeared. However, his strained relationship with fellow cast members continued throughout the show's run. Larry Wilcox eventually found working with Estrada too difficult, and he left the show before its final season. Wilcox was replaced by actor Tom Reilly, who played Bobby Nelson, Ponch's new partner. Before the final season was out, however, Reilly, too, had fallen out of favor with Estrada and was replaced for the show's last few episodes by Bruce Penhall.

Dubbed one of "the 10 sexiest bachelors in the world" by *People* magazine in November of 1979, Estrada admitted frankly in his autobiography that attracting women had never been a problem. "I'd take one girl out on a date and end up with another before the night was over," he wrote. However, he also admitted candidly that experience had shown him he was not always the best judge of character in the women he dated. His first two marriages—to Joyce Miller and Peggy Rowe—ended unhappily, although his marriage to Rowe produced two sons, Anthony Eric and Brandon Michael-Paul. Estrada is currently married to Hollywood sound technician Nanette Mirkovich, with whom he has a daughter, Francesca Natalia. The couple and their children live in a hilltop home in the San Fernando Valley, not far from Universal Studios and Burbank Airport.

Won New Popularity with Latinos

After six seasons, the public's appetite for *CHiPs* and its stars had apparently been sated. In the face of falling ratings, NBC cancelled the show at the end of its 1982-1983 season. Working during hiatus from *CHiPs*, Estrada had kept his movie career alive with appearances in such films as *I Love Liberty* and *The Line*. He'd also won critical praise for his portrayal of a young boxer in the made-for-TV movie *Honey Boy*, which he also produced. With his hit series cancelled, Estrada returned to New York, where he starred in an off-Broadway production of *True West*. He also managed to win his fair share of roles in film and television productions—most of them largely forgettable—throughout the remainder of the 1980s and into the early 1990s.

Things turned around for Estrada in 1993, when he was picked to star in a telenovela produced by Televisa, the Mexican-based producer of numerous soap operas for the Spanish-speaking television audience. In *Dos Mujeres, Un Camino*, Estrada played Juan Daniel Villegas, better known as Johnny, an easygoing Tijuana truck driver in his forties. Happily married to Ana Maria, Johnny meets and falls in love with Tania, a small town girl determined to become a famous singer. To further complicate Johnny's life, his wife and Tania subsequently meet and become close friends. The show quickly became a big hit among Latino audiences, propelling Estrada to stardom with a whole, new audience. Although Estrada had grown up in Spanish Harlem and spoke some Spanish, the show's producers decided he needed to improve his fluency in the language and enrolled him in classes before shooting began.

Estrada's role in *Dos Mujeres* brought him renewed popularity on a scale he hadn't enjoyed since *CHiPs*. It also gave him a new appreciation for his Latin heritage, about which he wrote extensively in his autobiography. "I wish I could say that I was aware of my heritage, proud of my people, and ready to be an example for everyone who saw me as one of their own. But the truth is, for a long time I never really thought of myself

in terms of my cultural credentials. I guess the best indication of that is the fact that, up until a few years ago, I never spoke anything more than pidgin Spanish. I never sought out spokesman status for causes that concerned Latinos. I never even thought of myself as breaking down race barriers in Hollywood. I was just happy to be working, whether I got the job for my talent or my skin tone."

Won Over New Generation

On the strength of his newfound popularity with Latino audiences, Estrada in the late 1990s mounted an effort to recapture the hearts of American audiences. In the last half of the decade he won roles in numerous films and made-for-TV movies, guest starred in a wide range of television series, and made the rounds of the talk shows. He played key roles in *Visions* and *Panic in the Skies!*, feature films which were released in 1996, and *Tom Sawyer* in 1998. He also showed up as a guest on such popular TV shows as *Baywatch*, *Martin*, *Pauly*, *Diagnosis Murder*, and *Sabrina, the Teenage Witch*.

The late 1990s saw a *CHiPs* reunion that brought together most of the members of the show's original cast, including Estrada, Larry Wilcox, and Bruce Penhall. *CHiPs '99*, a two-hour made-for-TV movie, first aired on the TNT cable television network on October 27, 1998. It also heralded a revival in interest about the original *CHiPs*, about which many young viewers in the late 1990s knew nothing. To satisfy the calls for more, TNT's sister station TBS began rebroadcasting episodes of the original series on its early-morning schedule. Of the role that made him a household name, Estrada has this to say on his official website: "I always loved Ponch. It was so much fun for me to be him, to put on his duds, get on that bike, and bust the bad guys, help out the kids, and to get the babes."

Selected works

Film

The Cross and the Switchblade, 1972.
Airport 1975, 1974.
Trackdown, 1976.
The Demon and the Mummy, 1976.
The Line, 1980.
I Love Liberty, 1982.
Il Pentito, 1985.
Hour of the Assassin, 1987.
Caged Fury, 1989.
Twisted Justice, 1990.
The Last Riders, 1991.
The Naked Truth, 1992.
The Final Goal, 1995.
Visions, 1996.
King Cobra, 1999.
Oliver Twisted, 2000.
Van Wilder, 2002.

Television

Fire!, 1977.
CHiPs, 1977-1983.
Honeyboy, 1982.
Dirty Dozen: The Fatal Mission, 1988.
She Knows Too Much, 1989.
Earth Angel, 1991.
Dos Mujeres, Un Camino, 1993.
Noi Siamo Angeli, 1996.
CHiPs '99, 1998.
The Bold and the Beautiful, 2001.

Writings

My Road From Harlem to Hollywood, William Morrow & Co., 1997.

Sources

Books

Complete Marquis Who's Who, Marquis Who's Who, 2001.

Estrada, Erik, *My Road from Harlem to Hollywood,* William Morrow & Co., 1997.

Periodicals

Entertainment Weekly, October 4, 1996; April 25, 1997.
Publishers Weekly, March 10, 1997.

On-line

"CHiPs," *TV Tome,* www.tvtome.com/tvtome/servlet/ShowMainServlet/showid-83 (May 21, 2003).
"CHiPs Online," *Adequate,* www.adequate.com/CHiPs (May 21, 2003).
"Erik Estrada," *Internet Movie Database,* ww.imdb.com (June 11, 2003).
"Erik Estrada," *Yahoo! Movies,* http://movies.yahoo.com/shop?d=hc&id=1800015234&cf=biog&intl=us (May 21, 2003).
Erik Estrada Official Website, www.erikestrada.com (May 21, 2003).

—Don Amerman

Rene Favaloro

1923-2000

Heart surgeon

Argentine heart surgeon Rene Favaloro made his name in America where, in 1967, he performed the world's first documented heart bypass surgery. Favaloro was a rural doctor in his native Argentina, but became a pioneer of coronary surgery in the United States before returning to his homeland. During his career, he would claim to have performed some 18,000 heart bypass operations. In the end, the state of the Argentinean health system would prove too much for Favaloro. The doctor devoted his life to the provision of free, quality health services there. Increasing frustration and financial desperation led him to take his own life in 2000.

Interest in Medicine Began Early

Rene Geronimo Favaloro was born July 14, 1923, and raised in a modest home in La Plata, Argentina. His mother, Ida Y. Raffaelli, was a dressmaker, and his father, Juan B. Favaloro, was a carpenter. Favaloro's uncle was the only person in the family to have earned a university education, and he had become a doctor. Favaloro was convinced even as a boy that his own destiny lay in medicine, as well. He studied medicine at La Plata University, graduating in 1948. In 1950 he took a temporary post working as a country doctor in Jacinto Arauz, a small, impoverished town in the province of La Pampa, 300 miles west of Buenos Aires. He ended up staying in Jacinto Arauz for 12 years. "The lessons of his rural practice were never lost on him," Pearce Wright wrote in a London *Guardian* obituary, "and he maintained that all doctors in Latin America should be required to work among the poor."

Favaloro left Jacinto Arauz for America to begin his post-graduate studies. When Favaloro arrived at the Department of Thoracic and Cardiovascular Surgery at the Cleveland Clinic in 1962, he spoke very little English. However, the language barrier did not hold him back. Favaloro soon established himself as a pioneer in his field, although he was prone to breaking into a string of Spanish expletives when things were not going his way in the operating room.

In 1967 Favaloro performed the world's first documented coronary bypass surgery. Eugene Pottenger, a 54-year-old produce wholesaler from Illinois, had been given just three months to live because of the severe

At a Glance . . .

Born Rene Geronimo Favaloro on July 14, 1923, in La Plata, Argentina; died on July 29, 2000, in Buenos Aires, Argentina; son of Ida Y. Raffaelli (a dressmaker) and Juan B. Favaloro (a carpenter); married Maria (deceased); children: raised four of deceased brother's children. *Education:* National College and Medical School at the University of La Plata, MD, 1948; Rawson Hospital, Buenos Aires, postgraduate coursework; Department of Thoracic and Cardiovascular Surgery, Cleveland Clinic, post-graduate studies, c. 1962.

Career: Instituto General San Martin in La Plata, intern, resident, staff position, 1940s; Jacinto Arauz, Las Pampas, Argentina, general practitioner, 1950-62; Cleveland Clinic, heart surgery and research, 1962-72; performed first documented coronary bypass surgery, 1967; author of more than 300 scientific papers, 1960s-2000; Favaloro Foundation, founder, 1992-2000.

blockage of an artery to his heart. Pottenger was hooked up to an artificial heart-lung machine, and Favaloro "harvested" a vein from the patient's leg to use as a replacement for the clogged coronary artery. The procedure has become "a mainstay of modern medicine," according to the London *Times,* and boasts survival rates of 20 years or more.

Others would claim to have already performed the procedure. In the world of medical achievement, however, nothing is accomplished until it is documented in a medical journal. Favaloro and the Cleveland Clinic were the first to appear in print, in the *Journal of Thoracic and Cardiovascular Surgery* in August of 1969. Favaloro maintained the procedure was nothing more than a logical next step from the work he and his team had been doing. "Medicine is only evolution and it doesn't matter who is first," he was quoted as saying in the London *Times.* Still, he added, "in this case there is no doubt that the Cleveland Clinic was first."

Returned to Argentina

The pioneering heart surgeon turned his back on a lucrative medical career in the United States in order to bring his expertise back to his homeland. "Although he could have had a brilliant medical career at one of the most prestigious and well-endowed medical centers in the United States—which would have made him very rich—Favaloro resigned," according to the London

Guardian. He returned to Argentina in 1972 to create a top-level teaching clinic and performed the nation's first heart-transplant operations. Favaloro raised the $55 million it took to found his heart clinic, the Favaloro Foundation, which opened its doors in 1992. There, he treated thousands of patients, often at no charge, and trained hundreds of surgeons.

The 25th anniversary of Favaloro's first bypass surgery was celebrated at the Cleveland Clinic in 1992. Pottenger, the first patient, was still alive at 79 and attended the event. Favaloro constantly downplayed his achievements. "I'm still a simple country doctor," he said in 1992, according to the London *Times.* "Despite the technology, the most important thing is to talk to the patient and make contact with the patient. The patient is not only the illness, he has a soul."

Favaloro was author of more than 300 scientific papers and wrote the study *Surgical Treatment of Arteriosclerosis* in 1970. He also wrote an autobiography, *The Challenging Dream of Heart Surgery: From the Pampas to Cleveland,* in 1994. While Favaloro was known and honored the world over for his achievements, he was disenchanted with this level of international success. Truth be told, his international renown contrasted sharply with the lack of recognition—and practical support—he received in Argentina.

Clinic Struggled With Financial Difficulty

Argentina has struggled with financial depression since the 1990s when, like many other Latin American countries, it instituted free-market reforms. Millions of Argentines lost their health-care coverage while the government slashed subsidies to Favaloro's clinic. The Favaloro Foundation was often the only hope for chronic patients, and the doctor refused to turn away those who could not pay. After years of championing the cause of universal health care, Favaloro was growing distraught. According to the national newspaper *La Nacion,* as quoted by the *Guardian,* the Favaloro Foundation was reportedly owed $18 million by state-owned medical centers and hospitals. His dream was on the brink of financial ruin. He pled for help from the government and private investors to no avail. According to the *Seattle Times* he wrote in a letter to a friend, "I am going through one of the worst moments of my life. I have become a servant knocking on doors looking for money to keep the foundation alive."

Favaloro died July 29, 2000, at age 77. He was found by his secretary in the bathroom of his Buenos Aires apartment. From the gunshot wound to his chest, the gun lying nearby, and letters of farewell found in the apartment, police attributed the death to suicide. Favaloro's wife, Maria, had died in 1998. Though they had no children of their own, they raised four children of one of Favaloro's brothers, who died young. Argentine

President Fernando de la Rúa, acknowledged Favaloro's "deep love and attachment to his country," according to the *Lancet,* and declared July 31 a day of national mourning.

Favaloro was honored in Europe for his work just weeks before his death. He attended the opening of the Georges Pompidou European Hospital in Paris on June 26 and 27, 2000. While there, he confided his troubles to fellow Argentine heart surgeon Juan Carlos Chachques, who is director of the Paris hospital. "I have no doubt that this tragedy is a direct consequence of the financial situation in which Argentina's health system is embroiled, Chachques is quoted as saying in *Lancet.* "Dr. Favaloro faced the appalling prospect that everything he had worked to achieve ... was on the point of disintegration."

Selected writings

Surgical Treatment of Arteriosclerosis, (study) 1970.
The Challenging Dream of Heart Surgery: From The Pampas to Cleveland, (autobiography) 1994.

Sources

Guardian (London, England), August 3, 2000, p. 22.
Lancet, August 5, 2000, p. 492.
Seattle Times, August 27, 2000, p. A25.
Times (London, England), July 31, 2000, p. 19.

—Brenna Sanchez

Emilio "El Indio" Fernández

1904-1986

Film director

Emilio "El Indio" Fernández has been called the father of Mexican Cinema. From his directorial debut in 1941 to his work as an actor in the 1960s and 1970s, he became a national symbol, struggling against the marginalization of Mexico's native population. "His films are moving …," wrote Julia Tuñón in *Mexican Cinema,* "because they address the difficulties of finding a place, and they are sincere because that struggle is the director's own." As his work shaped the development of film in his own country, it also brought international recognition to Mexican films. "A man of complex personality, withdrawn, and occasionally violent," wrote Carl J. Mora in *Mexican Cinema,* "Fernández was to be the founder of a 'Mexican school' that achieved international recognition in the late 1940s and 1950s."

Fernández was born in El Seco, Mexico in 1904, and received the nickname "El Indio" because of his mixed parentage of Mexican and Indian. He received a 20-year prison sentence for taking part in the Huerta rebellion in 1923, but he escaped and immigrated to the United States. During the 1920s and early 1930s, he lived in Hollywood, digging ditches and playing bit parts in movies. Living away from Mexico imbued Fernández with a deep love of his country, a feeling that he would later insert into his movies. "I was so nostalgic for Mexico," he told Tuñón, "that I would travel … to the frontier simply to see the desolation of the desert. I cried when I saw the Mexican side … I felt that I was missing half of my soul." In 1933 he returned home after receiving amnesty.

In 1934 Fernández received his first lead role in *Janitzio.* Because of his Indian features and athletic build, he was frequently cast as revolutionaries, bandits, and Mexican cowboys. In 1941 he directed *La Isla de la Pasión*, his first feature. "The debut of … Fernández was, in hindsight," Mora wrote, "perhaps the most significant event of the year." He would work closely with cinematographer Gabriel Figueroa to create a beautiful portrait of the natural Mexican landscape. "Fernández maintained that his purpose as a filmmaker," wrote Joanne Hershfield in *Mexico's Cinema,* "was to neutralize Hollywood's influence and to dramatize Mexico's past and present in order to portray what he believed was an authentic national identity."

Although Fernández's ultimate goal was to create a Mexican cinema, he imported many techniques from abroad. He had become familiar with the work of Russian filmmaker Sergei Eisenstein while staying in Hollywood, and admired the unfinished *Que Viva*

México! "This is what I learned," Fernández told Tuñón of his experience watching Eisenstein work. "The pain of the people, the land, the strike, the struggle for freedom and social justice. It was wonderful!" He was also familiar with Fred Zinneman's *Redes*, a film that likewise combined drama and ideology.

Fernández drew from these methods to dramatize his concerns for Mexico's native Indian population. "In all of Fernandez's films, race and class appear to be synonymous," wrote Hershfield. "Indians are at the bottom of the socioeconomic ladder." The Indianism movement of the 1930s, a movement that considered the native population as the ultimate representatives of Mexicaness, and Fernandez's own mixed parentage, also influenced his approach. "He elevated the Indians to mythic stature," wrote Hershfield, "romanticized their lives, and ... linked the meaning of *lo mexicano* visually and narratively to Mexico's indigenous roots."

Fernández worked quickly during the 1940s, and released a string of well-received films including *María Candelaria*, *La Perla*, and *Río Escondido*. On *La Perla*, he received support from author John Steinbeck, and two versions of the film—one in Spanish, one in English called *The Pearl*—were completed. *Flor Silvestre* represented the first of many collaborative efforts between Fernández, cinematographer Figueroa, screenwriter Mauricio Magdaleno, and actors Dolores del Río and Pedro Armendáriz. "This was the so-called 'golden age' of the Mexican cinema," Tuñón wrote, "the era in which national films were distributed throughout Latin America. ... Fernández's films benefited from this success but also, to a large degree, created it."

Fernández received his greatest acclaim as a director with *María Candelaria* in 1943. "This is a polished, smoothly told film," Bob Mastrangelo noted in *All Movie Guide*, "that reflects a director who has mastered studio storytelling at its finest." *María Candelaria* relates the tale of a young Indian girl who has been shunned by the local townspeople because her mother posed for a nude painting in her youth. "It remains a classic of the Mexican cinema," Mora wrote, "and the work that created an international following for 'El Indio.'" Although some criticized the film for presenting a "tourist" view of Mexico, Mora noted, "the film retains a simplicity and lyrical beauty that can still be appreciated over thirty-five years later." *María Candelaria* was screened at the Cannes Film Festival in 1946 and won the Grand Prix.

Fernández directed 17 films between 1950 and 1956, ceased directing during the late 1950s, and continued to make films sporadically through the 1970s. Critics complained, however, that his later work lacked the power of his best films of the 1940s. "When he began to have difficulty finding financial backers and accepted commissioned work," Tuñón noted, "his films escaped from the auteurist mould of his better moments."

Throughout Fernández' career, his colorful and volatile personality grew to mythic proportions. "We have to understand that Emilio Fernández," wrote Tuñón, "constructed his life with the same passion as he developed the characters of his films." Because of his reputation as violent, many directors cast him in the roles of brutal villains. Fernández served a six-month prison sentence after killing a farm laborer during an argument in 1976, and was "notorious in cinematic circles," wrote Hal Erickson in *All Music Guide*, "as the only prominent director who ever actually shot a film critic." Tuñón concludes, "in sum, we have to understand that he was a character worthy of his own films."

Fernández remained in demand as an actor during the 1960s and 1970s, and received parts in Sam Peckinpah's *The Wild Bunch* and *Bring Me the Head of Alfredo Garcia*, and John Huston's adaptations of *Night of the Iguana* and *Under the Volcano*. Over the course of his career, Fernández directed 42 films, received 16 international prizes, and won the Grand Prix at the Cannes Film Festival in 1946. Fernádez died on August 6, 1986, in his beloved Mexico City. His films remain beautiful portraits of the Mexican landscape and are synonymous with Mexico's golden age of film. "Fernández's films transcended frontiers," noted Tuñón. "They are considered representative of a hypothetical Mexican cinema school, which was, in fact, what he aspired to."

Selected filmography

La isla de la pasión, 1941.
Soypuro mexicano, 1942.
Flor silverstre, 1943.
María Candelaria, 1943.
Enamorada, 1946.
La Perla, 1947.
Río Escondido, 1947.
Pueblerina, 1948.
Del odio nació el amor, 1949.

Acapulco, 1951.
Nostros dos, 1955.
El impostor, 1958.
Pueblito, 1962.
La Choca, 1974.
Zona roja, 1975.

Sources

Books

Hershfield, Joanne, and David R. Maciel, editors, *Mexico's Cinema: A Century of Film and Filmmakers,* Scholarly Resources, 1999, p. 87.

Mora, Carl J., *Mexican Cinema: Reflections of a Society 1896-1980,* University of California, 1982, p. 58, 65.
Paranaguá, Paulo Antonio, editor, *Mexican Cinema,* British Film Institute, 1995, pp. 179-182, 184, 191.

On-line

"Emilio Fernandez," *All Movie Guide,* www.allmovie.com (May 3, 2003).
"Emilio Fernandez," *Biography Resource Center,* www.galenet.com/servlet/BioRC. (June 4, 2003).

—Ronnie D. Lankford, Jr.

Don Francisco

1940—

Television show host

Few television personalities have been as enduring and beloved as Don Francisco, the host of the weekly Spanish-language variety show *Sabado Gigante*. Debuting in 1962 in Chile, the show offered light comedy, music, and audience contests in a variety-show format centering on the genial and reassuring personality of its emcee. A mainstay of Chilean television for decades, *Sabado Gigante* relocated to Miami in 1986 and made its national debut in the United States on the Univision network the following year. Retaining its original format, *Sabado Gigante* proved as popular in the rest of the Latino world as it had been in its home country and became Univision's biggest hit. With an estimated 100 million viewers in thirty countries, *Sabado Gigante* indeed made Don Francisco into one of the best-known television personalities in the history of Spanish-language television.

The man behind the character of Don Francisco was born Mario Kreutzberger Blumenfeld on December 28, 1940, in the South American country of Chile. Kreutzberger's parents had emigrated to the country from Germany in the 1930s when, as Jews, their lives came under threat by the Nazi regime under Adolf Hitler. His mother had been a promising classical vocalist and his father worked as a tailor; both parents passed along their vocations to their son. His mother encouraged him to sing, and although the shy young man enjoyed performing in a neighborhood theater group in Santiago, where the family lived, it was not until he created the comical character of Don Francisco that he felt at ease performing. His father, who owned a menswear shop in Santiago, encouraged his son to follow in his trade and sent Kreutzberger to New York City around 1959 to study fashion design.

Kreutzberger spent two years in New York City, but most of his attention was focused on pursuing a new interest that he discovered there: television. "In my humble hotel room was something I never saw before: a radiant screen that you could watch and listen to at the same time," he told Jordon Levin of the Knight-Ridder/Tribune News Service in 2000, "It was my first television. When I saw that, I said, 'My father was wrong. This is the future.'" After returning to Chile, Francisco spent a year learning the technical side of television production at Channel 13, located at the Catholic University in Santiago, the country's capital. Putting together a variety show of skits, interviews,

At a Glance . . .

Born Mario Kreutzberger Blumenfeld on December 28, 1940, in Chile; married Teresa Muchnick, 1962; three children: Vivian, Francisco, and Patricio. *Religion:* Jewish.

Career: *Sabado Gigante,* host, 1962–.

Awards: Induction into Hollywood Walk of Fame, 2001.

Address: *Television studio—Sabado Gigante,* 9405 NW 41 Street, Miami, FL, 33178. Phone: (800) 345-7360; (305) 471-8262.

contests, and music, Francisco debuted *Sabado Gigante* (*Giant Saturday*) on August 8, 1962, in a fittingly stupendous eight-hour format. "It was my idea to make the program like a soup, to melt everything inside," Francisco recalled to Levin, adding, "People like change. When I started in TV, there was no remote control. So the idea was to try and do the remote control in people's minds." Although the length of the program was later reduced to a more manageable three hours, its format stayed essentially the same for the next forty years.

Sabado Gigante rapidly became the most popular program on Chilean television and Don Francisco became one of the most popular celebrities in the nation of 13 million people. Over time Francisco developed into a pop culture icon and his popularity endured despite the upheavals that transformed his native country in the 1960s and 1970s. Although Chile had enjoyed relative tranquility and a democratically elected civilian government through 1973, a military coup allegedly engineered by the Central Intelligence Agency against President Salvador Allende, a Communist who was elected to office in 1970, plunged the country into a period of repression. After General Augusto Pinochet took power and established a right-wing, anti-Communist dictatorship, the country enjoyed little political freedom or other civil liberties until his departure from office in 1993. Ruthless and corrupt, the Pinochet regime was responsible for the disappearance and presumed murders of an estimated 3,000 of its citizens.

Given the tense atmosphere, Francisco steered clear of political topics on *Sabado Gigante.* In 1978, however, he inaugurated a major philanthropic effort with his *National Telethon* to raise money to help crippled and ill children. The twenty-seven-hour telethon, which appealed to watchers for donations, became an annual

event on the first weekend of each December. The telethon raised Francisco's profile even further, as sociologist Maria Elena Valenzuela commented in a *Boston Globe* profile in 1985, "He's an omnipotent, semireligious figure who bestows gifts on people, and the poor can live the miracle as their own.... Everything in Chile is divided and tense, but Don Francisco unites people and makes them feel they have a chance."

After marrying the former Teresa Muchnick in 1962, Francisco and his wife raised one daughter, Vivian, and two sons, Francisco, and Patricio, in Santiago. In 1986, however, Francisco's career took a dramatic turn when Chilean native Joaquin Blaya, then head of the Miami-based Spanish-language Univision network, offered him a spot on the broadcast schedule. Filming *Sabado Gigante* in both Miami and Santiago, Francisco shuttled back and forth between the two cities for the first seasons of production. The hectic schedule paid off when the show became an instant hit. By the end of its first season *Sabado Gigante* was Univision's highest-rated show and was watched by an estimated 43 percent of Hispanic viewers in the United States. Eventually the show was broadcast in 30 countries and claimed a viewership of 100 million people. In 1991 Francisco relocated full-time to the United States, where he lived in a large home in an exclusive neighborhood in North Miami Beach. He also continued to travel around the world promoting *Sabado Gigante* and filming segments for the show.

The success of *Sabado Gigante* allowed Francisco to branch out into other television projects. In 1991 he appeared in *Noche de Gigantes* (*Night of Giants*), an interview show that featured Hispanic celebrities, singers, and comics. After cutting *Sabado Gigante* to just three hours, Francisco added *Fiesta Gigante,* another hour-long variety show, to the Univision line up in conjunction with his first show. He also continued to secure commercial endorsements for products ranging from Mazola Oil to American Airlines to Ford automobiles for his shows. Demonstrating the potency of Francisco as a commercial pitchman, his image was used beginning in 1998 to promote the launch of the Puerto Rico-based Banco Popular credit card in the United States. Chosen because his name and face were universally known and trusted among Hispanic consumers, Francisco's popularity among advertisers such as Banco Popular also demonstrated the power of the growing Hispanic consumer market. Already the largest ethnic minority in several Sunbelt states, Hispanic Americans were predicted by the U.S. Census Bureau to become the largest minority group in the United States no later than 2004.

As the largest Spanish-language network in the United States, the Univision network beamed *Sabado Gigante* into 90 percent of Hispanic-American homes by 2002, when Francisco marked the fortieth anniversary of his television career. Although he was still an inveterate traveler who claimed to have visited every region of the world except for a few remote places, Francisco reflected long enough on his success to write *Entre la espada y la TV,* published in English as *Don Francisco: Life, Camera, Action,* in 2002. The book was the second installment of Francisco's autobiography and traced the development of *Sabado Gigante* into a global broadcasting phenomenon.

Still conducting the *National Telethon* in Chile every year—with the exception of 1999, when the country held its presidential elections—Francisco was lauded for his television success and philanthropic efforts in 2001 when his name was added to the Hollywood Walk of Fame in Los Angeles. The event brought out one of the largest turnouts of fans that Walk of Fame organizers had ever seen and demonstrated that Francisco's international appeal had yet to ebb. Perhaps the secret to his success was best described by Francisco himself in a 1995 interview with Norma Libman of the *Chicago Tribune,* "If you scratch a little under the surface you will find people are similar everywhere, even if they look from the outside completely different," he commented. "There are differences in color, in religion, in culture, but everybody wants a good life, they want to build a family, they want to have a job and be successful, even in the Communist countries."

Sources

Periodicals

American Banker, October 19, 1998, p. 13.
Billboard, February 26, 2000, p. 8.
Boston Globe, December 16, 1985, p. 2.
Chicago Tribune, July 31, 1988, p. 3; October 7, 1991, p. 5; June 25, 1995, p. 20.
Críticas, July/August 2002, pp. 13, 44.
Daily Variety, June 14, 2001, p. 8.
Hollywood Reporter, February 22, 2000, p. 47.
Knight Ridder/Tribune News Service, June 5, 2000, p. K4418.
Los Angeles Magazine, August 2001, p. 24.
People, September 2, 1996, p. 61.
San Francisco Chronicle, June 8, 1998, p. E2.
Variety, November 1, 1999, p. M22.

On-line

"Biografía Don Francisco," *Sabado Gigante,* www.gigante.com/usa/biografia.shtml (March 29, 2003).

—Timothy Borden

Héctor Pérez García

1914-1996

Physician, civil rights advocate

Héctor Pérez García led the fight for civil rights for Mexican Americans for nearly 50 years. As the founder of the GI Forum, García became an advocate for the medical rights of Hispanic veterans during the years following World War II. His focus soon broadened to encompass larger issues of discrimination, including housing, education, jobs, and health care. He was a legendary civil rights advocate, advisor to presidents, and a hero to many Hispanics, especially in South Texas.

Gained Education and Army Experience

García was born on January 17, 1914, in Llera, Mexico, a small town in the border state of Tamaulipas. His father, José García, was a professor, and his mother, Faustina Pérez, was a teacher. The Mexican Revolution began just months after García's birth, and in 1917 his parents fled with their seven children to the United States to escape the violence. The family settled in Mercedes, Texas, a small South Texas town in Hidalgo County in the Rio Grande Valley. Because his father's teaching credentials were not recognized in the United States, José García provided for his family by running a dry-goods business with his brothers. The children pitched in by picking cotton and scavenging for discarded fruits and vegetables among the local packing sheds.

Reared in a close-knit family that stressed education, García was motivated by his father to move beyond the limited expectations and opportunities afforded Mexican Americans at that time. García, who attended Mercedes public schools, responded to this motivation by graduating as the valedictorian of his high school class. With the Great Depression sorely straining the family's finances, his father sold his penny-a-week life insurance policy to allow García to enroll in Edinburgh Junior College. García continued his education at the University of Texas, from which he graduated with a bachelor's degree in zoology in 1936. Wishing to pursue his medical degree, García applied to and was accepted by the University of Texas Medical Branch at Galveston, which only admitted one Mexican American student each year. After graduating from medical school in 1946, García was unable to find a medical internship program in Texas that would accept a Mexican American. He completed his two-year general and surgical internship at Creighton University's St. Joseph Hospital in Omaha, Nebraska.

The outbreak of World War II followed on the heels of García's internship, and he delayed his entrance into

At a Glance . . .

Born Hector Perez García on January 17, 1914, in Llera, Mexico; died on July 26, 1996, in Corpus Christi, TX; married Wanda Fusillo, June 23, 1945; children: Hector (deceased), Wanda, Cecilia, and Susana. *Education:* University of Texas, BA, zoology, 1936; University of Texas Medical Branch at Galveston, MD, 1946. *Military Service:* U.S. Army, 1942-46. *Religion:* Roman Catholic. *Politics:* Democrat.

Career: Physician, Corpus Christi, TX, 1946-96.

Memberships: GI Forum, founder and first chairman, 1948; Advisory Council of the Democratic National Committee, 1954; Political Association of Spanish Speaking Organizations, national president, 1960-64; National Advisory Council on Economic Opportunity in the United States, 1967; U.S. Commission on Civil Rights, 1968; U.S. Attorney General Benjamin Civiletti's Hispanic Advisory Committee on Civil Rights, 1979.

Awards: Medalla Al Merito, American GI Forum of Texas, 1952; Distinguished Service Award, National Office of Civil Rights, 1980; Presidential Medal of Freedom, 1984; The Hispanic Heritage Award, National Hispanic Leadership Conference, 1989; The Equestrian Order of Pope Gregory the Great, Pope John Paul II, 1990.

medical practice to enlist in the U.S. Army in 1942. His previous summertime service in Franklin D. Roosevelt's Civilian Military Training Corps allowed García to enter the U.S. army as an officer. He served first in the infantry before becoming an officer in the Corp of Engineers. He eventually served as a combat surgeon with the Medical Corps. Discharged in 1946 with the rank of major, García was awarded the Bronze Star with six battle stars for his service in North Africa and Italy. In late 1944, while serving in Italy, García met Wanda Fusillo, a graduate student at the University of Naples. They were married on June 23, 1945, just weeks after Fusillo completed her doctoral studies. The couple had three daughters: Wanda, Celia, and Susana. A son, Hector, died at the age of 13 after falling while running down the stairs of a mountain home.

Fought for Civil Rights With GI Forum

After his discharge from the U.S. Army in 1946, García started his medical practice in the South Texas town of Corpus Christi. He located his office near the Veterans Administration (VA) building and contracted with the VA to provide services to Mexican-American veterans. The VA paid García three dollars per patient. It quickly became apparent to García that Mexican-American veterans were not being treated fairly or equally by the VA. He heard many stories from veterans who had been denied treatment at the Naval Air Station hospital; others had been denied financial assistance for medical expenses and job training as prescribed by the GI Bill of Rights. To treat men and women who had faithfully served their country during the war as second-class citizens was unacceptable to García. In response, on March 26, 1948, he organized a meeting at Lamar Elementary School to discuss veterans' concerns. More than 700 attended the meeting. On that night, the GI Forum was founded. Elected as the organization's chairman, García began his lifelong role as activist, organizer, and community caretaker.

In 1949 García became involved with the burial of Private Felix Longoria. Longoria, a Mexican-American soldier from Three Rivers, a town near Corpus Christi, had been killed near the end of the war and interred in the Philippines. Three years later, Longoria's wife was asked if she would like to reinter her husband in Texas. Although she had since moved to Corpus Christi, Longoria's wife decided to bury her husband in his hometown of Three Rivers. Her decision set off a series of events that brought García and the GI Forum into the national spotlight. When Longoria's family was denied access to the only funeral home in Three Rivers, García stepped in to help. After hearing from the funeral home director himself that the only reason the family could not use the facilities was because Longoria was a Mexican American, García contacted the local media and then sent off a series of telegrams to everyone he could think of, including the newly elected senator to the U.S. Congress from Texas, Lyndon B. Johnson. With Johnson's intervention Longoria's remains were interred two months later in Arlington National Cemetery with full military honors.

With the Longoria incident behind him, García began to broaden his focus beyond veterans' concerns to address the wider spectrum of social inequalities facing Mexican Americans in his Coastal Bend community, including segregated education, housing, health care, poll taxes, and employment. He traveled the country, organizing new GI Forums. In the years before the rising popularity of the Martin Luther King, García's GI Forum was the leading civil rights organization in the country. During the early 1950s, novelist Edna Ferber spent time with García, and she used him as a model for the character of the Mexican-American doctor in her 1952 novel *Giant,* as well as the 1956 movie version.

Joining forces with the League of United Latin American Citizens (LULAC), an older civil rights organization also founded in Corpus Christi, García and the GI Forum took on several court battles to end discriminatory practices. In 1948 García was put in charge of raising funds to cover the legal expenses of Minerva Delgado and 20 other Mexican-American families in Bastrop, Texas, who filed a lawsuit to end segregated schooling and challenge the fictitious "separate but equal" policy. Although the decision ruled against segregation, the battle to implement integration had just begun. The LULAC and the GI Forum sued the Driscoll school district in 1957 for discriminating against Mexican Americans, winning once again. In another case, *Hernandez v. State of Texas,* LULAC and GI Forum lawyers took the case all the way to the Supreme Court in 1954 after Peter Hernandez had been found guilty by an all-white jury and given the death penalty. After Chief Justice Earl Warren discovered that not one single Mexican American had been called to jury duty in the county in 25 years, he ruled for Hernandez and reversed the conviction.

In the 1950s García became increasingly politically active. In 1954 he was on the Advisory Council of the Democratic National Committee, and in 1960 he was appointed chairman of the Mexican-Spanish section of the Nationalities Division of the Democratic National Committee. Following John F. Kennedy's nomination for the presidency, García served as national chairman of the "Viva Kennedy" clubs, intended to get Mexican Americans to the polls to vote the Kennedy-Johnson ticket. Following the election, Kennedy named García to the American delegation that signed a treaty between the United States and the Federation of the West Indies in 1961. García was also instrumental in establishing a nationwide Hispanic organization, which resulted in the formation of the Political Association of Spanish Speaking Organizations (PASSO). García served as PASSO's first president.

Generosity Mixed with Impatience

García was a benevolent man, who often did not collect for his medical services. Stories of García's generosity and kindness are plentiful. He never asked for payment from those who could not afford it, and when one of his advisors sent out collection letters requesting payment on the doctors' debts, García was horrified and immediately ended any attempt to be reimbursed, saying that sending a letter to people who did not have money would not give them money to pay. He simply expected that people would pay if they could. García also helped others when ever he could. Johnny De La Fuente, a recipient of García's generosity told the *Corpus Christi Times,* "He was the kind of person who helped the needy until the end."

Although García was well known for his generosity with the poor, even his friends admitted that García was likely to preach democracy but function more as an authoritarian at times. He had little patience for the decision-making process that involved motions, votes, and approvals. He felt he did not have time, and the slowness inherit in the democratic process frustrated him. "There's no question that Dr. García was impatient," Judge James Deanda, former legal council for the GI Forum, told *Justice for My People.* Deanda recalled the frustrated comments of a labor leader, who said of García, "the trouble with Hector is that he's teaching everybody the democratic system and how to participate in it, but after he teaches you, he will not let you participate."

During the Vietnam War the GI Forum supported the Mexican Americans with family members involved in the war, including helping with the burial of the dead. García personally attended nearly 200 funerals of local Hispanic servicemen, often speaking at the service. Yet his patriotic stance during the Vietnam War put García into conflict with more radical Hispanic groups who opposed the war and held no love for Johnson. García, on the other hand, was a proud veteran who expected all Mexican Americans to be honored to serve their country, and he held Johnson as a long-time personal friend since the days of the Longoria incident. His role as a moderator who worked from within the system was viewed by more radical groups as selling out to the Anglo culture. Yet no one denied García's impact on the Hispanic community. During the 1950s Texas movie theaters, restaurants, and hotels were desegregated. In the 1960s, barber shops and beauty parlors were opened to Mexican Americans, and in the 1970s swimming pools and cemeteries were desegregated.

Remembered as a Leader Among Leaders

In 1967 Johnson appointed García as an alternate ambassador to the United Nations, where he gave the first speech by an American before the United Nations in a language other than English. He also served on the National Advisory Council on Economic Opportunity. In 1968 he was the first Hispanic appointed to the U.S. Commission on Civil Rights. In 1972 he became a member of the Texas Advisory Committee on Civil Rights. After entering office in 1977, Jimmy Carter asked García to serve as a member of the U.S. Circuit Judge Nominating Commission for the Western Fifth Circuit Panel. The following year Carter invited García to participate in a high level briefing on the President's Tax and Economic Program. García traveled to Washington again in 1980 on Carter's request to attend high level briefings on Iran, Afghanistan, and Pakistan. In 1984 García was awarded the Presidential Medal of Freedom, the highest honor a civilian can receive in the United States. García was especially proud to receive the honor from Ronald Reagan, a Republican, proving that García's lifelong efforts crossed racial and political boundaries.

García continued his work to provide "first-class" rights for the Hispanic population. In 1987 he fought against an effort to declare English the official language of the United States. The following year he traveled to the *colonias,* inhabited by poverty-stricken workers along the U.S. and Mexican borders, to lobby for improved medical and sanitary services. Although he never received the national recognition awarded to Martin Luther King, García holds legendary status in South Texas.

By the 1990s García's health was fading. He had suffered a heart attack in 1980. He underwent open heart surgery shortly after the attack and again in 1985. During the late 1980s doctors discovered cancer and removed half of his stomach. In his later days, he spent a lot of time among his friends playing dominos, his favorite game at which he considered himself unmatched. He died at Memorial Medical Center in Corpus Christi on July 26, 1996, of pneumonia and congestive heart failure. The *Corpus Christi Caller Times* eulogized him, stating, "What this community owes Dr. Hector goes beyond his years of service as a physician or his role as a civil rights leader. He, perhaps more than any one single person, helped this community travel through a difficult period in its history, a time when ethnic and racial feelings were at a flashpoint. He did this by his appeal to higher ideals and his allegiance to the bedrock ideals of this country: fairness, equity, and patriotism. His was a remarkable life."

Sources

Books

Lamar, Howard R., ed. *The New Encyclopedia of the American West.* New Haven, CT: Yale University Press, 1998.
Meier, Matt. *Notable Latino Americans.* Westport, CT: Greenwood Press, 1997.

Periodicals

Corpus Christi Caller Times, August 11, 1996; January 22, 2002.
New York Times, July 29, 1996.

On-line

Handbook of Texas Online, www.tsha.utexas. edu/handbook/online (June 10, 2003).
"Hector P. García: A Texas Legend," *University of Texas Medical Branch, Galveston,* www.sga.utmb. edu/ulams/drGarcía (June 10, 2003).
Justice for My People, www.justiceformypeople.org (June 10, 2003).

Other

Additional information for this profile was obtained from transcripts of *Justice for My People: The Dr. Hector P. García Story,* a documentary produced by Jeff Felts of KET-TV, Public Television, in Corpus Christi, Texas.

—Kari Bethel

Juan Bosch Gaviño

1909-2001

Author, politician

Juan Bosch Gaviño, also known as Juan Bosch, was a most unusual man—successful and prolific in the world of literature and philosophy and prominent, if less successful, as a politician. His writings and his politics emphasized the gross inequalities between the poverty-stricken Dominican masses and the wealthy few. His creative writing focused on the struggle and sacrifices of Dominican peasants and celebrated their rich oral traditions. Although he was president of the Dominican Republic for barely seven months, "Professor Bosch," as he was widely-known, influenced Dominican politics for more than a half-century. He founded two powerful political parties and was instrumental in transforming the Dominican Republic from a closed society controlled by a wealthy, conservative elite, to an open democracy. A liberal, anti-communist democrat, Gaviño was respected as an intellectual of high integrity, as well as one of the greatest Latin-American short-story writers.

Gaviño was born on June 30, 1909, in La Vega, Dominican Republic. His father, José Bosch, was a stonemason from the Catalonian town of Tortosa in Spain, and his mother, Angela Gaviño Bosch, was Puerto Rican. They were lower-middle class artisans with strong interests in education, literature, and music. Gaviño's maternal grandfather was a farmer, an intellectual, and a poet. As a child in the rural tobacco-producing Cibao region, Gaviño witnessed first-hand the feudal relationship between large landowners and peasants. He also watched as the Dominican flag was replaced by the American flag, following the 1916 U. S. military intervention. Years later he wrote in The

Unfinished Experiment: "No one will ever know what my seven-year-old soul suffered at the sight."

Wrote Early Stories About Rural Peasants

Gaviño's primary school teacher in La Vega, musician Rafael Martínez, instilled in him a concern for the future of the country and the world. Gaviño was drawing, sculpting, and writing by the age of nine. As a teenager he published a small newspaper in La Vega and published his first short story at age 14. Gaviño graduated with a degree in literature from the University of Santo Domingo.

Gaviño's earliest short stories were published in the newspaper Listín Diario and the journal Bohoruco. A small publishing house in La Vega printed 500 copies of his first story collection, Camino real, in 1933. It included one of his best-known stories, "La mujer," about a woman who is abused by her husband after using their meager resources to feed their young son.

Gaviño's first nonfiction, Indios: Apuntes históricos y leyendas, was published in 1935. His first novel, La mañosa: Novela de las revoluciones, published in 1936, was semi-autobiographical. A classic of Dominican literature, it dealt with the political and social issues that became the hallmark of Gaviño's work.

Although Gaviño cited Don Quixote, The Brothers Karamazov, and Huckleberry Finn as important influences on his work, as a short-story writer he emulated

At a Glance . . .

Born Juan Bosch Gaviño on June 30, 1909, in La Vega, Dominican Republic; died on November 1, 2001, in Santo Domingo; son of José Bosch and Angela Gaviño Bosch; married second wife Carmen Quidiello, 1941; children: León, Patricio, Barbarita, and one other. *Education:* University of Santo Domingo, BA, literature, 1920s. *Religion:* Roman Catholic. *Politics:* Partido Revolucionario Dominicano, 1939-73; Partido de la Liberación Dominicana, 1973-01.

Career: Author of short stories, novels, essays, histories, biographies, political treatises, 1929-00; Cuban journalist, c.1939-52; Cuban government, advisor, c.1944-52; Institute of Political Education, San Isidro del Coronado, Costa Rica, professor, c.1952-58; Dominican Republic government, president, 1963; University of Puerto Rico, professor, c.1963-70.

Memberships: Partido Revolucionario Dominicano, founder, political committee head, and president, 1939-66; Partido de la Liberación Dominicana, founder and leader, 1973-94.

Awards: Juegos Florales Hispanoamericanos (Dominican Republic), first place award, 1940; Hernández Catá prize, 1943; FNAC Foundation (France), short story award, 1988; José Martí Order (Cuba), 1989; honorary degree, New York City College, 1993.

Rudyard Kipling, Guy de Maupassant, and Oscar Wilde. He was a part of the *criollismo*, a neorealist, Spanish-American literary movement that was influential between the end of World War I and the late 1940s. Like so many other Latin American authors, Gaviño linked his art to social and nationalistic issues. He emphasized plot over character development, used symbolism, poetic descriptions, and colloquial dialogue, while promoting Dominican popular culture. As campesinos began moving into the overcrowded capitals of Latin America, Gaviño incorporated this new urban underclass into his stories.

Exiled for 24 Years

Gaviño was 21 when General Rafael Leónidas Trujillo, one of Latin America's most notorious dictators, took control of the Dominican Republic in a military coup. In 1933 Gaviño was imprisoned for conspiracy against the regime. In 1937, following a Trujillo-ordered massacre of 15,000 Haitian squatters on the border between the two countries, Gaviño moved to Puerto Rico with his wife and children.

Gaviño modeled his life in literature and politics after the nineteenth-century Puerto Rican writer and patriot Eugenio María de Hostos. In 1939 he moved to Havana, Cuba, to oversee the publishing of Hostos's complete works. Gaviño also wrote two books on Hostos, *Hostos, el sembrador* and *Mujeres en la vida de Hostos*. In 1941 he married his second wife, the playwright Carmen Quidiello, who was from a prominent family in Santiago, Cuba. They had a son, Patricio, and a daughter, Barbarita.

A member of Cuba's intellectual and literary elite, Gaviño worked as a journalist and published in the Cuban magazines *Bohemia* and *Carteles*. For a time he was a medical representative for the Cuban Biological Institute and he continued to write short stories as well as nonfiction. Using a pseudonym Gaviño entered "El socio" in the Juegos Florales Hispanoamericanos of the Dominican Republic in 1940. This story about the plight of peasants under an evil landowner won first place. His story "Luis Pie," included in the collection *Ocho cuentos*, won the Hernández Catá prize in 1943. Trips to Bolivia inspired Gaviño's final novel, *El oro y la paz*, written in Puerto Rico in 1964, and his critically acclaimed story, "El Indio Manuel Sicuri," written in Chile in 1956. This story was made into a Bolivian film that played at the Cannes Film Festival.

Became Politically Active

In Cuba in 1939 Gaviño helped found the Partido Revolucionario Dominicano (PRD), the leftist Dominican Revolutionary Party. It became the most influential of the exiled anti-Trujillo organizations. Gaviño served as PRD president until 1966. He spent several months during 1942 doing party organizing in New York. In 1947 Gaviño helped organize the Dominican-Cuban Cayo Confites expedition, a failed attempt to overthrow the Trujillo dictatorship.

Between 1944 and 1952 Gaviño held various positions within the Cuban government, including secretary and advisor to President Carlos Prío Socarrás. However in 1952, threatened with deportation to the Dominican Republic by the new Cuban dictator Fulgencio Batista, Gaviño fled to Costa Rica, where he became a professor at the Institute of Political Education in San Isidro del Coronado, on the outskirts of San José. He also traveled throughout Latin America and Europe during the 1950s. Returning to Cuba in 1958, he was jailed by the dictatorship. After his release he moved to Venezuela. When Fidel Castro overthrew Batista in 1959, Gaviño returned to Cuba. However, he left again in disgust over the policies of the new communist government.

Following Trujillo's assassination in 1961, Gaviño returned to the Dominican Republic and built up his PRD party with peasants and laborers. Appearing on television weekly and with frequent radio broadcasts, his good looks and eloquent but plain speech won him wide popularity. Gaviño was a social democrat at a time when many political factions branded any type of socialism as communism. When a Spanish Jesuit called him a communist during the presidential election campaign, Gaviño withdrew from the race. However, after a four-hour nationally-televised debate, the priest retracted his charges and, two days before the vote, Gaviño re-entered the race. In December of 1962, in a landslide election, Gaviño became the first freely-elected president of the Dominican Republic in 38 years.

Short Presidency Impeded by International Factions

President Gaviño drew up a constitution, undertook land reform by limiting the size of landholdings, and strengthened the rights of agricultural and industrial workers. He also nationalized some businesses, initiated major public works projects, and promoted civil liberties and nationalism. He began routing out corruption in the government and cut government salaries. The right-wing, led by the Roman Catholic Church, was furious. Pro-Cuban communists were unhappy with Gaviño's form of socialism as well. He was widely criticized as politically inexperienced, impractical, and ineffective. Although Gaviño had been promised the full support of the United States, after only seven months in office he was ousted in a right-wing coup by a group of military officers and government officials, linked to Dominican industrialists and businessmen and to the United States. Gaviño went into exile and taught at the University of Puerto Rico.

The revolution in April of 1965, led by Gaviño's military supporters, would have returned him to power and restored the constitution of 1963. However, U. S. President Lyndon Johnson feared that Gaviño would establish another Cuban-like state in the Caribbean. The U. S. Federal Bureau of Investigation surrounded Gaviño's home in Puerto Rico to prevent him from returning to the Dominican Republic. The United States sent 22,000 marines to occupy Santo Domingo and civil war broke out.

Gaviño returned home to run in the elections of June of 1966. However, he did not campaign because of repressive electoral conditions, threats on his life by the military, and American support for his rival Joaquín Balaguer, an ultra-conservative, former ally of Trujillo.

Despite widespread allegations of electoral fraud, Gaviño did not contest his defeat.

Examined and Spoke Out Against Democracy

Gaviño went to Spain and entered a period of disillusionment and reflection. His years as a productive short-story writer ended. Rejecting representative democracy, Gaviño began writing about the concept of a "popular dictatorship." He was quoted in the *Seattle Times* as saying, "They [the United States] are insisting that our countries be democratic, and that we celebrate elections every four years. But in the United States they don't know the situations of people without schools, work or hospitals.... We Latin Americans have to search for a political way out that is adequate for us to confront the problems of our people."

Gaviño began examining the workings of capitalism in underdeveloped countries, analyzing class struggle, and calling for political reform. During the 1960s three of his books were translated into English and published in the United States. *The Unfinished Experiment: Democracy in the Dominican Republic* analyzed the class structure of Dominican society and the difficulty of establishing a democratic government there. In his review of the book for the *Journal of Politics,* Howard J. Wiarda called Gaviño "a magician with the Spanish language." *David: The Biography of a King* compared the Dominican Republic to Israel without the biblical King David. In *Pentagonism: A Substitute for Imperialism,* and in other books and essays, Gaviño criticized American foreign policy. He used the term "pentagonism" to describe the ever-expanding militarization of American society, arguing that American military operations around the world were used to justify the arms race that drove the American economy. *Viaje a los antípodas* criticized U. S. intervention in Vietnam. *De Cristóbal Colón a Fidel Castro* and *Composición social dominicana* were published in 1970 and *Breve historia de la oligarquía* appeared in 1971.

Gaviño returned to the Dominican Republic in 1970 and founded the socialist Partido de la Liberación Dominicana or Dominican Liberation Party (PLD) in 1973. He ran for president on the party's ticket in 1978, 1982, 1986, 1990, and 1994, losing to Balaguer every time. The 1990 election was very close and the 80-year-old Gaviño and 82-year-old Balaguer finally agreed to a recount brokered by former U. S. president Jimmy Carter. A Dominican pollster was quoted in *Time* Magazine as saying: "It appears that the elder of the dinosaurs has won." Ironically, in addition to their political rivalry, Gaviño and Balaguer competed for the title of the Dominican Republic's most important contemporary writer. Gaviño and Balaguer formed an alliance—the National Patriotic Front—that enabled the PLD candidate, a Gaviño protégé, to win the 1996 election.

Works Honored Before and After Death

Gaviño published more than 50 books, including novels, collections of short stories and essays, histories, and biographies, as well as contributions to anthologies and prologues for other texts. Many of his writings have been translated into various languages and reprinted often. Some of his books, particularly his biographies, are used as textbooks throughout Latin America. Many of his essays originally were published in the periodicals *Vanguardia del Pueblo, Politica—Teoria y Accion,* and *Hablan los Comunistas,* between 1974 and 1985. Excerpts from *Trujillo: Causas de una tiranía sin ejemplo* were published as *La fortuna de Trujillo* in Santo Domingo in 1985.

In 1988 Gaviño received a short-story award from the FNAC Foundation in France. During the 1980s he made several trips to Cuba and in 1989 Fidel Castro presented him with the José Martí Order. In 1993 he was awarded an honorary degree by New York City College. The Puerto Rican Traveling Theater of New York City produced a dramatization of five of Gaviño's short stories, including "The Beautiful Soul of Don Damián," in 1998.

Gaviño died of respiratory failure on November 1, 2001, in a Santo Domingo hospital. He laid in state at the National Palace and was buried in La Vega. For many Dominicans Gaviño embodied pride in their nation and hope for its future. Amy Coughenour Betancourt, of the Center for Strategic and International Studies in Washington, told the *Miami Herald:* "The Dominican Republic lost one of its greatest thinkers and visionaries of all time. Gaviño's legacy of literature, political thought, and leadership with regard to human rights, political rights and freedoms, and social and economic development is indelible. He has left behind a vision for what the country can become, and has left his mark on generations of leaders now and yet to come."

Selected writings

Fiction

Camino real, R. A. Ramos (La Vega, Dominican Republic), 1933; revised edition, El Diario (Santiago, Dominican Republic), 1937.

La mañosa: Novela de las revoluciones, El Diario, 1936.

Dos pesos de agua, cuentos A. Ríos (Havana), 1941.

Ocho cuentos, Trópico (Havana), 1947.

La muchacha de La Guaira; cuentos, Nascimiento (Santiago, Chile), 1955.

Cuento de Navidad, Ercilla (Santiago, Chile), 1956.

Cuentos escritos en el exilio y apuntes sobre el arte de escribir cuentos, Librería Dominicana (Santo Domingo), 1962.

Más cuentos escritos en el exilio, Librería Dominicana, 1964.

Cuentos escritos ante del exilio, Edición Especial (Santo Domingo), 1974.

El oro y la paz, Edición Especial, 1977.

Cuentos, Casa de Las Américas (Havana), 1983.

"The Beautiful Soul of Don Damián," in *Rhythm and Revolt: Tales of the Antilles,* Plume, 1995.

"Encarnacion Mendoza's Christmas Eve," in *The Oxford Book of Caribbean Short Stories,* Oxford University Press, 1999.

Nonfiction

Indios: Apuntes históricos y leyendas, La Nación (Santo Domingo), 1935.

Mujeres en la vida de Hostos, Asociación de Mujeres Graduadas de la Universidad de Puerto Rico, 1938.

Hostos, el sembrador, Trópico, 1939.

De espaldas a mi mismo: Conceptos laudatorios sobre la obra de gobierno del generalisimo Trujillo Molina, Partido Dominicano (Ciudad Trujillo, Dominican Republic), 1942.

Judas Iscariote: El calumniado, Prensa Latinoamericana (Santiago, Chile), 1955.

Trujillo: Causas de una tiranía sin ejemplo, Librería Las Novedades (Caracas), 1959.

Símon Bolívar: Biografía para escolares, Escolar (Caracas), 1960.

Apuntes para una interpretación de la historia costarricense, Eloy Morúa Carrillo (San José, Costa Rica), 1963; revised, *Una interpretación de la historia costarricense,* Juricentro (San José), 1980.

The Unfinished Experiment: Democracy in the Dominican Republic, Praeger, 1965.

David: The Biography of a King, Hawthorn Books, 1966.

Teoría del cuento: Tres ensayos, Universidad de Los Andes, (Mérida, Venezuela), 1967.

Pentagonism: A Substitute for Imperialism, Grove Press, 1968.

Composición social dominicana: Historia e interpretación, Colección Pensamiento y Cultura (Santo Domingo), 1970.

De Cristóbal Colón a Fidel Castro: El Caribe, frontera imperial, Alfaguara (Madrid), 1970.

Breve historia de la oligarquía, Impresora Arte y Cine, 1971.

Tres conferencias sobre el feudalismo, Talleres Gráficos (Santo Domingo), 1971.

El Napoleón de las guerrillas, Editorial de Ciencias Sociales (Havana), 1976.

Viaje a los antípodas, Alfa y Omega, 1978.

Articulos y conferencias, Alfa y Omega, 1980.

La Revolución de Abril, Impresora Mercedes (Santo Domingo), 1981.

La guerra y la restauración, Corripio, 1982.

Capitalismo, democracia y liberación nacional, Alfa y Omega, 1983.

La fortuna de Trujillo, Alfa y Omega, 1985.

Capitalismo tardio en la República Dominicana, Alfa y Omega, 1986.

El estado, Alfa y Omega, Santo Domingo, 1987.

Capitalismo y democracia, Alfa y Omega, 1988.
El PLD: Partido nuevo en América, Alfa y Omega, 1989.
Temas económicos, Alfa y Omega, 1990.
Breve historia de los pueblos arabe, Alfa y Omega, 1991.
(With Avelino Stanley Rondon) *Antologia personal,* University of Puerto Rico Press, 1998.
En primera persona: Entrevistas con Juan Bosch, Comision Permanente de la Feria del Libro, 2000.

Sources

Books

Peacock, Scot, editor, *Hispanic Writers,* 2nd ed., Gale Group, 1999, pp. 110-112.

Periodicals

Financial Times, (London) November 2, 2001, p. 12.
Journal of Politics, August, 1965, pp. 671-673.
Miami Herald, November 2, 2001.
NACLA Report on the Americas, March-April 1997, pp. 24-25.
New York Times, November 2, 2001, D9.
Seattle Times, September 9, 1986, A12.
Time, May 28, 1990, p. 39.

On-line

"Juan Bosch," *Afiwi,* www.afiwi.com/people2.asp?id=162 (April 7, 2003).
"Juan Bosch: The Long Road to Transcendence," *Granma International,* http://granmai.co.cu/ingles/septiem4/30Gaviño-i.html (April 7, 2003).

—Margaret Alic

Felipe González Márquez

1942—

Spanish prime minister

Felipe González Márquez, Spanish prime minister from 1982 to 1996, helped transform his country's government from a repressive dictatorial regime into an open, progressive democracy. For nearly half a century before González's election, Spain was isolated from the rest of the world, economically and (to a lesser extent) culturally. Under his leadership, Spain regained its position as an integral member of the European community and strengthened its ties with countries in Central and South America.

Found Socialism During College

González was born on March 5, 1942, in Seville, the largest city in the southern Spanish province of Andalusia. His parents, Felipe González Helguera and Juana Márquez, owned a small dairy. The family made a relatively respectable living, but Spain in the 1940s was a difficult place to live. In the mid-1930s the country was split by a bloody civil war that left a military dictatorship in charge, with Generalissimo Francisco Franco as its head. Spain did not participate in World War II, but Franco's regime eliminated many civil liberties for Spaniards. All political parties were banned, as were all trade unions except those sanctioned by the state. There was no free flow of information, and those who opposed Franco risked detention in prison labor camps. Many of those prisoners were eventually executed.

One of Franco's labor camps was near the González family farm, and young González and his family heard tales of repression from former prisoners who had served out their sentences. This experience, combined with a strong sense of values instilled in González by his parents (particularly his mother, whom he once described as a "driving force" in the family), set the stage for his later political activity. González attended local schools run by the Claretian order of priests. He was not an inspired student and he studied little, yet he displayed a strong sense of purpose and drive for things that interested him, such as middle- and long-distance running which he took up despite childhood asthma. This drive, along with encouragement from his parents, propelled González through high school and into college; the only one of the four González children to attend.

It was during his college years that González became interested in politics—in particular, socialism. Although socialism was officially banned in Spain, college campuses throughout Europe were being exposed to a

At a Glance . . .

Born on March 5, 1942, in Seville, Spain; married Maria Carmen Romero, 1969; children: Pablo, David, Maria. *Education:* University of Seville; BA, 1966; Belgian Catholic University, 1966-67.

Career: Spanish Socialist Party (PSOE), executive commission member, 1970-74, party leader, 1974-97; Spanish prime minister, 1982-96.

Awards: Charlemagne Prize, 1993; Great Golden Cross for Merit, Republic of Austria, 1997.

Address: *Office*—Socialist Workers Party of Spain, Ferraz 68 y 70, 28008, Madrid, Spain.

variety of political ideas, some of them radically different then the ruling government. Even the campuses of politically repressive Spain were not immune to the flow of ideas. In 1962 González joined the Socialist Youth movement, which was then an illegal underground movement. Through Socialist Youth he met Alfonso Guerra, a like-minded student who became his close friend (and who would later become his deputy prime minister). In 1964 González joined the Socialist Workers Party (PSOE), another illegal group. After graduating from the University of Seville in 1966 with a degree in law, González won a scholarship to the Belgium Catholic University where he continued his studies for two years. While at college in Belgium, González was able to gain access to books and other information that was banned in Spain. The experiences of his college years helped inform his political beliefs, and they furthered his resolve to help change his government.

Garnered Support for the PSOE

Spain in the 1960s was far less isolated from the world than it had been during and immediately after World War II. Culturally and economically Spain appeared much more open. Politically, however, the Franco regime was still in total control, and there was still no legal way to oppose or even question the government. The labor situation was not healthy, and employee-labor disputes became increasingly common. Labor slowdowns, lockouts, and strikes took their toll and became more frequent even though such actions were illegal.

The PSOE during these years was virtually powerless to offer any real guidance. The party had been in exile for decades, and its leadership had grown old and inflexible. The bigger problem was that the PSOE leaders had lost touch with the needs of Spain. González and his younger colleagues mobilized beginning in the 1970s to make socialism a viable force in Spanish politics—no small task considering that the PSOE was still illegal. During these years González conducted all of his PSOE business under the assumed name "Isidoro."

González was elected to the PSOE's executive commission in 1970 during the party's 11th congress. In 1974, during its 13th congress, González became PSOE's first secretary-general. As González rose in power, he and his colleagues began moving the party forward to make it more relevant to contemporary issues.

The real test for the PSOE came in November of 1975 when Franco died. With him died at least some of the political repression that had crippled Spain for nearly four decades. González and his colleagues felt that the best way to legitimize the PSOE in Spain would be to gain support from socialists throughout Europe. All during 1976 González worked to build bridges between the PSOE and established socialist political organizations in other countries. One reason for his success was his own personal charm. A charismatic speaker who projected a friendly, open demeanor, González won popular support for his cause almost as much for his personality and message.

Change and Victory for the PSOE

In June of 1977 Spain held its first free elections in more than 40 years. The PSOE won 30 percent of the vote, making it the majority opposition party. González's commitment to socialism was tempered by a belief that the transition to a democratic government in Spain would be best served by a more centrist approach. He worked to build a good working relationship with the centrist government led by Adolfo Suarez.

Many Spanish socialists, however, felt that the government needed to adopt a more radical political agenda. During the party's 28th congress in May of 1979, González made a motion to remove the word "Marxist" from the party's official platform. The motion was rejected, and González stepped down as party leader. The party had a change of heart, and a mere four months later it adopted González's motion and reinstated him as leader. Those from the left wing of the party were not pleased by the push toward the center, but the centrists were certain that only by embracing a moderate agenda could they win more seats in the Spanish parliament. Even a centrist approach was too radical for some; on February 23, 1981, military troops under the leadership of Colonel Antonio Tejero stormed Spain's parliament building and took a number of legislators hostage, including González. The coup failed, in part thanks to the personal intervention of Spanish King Juan Carlos I.

In the October 1982 elections the Spanish public came out in a strong show of support of solidarity with

González and the moderates. The PSOE won 46 percent of the vote, which gave it a parliamentary majority. Soon after, González was sworn in as the nation's first socialist prime minister.

Took Spain in a New Direction

Under González's rule, Spain shook off the last vestiges of isolation from the Franco days. Spain had joined the North Atlantic Treaty Alliance (NATO) only six months before the 1982 elections, a move that the PSOE had initially opposed. González, taking a longer-term view, expressed his support for the move, and the government agreed to maintain the alliance. The country voted in a 1986 referendum to continue Spain's NATO membership. González led Spain into the European Economic Community in 1986, a significant move that further strengthened ties with the rest of Europe and that helped strengthen Spain's economy. He also managed to attract a considerable amount of foreign investment into the country, a move that won him allies among the business community (not normally known for its friendly attitude toward socialism). While Spain under González did not attempt to ally itself specifically with either the United States or the Soviet Union, the government did work to maintain good relations with the United States. In the mid-1980s Spain and the United States reached a key agreement reducing the number of American military forces stationed in Spain.

Socialism was riding a wave of popularity in Europe when González became Spanish prime minister, and he capitalized on that popularity to develop good relationships with socialist leaders. His brand of socialism, known in some circles as *Felipismo,* was conservative by traditional socialist measurements, and during his tenure as prime minister both supporters and foes noted that he became increasingly conservative. González answered critics by explaining that he preferred a pragmatic rather than a doctrinaire approach to governing.

Domestically, González's policies met with mixed results. His push to include Spain in the EEC did improve the Spanish economy; inflation in Spain dropped from 15 percent in 1982 to under five percent in 1988, and Spanish gross domestic product grew at a respectable rate. The González government was unable, however, to reduce unemployment demonstrably. The unemployment rate in Spain hovered around 20 percent during much of his tenure. González tried various means of cost-cutting including a freeze on social benefits. A growing trade deficit, coupled with higher interest rates, cost him some of the good will he had garnered from the business community when he first took office. Nevertheless, he remained personally popular.

Continued to Promote Spain After Term

A number of party scandals during the early 1990s weakened the González government, but his party won a narrow victory in the 1993 elections. By 1996 enough of his traditional base had eroded, and in the elections that year the conservative Popular Party took charge, with José Maria Aznar the new prime minister. González remained socialist party leader but stepped down in 1997. That year, charges were filed against several members of his government for waging what was termed a "dirty war" against Basque separatists. The Basques, who live primarily in northern Spain, had frequently made demands for more autonomy from Spain, and at times these demands were backed by violence from the most militant factions. In the 1980s and 1990s, the government used questionable tactics in trying to crush the Basques. A dozen officials from González's government received jail sentences for their role in the dirty war, but González was not charged with any wrongdoing. His interest in Spain and its role in Europe and the world remained his chief concern after his term of office expired, and into the 21st century he was traveling and lecturing frequently about international affairs.

González married Maria Carmen Romero, a schoolteacher he met while involved in Socialist Youth, in 1969. She later served in the Spanish parliament as a member of the PSOE party. The couple had two sons and a daughter. González received the Charlemagne Prize in 1993 and the Great Golden Cross for Merit of the Republic of Austria in 1997.

Sources

Books

Current Biography, H. W. Wilson Co., 1977.
Encyclopedia of World History, Houghton Mifflin Company, 2001.

Periodicals

Economist, May 4, 1991.
New York Times, October 30, 1982.
Time, October 23, 1989.
Washington Post, January 31, 1993.

On-line

"Felipe González Márquez," *Leading Authorities,* www.leadingauthorities.com (June 10, 2003).

—George A. Milite

Jimmy Gurulé

1951—

Prosecutor, law professor

In the field of criminal law there is no one more renowned than Jimmy Gurulé. During his more than 20 years as a law professional, Gurulé has earned a reputation as a crusader for justice—a man who goes full-tilt in his efforts to use the law as a means to help those victimized by society. Gurulé first gained prominence in the late 1980s as a federal prosecutor in the U.S. Attorney's Office in Los Angeles when he successfully brought down a Mexican drug ring. A solid, driven prosecutor, Gurulé was called up to Washington, D.C., in 1990 during the presidency of George H. W. Bush to serve as assistant attorney general in the Department of Justice, the first Hispanic to hold that post. Gurulé went on to become the Department of the Treasury's undersecretary for enforcement in 2001. In this capacity, he was the highest-ranking Hispanic law-enforcement official in the country. After the September 11, 2001, attacks on the United States, Gurulé went to work untangling the web of terrorist finances and has helped freeze more than $125 million in assets. He has since returned to Notre Dame to teach criminal law and pass his knowledge on to others. Now, Gurulé serves as an expert, a teacher, and a role model to other Hispanic Americans.

Michael Olivas, a University of Houston Law Center professor and friend of Gurulé's, told *U.S. News &* *World Report* that Gurulé has always worked hard to bolster the image of the Hispanic-American and believes in always being the best no matter what he is doing. "He was always the first. That meant always realizing he was a role model and had to be better than everyone else around him. And he usually is."

Heavily Influenced by Maternal Role Models

Gurulé (pronounced gur-ooh-LAY) was born June 14, 1951, in Salt Lake City, Utah, to Rita (Cabrera) and George Gurulé. His father was from New Mexico, where the Gurulé bloodline could be traced back 300 years. The Gurulés were one of the original families to settle the areas of Albuquerque, New Mexico, and Santa Fe, New Mexico. Gurulé's parents divorced when he was young, and he grew up splitting his time between Santa Fe, New Mexico, where his father lived, and Salt Lake City, Utah, where his mother's family lived. To make ends meet, Gurulé's mother worked two jobs. Though she spent her days at a telephone company and her nights working as a waitress, she dedicated her free time to her son and became a driving influence in Gurulé's life. Neither of Gurulé's parents graduated from high school, but they recognized the

At a Glance . . .

Born Jimmy Gurulé on June 14, 1951, in Salt Lake City, UT; married in November 1980; three children. *Education:* University of Utah, BA, 1974; University of Utah College of Law, JD, 1980.

Career: Salt Lake County, UT, prosecutor's office, deputy attorney, 1983-85; U.S. Attorney's Office, Los Angeles, major narcotics division, federal prosecutor and deputy chief, 1985-89; Notre Dame Law School, professor, 1989-90, 1992-01, 2003–; Department of Justice, assistant attorney general, 1990-92; Department of the Treasury, undersecretary for enforcement, 2001-03.

Memberships: Harvard Journal of Hispanic Policy editorial advisory board, 1996–; Notre Dame Latino Studies Program advisory board, 1987–; LEXIS-NEXIS Advisory Board for Criminal Justice Publications, 1998–; National Criminal Justice Trial Advocacy Competition advisory board, 1990–.

Awards: Drug Enforcement Administration's Administrator's Award; Attorney General's Distinguished Service Award; Edmund J. Randolph Award for service to the U.S. Department of Justice, 1991; Hispanic National Bar Association President's Award for Outstanding Leadership in the Hispanic American Community and Legal Profession, 1993; Treasury Medal, Department of the Treasury.

Address: *Office*—212 Law School, PO Box R, Notre Dame, IN 46556.

merits of an education and believed that hard work would take you places. "My mother was a strong force in my life," Gurulé said in an interview with *Contemporary Hispanic Biography (CHB)*. "She always stressed to me that you could accomplish great things if you worked hard."

In 1969 Gurulé graduated from Murray High School in Murray, Utah, a suburb of Salt Lake City, and entered the University of Utah, earning a bachelor's degree in 1974. Next, he enrolled in law school. Gurulé recalled that he wanted to study law because he had an idealistic notion—which he still possesses today—that lawyers are the instruments of justice in our society. Back then, Gurulé saw lawyers as the "crusaders" who would help those victimized by crime, society, the government, or

large corporations. He told *CHB*, "I believed then that a training in the law and an understanding of the law would provide me with the training and tools needed to advocate and defend the rights of the disadvantaged—the victims of society."

But before he could advocate for others, Gurulé had to learn to advocate for himself. As one of only two Hispanics in his class at the University of Utah College of Law, Gurulé felt like an outsider. Whenever he was down, his grandmother, Frances "Pancha" Yanez-Gonzalez, pulled him back up. Growing up, Gurulé spent a great deal of time under Pancha's care. She spoke to him in Spanish and instilled in him an appreciation for his culture as a Latino. Pancha spent her life as a migrant worker, picking sugar beets in fields across Utah and Idaho. In the Hispanic district in Salt Lake City where she lived, her home served as the social center of the neighborhood. Gurulé remembered that his grandmother's kitchen was always filled with neighbors sitting around, seeking advice and help. From his grandmother, Gurulé learned the virtues of helping others.

As Gurulé told *Notre Dame Magazine*, "She was a saint, one of the wisest people I ever met, wiser certainly than the vast majority of judges I've appeared before. ...she's the most upbeat person I've ever known, someone who had very little material wealth but who was determined to always, always leave you feeling upbeat and positive whenever you went for a visit." Whenever Gurulé expressed doubt or frustration, Pancha invited him over and after a session of coffee and counseling, he would leave feeling better, "like the weight of the world was lifted off my shoulders."

Developed an Interest in Criminal Law

Following his second year of law school, Gurulé worked a summer internship at the Salt Lake County prosecutor's office and developed a passion for criminal law. While working in the prosecutor's office, Gurulé got to see firsthand how crime victims struggled to overcome their wounds. The victims came to be interviewed by prosecutors who were trying to figure out what charges could be filed. One day, Gurulé spoke with a woman who had been battered by her live-in boyfriend. As he listened to the painful retelling of her story, Gurulé noted her broken nose and arm and felt a tug in his own heart toward helping victims of crime. "I was very touched that here was a criminal justice system available to her irrespective of her economic status—a justice system that would address the wrongs that had been done to her," he told *CHB*. At that moment, Gurulé came to realize that criminal law would allow him to impact people's lives in a positive way daily.

After earning his law degree in 1980, Gurulé became a member of the Utah bar and headed to Washington,

D.C., to work for the Department of Justice as part of an honors program. The prestigious program was the only way attorneys could join the justice department right out of law school. Gurulé was one of about 1,000 applicants for the 12 slots awarded in the program. Along the way he married, in November of 1980, and in 1982 returned to Salt Lake City where he joined the narcotics division of the Salt Lake County prosecutor's office.

In 1985 Gurulé moved to California to work as a federal prosecutor in the U.S. Attorney's Office in Los Angeles, which, at the time, was the second-largest U.S. Attorney's Office in the United States. Again, Gurulé worked in the narcotics division, and his high-octane drive propelled him upward. Soon, Gurulé was promoted to deputy chief of the major narcotics division. In the late 1980s Gurulé gained prominence during a complex and sensitive three-year investigation of a Mexican drug ring suspected of torturing and killing Enrique "Kiki" Camarena, a Drug Enforcement Administration (DEA) agent. After months of daily battle in the courtroom, lead prosecutor Gurulé secured convictions of three men involved in the murder. For his service, Gurulé earned the DEA Administrator's Award, the highest award conferred by the DEA, as well as the Attorney General's Distinguished Service Award. Soon after, Gurulé, looking for a change of pace, accepted an offer to teach at Notre Dame. He joined the faculty in 1989.

Worked High-Profile Jobs in Washington

In 1990 Gurulé was nominated to become assistant attorney general of the Department of Justice by then-President George Herbert Walker Bush. Gurulé became the first Hispanic to serve in that position, and his grandmother was so proud that she flew to Washington, D.C., for his swearing-in ceremony. Not only was Pancha proud that her grandson had become the first Hispanic to serve in that capacity, she was aware of the broader consequences his success had for the Hispanic community as a whole.

Gurulé stayed in Washington for two years, returning to Notre Dame in 1992 when President Bill Clinton took over and made his own appointments. In 2000 Gurulé joined a criminal advisory committee for then-presidential candidate George W. Bush. Gurulé helped the Bush campaign by developing position papers and giving Bush advice on criminal justice issues. Later, after Bush won the presidency, he nominated Gurulé to become undersecretary for enforcement in the Department of the Treasury. Gurulé was sworn in on August 7, 2001, and became the highest-ranking Hispanic in U.S. law enforcement. As undersecretary for enforcement, Gurulé oversaw about 30,000 employees within the Secret Service, the U.S. Customs Service, the Bureau of Alcohol, Tobacco and Firearms, the Finan-

cial Crimes Enforcement Network, and the Office of Foreign Assets Control, and worked with a budget of around $5 billion.

Following the September 11, 2001, attacks on the United States, Gurulé was called in to help fight the war on terrorism. His job was to figure out where the terrorists got their money and use the information to develop a strategy to cut off terrorist financing to deter future attacks. Gurulé worked tirelessly to get U.S. allies to freeze accounts in foreign banks worldwide. In the 12 months following 9/11, Gurulé visited 15 countries, some multiple times. After 18 months on the job, Gurulé resigned as undersecretary and returned to Notre Dame in 2003. Part of the reason he left was because Congress created the new Department of Homeland Security, which took away some of his responsibilities and gave them to department director Tom Ridge. When he left, Gurulé was awarded the Treasury Medal, one of the department's highest honors, for his role in helping the government implement new policies to choke off terrorist funding.

At Notre Dame, Gurulé serves as the faculty advisor to the Hispanic Law Students Association. He urges Hispanics to set for themselves the objective of accomplishing something great in their lifetimes. He told CHB that he urges his students to do as he has, "Set high expectations for yourself—If you set high expectations for yourself and come up short, you will still come up with something significant, rather than settling for the middle of the road."

Selected works

Articles

"The Ancient Roots of Modern Forfeiture Law," *Notre Dame Journal of Legislation*, 1995.
"The Money Laundering Control Act of 1986: Creating a New Federal Offense or Merely Affording Federal Prosecutors an Alternative Means of Punishing Specified Unlawful Activity?" *American Criminal Law Review*, 1995.
"Terrorism, Territorial Sovereignty, and the Forcible Apprehension of International Criminals Abroad," *Hastings International and Comparative Law Review*, 1994.

Books

(with S. Guerra) *The Law of Asset Forfeiture*, Lexis Law Publishing, 1998.
(with M. C. Bassiouni, J. Paust, M. Scharf, S. A. Williams, and B. Zagaris) *International Criminal Law: Cases and Materials*, Carolina Academic, 1996.
Complex Criminal Litigation: Prosecuting Drug Enterprises and Organized Crime, Michie, 1996.
(with R. J. Goodwin) *Criminal and Scientific Evidence: Cases, Materials and Problems*, Michie, 1997.

Sources

Periodicals

Newsweek, October 29, 2001, p. 30.
U.S. News & World Report, December 31, 2001, p. 57.

On-line

"Jimmy Gurulé," *Notre Dame Faculty,* www.nd.edu/ ~ndlaw/faculty/facultypages/gurule.html (June 10, 2003).
"Dollar Signs: Jimmy Gurulé heads the hunt for Al Qaeda's paper trail," *Notre Dame Magazine,* www.nd.edu/~ndmag/au2002/gurule.html (June 10, 2003).

Other

Additional information for this profile was obtained through a personal interview with *Contemporary Hispanic Biography* on May 23, 2003.

—Lisa Frick

Carlos M. Gutierrez

1953—

Corporate executive

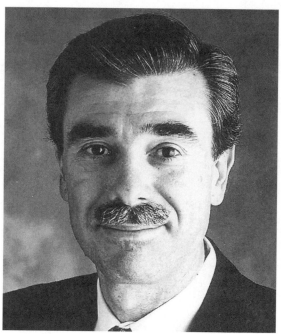

When Cuban-born Carlos M. Gutierrez ascended to the top spot at the Kellogg Company in 1999 he became not only the youngest chief executive officer (CEO) in company history but also the firm's first Hispanic CEO. According to *Hispanic Online*, the Hispanic Association on Corporate Responsibility stated that he was one of just 14 Hispanics wielding serious power in Fortune 1000 companies. Gutierrez's multicultural background has been a plus at Kellogg which has production facilities on six continents and distributes products to 160 countries. "It's been incredibly helpful," he told the Knight Ridder/Tribune Business News. "I must be the only CEO in the country who takes calls and writes letters in Spanish." While unabashedly proud of his heritage, Gutierrez told *The Florida Times Union* that he preferred to be recognized for his business acumen than as "the Hispanic CEO." Considering his track record at Kellogg, Gutierrez has nothing to worry about. When he took over Kellogg, the nearly century-old cereal giant was in trouble. Sales were down and shareholders were worried. Home of Frosted Flakes, Rice Krispies, and Raisin Bran, Kellogg had gone stale. Gutierrez didn't flinch. Through some very bold, and often unpopular moves,

he prodded Kellogg back to life. By 2003 the company's profits had risen seven percent above the previous year, beating Wall Street's per-share forecasts by one cent. Though Gutierrez told the *Battle Creek Enquirer,* "To be able to turn in this type of sales and earnings performance is a real credit to our whole organization," business analysts all point to Gutierrez's gutsy leadership as the driving force behind the company's resurgence.

Carlos Miguel Gutierrez was born in Havana, Cuba, on November 4, 1953, to Pedro Gutierrez and Olga Fernandez. The elder Gutierrez owned a successful pineapple plantation which provided the family with a very comfortable life. While Olga minded their large home, Carlos and his older brother attended Catholic school. In a country run into poverty by the corrupt regime of dictator Fulgencio Batista, the Gutierrez's enjoyed a relatively idyllic life. Then, in 1959, Fidel Castro took power and within a year began to implement a fierce brand of communism. Private businesses such as the Gutierrez family plantation were seized by the government. During this tumultuous time Gutierrez's father was briefly jailed for alleged anti-government activities.

Upon his release the family fled to Miami to wait for Castro's ouster. It never came. Gutierrez's father realized they would have to begin a new life in a new country. The transition was a blow to the family, long used to both wealth and influence in their homeland. For a while they lived in a hotel in Miami. It was there that six year-old Gutierrez learned English from a bellhop.

Early Learned Work Ethic Paid Off

Gutierrez and his family soon embarked on a sort of nomadic existence, moving as his father's job dictated. By the time he reached high school, Gutierrez had lived in Fort Lauderdale, Miami, New York City, Mexico City, and Tampico, Mexico. Though the elder Gutierrez eventually became head of Heinz Company's Latin American fruit operations, the family never did regain the level of prestige it knew in Cuba. This loss has long inspired Gutierrez. He told *The Detroit News,* "It motivated me to know the worst that could happen and that I should always be ready for it. After losing everything, I wanted to create a better life."

While Gutierrez was in high school he began selling magazine subscriptions door-to-door, capitalizing on his natural sales ability. After graduating, he took a job with his father's company in Mexico City. However, when he heard of a sales position opening with Kellogg Mexico, he wasted no time in applying. He was hired in 1975 as a sales and marketing trainee and promptly began moving up the ranks, impressing both co-workers and supervisors. "He had a leadership quality that came out early," Bill LaMothe, a former CEO of Kellogg told *The Detroit News.* Gutierrez moved to Queretaro, Mexico, for the company and there began to study business administration at the well-respected Monterrey Institute of Technology. However, he would not be able to finish his degree. In 1982 Kellogg brass, impressed with Gutierrez's skill, brought him to company headquarters in Battle Creek, Michigan, and made him supervisor of Latin American marketing. Again, his hard work brought recognition and the following year he was promoted to manager of international marketing services.

In explaining his work ethic, Gutierrez told *Hispanic,* "I always felt I had to work a little harder or show a little bit more commitment than the average executive because I did have a different background." Unlike most other junior executives, Gutierrez did not complete college. He explained to *Hispanic,* "It was something that drove me perhaps to work harder, to read more, to be a bit more curious." In addition, when he arrived in Battle Creek there were no minorities in the company's top ranks. He knew if he were to earn a corner suite he would have to go above and beyond to prove himself. Fortunately Gutierrez loved to work, admitting to *The Detroit News* that working was his favorite pastime. That hobby nudged him further up the corporate ladder. In 1984 Gutierrez was promoted general manager of Kellogg Mexico and he moved back to Mexico City. There he found a company in dire straits. Sanitation levels at Kellogg's production facility were dangerously low, threatening product quality. At the same time costs were sky high, seriously impairing profitability. With a stroke of boldness that would come to characterize his management style, Gutierrez shut the plant down for 90 days to revamp operations. His move paid off. Upon reopening, the plant became one of the cleanest and most efficient of Kellogg's facilities worldwide. This ability to resolve a problem would also come to characterize his work. "His whole career has been one of many successes in almost any situation we threw him into," LaMothe told the *The Florida Times Union.*

Led Kellogg Divisions Worldwide

After his coup in Mexico, Gutierrez shot up the corporate ladder. In 1989 he became president and CEO of Kellogg Canada. The following year he returned to Battle Creek where he was made corporate vice president for product development. Six months later he was promoted vice president of Kellogg Company and executive vice president for sales and marketing of Kellogg USA. In 1992 he became general manager of Kellogg USA's Cereal Division. The following year he was sent back overseas, this time as president of Kellogg Asia-Pacific, based in Australia. In each position, Gutierrez was admired for his ability to implement changes that resulted in better profitability and increased efficiency. However, he also drew praise for his professional manner. "He's gentle, tactful, polite," a former Kellogg newsletter editor told *The Detroit News.* "When you're with him you get a feeling of his strength, but it's very quiet strength. He just knew how to get along with people." That included everyone from fellow executives to hourly factory workers. His demeanor also won respect outside the walls of Kellogg. The mayor of Battle Creek told *Hispanic,* "It would be very easy for him to be self-important or self-aggrandizing, but he doesn't do that."

After a lifetime spent moving, first as an exiled child of Cuba and then as a busy corporate executive, Gutierrez finally settled down in 1996 when he transferred back to Battle Creek and moved into the upper-echelons of Kellogg management. The title on the door of his corporate suite originally read executive vice president for business development. It was changed to chief operating officer in 1998, a position which had been vacant for six years. Gutierrez's name was soon splashed across the business press and industry analysts agreed that the post was Gutierrez's last stop on his way to CEO. Their predictions came true the following year. In April of 1999, after nearly a quarter of a century with Kellogg, Gutierrez took the helm of the cereal dynasty as CEO and president.

When Gutierrez inherited Kellogg, the company had annual sales of $7 billion and employed over 14,000 workers worldwide. However, the company was in trouble. *The Financial Times* wrote in 1998 that "Kellogg has been going nowhere for most of the last decade. Its market share has declined, profits have bobbed up and down, and its share price performance has been as soggy as a bowl of old corn flakes." Busy consumers wanting their morning meal on-the-run were opting for breakfast bars, bagels, and bagged donuts. In addition price wars between cereal manufacturers cut into what little profit remained. Gutierrez faced an uphill battle to turn around the company, but it was a challenge he was ready for. In an oft-quoted comment made at a press conference following his appointment as CEO, Gutierrez boldly promised to boost profits by at least ten percent a year. Business

analysts and stockholders alike wanted to know how. Change was his answer. "I think what the board wanted to see was leadership from someone who can really put the institution first," he was quoted in *The Florida Times Union.* "They know I love this institution ... but they also know I've demonstrated a willingness to change."

Took Bold Steps to Save Company

One of the first changes that Gutierrez implemented sent shock waves through the Kellogg empire. He decided to close down the original Battle Creek-based factory saying that it had become outdated and inefficient. The plant founded by W.K. Kellogg in 1906 was as potent a symbol of the company as Tony the Tiger. In addition in the close knit community of Battle Creek—nicknamed Cereal City—the closure would mean a loss of 550 jobs. It was a difficult decision as Gutierrez and his wife lived in Battle Creek and their three children attended its schools. "I care very much about this company and community," Gutierrez told *The Florida Times Union.* "These are painful but necessary decisions to make." However, they also brought him respect. "This is probably one of those decisions that should have been made years ago," a Michigan economist told *The Florida Times Union.* "But no one else had the guts to do it." Gutierrez's gutsy move resulted in an initial rise in profits by January of 2000. However, Kellogg was still in trouble as its sales slipped behind rival General Mills for the first time since the company's founding.

With over 75% of Kellogg's business dependent on downward-spiraling cereal sales, Gutierrez realized that the company had to expand beyond the cereal aisle if it wanted to survive. His solution would prove the most daring step of his career. In 2001 Gutierrez negotiated Kellogg's $4.4 billion purchase of snack food giant Keebler. "Carlos is betting his career on Keebler," a food industry analyst told *Newsweek.* "But if he'd relied on cereal alone, he was almost sure to lose." The purchase was costly for the ailing company and shortly after the deal was done Gutierrez announced that Kellogg was lowering its annual profit growth targets. However with Keebler, Kellogg's dependency on cereal sales dropped to 40%, a change that Wall Street liked. The general response was summed up by an analyst quoted in *Hispanic:* "These moves have inspired more confidence on my part that Kellogg's is now moving in the right direction."

By 2003 Wall Street's predictions had come true. Kellogg was back on an upward swing. Net earnings for the first quarter of the year were $163.9 million, a full seven percent above the first quarter of 2002. Cost per share of the company had increased by eight percent. The company had also achieved four percent in sales growth and amassed a $1 billion cash flow. Kellogg's board of directors were pleased and rewarded Gutierrez handsomely. His compensation package for 2002 totaled over $2.8 million dollars. Quite a difference from his days as a young Cuban exile living in a hotel with his displaced family. Some would say that Gutierrez's rise to the top of one of America's most respected corporations is an example of the American Dream come true. Gutierrez, with characteristic directness, might credit his achievement to something his father once told him. "Success is about results. Anything else is a bit fluffy," he recalled to *The Florida Times Union.* His drive for results has propelled his career since his eager days as a sales trainee and has resulted in Gutierrez becoming one of the most admired leaders—Hispanic or otherwise—in the business world.

Sources

Periodicals

Battle Creek Enquirer, April 26, 2003, p. A1; March 15, 2003, p. A1.

Cosmetics International, February 10, 2002, p.15.
Detroit News, January 28, 2000, p. 1; May 15, 2000 p. 1.
Financial Times, September 23, 1998, p. 31.
Florida Times Union, September 6, 1999, p. D1.
Hispanic Magazine, March 2002.
Knight Ridder/Tribune Business News, March 28, 2000.
Newsweek, November 6, 2000 p. 56.

On-line

"Thinking Out of the Box," *Hispanic,* www.hispanic online.com/magazine/2002/march/Features/kel loggs.html (May 15,2003).
"Carlos M. Gutierrez," *Kellogg Company Official Website,* www.kelloggs.com (May 19, 2003).

—Candace LaBalle

Alejandra Guzmán

1968—

Rock singer, songwriter

She's been called the Mexican Madonna and the bad girl of Latin pop. Mexican rock star Alejandra Guzmán indeed gained tabloid notoriety for her flesh-baring displays on stage and for a series of controversial moves and wrong turns in her personal life. Yet another way to regard Guzmán's career would be to identify her as a performer who has broken new ground for women in Latin American music. Guzmán's low, raspy voice is a distinctive instrument widely recognized all through the Spanish-speaking Americas, and she brought a new level of sexual frankness to Mexican popular music. In a world where female performers often act out the ideas of male impresarios, Guzmán has generally controlled the direction of her own career.

Born February 9, 1968, in Mexico City, Alejandra grew up in a hothouse atmosphere where her performing instincts were encouraged, making her first appearance on television at the age of two months and often traveling with her mother's dramatic company. "I was influenced by being born to two big stars," Guzmán told the San Antonio Express-News. Her father, Enrique Guzmán, was a Venezuelan-born performer who was one of the pioneers of rock en español in the 1960s and 1970s, and her mother, Silvia Pinal, was an actress who sang duets with her husband on their television

program Silvia y Enrique—something like a Mexican Sonny and Cher. As a teenager she was cast along with her mother in a production of the musical Mame and decided that she wanted to make singing a career. Her parents insisted only that she finish high school.

Guzmán appeared for a few years in Mexican television soap operas while looking for a way to break into the music business. Her musical career took off in 1989 when she convinced Latin producer Miguel Blasco to helm her debut album Bye Mama. From the start Guzmán, who named the Rolling Stones and the throaty-voiced Janis Joplin and Billie Holiday as major influences, made a strong impact. It wasn't long before Mexican fans had proclaimed her "La Reina del Rock" or "The Queen of Rock."

Guzmán's second album Dame tu Amor, featuring classic-rock covers, eclipsed even its predecessor's strong showing and marked the beginning of her sexy stage show, featuring short miniskirts and a set of sensual dance moves that were explicit even by Latin pop standards. She accumulated a set of tattoos in the bikini-line area that male fans shouted for her to display as her concerts unfolded, and her daring image stoked her record sales as the Fonovisa label released roughly one Guzmán album a year. Her best-selling release was her third album, *Eternamente Bella,* which reportedly hit sales of a million copies within a year of its release. Guzmán's outrageous persona went from image to reality in 1992, however, when she announced that she was pregnant out of wedlock with her daughter Frida Sofía.

That caused major controversy, but Guzmán bounced back undaunted after a short hiatus, releasing a song called "Mala Hierba" as the leadoff single of her RCA-label album *Libre* and, more controversially still, posing semi-nude in a 1994 issue of *Playboy* magazine's Mexican edition. Guzmán defended her photo spread to the *Houston Chronicle* saying, "My intention was to do it with artistry, not something vulgar or horrible…. Also I did not show the expensive things, because for that I would have charged an incredible sum." Regardless of the controversial publicity, *Libre*, which featured songwriting contributions by Guzmán and reflected her heavy involvement in song selection and production, did well, landing in the top ten of Mexican album sales charts.

Nevertheless, Guzmán's career began to run into trouble as the 1990s wore on. She entered a rehab program for drug addiction, finally swearing off drugs permanently in 1997. Her music deepened as she began to include elements such as Middle Eastern and Indian instruments, and after the release of her 1996 album *Cambio de Piel* she began to gain fans in the United States beyond the usual circuit of Latin concert venues and compact disc shops. Guzmán married U.S. citizen Farrell Goodman in 1998, but the marriage didn't last—her husband was arrested and convicted on drug trafficking charges in Germany. Tabloid newspapers had a field day as Guzmán protested that she knew

nothing of his illicit activities. To make things worse, Guzmán's daughter became the target of an unsuccessful kidnapping attempt.

Guzmán tried to get back to her roots and recharge by appearing on stage with her mother in the musical *Gypsy*, but her label RCA had become leery of the negative publicity surrounding its troubled rock star and put only desultory efforts into promoting her 1999 album *Algo Natural*. The company was also undergoing a reorganization at the time, leaving no one in charge of Guzmán's career. The album won critical praise and a Latin Grammy nomination, but it bombed commercially. Though *People en Español* had named Guzmán one of its "Year's Most Intriguing People" in 1998, she was displaced from her spot at the top of Mexico's gossip columns by singer Gloria Trevi, who was imprisoned in Brazil after being indicted on kidnapping and sexual assault charges.

Guzmán, having reached an age that few rock-star careers survive, could have given up. But she soldiered on, undertaking a U.S. tour and promoting the *Algo Natural* album on her own. After a time, things began to turn around. Mexican audiences warmed to her account of the Farrell Goodman fiasco, allowing her to make some degree of transition from bad girl to victimized spouse. And Guzmán drew on a large reservoir of fans who still flocked to her live appearances. An appearance at the Centro de Bellas Artes in Santurce, Puerto Rico, in February of 2001 mushroomed into a three-night stand as tickets were snapped up, and Guzmán's energetic performances were the talk of the Latin music industry.

Hiring Puerto Rican entertainment lawyer Alfredo Castellanos as her manager, Guzmán launched a full-scale comeback. Re-signed to RCA/BMG for a lucrative three-album deal, she recruited veteran Cuban-American rock producer Desmond Child for her next album, *Soy*; Child in turn brought on board guitarist Joe Satriani and songwriters Steven Tyler and Joe Perry from the rock group Aerosmith. Guzmán helped to translate the Tyler-Perry contribution, "Soy tu Lluvia," into Spanish, and she herself co-authored the party anthem "Diablo." The album earned Guzmán a Latin Grammy award in 2002 for Best Female Rock Vocal Performance, and she gained a newly respectable image as a guest anchor for the Mexican network Televisa, at the 2002 Winter Olympics in Salt Lake City, Utah.

Guzmán toured the continental United States, Mexico, and Puerto Rico in 2002 and worked on a new album that was tentatively planned to include some English-language lyrics. Her concert schedule in 2003 included a May appearance with her father at Mexico City's National Auditorium. As Guzmán entered her second decade of stardom in the early 2000s, she had outlasted the idea that she had nothing more to offer than raunch or sensationalism.

Selected discography

Bye Mama, Fonovisa, 1989.
Dame tu Amor, Fonovisa, 1989.
Eternamente Bella, Fonovisa, 1990.
Lo Mas Prendido, Fonovisa, 1991.
Libre, RCA, 1993.
Enorme, RCA, 1994.
Al Borde de la Locura, Fonovisa, 1994.
De Piel Negra, Fonovisa, 1996.
Cambio de Piel, RCA, 1996.
La Guzmán (live), 1997.
Algo Natural, RCA, 1999.
Soy, RCA, 2001.
Alejandra Guzmán, Fonovisa, 2002.
Ellas Cantan Así, RCA, 2003.

Sources

Periodicals

Boston Globe, December 4, 1998, p. C6.
Chicago Sun-Times, November 18, 2000, p. 22.
Houston Chronicle, November 28, 1993, p. Zest-20; November 25, 2001, p. Zest-7.
Miami New Times, February 21, 2002.
San Antonio Express-News, February 21, 2003, p. H14.

On-line

"Alejandra Guzmán," *All Music Guide,* www.allmusic-.com (May 22, 2003).
"Biografía," *Alejandra Guzmán website,* www.aleguzman.com (May 22, 2003).

—James M. Manheim

Edward Hidalgo

1912-1995

U.S. Secretary of the Navy

Edward Hidalgo was the first Hispanic to serve as U.S. Secretary of the Navy. He was named to the position in October of 1979 after a long and distinguished legal and naval career. Although his tenure as secretary was short (15 months), he nonetheless made significant contributions to the Navy Department. In particular, he advocated recruiting more Hispanics into the Navy and encouraging more Hispanics to consider a naval career.

Originally named Eduardo Hidalgo, he was born in Mexico City on October 12, 1912, to Egon and Domita Kunhardt Hidalgo. The family moved to New York in 1918 and a few years later young Hidalgo became a United States citizen and anglicized his name. He attended Holy Cross College in Washington, D.C., graduating with honors in 1933. From there he went to Columbia Law School, where he received a J.D. in 1936.

Hidalgo served as a law clerk in the Second Circuit Court of Appeals in New York until 1937, when he became an associate at a New York law firm. Then America entered World War II where Hidalgo was introduced to the Navy, serving as a lieutenant in the U.S. Naval Reserve from 1942 to 1946. In this capacity he held several positions. From 1942 to 1943 he served in Montevideo, Uruguay, as a legal advisor to the ambassador to the Emergency Advisory for Political Defense. For the remainder of the war he was assigned to the carrier Enterprise as an air combat intelligence officer. He was awarded a Bronze Star for his service.

When the war ended in 1945, Hidalgo was named to the Eberstadt Committee, a special group charged with providing recommendation for unifying the branches of the military. Before World War II there had been no formal unification; the various branches of the military operated independently. The success of the armed forces through close but informal coordination during the war convinced military and government leaders that a formal coordination was essential for military strength. As a lawyer with naval experience, Hidalgo was a natural addition to such a group. Hidalgo received a special commendation for his contribution to the Eberstadt Committee, and he finished out his service as a special assistant to Navy Secretary James V. Forrestal.

At a Glance . . .

Born Eduardo Hidalgo on October 12, 1912, in Mexico City, Mexico; died on January 21, 1995, in Fairfax, VA; divorced twice; married third wife Belinda Bonham; children: Edward, Jr., Joanne, Ricardo, Tila. *Education:* Holy Cross University, BA, 1929-33; Columbia Law School, JD, 1933-36; University of Mexico Law School, civil law degree, 1959. *Military Service:* U.S. Naval Reserve, lieutenant, 1942-46; U.S. State Department, advisor, 1942-43, air combat intelligence officer, 1943-45; U.S. Navy secretary, special assistant, 1945-46.

Career: Second Circuit Court of Appeals, New York, law clerk, 1936-37; Wright, Gordon, Zachry & Parlin, associate, 1937-42; Curtis, Mallet-Prevost, Colt & Mosle, partner, 1946-48; Hidalgo, Barrera, Siquieros & Torres Landa, founder and partner, 1948-65; U.S. Navy Secretary, special assistant, 1965-66; Cahill, Gordon, & Reindel, partner, 1966-72; U.S. Information Agency, special assistant for economic affairs, 1972, congressional liaison, 1973-76; assistant secretary of the navy, 1977-79; secretary of the navy, 1979-81; consultant, 1981-95.

Awards: Bronze Star, U.S. Navy, 1943; Special Commendation Ribbon, U.S. Navy, 1945; Knight of the Royal Order of Vasa, Kingdom of Sweden, 1963; Order of the Aztec Eagle, Republic of Mexico, 1980.

After he left the Navy, Hidalgo returned to the law, founding his own law firm in Mexico City in 1948. In 1958 he wrote a book, *Legal Aspects of Foreign Investments,* which was published in Mexico. He also received a Mexican civil law degree from the University of Mexico Law School in 1959. In 1965 Hidalgo returned to the navy, serving for a year as a special assistant to Navy Secretary Paul H. Nitze. He took up law again in 1966, practicing in the Paris offices of a New York firm for the next six years. Then, in 1972, he accepted a position as special assistant for economic affairs for the United States Information Agency (USIA). A year later he was named USIA's general counsel and congressional liaison.

In 1977 Hidalgo returned once again to the Navy, this time as assistant secretary. Two years later, in September of 1979, President Jimmy Carter nominated him to replace outgoing Secretary W. Graham Clayton, Jr. He was confirmed as secretary of the Navy in October of that same year.

One of Hidalgo's top priorities during his tenure as secretary was recruiting more Hispanics into the Navy. He felt that a naval career could provide young Hispanics with valuable education and experience that they could parlay into long-term service in the Navy, and also use to their advantage once they returned to civilian life. He was particularly interested in encouraging more Hispanic members of the Navy to apply for officer positions. (In 1976 there were only five Hispanic cadets enrolled in the U.S. Naval Academy.) In December of 1980 Hidalgo convened the Hispanic Officer Recruitment Conference (HORC) to help identify ways to make naval careers more attractive to Hispanics. One result of HORC was the establishment of the Association of Naval Service Officers (ANSO). This group, created to enhance recognition and advancement of Hispanics in the Navy, provided encouragement and mentoring for young Hispanics who might want to get onto a career track as a naval officer. The efforts ultimately paid off; by 1986 there were 200 Hispanic naval cadets at the Academy. Under Hidalgo's direction, the Navy also created an advertising recruiting campaign aimed at Hispanics.

Hidalgo left his position in January of 1981 after Ronald Reagan was sworn in as president. Less than a year later he took a consulting position with General Dynamics Corporation, a major contractor with the U.S. Navy. This raised some concerns because during his years in the Navy Department, Hidalgo had helped negotiate a settlement for General Dynamics. The company had filed an $843 million claim against the Navy for cost overruns on attack submarines because of costly design changes. The Navy ultimately settled with General Dynamics for $643 million. Hidalgo was called to testify before a Congressional committee in 1985. The committee determined that Hidalgo had done nothing improper in taking the General Dynamics job, since the division he worked for had nothing to do with the Navy.

In 1989 Hidalgo was named to the President's Commission on Aviation Security and Terrorism. From 1991 to 1993 he served as a consultant to the Mexican government on the North American Free Trade Agreement (NAFTA). In 1994 he was recognized by ANSO when a new Washington, D.C., chapter was established. In addition to his military awards from the U.S. Navy, Hidalgo was made an honorary knight of the Royal Order of Vasa by the Swedish government in 1963, and he received the Order of the Aztec Eagle from his native Mexico in 1980.

Hidalgo was married three times; his first two marriages ended in divorce. He had two daughters and two sons. A Washington resident in his later years, he died on January 21, 1995, in Fairfax, Virginia. According to the *Navy News Service,* at the time of his death, Navy Secretary John Dalton remembered Hidalgo as "a superb Secretary of the Navy ... whose years of government service and love for the sea services never ended."

Sources

Books

Sweetman, Jack, *American Naval History: An Illustrated Chronology of the U.S. Navy and Marine Corps, 1775-Present,* Naval Institute Press, 2002.

Periodicals

Hispanic Times, September 1994.
Miami Herald, May 6, 1984.
New York Times, January 23, 1995.

On-line

Navy News Service, www.chinfo.navy.mil/navpalib/news/navnews/nns95/nns95004.txt (July 5, 2003).

Other

Additional information for this profile was obtained from the Federal Register Division of the National Archives and Records Service and from the *Public Papers of the Presidents of the United States, Jimmy Carter, 1977, 1979,* obtained from the Government Printing Office in Washington, D.C.

—George A. Milite

Pedro Infante

1917-1957

Actor, singer

During his career Mexican screen idol Pedro Infante made more than 50 films and recorded hundreds of popular songs. His adoring fans nicknamed him the 'Idol of Guamuchil,' after the village he was born in, as well as the 'the King.' Though he made millions as an actor, rode an American Harley Davidson, and flew airplanes, to the Mexican public he always remained the kind-hearted carpenter from the pueblo. "Infante was a symbol of someone who had worked himself up from nothing," noted *Fiesta Del Mariachi*. Women wanted to marry him. Men wanted to befriend him. Children worshipped him. When he died at the age of 39, all of Mexico mourned. On the 25th anniversary of his death, they were still mourning as 10,000 people made the pilgrimage to his Mexico City gravesite. The *Cine Mexicano* website noted, "As the new century begins, Pedro Infante continues to be the most important figure of our cinema. It is hoped that 'the King' will continue to reign for many more years."

Came From Talented Family

Pedro Infante Cruz was born on November 18, 1917, in the port town of Guamuchil, part of the larger city of Mazatlán located in the Mexican state of Sinaloa. He was the second of nine sons born to Delfino Infante Garcma and Refugio Cruz. The couple also had six daughters. Two of Infante's brothers, Angel and José, also found fame as actors and singers. Infante's father, Delfino, was a professional musician but had trouble making ends meet. When Infante was in fourth grade he had to drop out of school to help support his family.

He sold hardware, ran errands, and waited tables, however his most consistent job was as a carpenter. That is, until he fell in love with music. His father taught him the basics of music and with his carpentry skills he soon built his first guitar. He learned how to sing by imitating songs he heard on the radio.

Infante's first musical experience was with a group he formed called La Rabia. They played in local night clubs, performing rancheras and boleros—popular forms of Mexican music. In 1932 he joined the more famous Orquesta Estrella de Culiacán in Sinaloa's capital city. After a 1937 performance at a local festival, Infante's first wife, María Luisa León, insisted that he move to Mexico City to pursue his musical career. Within two years he had a contract to perform on a local radio show. Four years after that, in December of 1943, Infante recorded his first album, *El soldado raso*. He would go on to record more than 50 albums and hundreds of songs. He made the bolero musical form famous, earning the nickname King of the Bolero.

The Houston Chronicle noted that because he lacked formal training, "Infante's voice was unrefined, yet it was filled with emotion." The songs tugged at the heartstrings, telling tales of love found and lost, friendships built and broken, families together and apart. There wasn't a soul in Mexico who couldn't relate. *The Houston Chronicle* went on to say, "Infante's signature tunes included the exquisite heartbreaker 'Cien años,' a song about devotion from afar. The male protagonist sings about walking by an ex-love on the street. She looks right past him. He calls her name; she pretends not to hear. Her air of indifference hurts. Despite this indignity, he vows that, though 100 years may pass, he will never stop loving her, so intertwined were their lives." Some of his other popular songs include the bolero "Amorcito corazon," which was played repeatedly at his funeral by hundreds of mariachi bands as well as "La que se fue," and "Asi es la vida."

Became the Common Man's Star

The 1930s to the mid-1950s was the golden age of the Mexican film industry. Five major Mexican film studios pumped out thousands of films "[spreading] tales of machismo, glamour and rustic innocence to every corner of the Latino world," according to an article in *The Buffalo News*. Infante had arrived in Mexico City, the center of the country's film industry, at a perfect time to become a star. He had roles in two short films before appearing in his first feature as an extra in 1942. He appeared in three more films that year, including a starring role in *Jesucita en Chihuahua*. Over the next five years he starred in or had major roles in over a dozen more films including the 1946 comedy *Los tres García* and its sequel *Vuelven los García* released that same year. In 1947 the film that catapulted Infante to stardom and is still considered a must-see of Mexican cinema, *Nostros los pobres*, was released. In *Nosotros los pobres* Infante introduced the poor-but-proud character Pepe el Toro, struggling haphazardly through his urban life. The film combined musical comedy with gritty imagery and drama and was so popular that two sequels were made. The film is also a good illustration of Infante's acting style. Rather than lose himself in a role, he remained very connected to the audience. During songs he would often look straight at the camera and wink. His fans loved it. It also

didn't hurt that he was dashingly handsome, often eliciting comparisons to Clark Gable.

Infante often portrayed the common man that everyone could relate to. "He was the good friend, the good son, the romantic in love, the caring father, the sexy singer, the 'macho' with a heart," noted a biography of Infante on the *Lonestar* website. Infante's rise from poor carpenter to cinema star was well-known and it seemed as if onscreen he were portraying himself—the good-hearted worker eager to succeed. He was so revered for these types of characters that movies were specifically written for him with just these sorts of roles in the lead. They proved to be a sure-thing at the box office and continued to draw fans nearly fifty years after his death. They also helped propel Infante to superstardom, making him the most famous Mexican in recent history. Though many of his films were limited to strictly popular success, several also garnered critical acclaim. In 1947 Infante received the nomination for best actor from the Academy of Cinemagraphic Science and Art of Mexico for his role in *Cuando lloran los valientes*. He was again nominated in 1948 for *Los tres huastecos* and in 1953 *Un rincón cerca del cielo*. He finally won the prestigious award in 1956 for his portrayal of Pablo in *La vida no vale nada*. In all Infante appeared In 59 films, including *Tizoc* a color film made just before his death for which he received the Best Actor nod at the Berlin Festival in 1957.

Like many stars, Infante was larger-than-life off screen as well as on. He was known as quite the ladies man and by some accounts fathered over a dozen children. Three of them, Pedro Infante Jr., Cruz Infante, and Irma Infante, followed their father's footsteps into acting. He divorced María Luisa, his first wife from Sinaloa and married Lupita Torrentera with whom he had two children. When that relationship ended, he married Irma Dorantes, a fellow actor with whom he also had children. However, being a firmly Catholic country, his divorce from María Luisa was never legal and following his death, his marriage to Irma was challenged, most likely in the course of the division of his estate. Though he made a lot of money during his career, his parents, 14 brothers and sisters, three wives, and many children, relied on him. "His bills were exorbitant," noted *Virtualorbe*. "During the 1950s he was signing over 50 checks a month for his relatives' personal expenses." Nonetheless, Infante found funding for his two hobbies—his Harley Davidson motorcycle and flying. He often said it was his first wife who made him an actor when she insisted he leave Sinaloa for Mexico City, but that it was God who had made him a pilot. That is questionable as he was not a very good pilot. He flew recklessly and had two accidents by 1949, one quite serious. He had crashed his plane and suffered head injuries that nearly killed him. Mexico prayed during a tricky three-hour operation and finally breathed a sigh of relief when Infante came out of it okay.

His Death Mourned, His Legacy Launched

On April 15, 1957, Infante wasn't so lucky. According to *Fiesta Del Mariachi*, "Infante woke up early and rode his Harley Davidson motorcycle to the airport." It would be his last ride. Shortly after he crashed his plane near the city of Merida in the Mexican state of Yucatan. At quarter past eleven in the morning, the famed Mexican radio station XEW announced that Pedro Infante was dead. He was 39 and at the peak of his career. He had several more films in the works including possible appearances in American films opposite John Wayne, Joan Crawford, and Marlon Brando. Mexico was devastated. The government declared a national day of mourning. Throughout Latin America and in the Mexican-American communities in the United States, radio and television stations preempted regular programming to play day-long homages to Infante. His death was as traumatic for Mexico as the death of Princess Diana would be for Great Britain decades later. Thousands visited his body, laying a blanket of flowers and shedding a sad river of tears.

Infante left behind a very large legacy including his many films, hundreds of recordings, and large family. Each has helped keep Infante's memory and spirit alive. Compilation albums of his work continue to be released and are readily available in most major record stores. His films are in regular rotation on stations throughout Mexico and Latin America as well as on Spanish-language networks in the United States. One of his descendents living in the tequila-making state of Jalisco, Mexico, created a tequila called "Pedro Infante." Four films have been made about his life, one as recently as 1998. In 2001 acclaimed Mexican-American author Denise Chavez introduced Infante to a whole new legion of America fans when she published her novel *Loving Pedro Infante*. However, for Mexicans, Infante's memory need not be constantly rekindled. In Mexico, he will always remain an idol and a king, someone far more than a mere actor or singer. "For [us], Infante represented all that a Mexican should be," commented *Cine Mexicano*. "A respectful son, an unconditional friend, a romantic lover, and a man of his word."

Selected works

Films

Jesusita en Chihuahua, 1942.
Cuando habla el corazón, 1943.
Escándalo de estrellas, 1944.
Cuando lloran los valientes, 1945.
Los tres García, 1946.
Vuelen los García, 1946.
Nosotros los pobres, 1947.
Los tres huastecos, 1948.
Ustedes los ricos, 1948.
Sobre las olas, 1950.
A toda máquina, 1951.
Un rincón cerca del cielo, 1952.
Ahora soy rico, 1952.
Dos tipos de cuidado, 1952.
Pepe El Toro, 1952.
La vida no vale nada, 1954.
Escuela de música, 1955.
Tizoc, 1956.

Singles

"El Soldado raso," 1943.
"Noche plateada," 1944.
"Ramito de azahar," 1945.
"Vieja Chismoas," 1946.
"Maldita sea mi suerte," 1947.
"La Barca de Oro," 1948.
"Amorcito Corazon," 1949.
"Cuartro caminos," 1950.
"El Lavadero," 1950.
"La que se fue," 1950.
"Ahora soy rico," 1952.
"Corazon, Corazon," 1952.
"Tu recuerdo y yo," 1952.
"Cien años," 1953.
"Las tres hermanas," 1955.
"Pos Cui-cui-ri," 1956.

Sources

Periodicals

Buffalo News, February 22, 1996, p. B5.
Houston Chronicle, April 18, 1999, p. 18.

On-line

"A Tribute to Pedro Infante," *Fiesta Del Mariachi,* www.fiestaweb.org/Biographies/Pedro.cfm (June 19, 2003).
"Pedro Infante," *Cine Mexicano,* http://cineexicano.mty.itesm.mx/estrellas/infante.html (June 19, 2003).
"Pedro Infante," *Lonestar,* http://lonestar.utsa.edu/rlwilson/PedroInfante.html (June 19, 2003).
"Pedro Infante," *Virtualorbe,* www.virtualorbe.com/PedroInfante/pinfante/biografia.html, (June 19, 2003).

—Candace LaBalle

Juan Carlos de Borbón y Borbón

1938—

King of Spain

Spain's King Juan Carlos I has ushered his country through an unusual political evolution: handpicked by military dictator Generalissimo Francisco Franco to succeed him, the new monarch quickly moved to restore Spain to a democratic constitutional government in the late 1970s. In doing so he gave up much of his own power, and within a decade had brought the Iberian Peninsula nation into the pan-European political community. "The transfer of power in Spain was a model," observed *UNESCO Courier* writer Ramón Luis Acuña, "a source of inspiration for guiding democratic changes not only in a number of Latin American countries but also, and despite a very different political situation, in the Eastern bloc countries, including Russia."

The future king was born Juan Carlos Alfonso Víctor María de Borbón y Borbón in Rome, Italy, on January 5, 1938. His grandfather had fled Spain after the country was proclaimed a republic in 1931, an act that served to oust a Borbón dynasty whose rule in Spain dated back to 1700. The family had long, complex ties to the royal houses of Europe: the Borbón line was originally a French one, there was princely German blood as well, and Juan Carlos' grandmother was the granddaughter of England's Queen Victoria. Juan Carlos' father, Don Juan de Borbón y Battenberg, became

regent-in-exile in 1941 after the grandfather, King Alfonso XIII, abdicated in Don Juan's favor that year. By then, Spain had become a military dictatorship under Franco. The exiled royal family moved to Lausanne, Switzerland, during World War II, but after the war's end settled in Estoril, Portugal. In 1947 Franco announced that he planned to choose his posthumous successor from the Borbón line. Franco then informed Juan Carlos' father—a bitter foe of the Generalissimo—that in order for his son to be considered, Juan Carlos would have to return to Spain for his schooling.

Attempted to Bridge Gap in Politics

In November of 1948 the ten-year-old Juan Carlos set foot for the first time on Spanish soil. He was schooled in Madrid and San Sebastián, finishing with a *bachillerato* in 1954. Against the wishes of his father, he agreed to attend Spain's three military academies at Franco's urging. His education was completed in 1961 at Madrid University with courses in law, political science, and philosophy. Eight years later, Franco formally proclaimed him successor, bypassing Don Juan and causing a rift that would endure for years. Juan Carlos' father refused to abandon his claim to the

At a Glance . . .

Born Juan Carlos Víctor María de Borbón y Borbón, on January 5, 1938, in Rome, Italy; son of Don Juan de Borbón y Battenberg and Maria de las Mercedes de Borbón y Orleans; married Sofia de Grecia de y Hannover, May 14, 1962; children: Felipe, Elena, Christina. *Education:* Graduate of Spain's three military academies, late 1950s; Madrid University, BA, 1961. *Religion:* Roman Catholic.

Career: King of Spain, 1975–.

Awards: Charlemagne prize, 1982; UNESCO, Bolivar prize, 1983; Candenhove Kalergi prize, Switzerland, 1986; Nansen medal, 1987; Elie Wiesel Humanitarian award, 1991; UNESCO, Félix Houphouët-Boigny Peace prize, 1995; Franklin D. Roosevelt Four Freedoms award, 1995.

Address: *Office*—c/o Embassy of Spain, 2375 Pennsylvania Ave. NW, Washington, DC 20037.

throne, and claimed that Juan Carlos sided with Franco's fascist politics. On the other hand, supporters of the Franco regime believed that Juan Carlos harbored leftist views, and because he made almost no political pronouncements that would jeopardize his neutral stance, he was sometimes derided as the *idiota perdido,* or "lost fool."

Juan Carlos did say later that he realized there was a great generational chasm between him and his father. Should Franco have appointed a successor from the ranks of Spain's military brass, it would have brought permanent military rule to the country. Yet he also realized that the imperial era that his father had known—that of King Alfonso XIII, which dated back to 1886—was a long vanished one after two world wars had sundered Europe. "I realized the Spain my father was always talking about no longer existed," he recalled of this moment in an interview with *Europe* journalist Robert Latona. "The men and the women I met were nothing like those my father had known when he was 18 and had to go off into exile."

In the six years between his formal proclamation and Franco's 1975 death, Juan Carlos clandestinely began courting members of Spain's intelligentsia—the liberal politicians, writers, and other estimable personalities who had either been forgotten or harassed by the authoritarian Franco regime. Sometimes they were even smuggled into the Zarzuela Palace, a hunting lodge outside of Madrid that Juan Carlos had made his

family home after his 1962 marriage to Sofía de Grecia de y Hannover, a princess of Greece. The couple had three young children by the time Juan Carlos ascended to the throne on November 22, 1975, giving Spain its first monarch since 1931.

Juan Carlos promptly announced himself the "king of all Spaniards"—meaning those who had fought on the losing Republican side during the bloody Civil War of the 1930s, and the Francoists who were victorious. His investiture speech made some hints at democracy, but it was his appointment of Adolfo Suárez, once a Franco acolyte, as prime minister in 1976 that served as the beginning of the end of fascism in Spain. Unbeknownst to many except the king, Suárez had democratic leanings, and the two began making sweeping changes. The important Law of Political Reform was passed by the Cortes, or Spanish parliament, in November of 1976, and this formally ended the military dictatorship. It established a two-chamber legislature to be elected by universal suffrage, and within a few months the political parties outlawed under Franco were legalized. In June of 1977 the country held its first free, multiparty elections in 41 years.

Faced Challenges to Prosperous Reign

In 1978 Spain's new constitution was formally sanctioned on December 27 after a national referendum. It granted Juan Carlos little political power, save for the right to appoint the prime minister, but even this was subject to the approval of the Cortes. "This Constitution is in many respects one of the most advanced in Europe, particularly concerning regional political freedoms and the defence of the rights of cultural minorities," noted Acuña in the *UNESCO Courier* article. Both the Basque region and Catalonia were made autonomous regions in an attempt to eradicate longstanding cultural hostilities.

Juan Carlos' new Spain faced its greatest challenge on February 23, 1981, when the Cortes was stormed by military units during a vote for a new prime minister. The politicians were held hostage, and martial law was declared. The coup was fomented by some of the army's top generals, still loyal to the Franco ideal, and its leaders mistakenly believed that the king would either give his support or tacitly remain silent. Instead, Juan Carlos summoned a television crew to the Zarzuela Palace, put on his formal military uniform as commander-in-chief of all Spain's armed forces, and told the nation that the move against a constitutional government was an assault on the crown, and that the coup would succeed only in the event of his death. Privately, Juan Carlos personally appealed to the generals who had instigated it, as well as others who had not yet sent in their regiments, for he knew many of them from his years at Spain's military academies in the late 1950s. Within hours, democracy was restored and the coup leaders were arrested.

The 1981 crisis would remain Juan Carlos' finest hour. Just five years later, Spain was able to enter the European Economic Community, and in 1992 welcomed the world to Barcelona for a festive Summer Olympics. The king consistently polls as the most respected political figure in the country, and earns high marks for eschewing any pomp and pageantry due him and his family. Nobel laureate Camilo Jose Cela remarked to *Europe* journalist Latona, "We have a better King than we deserve." Juan Carlos and the Reina Sofía still live at Zarzuela, with Madrid's far more opulent Palacio Royal the haunt of tourists. He receives an annual household budget of $5 million, but must pay taxes on it. He has also won praise for his role in forging ties to Latin America; relations across the Atlantic had disintegrated considerably after the end of Spain's once-mighty colonial empire. His role as a goodwill ambassador has had so much success that he is sometimes affectionately referred to by some South Americans as "the king."

Juan Carlos is an avid sailor, as is his wife. Their children are the Infantas Elena and Christina, and Felipe, Prince of Asturias and heir to his father's throne. Felipe was 13 years old when the 1981 coup erupted, and at the time Juan Carlos kept him near his side. He reportedly told him, according to the *Europe* article by Latona, "Watch closely. Nobody ever said this king business was easy, and someday it will be your turn."

Sources

Books

Dictionary of Hispanic Biography, Gale Research, 1996.
Encyclopedia of World Biography, second edition, 17 vols., Gale, 1998.

Periodicals

Economist, September 21, 1996, p. 54.
Europe, October 1993, p. 18; October 2000, p. 39.
Life, December 1985, p. 4, 46.
New Leader, October 6, 1997, p. 8.
UNESCO Courier, November 1995, p. 33.
U.S. News & World Report, April 27, 1992, p. 54.
Weekly Compilation of Presidential Documents, February 28, 2000, p. 362.

—Carol Brennan

Ricardo Lagos

1938—

Chilean president

The political history of Chilean President Ricardo Lagos will always be defined in relation to former dictator General Augusto Pinochet. In 1973 when Pinochet seized control of the country and installed a right-wing dictatorship, Lagos was forced to flee into exile. When Lagos returned he rose to prominence as an outspoken critic of Pinochet. In 2000, when Lagos was elected to the presidency, his inauguration shared top billing with Pinochet's return to Chile after being detained in London for human rights violations. Lagos inherited a country obsessed with the former dictator. Half the country called for Pinochet to be tried while the other half wanted to let the matter rest. Meanwhile, Lagos faced pressing domestic problems: an economic recession, an antiquated constitution, and an unequal distribution of wealth that left nearly a quarter of Chileans in dire poverty. Lagos knew to move forward he had to escape Pinochet. His mantra as quoted by *Institutional Investor* became, "I was elected not to administer what happened in the past, but to write the new lines of the future." In a country whose history, economy, and government is also deeply defined by Pinochet, this would not prove to be easy.

Established Academic Career as Economist

Ricardo Lagos Escobar was born on March 2, 1938, to Froilán Lagos and Emma Escobar. Lagos's father, a landowner, was some thirty years older than his mother, and he died when Lagos was just eight years old. Escobar, a piano teacher, raised Lagos on her own. A precocious child, Lagos raced through his primary education and entered the University of Chile at the age of 16 where he studied law. Following his 1960 graduation he married Carmen Weber and moved to the United States where he had a scholarship to Duke University. He earned a doctorate in economics and returned to Chile where he and Weber divorced. Lagos began an academic career at the University of Chile working in the Institute of Economics. In 1967 he was named director of the School of Political Science, a post he held until 1969 when he was appointed secretary general of the university. In addition he taught economics and from 1971 to 1972 served as the director of the economics department. In 1971 he married his second wife, Luisa Duran.

At a Glance . . .

Born Ricardo Lagos Escobar on March 2, 1938; son of Emma Escobar (piano teacher) and Froilán Lagos (a landowner); married Carmen Weber, 1960s (divorced); married Luisa Duran, 1971; three children, two stepchildren. *Education:* University of Chile, law degree, 1960; Duke University, PhD, economics. *Politics:* Moderate Socialist. *Religion:* Agnostic.

Career: University of Chile, School of Political Science, director, 1967-69, secretary general, 1969-71, director, Economics Department, 1971-72; appointed Chilean ambassador to Moscow, 1972 (post never assumed); University of North Carolina, professor of economics, 1973-75; United Nations, economist, 1976-84; Alianza Democratica, president, 1983-84; Partidos por la Democracia, founder and president, 1987-90; Chilean government, minister of education, 1990-93, minister of public works, 1994-98; president of Chile, 2000–.

Memberships: Partidos por la Democracia. Has also belonged to other left wing political parties in Chile including: Alianza Democratica, Partido Socialista, and Partido Radical.

Addresses: *Office*—La Moneda, Presidential Palace, Santiago, Chile. *Website*—www.presidencia.cl.

As Lagos' academic career developed so did his interest in politics and by 1972 he was aligned with the Partido Socialista, the country's ruling socialist party. At the time Chile was governed by Salvador Allende, a devoted Marxist who enjoyed the support of the Partido Socialista. Allende soon tapped Lagos to serve in his government, nominating the young economist as ambassador to Moscow. However, Lagos would never make the trip abroad. On September 11, 1973, Pinochet—with heavy backing from the United States—stormed the presidential palace and ousted Allende. Pinochet dissolved Congress, suspended the constitution, and imposed censorship. He named himself president, but began ruling as a dictator with absolute power. Those who spoke out against him were tortured, executed, or simply made to disappear. It is estimated that over 3,000 people disappeared during Pinochet's reign. Lagos and other former government officials fled to the relative safety of exile. Back in the United States, Lagos became a professor of economics at the University of North Carolina. In 1976 he left that post to work as an economist for the United Nations.

Returned to Chile to Fight for Democracy

Lagos returned to Chile in 1978 with a U.N. passport. His official job was economist for the U.N.'s Regional Employment Program for Latin America and the Caribbean, however, he began to become more involved in Chile's left wing politics. He was an early founder of the Alianza Democratica, a party that called for Chile's return to democracy. In 1983 Lagos was elected president of this group and became the left's most public figure. The following year Lagos left the United Nations to devote himself full-time to politics. In 1986, after an assassination attempt against Pinochet, the dictator cracked down on the left and conducted massive arrests. Though Lagos had nothing to do with the murder plot, he was detained and interrogated. After a great outcry by the Chilean people as well as pressure from abroad, Lagos was released 20 days later.

In 1987 Lagos founded the Partidos por la Democracia, another party which pressed for Pinochet's ouster. Lagos was also instrumental in forming the Concertación para la Democracia (Concert of Parties for Democracy), an alliance made up of several leftist political parties, from the centrist Partido Democracia Cristiana (Christian Democrats) to the Partido Socialista. This unified opposition, along with international condemnation of Pinochet's human rights violations forced the Chilean government to call for a plebiscite—a national yes/no vote in which the Chilean people could allow Pinochet to remain in power or demand he step down. Lagos called out loudly and defiantly, "No." In a famous television appearance Lagos turned to the camera and thrusting his index finger at it, spoke directly to Pinochet. In front of a Chile long terrified into silence by secret police, midnight arrests, and the constant threat of disappearance, Lagos accused the dictator of "torture, assassinations, and human rights violations," according to the *Presidencia de la Republica* website. The bold accusation brought Lagos increased political fame and helped break the grip of fear that paralyzed the Chilean people. In October of 1988, the country voted no against Pinochet. He stepped down as requested but he retained his role as commander of the armed forces. In addition during his reign he had created nine seats-for-life on the senate and peopled them with his supporters. Pinochet was also entitled to one of these positions. The seats were protected by the Chilean constitution—also created by Pinochet's government—which provided the senators with immunity from criminal prosecution. Pinochet was not going to give up power easily.

Appointed Minister in New Democratic Government

In 1990 Chile enjoyed its first free elections in two decades. Patricio Aylwin, a Concertación member from the Christian Democrat party was elected president. Despite his prominent role in the return of democracy, Lagos was unable to obtain a senate seat in Aylwin's government. The problem was his socialist leanings. Despite the atrocities with which Pinochet governed, he had brought economic competition to Chile, resulting in what *Institutional Investor* called, "Chile's 'free-market miracle,' some two decades of extraordinary economic success." With that success had risen powerful middle- and upper-classes dependent on private business and enterprise. They feared that Lagos would work to limit the free market. Unable to gain an elected seat, Lagos accepted an appointment as minister of education. Lagos began initiating reforms to reduce the educational gap between poor and rich schools. Lagos wrote in *Socialist Affairs Online,* "I believe that the future of Chile depends to a large degree on deeper educational reform. We must discriminate in favor of those who have less in their access to education and training." He also reversed a law banning pregnant girls from attending school.

As Chile's second free presidential elections rolled around, Lagos put in his bid for the Concertación candidacy with the backing of the Party for Democracy. However, in the primary Concertación members chose Eduardo Frei, another Christian Democrat, as their candidate. After winning the presidency, Frei appointed Lagos his minister of public works in 1994. During this appointment Lagos was able to alleviate some of the fears of the business world by demonstrating he was not bound to socialist dogma. For example, *Institutional Investor* noted, "[Lagos] won plaudits for privatizing Chile's highway system." In 1998 Lagos left his government post to gear up for the 2000 presidential elections. The same year, a Spanish judge learned that Pinochet was in London and issued a warrant for his arrest on charges of human rights violations. British officials detained the aging dictator and an international media frenzy ensued. Chileans were hysterical. Many took to the streets in support of Pinochet's arrest, brandishing pictures of loved ones who died or disappeared under the dictator. Others, mainly from the conservative right and the business realm, decried the arrest as illegal and demanded Pinochet be returned to Chile. It was in this environment that Lagos won the Concertación's candidacy by over 70%. Unfortunately his run for the presidency would not be so easy.

Under the two Concertación presidencies, Chile enjoyed some remarkable growth. Neither Aylwin nor Frei altered the country's successful free market system. Instead they instituted "a mixture of gentle social reform," according to *The Washington Quarterly* with the result being "Per capita income has almost doubled, the business neighborhoods of Santiago have filled with opulent glass-and-marble office blocks, and even the roads—always a blot on Chile's copybook—improved, thanks to a private concessions program." Nonetheless, voters had lost confidence in the party. The source

of this loss stretched back once more to Pinochet. The nine senatorial seats he had installed during his reign were preventing the Concertación government from reforming the military-focused constitution. "This failure has fueled voter frustration and helped to discredit politicians and the government." Nearly a decade after stepping down, Pinochet was still manipulating Chile. The opposition's presidential candidate, conservative Joaquin Lavin, took advantage of this irony to promote his campaign under the slogan of "Change." Lavin's strategy almost worked. He forced Lagos into a run-off election which Lagos won by barely 30,000 votes.

Became New President for New Millennium

Lagos became president of Chile in March of 2000. A journalist described his inauguration in *The Economist:* "Car horns were honked. The red, white, and blue Chilean flag was draped out of windows, trailed from cars and waved in the streets. It was one of the biggest spontaneous political celebrations Chile had seen since 1988, when General Augusto Pinochet lost the plebiscite that ended his rule." It was a joyous moment and political analysts worldwide agreed that Lagos's ascension to the presidency marked Chile's final transition into democracy. Lagos agreed. "This is a fiesta for democracy," the *Miami Herald* quoted him as saying. "Chileans should come celebrate to applaud the beginning of a new century, new government." However, when the party ended Lagos faced one of the country's biggest problems—the ever-present rift between rich and poor. Also, Chile had entered its first economic recession in decades in 1999. In addition, like his predecessors Lagos would find it difficult to make changes with the ghost of Pinochet still strangling the constitution. Finally, there was the problem of Pinochet himself. After his arrest in London, Chileans pushed for an investigation into Pinochet's actions as dictator. Through a loop in the constitution, the Chilean courts were able to indict him despite his senatorial immunity. By 2000, under investigation for dozens of human rights violations, Pinochet continued to mire the country in the past.

Some of Lagos' first actions as president carefully straddled socialism and capitalism. An economist by training, Lagos has resoundingly supported the free market system and the wealth it has brought to Chile. "We have the highest growth in Latin America," he told *Institutional Investor.* In support of that growth, Lagos secured lucrative free-trade deals with the United States and the European Union. However, he also acknowledged that the free market was ineffective in solving social ills as deeply wrought as those in Chile. "The market is the right place for allocating resources, but it shouldn't be the model on which society is built," he was quoted in *The Economist.* To that end he vowed to pump more funds into social programs such as health care, housing, and education. Lagos also proposed labor reforms including bargaining and striking rights. For this he received heavy criticism from the conservative business fronts. He countered this by explaining to *Institutional Advisor,* "All I am trying to do is have the kind of legislation that is normal in a developed country, no more than that." He also introduced an unemployment insurance program. Despite his efforts, by 2003 consensus on Lagos's presidency was mixed. Rifts were forming in the Concertación, the economy was still sluggish, and the trials of Pinochet continued to divide the nation. Many agree that Lagos has the skills to resolve these problems. One Chilean business analyst told *Institutional Investor,* "Lagos is the brightest president we have had in a long time." However, in a country where history still polarizes politics and blurs economics, being bright might not be enough. Though the outcome of his presidency is still yet to be written, his place in history is firmly assured. Lagos will always be known as the man who helped topple Pinochet, leading Chile out of bloodshed and fear and into the light of democratic freedom.

Sources

Periodicals

Economist, January 22, 2000, p. 37; March 11, 2000, p. 41; October 14, 2000, p. 43; March 8, 2003.
Institutional Investor, March 2001, p. 69.
Miami Herald, March 12, 2000, p. 11A.
Progressive, May 2000, p. 24.
Washington Quarterly, Autumn 1999, p. 181.

On-line

"Biografia de Ricardo Lagos," *Gobierno de Chile, Presidencia de la Repulica,* www.presidencia.cl (May 23, 2003).
"Chile's Lagos Takes Oath, Begins 2-Day Celebration," *Miami Herald,* www.herald.com (May 20, 2003).
"Looking towards the future," *Socialist Affairs On-line,* www.socialistinternational.org/9SocAffairs/1-V48/eLagos.html (May 22, 2003).

—Candace LaBalle

Libertad Lamarque

1908-2000

Actor, singer

Argentine actor and singer Libertad Lamarque was "the second biggest export from South America, the first being Carmen Miranda (and she was born in Portugal)," according to Austin Mutti-Mewse of the London *Independent*. She got her start singing popular Argentine tangos, began her film career in 1929, during the silent film era, and was popular for the next seven decades. Lamarque made more than 60 motion pictures and 2,000 recordings, and performed on stage and in television in her native Argentina, her adopted Mexico, and the United States, though she never learned to speak English. She turned down offers to appear in Hollywood films, and was forced to take her career to Mexico after being banned in Argentina by First Lady Eva Perón.

Lamarque was born Libertad Lamarque Bouza on November 24, 1908, in Rosario, Argentina. She was the youngest of ten children born to Gaudincio Lamarque, a Uruguayan tinsmith and contortionist, and Josefa Bouza, a seamstress and Spanish immigrant. Lamarque's father was a militant anarchist and was in prison when she was born for voicing his political beliefs. Upon hearing his daughter had been born, he sent his request from prison that she be named Libertad, the Spanish word for "liberty." Lamarque began performing in front of her family for flowers and coins as a young girl, and soon discovered she loved performing for an audience.

Debuted in Argentine Silents

Lamarque first took the stage at the age of eight. After moving with her family to Buenos Aires in 1922, she began working in the theater. She garnered notice and applause for her first official professional role as the heroine in a three-month run of *Madre Tierra* in 1923. The *Madre Tierra* stage manager introduced Lamarque to producer Emilio Romero to record an album of tangos with her. The album was a success and Lamarque married Romero in 1927, when she was just 18. She had her only child, a daughter named Mirtha, the following year. Before long, Lamarque's career took its toll on the marriage. Romero could not tolerate her long studio hours and was jealous of the actors she was seen with. Divorce was not legal in Argentina at the time and it took Lamarque 12 years to have the marriage officially dissolved. A string of stormy romances followed her split with Romero. One story recalls her, heartbroken,

At a Glance . . .

Born Libertad Lamarque Bouza on November 24, 1908, in Rosario, Argentina; died on December 12, 2000, in Mexico City, Mexico; daughter of Gaudincio Lamarque (a Uruguayan tinsmith and contortionist) and Josefa Bouza (a Spanish seamstress); married Emilio Romero, 1927 (divorced); married Alfredo Malerba (died 1994); children: Mirtha.

Career: Actress, 1916-00; singer, 1920s-00; made more than 60 films and 2,000 recordings.

Awards: Mexican Cinema Arts and Sciences, 2000; Hispanic Film Makers Board, Lifetime Achievement Award; Hispanic Film Festival of Miami, honoree, film retrospective; Santa Fe Film Festival, honoree.

jumping out of a hotel window while on tour in Chile. She happened to land on a dentist who was walking by, and he became a Latin American hero.

Lamarque's music was a mix of soulful tangos, boleros, waltzes, milongas, and Mexican rancheras. She influenced such artists as Jennifer Lopez, Tom Jones, Paul McCartney, and Nat King Cole. Her home for most of her musical career was the RCA (later BMG) record label. She recorded her biggest hits, "Chilenito" and "Gaucho Sol" for the label in 1926. Her 1991 album, *Nadie Se Va del Todo*, was also immensely successful. "I believe Madonna played second fiddle in the music charts when it was released," she was quoted as saying in the *Independent*.

The young singer made her screen debut in the 1929 silent film *Adios Argentina*, directed by Luis Moglia Barth. When Barth was hired to direct Argentina's first sound film, *Tango* in 1933, he again chose Lamarque as his star. Lamarque would continue throughout her career as the leading lady in such films as *Aydame a Vivir, Besos Brujos, La Ley que Olvidaron, Madreselva*, and *Puerta Cerrada*.

Beckoned by Hollywood, Banned by Perón

Before long, Lamarque's success in Argentina became known, and Hollywood beckoned. Both Paramount and MGM studios offered her lengthy contracts in 1940, but she turned them down. Her Latin-American contemporaries, such as Lupita Tovar and Mona Maris, had found success in Hollywood, but were often typecast as evil or wild women. Lamarque spoke no English and did not want to be taken advantage of in Holly-

wood, though she later would travel to perform there. "I have no regrets," she is quoted as saying in the *Independent*.

A petty catfight between Lamarque and costar Eva Duarte on the set of 1944's *La Cabalgata del Circo*, left Lamarque unable to find work in Argentina for a time. The two actors squabbled frequently over costumes and the script. The tension between them peaked when Duarte emerged from her dressing room wearing Lamarque's dress. Lamarque slapped her costar across the face. Duarte married Juan Perón the next year. When she became Argentina's influential first lady in 1946, Eva Perón made it virtually impossible for Lamarque to get work in Argentina. She forbade the nation's radio stations and film studios to play her music or hire her. Lamarque has denied the event ever took place, "but her career in Argentina clearly ended when Peron came to power," Myrna Oliver wrote in the *Los Angeles Times*.

The ban took its toll on Lamarque who, with her second husband, industrialist Alfredo Malerba, eventually moved to Mexico, where she found enormous success in films, records, and concerts. She broke box-office records there with such films as *Gran Casino* in 1947 and *Escuela de Musica* in 1957. She was part of Mexican cinema's Golden Age of the 1940s, along with such Mexican movie legends as Jorge Negrete, Dolores del Rio, Pedro Infante, Arturo de Cordoba, Jorge Rivero, and Julio Aleman. "Strangely, even with a strong Argentine accent that never quite went away, she became the darling of Mexican cinema," Carl Mora, an expert on Latin American film, told the *New York Times*. "Her magnetic presence made for quite a life trajectory." She performed in New York City's prestigious Carnegie Hall in 1947.

Returned Home to Career in Soaps

Lamarque's 1960 return to Argentina was heralded by her fans, who met her at the airport, bearing signs that read "Welcome Back" and "Long Live Libertad." Television beckoned when Lamarque returned to Argentina, and she answered the call. She was a favorite guest on talk shows, reflecting and telling anecdotes from her long film career. She joined Mexican entertainer Cantinflas and actor Dolores del Rio to make director Nancy Cardenas' 1977 documentary about Mexican film. Lamarque got her start in television soap operas in 1981 when Cardenas cast her in *Soledad*. In 1998 she joined the cast of *La Usurpadora*.

Lamarque died in Mexico City on December 12, 2000. Earlier that year, Lamarque was honored by the Mexican Academy of Cinema Arts and Sciences, which gave her the Mexican equivalent of an Oscar for her work. She also received a Lifetime Achievement Award from the Hispanic Film Makers Board, and was honored at the Hispanic Film Festival of Miami, which featured a retrospective of her films. Two weeks before her death, she filmed the Christmas episode of *Carita de Angel,* the Mexican soap opera she had been working on. She was invited to receive an honor at the Santa Fe Film Festival as a pioneer of Latin-American film, but Lupita Tovar, Lamarque's contemporary who also was honored, accepted the award on her behalf. Just one month before her death, Lamarque was quoted as saying, "I'll work forever," according to Austin Mutti-Mewse in the *Independent.* "As long as I have a good pulse to put my make-up on, I'll keep working."

Selected works

Albums

"Chilenito," 1926.
"Gaucho Sol," 1926.
Canta Canciones de Maria Grever, RCA, 1978.
Nadie Se Va del Todo, BMG, 1991.

Film

Adiós Argentina, 1930.
Tango, 1933.
El Lma de Bandoneón, 1935.
Ayúdame a Vivir, 1936.
Besos Brujos, 1937.
Madreselva, 1938.
Puerta Cerrada, 1939.
Gran Casino, 1947.

Arrullo de Dios, 1967.
La Mamá de la Novia, 1978.

Stage

Madre Tierra, 1923.

Television

Show de Libertad Lamarque, 1964.
Soledad, 1981.
La Usurpadora, 1998.
Carita de Ángel, 2000.

Sources

Periodicals

Daily Telegraph (London, England), December 14, 2000.
Independent (London, England), December 19, 2000, p. 6.
Guardian (London, England), January 26, 2001, p. 24.
Los Angeles Times, December 15, 2000, p. B6.
New York Times, December 25, 2000, p. B6.
Washington Post, December 16, 2000, p. B7.

On-line

"Libertad Lamarque," *All Music Guide,* www.allmusic.com (April 7, 2003).
"Libertad Lamarque," *Internet Movie Database,* www.imdb.com (April 7, 2003).

—Brenna Sanchez

Luis Leal

1907—

Scholar, literary critic

On the same day Charles Lindbergh completed his historic crossing of the Atlantic Ocean—May 21, 1927—Luis Leal stepped off the train at Union Station in Chicago. As with Lindbergh, this Mexican native would become known as a pioneer in his field. Professor Leal helped develop the study of Latin American literature and is considered one of the founders of the field of Chicano/Chicana (Mexican American) literary studies. His extensive works include books, bibliographies, anthologies, and hundreds of journal and newspaper articles and essays, published for both U.S. and Latin American audiences. Much of Leal's works put Mexican, Chicano, and Latino literature and writers in historical context. They reflect his view that research is part of a dialogue on how to advance community or social issues. Affectionately called Don Luis, Leal also helped develop scholarship by working with students who wrote the first dissertations on world-renown Mexican and Chicano writers.

Just three years before the outbreak of the Mexican Revolution, Leal was born into a wealthy family of cattle ranchers that lived in the town of Linares, Mexico, on September 17, 1907. He, two brothers, two sisters, five aunts, and his parents inhabited a large

house taken care of by servants. His father supported the uprising against dictator Porfino Díaz, but when the fighting drew near their home in 1915, he moved his family to Mexico City for three years before returning to Linares in 1918. During the Revolution, Leal witnessed some executions and his family had cattle stolen. Mario T. García remarked in *Luis Leal: An Auto/Biography,* that the exposure gave "Don Luis a humanistic worldview and a sympathy for social justice." The idea of revolution would become an important research theme for Leal.

Need for Education Sparked Self-Motivation

Leal attended Catholic school as a child, where he read translations of Italian stories. The school taught no foreign languages; however, the stories sparked an interest that he pursued by minoring in Italian as a university graduate student. The options open to Leal following high school were limited because many universities in Mexico were not operating. For a few years he studied at home, reading texts selected by his mother and father. His father, who had studied

At a Glance . . .

Born on September 17, 1907, in Linares, NL, Mexico; married Gladys Clemens in 1936; children: Antonio and Luis Alonso. *Education:* Northwestern University, BS, Spanish, 1940; University of Chicago, MA, Spanish, 1941; University of Chicago, PhD, Spanish and Italian, 1950. *Military Service:* U.S. Army, 1943-45.

Career: University of Chicago, instructor, 1942-43, 1946-48, assistant professor, 1948-52; University of Mississippi, associate prof, 1952-56; University of Arizona, visiting prof, 1955-56; Emory University, assoc prof, 1956-59; University of Illinois, Urbana, assoc prof, 1959-62, prof, 1962-76, professor emeritus, 1976–; University of California, Santa Barbara (UCSB), visiting prof, 1976-77, 1985-91, 1993-94, 1997–; University of California, Los Angeles, visiting prof, 1977-78; UCSB Center for Chicano Studies, research scholar, 1978-80, 1984-85, acting director, 1980-83, *Ventana Abierta: Revista Latina de Literatura, Arte y Cultura*, editor, 1990s–; Stanford University, visiting prof, 1985, 1991-93; UCSB Department of Chicano Studies, endowed chair, 1994-96.

Memberships: Academia Norteamericana de la Lengua Española; Academia Española; Modern Language Association of America.

Selected awards: Scholar of the Year, National Association for Chicano Studies, 1988; Aguila Aztec Award, Mexican government, 1991; University of California, Santa Barbara, Luis Leal Endowed Chair of Chicano Studies, 1994; National Humanities Medal, President Bill Clinton, 1997; honorary doctor of literature, University of Illinois, Urbana-Champaign, 2000.

Addresses: *Home*—542 Wessex Ct., Goleta, CA 93117-1600.

After arriving in Chicago, Leal went to live with a family from Mexico in a poor west side neighborhood made up of mostly European immigrants. His lack of English skills delayed his entrance into the university for several years. He gradually improved his English with the help of Gladys Clemens, whom he married in 1936, and by watching movies and auditing classes. During this time, he also worked as a Spanish proofreader, read Spanish novels, and developed friendships with other Latin Americans, including the Spanish consul.

Once Leal entered Northwestern University, he found himself taking more Spanish classes than mathematics courses. When a Spanish professor suggested he change majors, he began studying literary criticism and literary history. By the time he earned his bachelor of arts degree in 1940, Leal had decided to become a professor. The following year he completed his master's degree at the University of Chicago, writing his thesis, a literary history, on Amado Nervo. Because he identified himself as a *norteño*, Leal also wrote a few papers while a student on the themes and other characteristics of northern Mexican writers.

Began to Study Mexican Literature

The second World War interrupted Leal's pursuit of a doctorate degree. Since he had become a naturalized citizen, the U.S. Army was able to draft him in 1943 and sent him to the Pacific theater. He served with forces that retook the Philippines from Japan. Two years later he resumed his studies upon his return to the United States. Before he had left, Professor Carlos Castillo asked Leal to collaborate with him on the first anthology of Mexican literature published in the United States. The *Antología de la literatura mexicana* was published in 1944. That same year, Leal also edited short stories for high school students under the title *Cuentecitos: Retold and Adopted from the Spanish of Vicente Riva Palacio* and condensed the first novel published in Mexico, *El periquillo sarniento* for educational publication.

Leal learned to do research and apply literary criticism while working on his Ph.D. dissertation. His advisor was from Argentina and emphasized Latin American literature, a departure from the Spanish peninsular literature emphasized by his undergraduate professors. For his dissertation Leal focused on the origins of the Mexican short story, and specifically, wrote Garcia in Leal's biography, the "fictional elements contained within the chronicles written by the Spanish after conquest of the Aztec empire."

While in Chicago Leal was active in Spanish cultural and Latino community-based organizations. He and his friends formed the *Sociedad Española*, a Spanish American literary club. He presented one of his first papers there, which he later published. However, Leal did not yet think Chicano literature deserved university study, although he read Spanish-language newspapers

engineering, introduced Leal to nineteenth century Spanish novels and discussed newspaper articles with him daily. Eventually, despite knowing little English, Leal applied to and was accepted by Northwestern University, a school many of his hometown friends had attended. He set out to study mathematics.

featuring such stories. Together with activist Frank Paz and with the support of the City of Chicago, Leal founded the Mexican American Council to assist people coming from Mexico.

Moved From University to University

The University of Chicago employed Leal as an instructor and made him an assistant professor prior to his earning his Ph.D. in 1950. In 1952, because he was already published, the University of Mississippi offered him a tenured position as an associate professor in its Romance language department. At Mississippi Leal focused on Mexican and Latin American short stories. He also produced *México: civilizaciones y culturas* in 1955, a book based on lectures he had given at the University of Chicago on periods in Mexican culture.

Wishing to get away from the civil unrest in the South, in 1956 Leal accepted an associate professor position at Emory University he had been offered shortly after his arrival at the University of Mississippi. At Emory he became a literary historian. His works *Breve historia del cuento mexicano*, *Antología del cuento mexicano*, and *Bibliografía del cuento mexicano* reflected his particular interest in Mexican short stories. Also at Emory he studied Mexican fables, or *fábulas,* most of which criticized the Spanish colonial administration.

In 1959 Leal joined the faculty of the University of Illinois. The move put him in the largest Spanish-language department in the Midwest and provided him access to a vast library of Spanish and Latin American materials. He concentrated his research on Mexican literature, while teaching and mentoring graduate students, including 44 who completed their doctoral degrees. He also often hosted *tertulias* where colleagues, friends, and students discussed life, literature, and art.

Made Significant Publications

While at the University of Illinois, Leal expanded his research focus from short stories to include novels and major Mexican and Latin American writers. He became especially interested in writers of the Mexican Revolution. Leal published extensively and read papers at scholarly conferences, often about disregarded subjects. Among the more than 200 articles he wrote for U.S. and Latin American audiences was a long piece on the first novel published in Spanish in the United States, in which he identifies the author of *Jicotencal.* In the 1960s he contributed essays to a Mexico City newspaper's Sunday literary supplement and to such scholarly journals as *Cuadernos Americanos* and *Historia Mexicana*. He also completed more than 30 definitive books on Latin American and Chicano literature. He expanded an essay written for *Encyclopaedia Britannica* in the 1950s on Mariano Azuela, the creator of the novel of the Mexican Revolution, into a full-length study based on reviews of Azuela's published

works, personal papers, and interviews with his widow. Leal's literature surveys included *Panorama de la literatura mexicana actual*, an assessment of twentieth century Mexican literature, and *Breve historia de la literatura hispanoamericana.*

The Chicano movement of the mid-1960s made Leal aware of the cultural and artistic contributions of Mexican Americans. He developed an interest in Chicano literature, which traced its roots from the Spanish colonial period. Garcia explained, "Don Luis became not only one of the first senior scholars in the country to champion this new writing and research, but he also became one of its first scholars. His previous work in Mexican and Latin American literature contributed to helping establish the cultural linkages between Hispanic literature south of the border and Chicano literature north of it. Moreover, his stature and importance in the early days of Chicano literary criticism made it difficult for others to dismiss this research area as nothing more than political rhetoric." Leal participated in one of the first sessions on Chicano literature at a Modern Language Association meeting; he read a paper that commented on the poets José Montoya, Alurista, and Ricardo Sánchez. He also wrote and edited numerous books and articles on the new genre. Book-length works include *Corridos y canciones de Aztlá, A Decade of Chicano Literature (1970-1979), Aztlán y México: Perfiles literarios e históricos*, and *No Longer Voiceless*. His book on *Juan Rulfo* put the Chicano author's works in literary, historical, and social context. In 1988, Salvador Guereña compiled *Luis Leal: A Bibliography with Interpretative and Critical Essays,* which covers his published works.

Continued Working After Retirement

In 1976 the University of Illinois had a mandatory retirement policy that forced Leal to end his professional career there. However, that circumstance also enabled him to further advance contemporary Chicano literary criticism. He and his wife moved to Santa Barbara, where he continued his research and taught courses in Chicano literature and Mexican cultural traditions for the Department of Chicano Studies at the University of California, Santa Barbara (UCSB) campus. As senior research fellow at UCSB's Center for Chicano Studies, he served as its acting director in the early 1980s to keep it open. UCSB honored him by naming the first chair in the United States dedicated to Chicano studies after him. Leal has also been honored by being the subject of the Spanish-language books *Homenaje a Luis Leal: estudios sobre literature hispanoamerica* and *Don Luis Leal: una vida y dos culturas/conversaciones con Victor Fuentes.*

Now in his nineties, Leal continues to share his scholarship as a visiting professor at UCSB. He also edits a literary periodical sponsored by the Center for Chicano Studies called *Ventana Abierta: Revista Latina de Literatura, Arte y Culrura*. It is the only literary journal in the United States published in Spanish.

Selected writings

(With Carlos Castillo) *Antología de la literatura mexicana*, 1944.

(Editor) *Cuentecitos: Retold and Adopted from the Spanish of Vicente Riva Palacio*, 1944.

(Editor) *El periquillo sarniento*, 1946.

México: civilizaciones y culturas, 1955, rev. 1971.

Breve historia del cuento mexicano, 1957, 1990.

(Editor) *Antología del cuento mexicano*, 1957.

Bibliografía del cuento mexicano, 1958.

(Contributor) *Cuardenos Americanos*, 1960s.

(Contributor) *Historia Mexicana*, 1960s.

Mariano Azuela, vida y obra, 1961.

Panorama de la literature mexicana actual, 1968.

(Editor with Joseph Silverman) *Siglo veinte*, 1968.

Breve historia de la literature hispanoamericana, 1971.

Mariano Azuela, 1971.

Corridos y canciones de Aztlá, 1980, 1986.

(Editor with others) *Día de los muertos*, 1983.

Juan Rulfo, 1983.

Aztlán y México: Perfiles literarios e históricos, 1985.

No Longer Voiceless, 1995.

(Editor) *Ventana Abierta: Revista Latina de Literatura, Arte y Cultura*, 1996-.

(With Victor Fuentes) *Don Luis Leal: Una vida y dos culturas. Conversaciones con Victor Fuentes*, 1998.

(With Mario T. Garcia) *Luis Leal: An Auto/Biography*, 2000.

Sources

Books

Dictionary of Hispanic Biography, Gale Research, 1996.

Luis Leal: An Auto/Biography, University of Texas Press, 2000.

On-line

"Don Luis Leal: One Life, Two Cultures," *Latina/Latino Studies Program at the University of Illinois at Urbana-Champaign*, www.lls.uiuc.edu/newsletter/don_luis.htm (June 12, 2003).

"Luis Leal," *Contemporary Authors Online*, reproduced in Gale's *Biography Resource Center*, www.galenet.galegroup.com/servelet/BioRC (June 12, 2003).

"Luis Leal," *Biography Resource Center*, www.galenet.galegroup.com/servlet/BioRC (June 12, 2003).

Other

Additional information for this profile was obtained through a curriculum vitae provided by Dr. Luis Leal on December 13, 2002.

—Doris Morris Maxfield

Wendy Lucero-Schayes

1963—

Olympic diver

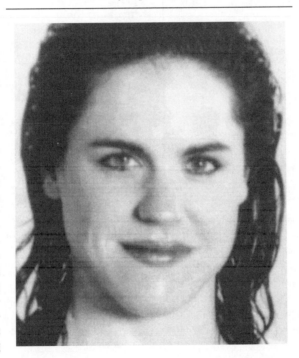

Olympic springboard diver Wendy Lucero-Schayes' life-long desire to succeed as an athlete led to an impressive career that included nine national titles, three U.S. Olympic Festival medals, and participation in the 1988 Olympics. She flourished as a diver in the early 1990s, demolishing the competition in almost every event that she entered between 1988 and 1992. While she was kept from competing in the 1992 Olympics due to an intestinal problem which lead to her retirement from the sport, Lucero-Schayes fell back on a long time career in sports broadcasting for major networks like ABC and ESPN and has remained an active voice in the world of women's sports.

Wendy Lucero was born on June 26, 1963, in Denver, Colorado, the daughter of Don Lucero, an electrician, and Shirley Lucero, a homemaker, both immigrants from Spain. As a young girl, Wendy admired her older sister's athleticism, competing against her whenever possible—and often coming in as runner-up—but Wendy remained persistent. She recalled to *Great Women in Sports* that finishing second "kept me in a 'trying to achieve mode.' I would always strive to be the best I could be because I wanted to grasp what my sister was attaining." Once she caught up to and matched her sister's sports success, Lucero-Schayes went on to test unexplored athletic challenges.

At the age of nine, Lucero-Schayes began dreaming of competing in the Olympics. Her talents lay in gymnastics, figure skating, and spring-board diving. Having begun gymnastics and ice skating lessons at a relatively late age, however, put her at a disadvantage in those sports. An even bigger challenge to the young athlete was her family's inability to afford the high cost of premium skating or gymnastics training essential to developing an Olympian. So Lucero-Schayes turned to springboard diving, a sport she first tried as a pre-teen. Her gymnastics training lent to her diving abilities, and she became remarkably competitive in springboard events. During her sophomore year of high school, Lucero-Schayes came in fourth in Colorado's state diving championships and she finished in second place her senior year. A promising springboard diver, she also competed in national events as a high school student, placing sixth in the three-meter diving event at the Junior Olympic Championships when she was a senior.

An Academic All-American, Lucero-Schayes received a full scholarship to the University of Nebraska, where she won the 1985 NCAA championship on the one-

At a Glance . . .

Born Wendy Lucero on June 26, 1963, in Denver, CO; married Dan Schayes in 1991. *Education:* University of Nebraska, BA, 1986.

Career: Diver, 1984-92; sports broadcaster, 1986–.

Awards: Phillips 66 Outdoor Championships, first place, 1984,1985; NCAA championship on one-meter springboard, first place, 1985; U.S. Olympic Festival, gold medal, 1987, 1989, 1990; American Cup II tournament, gold medal, 1987; McDonald's International, bronze medal, 1987; National Championships, one-meter and three-meter events, first place, 1989, 1990; National Indoor Championship, first place, one-meter and three-meter events, 1991; National Outdoor Championship, first place, one meter, second place, three meter, 1991; World Championship, silver medal, 1991; Alamo International Competition, silver medal, 1991; voted U.S. Female Diving Athlete of the Year, 1990, 1991.

Address: *Home*—Orlando, FL.

meter springboard and placed first at both the 1984 and 1985 Phillips 66 Outdoor Championships. In 1986 she earned a bachelor's degree in television sales and management and worked as a production assistant for televised sporting events. She began a career as a freelance sportscaster for ABC, NBC, and ESPN, and hosted "Focus Colorado," a Denver talk show. In the meantime, she continued to rigorously train for the 1988 Olympics.

In preparation for the 1988 Olympics in Seoul, Korea, Lucero-Schayes moved from the one-meter springboard to the three-meter springboard. In 1987 she won a gold medal at both the U.S. Olympic Festival and the American Cup II tournament. The same year she earned a bronze medal at the McDonald's International. Yet believing her performance could improve, she changed coaches and tried new training techniques. During this time Lucero-Schayes also learned that her mother had cancer. While this would have caused many athletes to falter, Lucero-Schayes used it as motivation to win the Olympic medal, not for herself, but for her mother.

Considered an underdog competitor in the 1988 Olympic Trials, she finished in second place at the 1988 Olympic Trials. In Seoul she came in sixth in the three-meter springboard event, a more than respect-

able performance that further enhanced her profile in sports as well as in the Hispanic community. Afterwards, she returned to Denver and continued her work in broadcasting. She met NBA basketball pro Dan Schayes at a charity event and the two married in 1991. For a time she divided her personal and training time between Milwaukee and Denver—where her husband played for the Nuggets—as well as Ann Arbor, Michigan, where she practiced with coach Dick Kimball.

Wendy Lucero-Schayes' best years as a diver came following the 1988 Olympics. She won the Olympic Festival titles in 1989 and 1990, the same years she also took the national championships in both the one-meter and three-meter events. In 1991 she won both springboard events in the national indoor championships, placed first in the one-meter and second place in the three-meter outdoors, and seized a silver medal at the world championship and Alamo International competitions. These impressive accomplishments led to her being voted the 1990 and 1991 U.S. Female Diving Athlete of the Year.

In the early 1990s Lucero-Schayes received a small bit of humorous media attention because of the fact that she shared the same name, Wendy, with two other world-class-level springboard divers. One of them, Wendy Wyland, would become yet another Wendy Lucero when she married Lucero-Schayes' younger brother Chad. Olympic Coach Ron O'Brien said it was especially difficult to have three Wendys on the U.S. team. He told the *Seattle Times*, "It was a bit of a problem when they were all three in the same training group. We used to have to use names other than Wendy."

The humor ended, however, when while preparing for the 1992 Olympics, Lucero-Schayes came down with a severe intestinal infection. The illness hampered her training, and as a result, she managed to only finish third in the Olympic trials, losing the opportunity to go to Barcelona, Spain. Though disappointed to miss participating in an Olympics held in her parents' native country, Lucero-Schayes remained proud of her diving career. She told *Great Women in Sports,* "Diving has been wonderful to me. Not only did it pay for a college education, but I was able to travel around the world, nothing that my parents were ever financially capable of doing."

After her husband retired from the NBA, the Schayes made their home in Orlando, Florida, with their cats. Exposure and success as an outstanding, world-class athlete also benefited Lucero-Schayes in her communications career. With broadcast work that included covering the diving world championships on ESPN, she finds pleasure and purpose working in television and speaking to audiences on motivational topics. She told *Great Women in Sports,* "The success I've had in sports overcoming those people who didn't think that I could [succeed] has made me like myself better and find out, 'Yeah, I am capable, and I'm not going to let them determine what I can do.' Hopefully I can share that with others."

Sources

Books

Great Women in Sports, Visible Ink Press, 1996.

Periodicals

Seattle Times, May 14, 1990.
Sports Illustrated, January 14, 1991.
USA TODAY, August 3, 1990; June 17, 1992.

On-line

"Wendy Lucero-Schayes," *Biography Resource Center,* www.galenet.com/servlet/BioRC (June 12, 2003).

—Kim Burton

Michael A. Mares

1945—

Mammologist, field biologist

Mammalogist Michael A. Mares has a rodent, a bat, and a parasite named after him. Mares, the world's foremost expert on the natural history of desert rodents, is responsible for the discovery of the three creatures. When he isn't setting up field research in the deserts of Argentina, Iran, Egypt, or the United States, Mares is a professor at Oklahoma University and, until 2003, was director of the Sam Noble Oklahoma Museum of Natural History. Under Mares' leadership, the museum underwent an extensive overhaul that resulted in sky-rocketing attendance.

Mares was born on March 11, 1945, in Albuquerque, New Mexico, to Ernesto Gustavo and Rebecca Gabriela (Devine) Mares. Mares grew up in New Mexico and enrolled as an undergraduate biology major at the University of New Mexico in Albuquerque in 1963, with his sights set on a career in medicine. Less than two years later, his focus had shifted to zoology, and he took his first foreign field-research trip to Mexico in 1966. Mares returned from the trip with an infectious disease he picked up in a bat cave. The infection landed him in the hospital and almost killed him, but did not deter him from his developing passion for field biology.

The disease did get in the way of Mares getting drafted to fight in the Vietnam War, however; he was given a permanent deferment because of damage to his lungs. He married Lynn Ann Brusin, now an attorney, in 1966. The couple has two sons, who were born on their parents' field trips to Argentina.

Studied Desert Life During Field Research

After graduating from the University of New Mexico, Mares pursued his master's degree at Fort Hays State College in Hays, Kansas. There, he received thorough training in what he referred to as the "ologies" in *A Desert Calling: Life in a Forbidding Landscape*: mammalogy, herpetology, ornithology, ichthyology, plant and animal ecology, wildlife ecology, field biology, human ecology and conservation, the biology of the Southwest, and comparative physiology. He was then accepted to the Ph.D. program at the University of Texas at Austin, where he was sent into the deserts of South America to study mammals. Mares claimed mammalogist Oldfield Thomas as his hero; Thomas named nearly 3,000 species and subspecies of mammals during his lifetime.

At a Glance . . .

Born on March 11, 1945, in Albuquerque, NM; son of Ernesto Gustavo and Rebecca Gabriela Mares; married Lynn Ann Brusin, August 27, 1966; children: Gabriel Andres, Daniel Alejandro. *Education:* University of New Mexico, BS, 1967; Fort Hays Kansas State College (now University), MS, 1969; Univ of Texas at Austin, PhD, 1973.

Career: Universidad Nacional de Cordoba, Argentina, adjunct professor of zoology, 1971; Universidad Nacional de Tucumán, Instituto Miguel Lillo, Tucumán, Argentina, adj prof of zoology, 1972, visiting professor of ecology, 1974; Univ of Pittsburgh, assistant/associate prof of biological sciences, 1973-81; Univ of Arizona Tucson, visiting prof of ecology and evolutionary biology, 1980-81; Univ of Oklahoma, Department of Zoology, assoc prof of zoology, 1981-85, Stovall Museum, assoc curator of mammals, 1981-85, OK Museum of Natural History, director, 1983-03, curator of mammals, 1985–, Department of Zoology, prof of zoology 1985–, distinguished research professor, 2003–; Sam Noble OK Museum of Natural History, distinguished research curator, 2003–.

Selected memberships: American Association for the Advancement of Science; Amer Society of Mammalogists; Assn of Science Museum Directors; Ecological Soc of America; Sociedad de Biología de Chile; Southwestern Association of Naturalist.

Selected awards: Fulbright-Hays Research Fellow, 1976; National Chicano Don W. Tinkle Research Excellence Award, Southwestern Assn of Naturalists, 1989; C. Hart Merriam Award, Amer Soc of Mammalogists, 2000; OK Higher Education Hall of Fame, 2002; AAAS Fellow, Amer Assn for the Advancement of Science, 2002.

Addresses: *Home*—3930 Charing Cross Court, Norman, OK 73072. *Office*—Sam Noble Oklahoma Museum of Natural History, University of Oklahoma, Norman, OK 73072.

Mares has devoted much of his career to studying desert mammals and how they have adapted to survive in what is commonly seen as a hot, dry wasteland. To the average observer, it might seem that Mares' job is a tedious and boring one. "The animals that I study are not as charismatic as the African lions ...," Mares wrote in *A Desert Calling*. "I have focused instead on the uncharismatic, the rodents and other small mammals that pass remarkable lives mostly hidden from view...." What keeps Mares intrigued, he continued, is that "Field biology involves daily encounters with the wondrous."

Field biologists, especially those who work in foreign countries, face disease, accidents, bureaucratic glitches before their work even starts, often for months or years at a stretch. While many scientists deplore fieldwork, because it often takes place under appalling and dangerous conditions, Mares thrives on it. "Mares has put himself into great discomfort and occasional danger in nearly every desert of the world, largely because he is consumed by a personal quest to understand ...," colleague Stephen Jay Gould wrote in his foreword to *A Desert Calling*.

Wrote Field Narratives While Teaching

What also sets Mares apart from other scientists is his lively and engaging writing style. The author constructed *A Desert Calling: Life in a Forbidding Landscape* to be both informative and descriptive of his field experience, but the book also succeeded in being entertaining and autobiographical. His tales of both the hardships and rewards of field work prove his worth as a storyteller, as well as a scientist. Mares "paints amazing portraits" of desert animals and the ways they have adapted to survive, according to *Science News*. Tim Markus of *Library Journal* elaborated: "It is a testament to his love of biology and his abilities as a writer that he is able to convey the excitement that accompanies the discovery of a new species after surviving the numerous hardships of extended fieldwork."

"Field narratives have certain conventions," Gould observed in his foreword, "and Mares follows them there, but with a verbal freshness (and a fine sense for a good yarn) that will delight even the most sophisticated urbanite." Of the two major requirements of the field-narrative genre, Gould continued, "one must first tell terrific stories about animals—as Mares does again and again. Second, one must relate the tales of danger, biting bugs, venomous snakes, near drowning, strandings in the desert, and meetings with weird and dangerous people—the occasional but inevitable incidents that no one really loves when they are happening, but that more than repay the debt in the pleasure of later telling." Mares is also the author of more than 155 articles, as well as reviews, lectures, addresses, grants, and contracts. He has served as editor of numerous books and scientific publications.

In addition to his research work in barren desert environments, Mares has spent his career thoroughly entrenched in academia. A string of assistant and associate professorships led to his title as distinguished research professor in the department of zoology at the University of Oklahoma. Mares also is distinguished research curator for the University-affiliated Sam Noble Oklahoma Museum of Natural History, a post he took in 2003 after stepping down as the museum's director.

Shared Wondrous World Through Museum

Mares became the director of the Sam Noble Oklahoma Museum of Natural History in 1983. After struggling for some years with both an up-and-down economy and shifts in university and museum administration, Mares undertook a $40 million renovation of the museum. Mares himself worked to raise the money from public and private donors. In the end, the museum became a state-of-the-art attraction and educational facility. The museum included classrooms for Oklahoma University graduate and undergraduate students, and featured digital and interactive exhibits that left the old, yellowed bones of yesterday's natural history museums in the dust. "You can't present this stuff in a dry manner anymore," Mares told the *Wall Street Journal*. "People won't come and see it." But come and see it they did; in the first two months after its reopening, the museum attracted 100,000 visitors—more people than had previously attended the museum in a year.

Gould summed up Mares' achievements in his foreword to *A Desert Calling:* "Mares has truly proven ... that we live on a most wondrous planet, a place where every nook of space and every sentient object (even the insentient ones, for that matter) loudly proclaim the truth of Shakespeare's appended examples for his famous proclamation about the sweet uses of adversity: 'sermons in stones, and good in every thing.'"

Selected writings

(Editor, with H. H. Genoways) *Mammalian Biology in South America,* Pymatuning Laboratory of Ecology, Special Publication, 1982.

(Editor) Charles Banks Wilson's *Search for the Purebloods,* Special Publication, 1983.

Heritage at Risk: Oklahoma's Hidden Treasure, Special Publication, Oklahoma Museum of Natural History, 1988.

(With R. A. Ojeda, and R. M. Barquez) *Guide to the Mammals of Salta Province, Argentina,* The University of Oklahoma Press, 1989.

(With Caire, W., B. P. Glass, J. T. Tyler) *The Mammals of Oklahoma,* The University of Oklahoma Press, 1989.

(Editor, with D. J. Schmidly) *Latin American Mammalogy: History, Biodiversity and Conservation,* The University of Oklahoma Press, 1991.

(With Barquez, R. M. and R. A. Ojeda) *The Mammals of Tucumán (Los Mamíferos de Tucumán),* Special Publication, Oklahoma Museum of Natural History, 1991.

(With Barquez, R. M., and N. Giannini) *Guide to the Bats of Argentina (Guía de los Murciélagos de Argentina),* Special Publication, Oklahoma Museum of Natural History, 1993.

(Editor) *Encyclopedia of Deserts,* University of Oklahoma Press, 1999.

(Editor, with Barquez, R. M. and J. K. Braun) *The Bats of Argentina,* Special Publications, Museum of Texas Tech University, Lubbock, Texas, 1999.

(Editor) *A University Natural History Museum for the New Millennium,* Sam Noble Oklahoma Museum of Natural History, 2001.

A Desert Calling: Life in a Forbidding Landscape, Harvard Univ. Press, 2002.

Also is the author of more than 155 articles, as well as reviews, lectures, addresses, grants, and contracts. In addition, wrote and produced the video *Behind the Rain: The Story of a Museum,* in 2002.

Sources

Books

Mares, Michael A., *A Desert Calling: Life in a Forbidding Landscape,* Harvard Univ. Press, 2002.

Periodicals

Journal Record (Oklahoma City, Oklahoma), September 28, 1994.
Library Journal, April 1, 2002, p. 135.
New Scientist, May 4, 2002, p. 56.
Science, July 1, 1983, p. 49.
Science News, June 22, 2002, p. 399.
Wall Street Journal, June 30, 2000, p. W12.

Other

Additional information for this profile was provided by Michael A. Mares.

—Brenna Sanchez

Cheech Marin

1946—

Actor

Actor Cheech Marin is one of Hollywood's most recognizable Hispanic stars. Once half of the stoner-hippie comedy team Cheech and Chong, he enjoyed immense success in the 1970s, but went on to tackle a far wider range of roles. To the surprise of many, he has even played a police detective, and in 1992 released an album of children's songs. Marin has also become a renowned patron of Chicano art, and is thought to own the largest collection of such in private hands. "I personify all the changes our generation went through, in the extreme," he joked with a *People* interviewer in 1998.

The actor was born Richard Anthony Marin on July 13, 1946, in Los Angeles, the third generation in a Mexican-American family. English was his first language, and the accent he later used in the Cheech and Chong routines was wholly fabricated. His father was a Los Angeles police officer, and an uncle on the force was the LAPD's highest-ranking detective of Hispanic heritage for a number of years. The "Cheech" nickname came from an uncle, who peered at the infant in his crib and declared he resembled a chicharron, the Mexican deep-fried pork skin treat. Marin and his three

sisters grew up first in the South-Central area of Los Angeles, a rough section of the city. "By the time I was 7, I had seen three murders," he told *People* magazine. His parents then relocated to the San Fernando Valley area, settling in Granada Hills. "It was like moving from Nigeria to Knotts Berry Farm," Marin said in a *San Francisco Chronicle* interview with Jesse Hamlin.

Started Entertaining With Tommy Chong

As a teen, Marin earned top grades in school, and was increasingly drawn to art and art history. He possessed few artistic skills of the visual kind himself, however. "I was always a musician," he told *Austin American-Statesman* columnist Anne Hornaday. "I was a singer from a very early age, and music occupied my life. I came from a very funny family; everyone's very bright and funny, but I knew at a very early age that show business was going to be my life." He briefly detoured from that plan with a stint at California State University at Northridge, from which he earned an English degree. During his years there, he worked full-time in a factory that made kitchen units for aircraft.

At a Glance . . .

Born Richard Anthony Marin on July 13, 1946, in Los Angeles, CA; son of Oscar (a police officer) and Elsa (a secretary; maiden name, Meza) Marin; married Rikki Morley (a homemaker and actor), November 1, 1975 (divorced); married Patti Heid (a computer artist), 1984; children: (from first marriage) Carmine, (from second marriage) Joe, Jasmine. *Education:* California State University, Northridge, BA, English.

Career: City Works Improvisational Group, Vancouver, BC, Canada, late 1960s; formed comedy duo Cheech and Chong with Tommy Chong, c. 1970; recording artist, 1972–; actor, 1978–; screenwriter, 1978–.

Awards: Grammy Award for Best Comedy Album, the National Academy of Recording Arts and Sciences, 1973, with Tommy Chong, for *Los Cochinos.*

Address: *Agent*—Creative Artists Agency, 9830 Wilshire Blvd., Beverly Hills, CA 90212.

At twenty-one years of age in 1967, at the height of the Vietnam War, Marin was highly eligible for the draft, and fled to Canada for a time to escape it. He settled in Vancouver, British Columbia, and hoped to begin a writing career. As a record reviewer for a Canadian music magazine, Marin was introduced to a local musician and club impresario Tommy Chong, and the two became fast friends. Marin joined Chong's bizarre improvisational theater group called City Works in 1969. The act featured comedy skits and topless dancers. Chong's parents owned the club, and the exotic dancers were a ploy to lure patrons; Chong just wanted to have a place to perform his music. Marin described the City Works show as "hippie burlesque" in an interview with *Los Angeles Times* writer Candace A. Wedlan. "It had long hair and dope and nudity and sex and drugs but in a real kind of hostile environment at first because guys wanted to see naked chicks, not long-haired guys talking. It was really seen as absurd. I mean, it was surreal, you know, and that's where we got our chops."

Heading back to the States and dropping the rest of the entourage, he and Chong began touring as a rock/comedy duo, but their music was not as popular with audiences as their banter, which satirized hippie culture and poked fun at those whose brains seemed permanently addled by drug use. The routine contained numerous references to marijuana, and became hugely

popular with counterculture youth. A gig at L.A.'s Troubadour club caught the attention of a record-industry executive one night, and Cheech and Chong released their eponymous debut in 1972. Their third comedy album, *Los Cochinos* in 1973, won a Grammy Award for best comedy album of the year. The records sold in the millions, and were a staple of many teen record collections; not surprisingly, some parents tried to ban the duo's stoned banter from their households. The comedy routine gave way to feature films, beginning in 1978 with *Up in Smoke.* Over the next five years, the Cheech and Chong movies were hugely popular at the box office, but criticized by some in the Latino community as rife with negative stereotypes.

Branched Out From Drug Humor

Uninterested in reprising the stoner role any longer, Marin split from Chong not long after the 1984 release of *Cheech and Chong's The Corsican Brothers.* As Marin told *Entertainment Weekly* journalist Bruce Fretts nearly a decade later, he and Chong "ran out of drug jokes, and it wasn't politically correct anymore. I didn't want to play those chords—it was boring. I wanted to get the characters involved in dramatic situations. Tommy was real resistant." Marin landed a deal to make his own movie, and it was a surprising success: he wrote, directed, and starred in 1987's *Born in East L.A.*, a farce about a third-generation Hispanic American who is mistaken for an illegal immigrant and deported to Mexico, where he experiences enormous difficulties because he neither understands nor speaks Spanish.

Marin took other film roles over the next few years, including *The Shrimp on the Barbie,* and appeared in television commercials aimed at Hispanic buyers for Chevrolet. He served as producer for a 1991 comedy series on the Fox Television network that featured a Latino comedy team, Culture Clash, but it was cancelled after six episodes. The same fate befell a sitcom in which he was cast, *The Golden Palace,* a spin-off of the highly successful *Golden Girls* series. In a move that many termed surprising—given his previous work as the comedic, marijuana-addled voice of 1970s counterculture—Marin branched out into children's entertainment. He did voice-over work for animated feature films, including *FernGully: The Last Rainforest* and *The Lion King,* in the latter giving voice to Banzai the Hyena. He also appeared on *Sesame Street* and released an album of children's songs, *My Name Is Cheech the Bus Driver.* He also stunned many when he emerged as the grand prize winner on the celebrity edition of the television's tough trivia game show, *Jeopardy!* in 1992.

Marin's Hollywood success began in earnest when independent filmmaker Robert Rodriguez cast him in two films, 1995's *Desperado* and *From Dusk Till Dawn,* but it was not until a role opposite Kevin

Costner in the 1996 film *Tin Cup* that Marin finally hit his stride in Hollywood. After a few years of scarce offerings, the actor told *Sport* writer Randy Williams that he was grateful for his *Tin Cup* role as a faithful golf caddie. "I was looking to do anything that didn't have a big joint in it," he joked. *Tin Cup* reunited him with a friend from his more free-wheeling younger days, Don Johnson, and Johnson invited him to take one of the leads in his new cop drama for television, *Nash Bridges*. Johnson even tailored the part specifically for Marin: Joe Dominguez, a San Francisco private detective who was once the partner of Johnson's Nash character. The irony of his playing a former law-enforcement officer was not lost on Marin, but he stressed that his father and others in his family had been cops, so he felt at home in the role. "I ended up playing my father," he told reporter Christy Slewinski in an article that appeared in the *Buffalo News*. "All I have to do is open my mouth and my dad comes out."

Became Chicano Art Connoisseur

Though the CBS series earned critical praise and quickly developed a devoted following, *Nash Bridges* was cancelled in 2001. Marin's film career, however, continued to flourish: he appeared in 2001's *Spy Kids,* and reprised his character in its follow-up as well as in a sequel to *Desperado*. He also will reunite with Tommy Chong on a film project for New Line Cinema. The success of their act did enable Marin to buy a home in the posh celebrity beachfront enclave of Malibu, where he lives with his artist wife, Patti Heid, and their two children; the actor also has an adult daughter from a previous marriage.

Over the years, Marin has become an avid collector of Hispanic art, and reportedly owns the largest collection of Mexican-American paintings in the United States outside of a museum. His favorites include Patssi Valdez, Frank Romero, Carlos Al, and Glugio "Gronk" Nicandro, and Marin claimed that he is formidable in his acquisition deals. "I drive a hard bargain," he told Hamlin in the *San Francisco Chronicle* interview. "But I'm always out there supporting the artists. I'm the guy who puts my money where my mouth is over a long period of time. My niche is Chicano art, and I'm a propagandist for it. I want to promote these painters because they deserve a wider audience and attention." Some of the collection became part of a 2002-2003 art exhibit, "Chicano Visions: American Painters on the Verge," that made stops in several American cities, including El Paso, Albuquerque, and Washington, D.C.

Selected works

Discography

Cheech and Chong, Ode, 1972.
Big Bambu, Warner Bros., 1972.
Los Cochinos, Warner Bros., 1973.
Wedding Album, Warner Bros., 1974.
Sleeping Beauty, Warner Bros., 1976.
Up in Smoke, Warner Bros., 1978.
Greatest Hit, Warner Bros., 1981.
Get out of My Room, MCA, 1985.
"Born in East L.A." (single), MCA, 1987.
Let's Make a New Dope Deal, Warner Bros., 1991.

Filmography

Up in Smoke, 1978.
Cheech & Chong's Next Movie, 1980.
Still Smokin', 1983.
The Corsican Brothers, 1984.
After Hours, 1986.
Born in East L.A., 1987.
Oliver & Company, 1988.
Rude Awakening, 1989.
The Shrimp on the Barbie, 1990.
The Lion King, 1994.
Desperado, 1995.
From Dusk Till Dawn, 1996.
Tin Cup, 1996.
Paulie, 1998.
Spy Kids, 2001.
Spy Kids 2: Island of Lost Dreams, 2002.
Once Upon a Time in Mexico, 2003.

Screenwriting

Up in Smoke, 1978.
Cheech & Chong's Next Movie, 1980.
Cheech & Chong's Nice Dreams, 1981.
Things are Tough All Over, 1982.
Still Smokin', 1983.
Cheech & Chong's The Corsican Brothers, 1984.
Born in East L.A., 1987.

Television

The Golden Palace, 1992.
Nash Bridges, 1996-2001.
The Ortegas, 2003.

Sources

Books

Newsmakers 2000, Issue 1, Gale, 2000.

Periodicals

ADWEEK Western Edition, September 24, 1990, p. 4.
Austin American-Statesman, January 18, 1996, p. 48.
Back Stage, June 15, 1990, p. 6.
Buffalo News, August 16, 1996, p. B15.
El Paso Times, May 25, 2003, p. 1.

Entertainment Weekly, February 4, 1994, pp. 44-45; August 25, 1995, p. 90; August 16, 1996, p. 45; December 20, 1996, p. 82.

Los Angeles Magazine, November 2002, p. 36; April 2003, p. 17.

Los Angeles Times, May 10, 1999, p. 6; July 7, 2002, p. 12.

People, July 11, 1983, p. 26; September 14, 1987, p. 14; October 12, 1992, p. 9; April 27, 1998, p. 125.

San Francisco Chronicle, May 9, 1996, p. E1; February 2, 1999, p. E1.

Smithsonian, October 2002, p. 45.

Sport, December 1997, p. 92.

On-line

"Cheech and Chong Take Another Hit," *Excite/ Reuters Online,* http://entertainment.excite.com/ article/id/342273 | entertainment | 07-23-2003::08 :30 | reuters.html (July 24, 2003).

—Carol Brennan

Miguel Mármol

1905-1993

Union activist

A shoemaker by trade and a revolutionary by avocation, Miguel Mármol devoted his life to organizing the peasants and workers of El Salvador and Guatemala. He was a founding member of El Salvador's Communist Party (CP) and the Young Communist League. The Salvadoran National Guard called him the "Red Phantom," because he repeatedly avoided capture and disappeared, only to return again, most notably after surviving his own execution.

from garbage cans to sell to cardboard factories and washerwomen.

Mármol eventually learned that his father was Eugenio Chicas, a successful farmer. Chicas was also the mayor of Ilopango. In addition to his legitimate daughters, Chicas had fathered so many children that, as a young man, Mármol discovered that a woman he was considering for marriage was his half-sister.

Raised in Poverty

Mármol was born on July 4, 1905, in the San Salvador suburb of Ilopango. His grandmother, a native Indian, had evicted her unmarried daughter, Santos Mármol, at the first sign of her pregnancy. Mármol's mother refused to reveal his father's identity and he was left in the care of his half-sisters while Santos Mármol carried bales of tobacco on her back to San Salvador, ten miles away, twice a day. The family lived in a mud shack, surviving on donated corn. When Santos Mármol was able to work as a cook or servant in San Salvador, the family ate well; however she often was unemployed, so the children fished and stole food from farms to eat. Mármol's sisters left school to collect boxes and rags

Mármol enjoyed school, attended his grandmother's catechism classes, and became an excellent swimmer. However at age eleven, just as he was starting the fourth grade, he quit school to work as a fisherman's apprentice. Mármol also cleaned the local National Guard barracks. Soon he became official assistant to the commander of the National Guard. He exercised with the guardsmen and dreamed of a military career. When he became a soldier at age 13, Mármol's first mission was to help quell a civilian and army uprising against the hated Salvadoran dictatorship. After witnessing the vicious torture of prisoners, Mármol requested an immediate discharge. That night—the first time in months that he had not slept in the barracks—the earthquake of 1918 collapsed the buildings, killing all of the guardsmen and officers. It was the first of Mármol's many escapes.

At a Glance . . .

Born on July 4, 1905, in Ilopango, El Salvador; died on June 25, 1993, in San Salvador; son of Santos Mármol and Eugenio Chicas; married Carmencita Mármol; children: Hildilita, Hilda Alicia (Angelita), Oscar (deceased), Francisquito (deceased), Antonita (deceased), María Elena, Berta Lilliam, Miguelito, another son. *Politics:* Communist. *Military Service:* Salvadoran National Guard, 1918.

Career: Fisherman, 1916-18; shoemaker, late 1910s-44; political and trade union activist, 1921-93; Claridad School, Guatemala, teacher and writer, mid-1940s; Trade Union of Guatemalan Shoemakers, organizational secretary and publisher of *The Unionist,* mid-1940s; bread baker, early 1960s; National University of El Salvador, lecturer, late 1970s-80.

Memberships: Constitutional Party, local secretary, 1921; Regional Federation of Workers of El Salvador, 1920s; Salvadoran Communist Party, 1930s-93; Young Communist League, secretary, 1930; National Alliance of Shoemakers, president, 1940s; National Workers' Union, 1944; Guatemalan Workers' Party, 1940s; General Federation of Guatemalan Workers, 1940s; Political Bureau of the CP Central Committee, 1950s; National Peasant Commission, general secretary, 1960s; Farabundo Martí National Liberation Front, 1980s-93.

Learned Shoemaking and Politics

Santos Mármol was determined that her son learn a trade rather than become a farm laborer. Unable to afford the teacher's training school, he apprenticed as a shoemaker. First in small shops in Ilopango, and then at the largest factory in San Salvador, Mármol received a simultaneous education in shoemaking and politics.

Soon he was making specialty shoes and living in the factory owner's home, where he read adventure novels and communist propaganda to his illiterate employer. Secret political meetings at the shop and home raised his political awareness. In 1921 Mármol became active in the liberal Constitutional Party in the town of San Martín, where his mother was a cook for the National Guard. When his political activities endangered both Mármol and his mother, the local National Guard commander protected them until the crisis passed.

Mármol opened his own shoe shop in San Martín, working on an egalitarian basis with his operators. The shop served as a front for both political activity and community recreation. However, this peaceful period came to an abrupt end when Mármol's enemies had him arrested for rape, charging that he was living with his first cousin, Carmencita. Rescued through his father's intervention, an embittered Mármol returned to work in a San Salvador shoe factory, where Carmencita joined him and became his wife.

Joined the Workers' Movement

Mármol threw himself into the organized workers' movement. He read voraciously and studied at the People's University and at schools run by the Communist International. Dividing his time between San Salvador and San Martín, Mármol organized meetings and distributed *The Hammer*, a newspaper published by the Regional Federation of Workers of El Salvador.

Mármol helped organize the Ilopango Society of Workers, Peasants, and Fishermen. The group cared for the sick; built and repaired roads; established a People's University and cultural center; launched a campaign against alcohol; and built a loan fund so that the women fish sellers could borrow money at reasonable rates. The Society initiated a cooperative movement among the fishermen to create beach access and stop the use of dynamite and poisons. However, when Mármol began organizing similar unions in other communities, government persecution intensified and he was forced into hiding.

With other members of the Regional Federation, Mármol organized strikes against landowners and construction companies for better wages and improved working and living conditions. In 1930 they founded the Salvadoran CP and Mármol was elected secretary of the Young Communist League. His family shared a tiny rented room with another family—seven people in all. While the men organized, the women sold fruit and tortillas to survive.

Mármol traveled to Moscow in 1930 as the Regional Federation's first official delegate to the World Congress of Red Trade Unions. However, as a recognized communist, his return to El Salvador was difficult. After hiding in Paris for almost a month, he sailed for Cuba where he was arrested as a Japanese spy. He talked his way out of prison and returned to Guatemala where, after a month, he was able to enter El Salvador despite a warrant for his arrest. As he began relaying his Moscow experiences to large audiences, the authorities forced him underground. In hiding, he organized and directed the Young Communist League and local committees.

Survived His Execution

As the worldwide economic depression hit poverty-stricken El Salvador, coffee and sugar prices plummeted and peasants were thrown out of work. Popular unrest reached new heights, with mass demonstrations and strikes. The government retaliated, the jails filled with political prisoners, and a military coup placed General Maximiliano Hernández Martínez in power. In January of 1932 the CP decided to organize an armed insurrection, but before they could act, the communist leaders and their military supporters were arrested and executed. Over the next few weeks, some 30,000 men, women, and children—2.5% of the population—were massacred by government forces.

Mármol was arrested and faced a firing squad along with 17 comrades and innocent bystanders. It took many bullets for the nervous soldiers to complete the executions. Mármol was felled with four bullets and a Russian salesman died on top of him, making it appear that Mármol had been shot in the head. After the soldiers left, he managed to crawl to safety, eventually making his way to San Salvador.

With his comrades dead, in prison, or disappeared, Mármol moved to the eastern part of El Salvador where he eventually found work in shoe factories and formed a new communist cell. After more than a year, he returned to San Salvador, living underground and moving every few days. He helped reorganize the CP and the underground worker's movement, laboring in a shoe factory to feed his family, and staying one step ahead of the police. Once he was saved by a former lover, Adelita Anzora, with whom he had a daughter named Hildita. Later Mármol was arrested as he prepared to flee to Honduras. Shackled and held incommunicado, he was finally released in 1936 after staging a hunger strike.

Lived in Exile

Mármol, whose wife had left him, remained enmeshed in the internal conflicts of the weak and fragmented CP until the early 1940s. He eventually established his own shop, specializing in cheap sandals, and he became president of the National Alliance of Shoemakers. His opposition to the Nazis and fascists helped him develop relationships with the American and British ambassadors to El Salvador.

The 13-year reign of terror under Martínez came to an end in May of 1944 and Mármol joined the national organizational committee of the National Workers' Union. However, in October of 1944, another military coup forced Mármol to flee San Salvador. Hiding in a cave, he produced propaganda for the opposition. After serving as a delegate to the founding congress of the General Federation of Guatemalan Workers, Mármol stayed on in Guatemala. He worked with the Claridad School, a center for political and union education, and wrote for their newspaper. Mármol was elected organizational secretary of the Trade Union of Guatemalan Shoemakers and ran the newspaper *The Unionist*. He began organizing the textile and other industries and became a salaried professional within the union. He also was a founder and leader of the communist Guatemalan Workers' Party.

Over the next few years, Mármol traveled to Mexico and Cuba and worked with indigenous peoples in Guatemala and with the CP in El Salvador. In 1954 he found himself fifth on the Guatemalan execution list and clandestinely made his way back to El Salvador. During the populist movement of the 1950s, Mármol was a leader of the resurrected Salvadoran CP and a member of the political bureau of the party's central committee. Late in the decade he traveled to the People's Republic of China for a course on political and trade union leadership and peasant organizing. Mármol served as general secretary of the National Peasant Commission during the 1960s, with responsibility for rural organizations and the editing of publications. He supported himself with a bread business. In 1963 he was captured again by the National Guard, held incommunicado, and tortured for many months. When the workers' movement demanded his freedom, he was exiled to Mexico, where he requested political asylum before secretly returning to El Salvador.

Interviewed by Roque Dalton

In 1966 Mármol traveled to Moscow for the Soviet Communist Party Congress. In May he attended the Czech Communist Party Congress in Prague, where he met the Salvadoran communist poet Roque Dalton. Dalton interviewed Mármol daily and nightly for several weeks. The result was a *testimonio,* Dalton's transcription of Mármol's dictation. This remarkable first-person account of Mármol's life is regarded as a classic of Latin American autobiographical literature. Mármol declined to speak of his most recent 12 years, out of fear of identifying comrades or providing his enemies with information. Although Mármol's writings, including poems and memoirs, have been lost, several of his letters and an interview are included in the English edition of *Miguel Mármol.*

Mármol was detained by the Salvadoran authorities in 1968 and in 1970 he was forced underground. Between 1974 and 1976 he traveled to the Soviet Union, returning to El Salvador as a lecturer at the National University. He tried to join the Farabundo Martí National Liberation Front (FMLN), which was fighting a guerilla war in El Salvador, but was told that, at age 76, he was too old. The CP ordered him into exile for his own safety. Mármol left for Cuba in 1980, just a step ahead of the National Guard.

During the 1980s Mármol traveled to Europe, Mexico, and Nicaragua. He also made his only trip to the United States in 1988. He spoke to university audiences and gatherings of activists, and promoted the English-language edition of *Miguel Mármol.*

Mármol returned to San Salvador in August of 1992, as the 12-year-long civil war ended. He signed the document that transformed the FMLN from a guerilla army into a legitimate political party. Living with his niece in the back of a tiny store, Mármol watched the fall of communist regimes around the world. He told the *Seattle Times,* "They aren't real revolutionaries anymore like we were. They're orthodox."

Left a Legacy

Mármol died of pneumonia on June 25, 1993, at the age of 88. Hundreds of people turned out for his funeral. Although he had fathered a number of children with different women, at the time of his interviews with Dalton, his only surviving children were a daughter, Hilda Alicia (called Angelita), and two boys, Miguelito, age two, and another born in the summer of 1966 while Mármol was in Prague. Among his other children, Oscar and Francisquito died while he was underground and Antonita died at age five while he was away. Another daughter died in 1954, leaving him a grandson.

Miguel Mármol was a central figure in the final book of Uruguayan writer Eduardo Galeano's fictional trilogy, *Memory of Fire, Century of the Wind.* As a character who escapes death many times, only to re-emerge stronger, he is Galeano's metaphor for the history of Latin America. In his introduction to *Miguel Mármol,* Dalton wrote: "Comrade Mármol is the prototypical incarnation of the Latin American communist worker and peasant leader of what is usually called 'the classical period,' 'the heroic era,' of the parties that ... sprang up and developed in nearly every country on the continent." Curbstone Press awards an annual Miguel Mármol prize for a first book-length fictional work in English by a Latin American author that reflects intercultural understanding and respect for human rights and civil liberties.

Sources

Books

Dalton, Roque, translated by Kathleen Ross and Richard Schaaf, *Miguel Mármol,* Curbstone Press, 1987.

Periodicals

AP Weekend Entertainment and Arts, July 24, 1987.
Associated Press, June 29, 1993.
Boston Globe, May 16, 1988, p. 2.
Latin American Perspectives, fall 1991, pp. 9-21, 79-88.
Monthly Review, January 1989, pp. 22-34.
The Nation, September 12, 1987, pp. 240-2.
Newsday, June 23, 1988, p. 49.
Seattle Times, January 31, 1993, p. A2.

—Margaret Alic

Arthur C. Martinez

1939—

Businessman

Arthur C. Martinez is a businessman who is best known as the person who saved Sears, Roebuck, and Company (Co.). Prior to joining Sears Martinez worked for several companies, including RCA Records. He entered the retail business in 1980 when he became the chief financial officer for Saks Fifth Avenue. In 1992 Martinez became the head of the Sears Merchandise Group and three years later he became the chief executive officer of Sears, Roebuck, and Company. During his eight year tenure at Sears, Martinez initiated a major overhaul of the company's operations and made the company profitable again. He is best known for changing the company's marketing strategy to focus on women as well as men. Martinez retired in 2000, although he continues to serve on the boards of directors for several businesses.

Learned Value of Money From Parents

Arthur C. Martinez was the only child of Arthur F. Martinez and Agnes Caulfield Martinez. He was born on September 25, 1939, in New York, New York. His mother was an Irish immigrant who worked part-time as a department store clerk. His father, who had some Spanish ancestry, worked as a fish wholesaler. Martinez was raised in Brooklyn and attended Catholic schools. He had a modest upbringing and learned important life lessons, especially the value of money, from his parents. "My mom and dad instilled in me their social convictions and a sense of community while I was still very young," Martinez told Janet L. McCoy of the *Auburn University News* in December of 1999.

As a teenager Martinez worked as a stock boy. He was a math prodigy who graduated from high school at the age of 16. He then attended the Polytechnic University and earned a B.S. in 1960. He financed his education with help from the ROTC. Upon graduation he served as a lieutenant in the army for two years. "I still think the army is the world's greatest diversity training ground," Martinez reminisced in his 2001 autobiography called *The Hard Road to the Softer Side*. "I was surrounded by soldiers of all races: whites, blacks, Hispanics, Native Americans, Asian Americans. There were straight arrows, drunks, geniuses, fools—every description you can think of."

At a Glance . . .

Born Arthur C. Martinez on September 25, 1939, in New York, NY; son of Arthur F. Martinez and Agnes Caulfield Martinez; married Elizabeth Rusch on July 30, 1966; two children. *Education:* Polytechnic University, BS, 1960; Harvard Business School, MBA, 1965. *Military Service:* U.S. Army, 1961-1963.

Career: Enjay Chemical, 1965-66; International Paper Company, director of planning, 1967-69; Talley Industries, assistant to president, 1969-70; RCA Corporation, director of finance, 1970-73, vice president, 1973-80; Saks Fifth Avenue, CFO, 1980-84, exec. vice president, 1984-87, vice chairman, 1990-92; BATUS, Inc, senior vice president and CEO, 1987-90; Sears Merchandise Group, CEO, 1992-95; Sears, Roebuck, and Co., CEO, 1995-00; author, 2001.

Selected memberships: Board of directors: Liz Claiborne, Martha Stewart Living Omnimedia, National Urban League, and PepsiCo; chair: Chicago Urban League Business Advisory Council, Executives Club of Chicago, National Retail Federation board of directors; deputy chair, Federal Reserve Bank of Chicago.

Selected awards: International Quality of Life Award, Auburn University, 1999; Gold Medal for Excelling in Retail, National Retail Federation, 1998; Business Statesman of the Year, Harvard Business School, 1997; CEO of the Year Award, *Financial World,* 1996; honorary JD, University of Notre Dame, 1997.

Address: *Office*—Sears, Roebuck, and Co., 3333 Beverly Rd, Hoffman Estates, IL, 60179.

In 1963 Martinez enrolled in the Harvard Business School and earned an M.B.A. in 1965. The lessons he learned at Harvard were vital to his later work experiences. In particular, Martinez recalled in his autobiography that the most important lesson was that "myopia is fatal. Think boldly about what business you are in, think carefully about what customers you are serving now and how you will meet the needs of the customers of the next generation." While in school Martinez and a friend also published a small magazine to support themselves. In 1966 Martinez married Elizabeth Rusch and the couple later had a son and a daughter together.

Gained Corporate Experience

Martinez's first job after Harvard was for Enjay Chemical, which later became Exxon. After learning that career advancement in the chemical industry would be slow, Martinez became the director of planning for new ventures for International Paper in New York City in 1967. Two years later he moved to the mergers and acquisitions division of Talley Industries in Arizona. In 1970 Martinez accepted an offer as a director of business planning for RCA record company in New York City. Four years later Martinez was promoted to head the international division of RCA.

When Martinez was in business school he did not plan to build a career in the retail industry. However, in 1980 he received an offer to become senior vice president and chief financial officer for Saks Fifth Avenue. Martinez was interested in trying out retail as a new experience. While at Saks Martinez learned that store personality was an important aspect of the business. "Carving out that personality and making sure it was distinctive was crucial. You had to understand that philosophy, stay consistent with it, and not vacillate," Martinez explained in his autobiography.

In 1986 Martinez accepted a promotion to senior vice president and group chief executive for BATUS, Inc., the parent company of Saks Fifth Avenue. For nearly four years Martinez worked in Louisville, Kentucky, running the retail businesses of Saks, Marshall Field's, Ivey's Department Stores, and Breuners. Saks was eventually sold to Investcorp and Martinez was invited to return to Saks in New York City in 1990 as a vice chairman. Martinez became unhappy with the intrusive management style of Investcorp so he eventually left Saks in 1992.

Martinez had lined up a new job with Swiss company P.A. Bergner, which owned Bergner's in Milwaukee and Carson Pirie Scott in Chicago. He was going to help Bergner out of bankruptcy when he got a call from Herb Mines, an executive headhunter, while vacationing in Maine. Mines informed Martinez that Sears, Roebuck, and Co. wanted to talk with him about helping their flailing company. Martinez was reluctant to consider the offer with Sears because he already had a verbal agreement to join Bergner. However, after a visit from Sears CEO Ed Brennan, who assured Martinez that he would have the authority and money to make major changes at Sears, Martinez accepted the challenge to reinvent one of America's best known department stores. "There were only two reasons not to take the job," Martinez told John McCormick of *Newsweek*. "Either it couldn't be done or I couldn't do it."

Revamped Sears

In 1992 Martinez became the chairman and CEO of the Sears Merchandise Group. Sears started as a watch company in 1887, founded by Richard W. Sears and Alvah Curtis Roebuck, which quickly grew into a business supplying a wide variety of products. The core of the company was the Sears catalog that targeted rural America, which did most of its shopping by mail. In the 1920s Sears became a retail store under the leadership of Robert Elkington Wood. For the next several decades, Sears adapted to changes in American life, such as the growth of cities and the spread of automobiles, and to changes in the American consumer, and the company flourished. According to Martinez in *The Hard Road to the Softer Side,* "Sears became the business model for big-store retailing. It was offering the right products in the right places at the right prices."

However, in the 1970s and 1980s, Sears began to suffer financially. The company had begun selling banking services, insurance, real estate, and stocks instead of focusing on what it did best, which was selling merchandise. The company made two mistakes which were nearly fatal. First and foremost, Sears had ignored its customers. The company that was built around the idea of being in touch with its customers had abandoned them. Second, Sears lost track of its competition. Discount stores, such as Kmart and Wal-Mart, as well as specialty stores, such as Home Depot and Circuit City, were luring customers away from traditional department stores like Sears.

In the year that Martinez joined Sears, the company had lost $3.9 billion and $3 billion of that amount came from the merchandising department. "It would be presumptuous to say I knew exactly what I was going to do when I walked in the door, but it was pretty clear that dramatic action was called for. It was not a situation where incremental improvement was going to be sufficient," Martinez told Terry Savage of the *Chicago Sun-Times* about the state of Sears when he joined the company. Within the first one hundred days in his new position, Martinez made some dramatic changes at Sears. The company had already sold many of its other businesses, such as banking and real estate, which allowed Martinez to focus on retail. His first decision was to end the venerable Sears catalog, which had been in circulation for over 100 years. While it was a sentimental favorite among the Sears employees, the catalog was losing $1.5 billion annually. Additionally, Martinez closed 113 stores and laid off 50,000 people. Martinez was quickly dubbed "the man who killed the catalog" and "the ax from Saks," but he was convinced that these tough decisions were necessary to save the company.

Martinez also focused on changing the corporate culture at Sears, which had contributed to the company's poor performance. Martinez aimed to make managers accountable for how well their particular areas performed. He replaced the 29,000 page Sears rule book with a new and simpler mission. "We wanted Sears to be compelling to work for, to shop at, and to invest in," Martinez explained in his autobiography. He also invested in improving the company's infrastructure, particularly with respect to communications and computers.

Found the Softer Side of Sears

The most important aspect of Martinez's restructuring plan was returning the company's attention to the customer. Martinez analyzed data about Sears' customers and their lifestyles. While Sears had traditionally been considered a man's store that sold tools, car batteries, and lawn mowers, Martinez discovered that most of Sears' customers were actually women. "If women were making all of those buying decisions, if they had indeed become the chief financial officers of the American family, why were we continuing to ignore their needs, their desires, and their dreams? My own suspicion was that we just didn't know how to talk to them and had not created a store that was warming or at all intriguing for them," Martinez explained in his autobiography. In response to this revelation, Martinez hired the advertising firm of Young and Rubicam to target women as Sears' customers. They developed the slogan "the softer side of Sears" and the accompanying advertisements to appeal to female customers.

Martinez's strategies for restructuring Sears were successful. From 1992 to 1995 Sears sales increased 13 percent and earnings nearly tripled. "Sears' downsizing caused a lot of pain and suffering, but the $35 billion retailer is on firmer footing today," wrote Scott McMurray of *U.S. News & World Report* in May of 1996. Martinez was credited for Sears' turnaround and he became CEO of Sears, Roebuck, and Co. in 1995 after Ed Brennan retired.

In 1996 Martinez was given the CEO of the Year Award by *Financial World* magazine. While Martinez enjoyed his successes at Sears, he also recognized that the restructuring job was not over yet. "Our situation is not unlike building the first half of a bridge," Martinez explained to Barry L. Rupp of *Financial World* in April of 1996. "When you're over the deepest part of the river, it's no time to take momentum for granted." Martinez planned to turn Sears into a consumer-brands and services company. He wanted to focus on Sears name brands, such as Craftsman, Kenmore, and Die Hard. He also initiated a move away from big malls to building smaller Sears specialty stores. In 1997 he introduced Sears Home Central as a single source for all household services, such as appliance repairs and pest control.

Faced More Challenges Before Retirement

The turnaround of Sears was not a straight road to success. Along the way the company suffered some financial setbacks. However, by the end of the 1990s, it was clear that Sears was better off than it had been at the beginning of the decade. In 1998 and 1999 the company faced a new round of challenges as apparel sales declined. The company also experienced problems with credit card delinquencies, and more employees were laid off. Martinez had a new strategy to turn sales around. Recognizing the growing business of internet shopping, the company launched Sears.com to meet the needs of a new type of customer. Sears also opened up the Great Indoors chain, offering upscale home decor and remodeling.

In 2000 Martinez announced his plans to retire from Sears. Although he enjoyed his work at Sears and the company still needed to work on staying competitive and profitable, Martinez wanted to retire at the age of 60 so that he could enjoy his retirement while he was still in good health and so he could spend time with his grandchildren. Martinez was replaced by Alan Lacy, president of services at Sears. Since his retirement Martinez has continued to serve on the board of directors of several companies, including Martha Stewart Living and Liz Claiborne.

Martinez spent eight years at Sears overhauling the company's corporate culture, infrastructure, marketing, and merchandising. He redefined the role of the traditional department store for the 1990s and made Sears a profitable company after nearly two decades of decline. When asked about his secret to success by Terry Savage of the *Chicago Sun-Times* in April of 2001, Martinez explained that "success will not be driven by your board scores and your grade point average coming out of school. They'll be driven by your character and your intensity, and by your willingness and ability to continue to learn."

Selected writings

(With Charles Madigan) *The Hard Road to the Softer Side: Lessons from the Transformation of Sears,* Crown Business, 2001.

Sources

Books

The Complete Marquis Who's Who, Marquis Who's Who, 2003.

Periodicals

Business and Management Practices, November 4, 2002, p. 10.
Chicago Sun-Times, April 29, 2001.
Financial World, March 25, 1996, p. 48; April 8, 1996, p. 10.
Fortune, October 16, 1995, p. 96; April 28, 1997, p. 106.
Industry Standard, November 22, 1999.
National Home Center News, April 17, 2000, p. 4.
Newsweek, November 1, 1993, p. 42.
Plain Dealer, December 25, 1994, p. 5H.
PR Newswire, March 25, 1999; June 22, 1999; September 10, 2000; December 7, 2000; January 3, 2001.
Time, December 23, 1996, p. 52.
U.S. News & World Report, May 13, 1996, p. 61.

On-line

"Alan Lacy Chosen as Successor to Arthur Martinez at Sears, Roebuck, and Co.," *Sears, Roebuck, and Co. Investor Relations,* www.corporate-ir.net (May 26, 2003).
"Arthur C. Martinez," *Biography Resource Center,* www.galenet.com/servlet/BioRC (May 14, 2003).
"Remodeling Sears," *Cio,* www.cio.com/archive/120196/sears.html (May 26, 2003).
Sears, www.sears.com (May 26, 2003).
"Sears Chairman Receives International Quality of Life Award," *Auburn University News,* www.auburn.edu/administration/univrel/news/archive/12_99 news/12_99martinez.html (May 26, 2003).

—Janet P. Stamatel

Rafael Moneo

1937—

Architect

Spanish architect Rafael Moneo took one of his field's top honors in 1996 when he was awarded the Pritzker Architecture Prize. The first Spanish architect ever to win the a-ward, Moneo became part of an esteemed roster of winners that included I. M. Pei, Robert Venturi, and Philip Johnson. Six years later, Moneo won critical acclaim for the Cathedral of Our Lady of the Angels, the home church of Los Angeles's Roman Catholic diocese. Writing in the *New Yorker*, Paul Goldberger called Moneo "a designer of exceptional thoughtfulness and precision. Even though he almost always works in masonry, his buildings have a certain delicacy."

Moneo was born on May 9, 1937, in Tudela, a city in Navarra, Spain. His father was a structural engineer, but Moneo was originally interested in philosophy and painting before changing course and earning a degree from Madrid University's school of architecture in 1961. His first career post was with the firm of renowned Danish architect Jorn Utzon; at the time, Utzon was completing a commission in Australia for the Sydney Opera House, heralded as one of the world's greatest modern structures upon its completion

in 1973, and Moneo worked on-site during the first years of the 16-year project.

Worked on Many Spanish Projects

Moneo had come of age in a Spain that was under the control of a right-wing military dictatorship headed by Generalissimo Francisco Franco. Modernism was the style he initially favored, but a fellowship at the Academy of Spain in Rome from 1963 to 1965 awakened his interest in classical styles. In 1965 he finished his doctorate in architecture and opened his own practice in Madrid. His first commission was for a factory in Zaragoza, but over the next decade he gained increasing prominence for several notable structures. The first of these to win international attention was the Bankinter Building in Madrid, which he did with Ramón Bescós. He also taught at Madrid and Barcelona universities, and became known as a deft critic in his field, especially after launching an architectural magazine in 1974 called *Arquitectura Bis*.

Spain entered a new era in 1975 when Franco died and King Juan Carlos I ascended to the throne. The king quickly steered the country toward a constitutional

At a Glance . . .

Born Jose Rafael Moneo Vallés on May 9, 1937, in Tudela, Navarra, Spain; son of Rafael (a structural engineer) and Teresa Moneo; married to Belén Feduchi (a contemporary furniture company owner); children: three daughters. *Education:* Madrid University of Architecture, diploma, 1961, doctorate, 1965; studied at the Academy of Spain, Rome, Italy, c.1963-65. *Military Service:* Spanish Army, 1958, 1959, 1962.

Career: Worked for the firm of Jorn Utzon, Hellebaeck, Denmark, early 1960s; opened private practice in Madrid, 1965; Madrid University School of Architecture, associate professor, 1966-70, professor of composition, 1980-85; Barcelona University School of Architecture, Barcelona, Spain, professor of architectural theory, 1970-80; *Arquitectura Bis,* co-founder, 1974; Cooper Union Institute of Architecture and Urban Studies, New York City, visiting fellow, 1976-77; Princeton University, Princeton, NJ, visiting fellow, 1982; Harvard University, Cambridge, MA, chair, department of architecture, 1985-90, Josep Lluís Sert Professor of the Graduate School of Design, 1991–.

Awards: Premio de Roma, 1962; Arnold W. Brunner Memorial Prize, American Academy and Institute of Arts and Letters, 1993; Manuel de la Dehesa Prize, Spanish Ministry of Public Works/Council of Architectural Associations, 1994, for the most significant public building in Spain, 1983-93; Gold Medal of Architecture, International Union of Architects, and Gold Medal of Architecture, French Academy of Architecture, and the Pritzker Architecture Prize, the Hyatt Foundation, all 1996; Royal Gold Medal, Royal Institute of British Architects, 2003.

Address: *Office*—Cinca 5, Madrid 28002, Spain.

democracy, along the lines of Great Britain, and Moneo's style fit in perfectly with the new cultural spirit, which merged traditional elements with a progressive verve. Yet Moneo was also gaining an international reputation, and began accepting teaching posts in the United States. In 1985 he moved his family, which included his wife, Belén, and three daughters, to the Boston area when he became chair of Harvard University's department of architecture. In 1991 he became the Josep Lluís Sert Professor at Harvard's Graduate School of Design, named for an esteemed Barcelona-born architect of the mid-twentieth century who had also taught at the school.

Moneo, however, continued to work in Spain. For some time he commuted to Madrid every weekend to supervise the gutting and renovation of the city's main train station, Atocha. In 1986 work was completed on one of his most outstanding projects, the National Museum of Roman Art in Mérida. The museum covered an excavation of Roman ruins that dated back some two millennia. Mérida had been founded in 25 B.C.E. by Emperor Augustus, and it served as a trade center for the part of the Roman Empire known as Lusitania. There were many Roman edifices in Mérida still functioning, including a bridge and a theater, and Moneo's museum building connected the theater and another monument, a traditional Roman amphitheater, by tunnel to the excavation site, which featured a Paleo-Christian basilica, tombs, and a house. It won him the Spanish government's Manuel de la Dehesa Prize in 1994 for the most significant public building in Spain in a period of ten years. "New walls of Roman brick, laid tightly in a series of arched corridors, create an abstract pattern vaguely suggestive of a binary rhythm, touching history without re-creating it," wrote *Los Angeles Magazine* critic Greg Goldin of the Mérida museum.

Won Coveted Award and Cathedral Commission

There were other notable commissions for Moneo in Spain during the 1980s and 1990s. He won coveted jobs for the Thyssen-Bornemisza Museum in Madrid and a new Olympic stadium in Barcelona for its hosting of the 1992 Summer Games. He also completed a new terminal for Seville's airport, and the Pilar and Joan Miró Foundation, a small museum on the island of Mallorca. His style found acceptance in less Mediterranean climes as well: he designed a hotel/office complex for the historic Potsdamer Platz in Berlin, and an entirely new building for Stockholm's Moderna Museet, the city's premier collection of modern art.

Such works put Moneo on the short list for the prestigious Pritzker Prize, created by the family of the Hyatt Hotels fortune to address the lack of an architecture category in the Nobel Prize. He won it in 1996, and Moneo's ceremony in California coincided with the announcement that same week that he had beat out several other top architects for what would be only his second building in the United States to date: the Los Angeles cathedral. The original church had been damaged in the 1994 Northridge earthquake, and the leader of Los Angeles' Catholic community, Roger Cardinal Mahony, drummed up support as well as $163 million to build a new one. It was a project fraught with controversy from the start over the site itself and cost overruns, but heralded by architecture critics and ordinary Los Angelenos alike upon its completion in 2002.

Moneo's Cathedral of Our Lady of the Angels was significant just for the fact that it was a relatively stately, religious-themed building in the center of a major American city—it was said to be the first such structure to go up on such an urban site in more than half a century. It was modernist in flavor, but blended historical elements deftly: Moneo had tons of sand delivered from Spain to mix into the concrete, which gave the exterior a warm, topaz color reminiscent of the first Roman Catholic missions in California. Impressive bronze doors created by artist Robert Graham brought worshippers inside—but into the wrong end, near the altar. A processional walk then wound visitors through. Of the interior, wrote Goldberger in the *New Yorker*, "Moneo has made a sumptuous modern space, angled and asymmetrical but calming. It is the same adobe color as the exterior, and there is soft, even light from huge alabaster windows. Crisply modern rooms with no right angles are rarely this serene." The alabaster windows were five-eighths of an inch thick, and the critic for *Los Angeles Magazine* commented favorably upon them as well. "As the sun moves east to west, the veined pigments in the stone change hues, from green and ocher to russet and gold, the way a sinking sun transforms pillars of sandstone in a red rock canyon," Goldin remarked. The church, in downtown Los Angeles, serves a largely Hispanic congregation, and seats 2,600. Outside, a large plaza can hold 5,000 visitors. "I wanted both a public space and something else: what it is that people seek when they go to church," Goldin quoted Moneo as saying in *Los Angeles Magazine*.

In 2003, the Royal Institute of British Architects awarded Moneo its Gold Medal, another of his profession's top honors. Moneo still maintains his Madrid office. His wife runs a furniture design firm in the city. His eldest daughter, Belén, is also an architect.

Sources

Books

Newsmakers 1996, Gale, 1996.

Periodicals

Architecture, October 1999, p. 110.
Evening Standard (London, England), February 14, 2003, p. 31.
Los Angeles Magazine, October 2002, p. 144.
Los Angeles Times, June 13, 1996, p. 2.
New Yorker, September 23, 2002.
Progressive Architecture, June 1986, p. 73.
Time, September 2, 2002, p. 64.

—Carol Brennan

José Montoya

1932—

Artist, educator, writer

As a painter, poet, and activist, José Montoya has played a leading role in the Chicano cultural movement. He founded the Royal Chicano Air Force, a California arts collective renowned for its political murals and community projects. His poetry is widely anthologized and has promoted new interest in Chicano literature. Montoya, who was named poet laureate of the city of Sacramento in 2002, is recognized as a legendary figure in the movement for recognition of Chicano culture.

home interiors. As he commented to *Dictionary of Hispanic Biography* contributor Ann Malaspina, "I have vivid memories about hardships, but I was also endowed with a lot of affection and love."

Art and storytelling were important parts of Montoya's early childhood. He enjoyed watching his mother mix the colors she used in her work. "We used to go on excursions to look for materials and colors," he told Malaspina, "tapping various levels of arroyo creeks for the yellow ocher colors." He also recalled his fascination with the storytelling traditions of his village.

Fascinated by Art and Storytelling

Montoya was born on May 28, 1932, on a ranch near Albuquerque, New Mexico, where his Mexican great-grandparents had settled after receiving a federal land grant in the 1800s. He was one of nine children, seven of whom survived, born to Malaquías Montoya and Lucia Saiz Montoya. When the boy was still an infant, his father was sent to prison for making liquor during Prohibition. Montoya grew up with his great-grandmother and great aunts while his mother supported the family by painting decorative motifs on

In 1938, when Malaquías Montoya was released from prison, the family moved to Albuquerque, where Montoya started school. But Montoya hated the city, and his family sent him back to live with his grandparents in the mountains. In 1941 Malaquías Montoya accepted a job as a farm laborer in California, and the family undertook a long journey by car and train to join him there. Turned away from Bakersfield, they moved to the Sierra Vista Ranches near Delano. The young Montoya, only nine years old, toiled in the fields while his parents cooked for the farmhands. For the next few years, Montoya attended school now and then while he

At a Glance . . .

Born on May 28, 1932, near Albuquerque, NM; married Mary Prieto (divorced); married Juanita Jue; children: six from first marriage, three from second marriage. *Education:* San Diego City College, AA, 1956; California College of Arts and Crafts, BA; Sacramento State University, MFA, 1971. *Military Service:* US Navy, 1951-55.

Career: Artist, 1960s–; Wheatland High School, Wheatland, CA, teacher, 1963-69; Sacramento State University, teacher in department of art education, 1971-81, professor, 1981-96; author, 1972–; National Taskforce on Hispanic Art, 1977; poet laureate of Sacramento, CA, 2002–.

Memberships: Mexican American Liberation Art Front, founder, 1960s–; Rebel Chicano Art Movement (later the Royal Chicano Air Force), founder, 1970s–.

Awards: City of Sacramento Mayor's Award for poetry, Sacramento Metropolitan Arts Council, 1995; California Arts Council award, 1997; National Endowment for the Arts, Grand Award for Literature, Arts Writing Fellowship Grant, 1981.

Address: *Office*—Poet Laureate Program, Sacramento Metropolitan Arts Commission, 2030 Del Paso Blvd., Sacramento, CA 95815.

earned wages and helped to care for his younger siblings. He skipped a whole year of school when he was 13. Along with a few other families, the Montoyas moved frequently to follow seasonal jobs. During World War II the family settled near Oakland, where Malaquías found work in the shipyards. In 1950, however, Montoya's parents separated and his father returned to New Mexico.

Discovered a Facility With Words

Montoya's mother wanted her son to finish high school, but left the choice to him. "I decided to stay in school and work after school and weekends to help the family," he explained to Malaspina. His mother worked hard, and later went on welfare, so that her children could remain enrolled at Fowler High School. Montoya's English teacher, Adrian Sanford, recognized the young man's talent and urged Montoya to continue with his literary and artistic pursuits. An essay that

Montoya wrote about his father's humiliation in prison, where he had to be cleaned of lice, elicited particular praise from Sanford. In 1951 Montoya graduated from high school—the first member of his family to do so.

As a young man Montoya was drawn to the street culture of Fresno, where Chicano *pachucos* or "gangs" held sway. He was arrested a few times for fighting. After his second arrest, he was given a choice between joining the Marine Corps or being assigned to a road crew. Montoya chose the Marines. But the Marine Corps refused to take him because of a tattoo that identified him as a gang member. He changed the tattoo into the shape of an anchor, and was allowed to join the Navy. From 1951 to 1955, during the Korean War, he served on a minesweeper. At the same time, he continued to read widely, particularly admiring the books of John Steinbeck.

After his stint in the Navy, Montoya settled in San Diego with his first wife, Mary Prieto. He attended San Diego City College at night under the GI Bill while working at a window company during the day. He earned an associate of arts degree in 1956, then received a scholarship from the California College of Arts and Crafts in Oakland, where he obtained a B.A. in fine arts. Montoya stayed an extra year to earn teaching credentials, and in 1963 began teaching at Wheatland High School in Wheatland, California.

Founded RCAF

In the early 1960s, Montoya began working for the movement to unionize local farm workers. He also realized that his art could be a vehicle for social change. With Esteban Villa, Malaquías Montoya, Manuel Hernandez, and others, he formed the Mexican American Liberation Art Front (MALAF). At Sacramento State University, where Montoya was teaching after having earned an M.F.A. in 1971, he helped Villa and a group of students form the Rebel Chicano Art Front (RCAF). "The idea was to use art as an organizing tool for the movement," he told Malaspina. The group's motto, *La locura lo cura* meaning "Craziness is its own cure", showed its emphasis on humor and activism. Soon people began to notice that the group's acronym was identical to that of the Royal Canadian Air Force. The group then renamed itself the Royal Chicano Air Force.

The RCAF, which became a well-known collective, enjoyed this military image. They dressed as World War II bomber pilots and drove around in an old army jeep that a fan had donated. Other supporters even donated flying machines to the group. Yet art remained at the center of the collective's work. The RCAF engaged in activist art, creating posters for migrant workers, the United Farmworkers Union, cannery workers, and other community groups. The RCAF also founded the "Arts in the Barrio" program, which offered art classes to Chicano students and senior citizens in Sacramento.

The program met at the Centro de Artistes Chicanos, a cultural center that Montoya and others founded in 1972.

One of the most impressive achievements of the RCAF was its involvement with the Chicano Park Murals project at Barrio Logan in San Diego. This large project, which includes about 40 major murals painted on 24 concrete pillars and two abutments of the San Diego-Coronado Bay Bridge in Chicano Park, features powerful images of Chicano culture. As *Public Historian* contributors Martin D. Rosen and James Fischer described them, the murals "depict images of Mexican pre-Columbian gods, myths and legendary icons, botanical elements, animal imagery, the Mexican colonial experience, revolutionary struggles, cultural and spiritual reaffirmation through the arts, Chicano achievements, identity and bicultural duality," as well as images of such heroic figures as Cesar Chavez, Che Guevara, Pancho Villa, Emiliano Zapata.

Montoya and the RCAF contributed "Leyes" and "La Familia," both dated 1975. Another RCAF mural, "I Am Somebody," includes a poem by Joann Little. "The murals," according to Rosen and Fischer, "have deep transcendent values and constitute a historic resource for which the Barrio Logan community has an unusually strong attachment. The importance of the Chicano Park murals has been underscored by local, national, and international recognition of their artistic and social value."

Among Montoya's artistic influences were Mexican engraver José Guadalupe Posado, whose work combined the political and the surreal. Muralists Diego Rivera, José Clemente Orozco, and David Alfara Siquieiros were also major influences. In 1973 Montoya's work was included in one of the first national exhibitions of Chicano art at Trinity University in San Antonio, Texas. Among his most notable works is his *Pachuco Series* of 1977, which depict the Chicano street gangs of his youth. Montoya's paintings, drawings, and prints have been exhibited across the United States and in Cuba, Mexico, and Paris. In 1977 he was named to the National Task Force on Hispanic Arts.

Poems Published in Anthology

Montoya's first literary success came in 1969 when nine of his poems were published in the anthology *El Espejo*. He went on to publish poems in chapbooks, pamphlets, and small-press collections. His first book, *El sol y los de abajo and Other R.C.A.F. Poems,* appeared in 1972. Montoya's use of the hybrid *calo* language, which combines English and Spanish slang, attracted considerable attention. Many admired the expressive power of the language, but Montoya recalled that his writing teachers disapproved, urging him to write in either Spanish or English. Among his most famous poems is "El Louie," about a man with whom Montoya grew up. The poem described Louie's military service in Korea but his later involvement with drugs, which led to his death. Many critics consider "El Louie" to be a classic depiction of a *pachuco.*

In 1992 Montoya published *In Formation: 20 Years of Joda.* The book includes poetry from 1969 to 1989, as well as several sketches by the artist. *Nation* contributor Ray Gonzalez called it "perhaps the definitive collection of *calo* writing to be found anywhere." Gonzalez noted that Montoya's voice remains as politically charged as it had been in the early years of the Movement. "Montoya writes a now-rare 'in your face, vato!' kind of poetry Chicano poets abandoned ages ago," Gonzales observed. "In today's market-conscious literary world, this kind of street writing has nothing to do with multiculturalism. It is too pure and powerful. No New York editor would go for it, much less understand it." Gonzalez went on to say that "His poetry, twenty-five years after the marches, boycotts and brown berets, still cries out against the social injustice that binds his people.... In *Information,* Montoya accomplishes what no other Chicano poet wants to do anymore: He has the courage to question his own people and ask if they have lost sight of their goals."

In addition to visual and literary art, Montoya creates music. He formed a band, José Montoya y Casindio. The group released a recording, *A Pachuco Portfolio,* in 1998.

In 2002 Montoya was named poet laureate of the city of Sacramento. For his featured project as poet laureate, Montoya chose to organize a Festival de Flor y Canto, or "Festival of Flower and Song." This event, which celebrated poetry as a means of sharing cultures, has pre-Columbian roots in Aztec ritual and emphasized the role of poetry in expressing reverence for life and social justice.

Selected writings

El Sole y Los de Abajo, Edicciones Pocho-Che, 1972.
In Formation: 20 Years of Joda, Chusman House Publications, 1992.
The Bully, Red Wing Press, 2001.

Sources

Books

Dictionary of Hispanic Biography, Gale Research (Detroit, MI), 1996.

Periodicals

Nation, January 31, 1994, p. 131.
Public Historian, Fall 2001, p. 91.

On-line

"Artist, Poet, Musician Jose Montoya To Speak At UNLV," *University of Nevada-Las Vegas,* www.unlv.

edu/News_Bureau/News_Releases/1999/Mar99/
206.html (April 1, 2003).

"CAC Folk Arts Grant, Jose Montoya," *Taco Shop Poets,* www.webnetarts.com/folkweb/artist.
htm (April 1, 2003).

"Guide to the Jose Montoya Collection 1969-2001, Biographical Sketch," *California Ethnic and Multi-cultural Archives,* www.cemaweb.library.ucsb.edu/ (April 1, 2003).

"Jose Montoya lauded by Sacramento," *California State University,* www.csus.edu/news/032502jose.
htm (March 28, 2003.)

"Sacramento Poet Laureate," *Sacramento Metropolitan Arts Commission,* www.sacculture.com/poets mac.htm (April 1, 2003).

—Elizabeth Shostak

Adriana C. Ocampo

1955—

Planetary geologist

Adriana Ocampo, a senior research planetary scientist with the European Space Agency (ESA) in Noordwijk, the Netherlands, is an expert on remote sensing. Geologists and geographers use remote-sens-ing instruments on Earth to study surface terrain. Ocampo used remote-sensing instruments mounted on spacecraft to study Earth and other planets, moons, comets, and asteroids. Ocampo and other planetary geologists also study extraterrestrial remnants on Earth, such as meteorites. In more than two decades as a research scientist at the Jet Propulsion Laboratory (JPL) of the National Aeronautics and Space Administration (NASA), Ocampo worked on several space missions. She also co-discovered the impact crater on the Yucatán Peninsula in Mexico, where scientists believe that an asteroid or comet collided with the Earth 65 million years ago, setting off a chain of events that resulted in the extinction of more than 60% of the planet's species, including the dinosaurs. Ocampo has devoted her energies to improving international cooperation in space exploration and narrowing the space science gap between developed and developing nations.

Joined JPL as a Teenager

One of three daughters of Teresa Uria de Ocampo, a Montessori teacher, and Victor Alberto Ocampo, an electrical engineer, Adriana C. Ocampo was born on January 5, 1955, in Barranquilla, Colombia. She was raised in Buenos Aires, Argentina, where her interest in space exploration was evident at an early age. Ocampo turned her dolls into astronauts and built spaceships out of kitchen utensils. She never went to bed without looking at the stars and contemplating outer space. Her parents encouraged her interests.

Ocampo's family emigrated to the United States when she was 14. At school in Argentina Ocampo had been steered toward a career in business or accounting, but at her new high school in Pasadena, California, she was able to study physics and calculus. Still she found attitudes in the United States less conducive to female scientists than in Argentina. However, in 1973, after her junior year in high school, Ocampo got a summer job at JPL in Pasadena. She continued to work there part-time throughout college. She majored in

Worked on Numerous Planet Mapping Projects

On the Mars Observer project Ocampo was in charge of the thermal emission spectrometer (TES). TES was designed to measure the planet's heat so that cartographers could make more accurate maps of Mars' surface. However the mission failed in 1993 when a malfunction caused the spacecraft to spin out of control and all signals were lost.

On the Voyager mission to the outer planets, Ocampo was a member of the navigation and mission planning team. Her work included the development of the Saturn ephemerides—tables showing the changing positions of Saturn and its satellites—to be used for the Voyager's encounter with the planet. Ocampo also was a co-investigator on the Hermes mission to explore the planet Mercury.

Ocampo was also in charge of the Near Infrared Mapping Spectrometer (NIMS) on the Project Galileo space probe, as NIMS science coordinator for Galileo's Flight Projects Mission Operations. NIMS was one of four remote-sensing instruments mounted on Galileo for its mission to Jupiter. The space probe was launched in 1989, entering Jupiter's orbit in December of 1995. As it passed the asteroid Gaspra, NIMS scanned its surface, revealing that the asteroid was covered with pulverized rock and dust that was thinner than that of the moon. It also showed that the asteroid's peak temperature was about 230 degrees Kelvin. NIMS measured reflected heat and sunlight from Jupiter's atmosphere, providing data on the planet's composition, temperature, and cloud structure. It also provided information about the mineralogy and surface chemistry of Jupiter's moons. Ocampo was responsible for planning the observations of Jupiter's moon Europa and analyzing the data. She and her colleagues published their work on the surface composition of Europa and Ocampo contributed to a high school textbook that uses the Galileo spacecraft to teach mathematics.

Studied the Chicxulub Impact Crater

The theory that a large asteroid crashed into Earth, starting a chain of events that led to mass extinctions, was first proposed by the physicist Luis Alvarez, his son—geologist Walter Alvarez, and others in the early 1980s. The only evidence at the time was the existence of a thin layer of the rare element iridium in 65-million-year-old geological strata called the K/T boundary because it demarcates the geological shift from the Cretaceous to the Tertiary periods. Iridium is more prevalent in comets and asteroids than on Earth. The scientists postulated that the impact led to global fires, smoke, and dust clouds that blocked the sun, cooling the planet and preventing photosynthesis.

In 1981 oil geologists discovered the buried Chicxulub crater on the coast of Yucatán, estimated to be about

aerospace engineering at Pasadena City College and participated in a JPL-sponsored science program. Switching her major, Ocampo graduated from California State University at Los Angeles with a B.S. in geology in 1983, having specialized in planetary science. She went to work at JPL as a full-time research scientist.

While working at the JPL Multi-mission Image Processing Laboratory, Ocampo became an expert on processing images obtained via remote sensing. She was a member of the imaging team for the Viking mission to Mars, planning observations of the Mars moons, Phobos and Deimos, and searching for a ring and other Mars satellites. She worked on both sequence planning and data analysis of the Mars images and produced a photo atlas of Phobos. Published by NASA in 1984, it is the only atlas of Phobos and was used to plan the Russian Phobos mission.

120 miles (200 kilometers) in diameter. In 1989 and 1990 Ocampo, her then-husband Dr. Kevin O. Pope, and Charles Duller were using satellite images to map water resources in the Yucatán. They found a semicircular ring of sinkholes, called "cenotes," that Ocampo recognized as related to the crater. They hypothesized that the crater might be the K/T impact site and published their findings in the journal *Nature* in May of 1991.

Ocampo joined the Chicxulub Consortium, a joint venture by American and Mexican scientists, to study the crater. In 1991 Ocampo and Pope led an international expedition of scientists and volunteers, sponsored by the Exobiology Program of NASA's Office of Space Science and The Planetary Society (TPS) of Pasadena. The expedition discovered two new sites. The site in Alvaro Obregon, Mexico, consists of two layers of material, called ejecta, that were thrown out by the impact and flowed lava-like across the surface in fluidized ejecta lobes. Impact ejecta are very rare on Earth and these were the first such lobes to be observed directly. The surface exposure of ejecta at Alvaro Obregon is the closest to the Chicxulub crater that has been found and is the best example known from a big impact crater.

The discovery of the Chicxulub ejecta lobes has important implications for understanding Mars. Ejecta lobes cover much of Mars, since its surface has remained unchanged for billions of years, preserving the debris from rare impacts. Ocampo told the JPL newsletter "Stardust:" "The discovery of these new ejecta sites is very exciting. It is like seeing a bit of Mars on Earth."

Ejecta Studies Led to New Discoveries

The second new ejecta site in Belize contains tiny green glass spheres called tektites—rocks that were melted by the heat of the impact. The team collected about 900 pounds (400 kilograms) of samples and drill cores for paleomagnetic studies, as well as fossils to help date the site. Among their fossils was a new species of crab from the Late Cretaceous and a new species of gastropod. With sponsorship from TPS, Ocampo led further geological expeditions to Belize in January of 1995, 1996, and 1998. In 1996 she co-led a TPS expedition to Gubbio in Italy, to drill at the original discovery site of impact ejecta at the K/T boundary.

Ocampo has given numerous presentations on her Chicxulub research at universities and professional meetings. Scientists now believe that the Chicxulub crater was formed by the impact of an asteroid or comet that was six to eight miles (10 to 14 kilometers) in diameter. Since the impact rock is very rich in sulfur, it is postulated that the impact resulted in a global sulfuric acid cloud that caused the Earth's atmosphere to remain opaque for about 10 years. Ocampo earned

her master's of science degree in geology from California State University at Northridge in 1997 with a thesis on the Chicxulub impact crater. She was awarded a grant by NASA to continue her research on the impact's effects on Earth's biosphere and its relation to the mass extinction.

In 1996 Ocampo presented her team's discovery of a chain of impact craters in the central African nation of Chad. The craters were found using radar images taken by the Spaceborne Imaging Radar C/X-band Synthetic Aperture Radar (SIR-C/X-SAR) mounted on the space shuttle *Endeavor* in 1994. Ocampo told the JPL press office, "The Aorounga craters are only the second chain of large craters known on Earth, and were apparently formed by the break-up of a large comet or asteroid prior to impact. With ground confirmation, this second chain will provide valuable data on the nature and origin of small bodies that cross Earth's orbit." The craters are believed to have been formed by an asteroid or comet that was about one-tenth the size of the one that formed the Chicxulub crater.

The study of impact craters has become important for understanding how the Earth and solar system formed and how life has evolved. Ocampo estimated that the Chad craters are about 360 million years old, corresponding to another period of mass biological extinctions. Ocampo told JPL, "These impacts in Chad weren't big enough to cause the extinction, but they may have contributed to it. Could these impacts be part of a larger event? Were they, perhaps, part of comet showers that could have added to the extinction? Little by little, we are putting the puzzle together to understand how Earth has evolved."

Promoted International Involvement in Space Research

In an interview on the *Planetary Radio Show* on January 6, 2003, Ocampo explained that "space exploration is the ultimate tool for international cooperation." Under the sponsorship of TPS, she organized a program to bring planetary science to developing countries. The first course, held in Mexico City in 1987, proved so successful that TPS, the United Nations, and the ESA sponsored additional workshops in Costa Rica and Colombia in 1992, Nigeria in 1993, and Egypt in 1994. Ocampo worked with the United Nations to develop these workshops, which have now been conducted in various countries, including Argentina in 2002 and China in 2003. Ocampo also founded the Pan American Space Conference to promote international communication and cooperation in space science and technology. As a member of the JPL Speakers Bureau, she promoted space science and engineering in the United States and abroad, in English and Spanish.

Ocampo served on the board of the Society of Hispanic Professional Engineers for five years, as secretary for one year, and as vice president for two years. She also was a member of the society's space committee and chaired its international affairs committee, where she established cooperative technical programs and university student exchange programs between the United States and Mexico. Ocampo is a member of TPS's advisory council, which works to disseminate scientific results and increase awareness of planetary exploration among the general public.

In 1998 Ocampo moved to NASA headquarters in Washington, D.C., as a program executive in the Office of Space Science, where she worked on joint missions with the ESA, Russia, and Japan. She also worked in the Solid Earth and Natural Hazards Division of the Office of Earth Science. In NASA's Office of External Relations, Ocampo was desk officer for Spain, Portugal, Russia, and the former Soviet republics. She moved to the ESA's planetary division in 2002. There she is involved in the Mars Express mission, a Mars orbiter and lander that is carrying new types of radar.

At JPL Ocampo was a member of the Advisory Council for Women, reporting directly to the head of JPL. In 1996 she received JPL's Advisory Council for Women Award for her outreach and community work. Ocampo is a member of numerous professional organizations, including the Society of Women Engineers where she was involved in a mentoring program for girls. In 1992 Ocampo received a Woman of the Year Award in Science from the Comision Femenil of Los Angeles. In 1994 she represented JPL at the Leadership Conference for Women in Science and Engineering in Washington, D.C. Although Ocampo has not realized her dream of becoming an astronaut and space shuttle mission specialist, she believes that the future of humankind lies in space exploration and the establishment of colonies on the moon and Mars.

Selected writings

Books

(With Thomas C. Duxbury and John D. Callahan) *Phobos: Close Encounter Imaging from the Viking Orbiters,* NASA, 1984.

(With B. A. Ivanov, D. D. Badukov, O. I Yakovlev, M. V. Gerasimov, Yu. P. Dikov, and K. O. Pope) "Degassing of Sedimentary Rocks due to Chicxulub Impact: Hydrocode and Physical Simulations," *The Cretaceous-Tertiary Event and Other Catastrophes in Earth History,* Geological Society of America, 1996.

(With Kevin O. Pope and Alfred G. Fischer) "Ejecta Blanket Deposits of the Chicxulub Crater from Albion Island, Belize," *The Cretaceous-Tertiary Event and Other Catastrophes in Earth History,* Geological Society of America, 1996.

Periodicals

(With Kevin O. Pope and Charles E. Duller) "Mexican Site for K/T Impact Crater?" *Nature,* 1991.

(With Kevin O. Pope, Gary L. Kinsland, and Randy Smith) "Surface Expression of the Chicxulub Crater," *Geology,* 1996.

(With Francisco J. Vega, Rodney M. Feldmann, and Kevin O. Pope) "A New Species of Late Cretaceous Crab (Brachyura: Carcineretidae) from Albion Island, Belize," *Journal of Paleontology,* 1997.

(With Louis Friedman and John Logsdon) "Why Space Science and Exploration Benefit Everyone," *Space Policy,* 1998.

(With Fraser P. Fanale and 21 other co-authors) "Galileo's Multiinstrument Spectral View of Europa's Surface Composition," *Icarus,* 1999.

Sources

Books

Bailey, Martha J., *American Women in Science: 1950 to the Present, A Biographical Dictionary,* ABC-CLIO, 1998, pp. 291-2.

Notable Scientists: From 1900 to the Present, Gale Group, 2001.

Olesky, Walter, *Hispanic-American Scientists,* Facts On File, 1998.

Periodicals

Hispanic, September 1996, p. 36.

On-line

"Adriana C. Ocampo," *NASA,* http://ltp.arc.nasa.gov/women/bios/ao.html (May 25, 2003).

"Adriana C. Ocampo," *Women of NASA,* http://quest.arc.nasa.gov/people/bios/women/ao.html (March 24, 2003).

"Adriana Ocampo," *Profiles of Women at JPL,* www.jpl.nasa.go/tours/women/ocampo.html (March 24, 2003).

"Chain of Impact Craters Suggested by Spaceborne Radar Images," *Jet Propulsion Laboratory,* www.jpl.nasa.gob/s19/news80.html (April 7, 2003).

"Earth-Shattering Impacts," *Planetary Radio Show,* http://planetary.org/audio/pr20030106.html (April 19, 2003).

"More Evidence Points to Impact as Dinosaur Killer," *Stardust,* http://stardust.jpl.nasa.gov/news/news10.html (April 7, 2003).

Other

Information for this profile was obtained through personal communications between Adriana Ocampo and *Contemporary Hispanic Biography* in May of 2003; and the *Women of Hope/Latinas Abriendo Camino/12 Ground Breaking Latina Women,* Films for the Humanities, 1996.

—Margaret Alic

Tony Orlando

1944—

Singer

1970s phenomenon Tony Orlando made a name for himself churning out bubble-gum pop songs with a female duo called Dawn, performing such runaway hits as "Knock Three Times" and "Tie A Yellow Ribbon 'Round the Ole Oak Tree." The group sold nearly 30 million records, topped the Billboard charts three times, and had their own television variety show that lasted for two seasons. But with their demise and subsequent breakup in the late 1970s, Orlando faced numerous obstacles, including a sluggish career, a cocaine addiction, and a nervous breakdown. Despite these roadblocks, he's managed to entertain audiences for more than forty years and continues to build an impressive resume that includes theater, production, and music. In 2002 he released a memoir of his life titled *Halfway to Paradise* in which he documents the ups and downs of his show business career.

Had Short First Music Career

Orlando was born Michael Anthony Orlando Cassavitis in New York City on April 3, 1944, to a Puerto Rican immigrant mother and a Greek furrier father. His younger sister and only sibling, Rhonda Marie, had cerebral palsy. Orlando managed to avoid the dangers of drugs and alcohol—so prolific in his working-class Manhattan neighborhood—by devoting much of his youth caring for his sister.

Orlando fell in love with music at the age of 15 and spent much of his time singing doo-wop on the corner and in the subway with his friends from the neighborhood. With hopes of breaking into the business, he performed and recorded demos with local groups like the Five Gents. Hanging around the legendary Brill Building, the New York-based home of some of the leading pop songwriters of the day, he managed to snag an audition with record producer Don Kirshner, who hired him for a dollar a week to sing on songwriter demos. One tape, featuring the Carole King-penned tune "Halfway to Paradise," was considered good enough to release and hit the U.S. charts at number 39 in 1960. A couple of months later he recorded the Barry Mann-Cynthia Weil penned song "Bless You," which rose to number 15 in the United States and number five in the United Kingdom in the fall of 1961. Orlando became a minor-league teen idol and even made an appearance on Dick Clark's hugely popular

At a Glance . . .

Born Michael Anthony Orlando Cassavitis on April 3, 1944, in New York, NY; married second wife, Frannie Amormino, 1991; children: (first marriage) Jon, (second marriage) Jenny Rose.

Career: Singer, 1960–; April-Blackwood Music (publishing arm of Columbia Records), general manager, 1967-71; actor, 1974–; Yellow Ribbon Music Theater, Branson, MO, owner and operator, 1993-99.

Awards: Grammy Award nominations, "Song of the Year" and "Best Pop Group Performance," 1973; American Music Awards, "Favorite Pop Single," 1973, 1974, "Favorite Pop Group," 1975; People's Choice Award, "Favorite All-Around Male Entertainer," 1975; awarded a star on the Hollywood Walk of Fame in 1990.

Addresses: *Agent*—The Brokaw Company, 9255 Sunset Blvd., Suite 804, Los Angeles, CA 90069.

show *American Bandstand*, but his star quickly faded. Orlando did a British tour with Bobby Vee, Clarence "Frogman" Henry and others in 1962, but by the next year he had quit the business. His last record, "Happy Times (Are Here to Stay)," peaked at number 82 in the United States.

Orlando had married shortly before his retirement and he had to find a way to make a living, so he went behind the scenes to work for music mogul Clive Davis and became general manager of April-Blackwood Music, a publishing arm of Columbia Records. He loved the work and the opportunity it afforded him to work with stars such as James Taylor, Barry Manilow, and Blood, Sweat & Tears. At that time things seemed to be headed in the right direction for Orlando and he had no plans to return to show business.

Teamed Up With Dawn

In 1970 Hank Medress, a former Token (of "Lion Sleeps Tonight" fame) turned producer and songwriter, and co-producer David Appel brought "Candida" to Orlando telling him it needed a better lead vocalist. The song was for a new Detroit-based group called Dawn, named after the daughter of Bell Records boss Wes Farrell and featuring female vocalists Thelma Hopkins and Joyce Vincent. He agreed to do it as a favor only if Medress agreed to keep Orlando's identity under

wraps so his boss wouldn't know he was moonlighting for a rival company. Orlando cut the track without ever meeting Hopkins and Vincent, who had already recorded their parts in California.

"Candida" hit Billboard's number three spot by the end of the summer of 1970, and stunned Orlando who was sure it would disappear without a trace. In a 2002 *Today Show* interview with Matt Lauer he recalled, "I remember pulling off on the freeway and getting off the exit and listening to that record (on the radio), not being able to tell anybody because I was afraid to lose my job." Booking agents were offering Dawn gigs, but there would be no act until Orlando decided to give up his day job and step back into show business. He finally acknowledged that he was the voice of Dawn and left his job to join the group full time to record what became the rest of their debut album, *Candida*.

Medress and Orlando quickly collaborated on a follow-up, "Knock Three Times," a tale of two neighbors in adjoining apartments who communicate their love via a series of three knocks on the ceiling ("if you want me") and two on the pipe ("means you ain't gonna show"). The song hit number one in December of 1970 in both the United States and the United Kingdom. What followed were a couple of years of relatively minor hits, including "I Play and Sing," "Summer Sand," and "What are You Doing Sunday." The album that featured these songs topped the Billboard 200 at a disappointing number 178. It wasn't long, though, before the group struck gold again with a song based on a convict's release from prison.

Released Megahit

"Tie a Yellow Ribbon 'Round the Ole Oak Tree" was released in February of 1973, and by April it had become a hit, selling more than six million copies worldwide. Though the lyrics were written about a convict returning home to White Oak, Georgia, hoping to see if his wife still loved him, the song quickly became associated with veterans returning from Vietnam after the war ended in 1974. Later it came to symbolize anyone returning home after a crisis, with yellow ribbons sprouting up on trees during wartime or when someone was missing or being held against their will. In fact, the song would climb the charts again in 1981 when 52 Iran hostages were released after 444 days of captivity. "I never ever set out to be a novelty act, a singer associated with ditties or bubble-gum tunes, yet ... 'Yellow Ribbon' seemed like a novelty song to me," wrote Orlando in his autobiography, *Halfway to Paradise*. "Even though I knew it had hit potential it wasn't the kind of song I wanted to be defined by." Nevertheless, the song changed Orlando's life and became his signature theme song.

In 1974, after performing "Yellow Ribbon" at the 16th Annual Grammy Awards, CBS programming chief Fred Silverman offered the group their own variety show, *Tony Orlando and Dawn*, which became an instant hit. It featured some of Orlando's boyhood idols, including Jackie Gleason and Jerry Lewis. Orlando would forge a close friendship with Lewis and go on to guest and host his Labor Day Telethon for years to come.

With the success of their TV show, came a whirlwind of hit songs, including "Say, Has Anybody Seen My Sweet Gypsy Rose," "Who's in the Strawberry Patch With Sally," and "Steppin Out (Gonna Boogie Tonight)." The group moved over to Elektra Records with Bell promotion executive Steve Wax in 1975 and recorded a cover of Jerry Butler's 1960 Top Ten hit, "He Don't Love You (Like I Love You)." It became the band's third number one single and selling more than a million copies.

Hit Low Point in Career

A trio of hits followed in late 1975-76, including "Mornin' Beautiful," a version of Marvin Gaye and Tammi Terrell's "You're All I Need To Get By," and a cover of Sam Cook's "Cupid." But good fortune took a turn and the group began to lose the public's interest. After only two seasons, the TV show was cancelled in 1976 amidst reports that Hopkins and Vincent were dissatisfied with their contracts. Then the group disbanded the following year when Orlando suddenly announced during a performance in Colhasset, Massachusetts, that it would be his last day as a performer.

Orlando had started to experiment with cocaine shortly before his television show was cancelled. He used the drug for nine months, but it would haunt him for years to come. "What nine months of using the stuff can do is ruin my career, ruin my decision making, ruin my marriage, ruin my self respect, ruin my relationship with my audience, and I lost my television show," he told Mark Steines of *Entertainment Tonight*.

The announcement that he was retiring from show business came after he suffered from a complete nervous breakdown from the demands of his TV variety show. He had also had a tough year with the death of his sister and the suicide of his close friend Freddie Prinze, who starred in the sitcom *Chico and the Man*. "Freddie was one of those brilliant, brilliant, brilliant comedians. And to see him lose his life like that had a tremendous effect on me, when I had never seen anybody die in my own presence," he told Larry King in a CNN interview. "And there I was with his wife Kathy and his mom. And it was a horrific time. And it affected me deeply."

Returned to Show Business

After a long recuperation, that included a six-month stay in a psychiatric hospital to help him kick his drug

addiction and a brief period as a born-again Christian, Orlando decided to pursue a solo career. He became a staple in Las Vegas showrooms—25 weeks a year in his heyday—and recorded a solo album, *Sweets For My Sweet,* for Casablanca in 1979. He also dabbled in acting, debuting in the TV movie *Three Hundred Miles For Stephanie,* and making a guest appearance on *The Bill Cosby Show*. In 1980 he briefly took over the lead role in the Broadway show *Barnum*. Orlando has continued to perform regularly since then, including a 1988 reunion with Dawn in Atlantic City. He also teamed up with his friend Jerry Lewis for a series of shows in the early 1990s at the Las Vegas Hilton and Riviera hotels.

In 1993 Orlando moved to the Ozarks to perform in a variety show in Branson, Missouri, where he opened his own theater, the Yellow Ribbon Music Theater. It was grueling work—he would do 400 shows a year from April to December—but he enjoyed the enthusiastic audiences and change of pace that Branson offered his family. The Missouri residency also gave him time to produce two themed musicals with original songs, including a show based on the life of his grandfather, musician Leon Stanley.

Orlando hit the road again in 1999, taking another Broadway turn in *Smokey Joe's Café*. This came soon after he ended litigation with former friend and business partner Wayne Newton over a failed joint venture in Branson. Orlando's suit, which asked for more than $15 million and accused Newton of damaging his reputation and wrongly throwing him out of the theater they once shared, was settled with a gag order on both sides. He has been working on an album's worth of new songs with an autobiographical theme. One of the songs, "Carribean Jewel," is a nod to his Greek and Puerto Rican heritage. Another, "Papito Played the Trumpet," is about his grandfather. While his old hits with Dawn continue to sell records, Orlando realized that it may be difficult to sell another solo album.

Orlando married his second wife, Francine Amormino, in 1991. They have a daughter, Jenny Rose, and a son, Jon, from his first marriage. He continues to tour, performing about 150 nights a year. As Orlando told *Entertainment Tonight*, "Everybody has that new time in their life when they are the new act and hot. That moment in your career only comes once and you're probably not as good in your craft until you get to the point in your career where you say this is my 43rd year. So right now when I do a show I know what I am doing, and I have the same enjoyment now as I did when I had the dream. So how bad could it be? As I say in the book I am Halfway to Paradise."

Albums

Candida, Bell, 1970.
Dawn Featuring Tony Orlando, Bell, 1971.

Dawn's New Ragtime Follies featuring Tony Orlando, Bell, 1973.
Prime Time, Bell, 1974.
He Don't Love You … Like I Love You, Electra, 1975.
Tony Orlando and Dawn's Greatest Hits, Arista, 1975.
I Got Rhythm, Casablanca, 1979.
(Solo) *Sweets For My Sweet,* Casablanca, 1979.
The Best of Tony Orlando and Dawn, Rhino, 1994.
Big Hits, Intersound, 1995.
Tony Orlando and Dawn — The Definitive Collection, Arista, 1998.
Knock Three Times: The Encore Collection, Arista, 1999.

Books

Halfway to Paradise, St. Martin's Press, 2002.

Television

Tony Orlando and Dawn, 1974-1976.
Chico and the Man, 1976.
The Johnny Cash Christmas Special, 1976.
Bob Hope Presents a Celebration with Stars of Comedy and Music, 1981
Three Hundred Miles for Stephanie 1981.
Lynda Carter: Street Life, 1982.
Rosie: The Rosemary Clooney Story, 1982.
The Cosby Show, 1985.

Theater

Barnum, St. James Theater, New York, NY, 1980.
Hey, Look Me Over!, Avery Fisher Hall, New York, NY, 1981.
Smokey Joe's Café, 1999.

Sources

Periodicals

Las Vegas Review, January 25, 2002.
New York Daily News, December 29, 2002.
News-Press, December 6, 2002.

On-line

"Larry King interview with Tony Orlando," *CNN-Transcripts,* www.cnn.com/TRANSCRIPTS/0212/15/lklw.00.html (June 16, 2003).
"Tony Orlando: 'Halfway to Paradise,'" *Entertainment Tonight,* www.etonline.com/celebrity/a12705.htm (June 16, 2003).
"Tony Orlando Takes Wayne Newton to Court," *CNN-Showbuzz,* www.cnn.com/SHOWBIZ/News/9904/29/showbuzz/#story4 (June 16, 2003).

Other

Additional information for this profile was obtained through transcripts from *The O'Reilly Factor*, broadcast by Fox News on November 8, 2002, and *The Today Show*, broadcast by NBC, October 14, 2002.

—Kelly M. Martinez

Daniel Ortega

1945—

Former Nicaragua president, revolutionary

Daniel Ortega joined the revolutionary Sandinista National Liberation Front (Frente Sandinista Liberación National—FSLN) in 1963, dedicating himself to the overthrow of the oppressive Somoza dictatorship, which had been governing Nicaragua since the 1930s. After years of imprisonment and exile for his revolutionary activities, Ortega led the Sandinista revolution, which resulted in the collapse of the Somoza regime in 1979. Serving as president of Nicaragua from 1985 to 1990, throughout the years of bloody conflict between the leftist Sandinistas and the U.S.-backed contra rebels, Ortega secured himself a position as both an international icon and an influential leader of the Sandinista movement and Nicaraguan politics.

Learned Rebellion at an Early Age

José Daniel Ortega Saavedra was born on November 11, 1945, in the small Nicaraguan mining community of La Libertad. He was the third son of Don Daniel Ortega, who worked as an accountant for a local mining company, and Lidia Saavedra Ortega. When the mine closed down, the family moved to Juigalpa,

closer to Nicaragua's capital Managua, where his father began an import-export business and his mother opened a bakery. They had more children, two of which would also become Sandinista revolutionaries: Humberto (born 1948) and Camilo (born 1950). Camilo later died fighting in the revolution and Humberto became a top military strategist, appointed minister of defense by the revolutionary government in 1979.

Politically influenced by his parents, who had both been imprisoned under the Somoza dictatorship, Ortega became involved in politics at a young age. He attended private and Catholic schools, developing a deep devotion to his religion, but he received much of his education at home where his parents tried to thwart the widespread American influences stemming from the 24-year U.S. occupation of Nicaragua between 1909 and 1933. They shared stories of former Sandinista leader Augusto César Sandino (after whom the Sandinistas were named), who had resisted the U.S. occupation until his murder in 1934 when General Anastasio Somoza Garcia seized power in a military coup. In a 1997 interview with CNN, Ortega described his earliest motivations: "I had a Christian upbringing, so I would say that my main

At a Glance . . .

Born on November 11, 1945, in La Libertad, Nicaragua; son of Don Daniel and Lidia (maiden name, Saavedra) Ortega; married Rosario Murillo (a poet); seven children. *Politics:* Sandinista.

Career: Sandinista National Liberation Front (Frente Sandinista Liberación National—FSLN), Federation of Secondary Students organizer, 1963-65, National Directorate leader, 1965-66, 1975-79, Internal Front leader, 1966-67, Juanta for the National Reconstruction Government leader, 1979-85; Nicaraguan president, 1985-90.

Memberships: Nicaraguan Patriotic Youth, 1956-60; Nicaraguan Revolutionary Youth, co-founder, 1960-61; *El Estudiante*, co-founder and editor, 1965.

Address: *Office*—Frente Sandinista Liberación National, Costado oeste, Parque El Carmen, Managua, Nicaragua.

early influences were a combination of Christianity, which I saw as a spur to change, and Sandinism, represented by the resistance against the Yankee invasion."

After the assassination of Anastasio Somoza Garcia in 1956, Luis Somoza Debayle assumed his father's presidency and Anastasio Somoza Debayle took over the national guard, launching a major reprisal campaign during which political opponents were tortured and imprisoned, the press was censored, and civil liberties were suspended. This eventually ignited the opposition movement. Ortega took part in a widespread student struggle against the regime while still in high school, participating in protests organized by the Nicaraguan Patriotic Youth (Juventud Patriótico Nicaragüense—JPN), for which he was captured and tortured in 1960. He went on to establish the Nicaraguan Revolutionary Youth (Juventud Revolucionaria Nicaragüense—JRN) with FSLN's Marxist founders Carlos Fonseca Amador and Tomás Borge Martínez. He was arrested again in 1961, but this did not deter him from continuing his revolutionary activities.

Rose to Position of Power

Ortega began studying law at Managua's Jesuit-run Universidad Centro-Americana, but he soon gave up his formal education to follow in Sandino's footsteps and become a full-time revolutionary. Without any civic

channels through which they could achieve change, leaders of the Sandinista movement came to the conclusion that the only way to overthrow the Samoza dictatorship was through armed struggle. The success of the Cuban Revolution had a huge impact on the Nicaraguan revolutionaries, with Fidel Castro, Che Guevara, and Camilo Cienfuegos acting as their main role models. They were also spurred on by the wars in Algeria and Vietnam. Ortega joined the underground FSLN in 1963 and helped organize the Federation of Secondary Students (Federación de Estudiantil Revolucionario—FES). He was again arrested and tortured for his activities. He went on to co-found the official paper of the revolutionary student front, *El Estudiante*, and was named to the FSLN's top policy council Dirección Nacional by 1965.

Ortega was put in charge of the FSLN's urban guerrilla wing, the Internal Front, in 1966. During this time, Anastasio Somoza Debayle was elected president and remained as director of the National Guard, giving him absolute political and military control over Nicaragua. As corruption and political repression increased, opposition to the regime grew, igniting a spiraling cycle of response and counter-response that threatened to destroy the country's economy and society. Ortega's first assignment was to rob a branch of Bank of America, an effort to secure funds to arm the revolution. The group was also responsible for the 1967 assassination of Gonzalo Lacayo, an alleged National Guard torturer. It wasn't long before the Samoza's National Guard captured Ortega, and he was imprisoned at the El Modelo jail on the outskirts of Managua. Political prisoners were treated with appalling cruelty, deprived of food and often forced to stand all day. This likely had a permanent effect on Ortega's personality, which has been described as "lonely, solitary, mistrustful, and hard" by his former deputy Sergio Ramirez. Searching for an outlet during his incarceration, he began to write poetry and caught the eye of fellow poet Rosario Murillo, who visited him frequently in jail and later became his wife.

When Sandinista commandos kidnapped Somoza's lackeys and foreign diplomats in 1974, Ortega was released, after seven years in prison, and exiled to Cuba as part of a hostage exchange. While there, Ortega affirmed the similarities between Cuba and Nicaragua, likening the Samoza regime to the Batista regime, both of which were backed by the United States. "I really felt transported to a country that was challenging imperialism, that was putting forward an alternative to capitalism," he told CNN in a 1997 interview for their "Cold War" documentary series. "I mean, it was challenging world capitalism and also the heavy weight of international imperialism. And one came face to face with these very spiritual, moral people who had a great fighting spirit." Inspired by this desire for social change, he returned to Nicaragua four years later to fight in the war against the government, leading one of the three FSLN guerilla groups.

Led Sandinistas to Victory

With weapons being smuggled into Nicaragua from Cuba, the FSLN was able to take up an armed struggle which led to the resignation of Samoza in July of 1979. Ortega was one of the leading commanders of the forces that ousted Samoza and soon became the head of the ruling junta for the Government of National Reconstruction. He went to Washington and the United Nations that same year in an attempt to neutralize a confrontation with the United States. "[We took power] with great enthusiasm and a great desire to transform the country, but also with the worry that we would have to confront the United States, something which we regarded as inevitable," Ortega explained to CNN. "It's not that we fell into a kind of geopolitical fatalism with regard to the United States, but historically speaking the United States has been interfering in our country since the last century, and so we said 'The Yankees will inevitably interfere. If we try to become independent, the United States will intervene.'" While visiting with President Carter, Ortega requested economic aid and material support to build up a new army. However, the United States perceived Nicaragua's communist ties a threat and took an opposing position to the Sandinista government. So Ortega turned to Algeria and the Soviet Union for support.

In November of 1984 the Sandinistas were victorious in the country's first democratic national elections, and Ortega became Nicaragua's president with 60 percent of the vote. Opponents charged that the Sandinistas had manipulated conditions during the election campaign in such a way that, although clean at first sight, the vote was actually rather tainted. The U.S. government of Ronald Reagan shared the opposition's criticisms and further intensified U.S. support for the Contra rebels—a coalition of dissatisfied peasants, former Sandinista allies, and Somozistas. Nicaragua's civil war had become a cold war standoff, with the Marxist-Leninist vanguard supporting the Sandinista government and the United States supporting the Contra rebels, who unleashed armed guerillas across the countryside. The result was a cruel and costly civil war.

Arguably it was the five-year-long U.S. trade embargo that succeeded in strangling the Nicaraguan economy and undermining the Sandinistas, bringing the nation scarcity, rationing, and endless lines which the Nicaraguan people would associate with Ortega's rule for decades to come. Within a few years, though, U.S. support for the Contras was shaken by the Iran scandal, during which it emerged that Oliver North was a lynchpin in a CIA scheme to sell weapons to Iran illegally, using the proceeds to fund the Contra activities. But it didn't undo the damage done by years of civil war and the U.S. embargo. Desperate for legitimacy, Ortega was compelled to accept a peace plan and elections negotiated by Costa Rican President Oscar Arias Sánchez, launched in February of 1987. The FSLN and the Contras signed a ceasefire agreement in March of 1988.

Relinquished Presidency to Chamorro

In the February 1990 elections under the Arias agreement, with international monitors in place, Ortega and the FSLN lost overwhelmingly to the UNO (Union of National Opposition), a right-centrist coalition led by Violeta Barrios de Chamorro, whose husband, Pedro Chamorro, was assassinated by the Samoza regime in 1978 for voicing dissent against the Somoza dictatorship. Ortega relinquished the presidency the following April, blaming the U.S. attack on Panama for his defeat. "It wasn't a completely free election because there was open interference from the United States, from President Bush, in the form of financial and political support to our opponents, as well as threats that the blockade would not be lifted and all the rest of it if UNO didn't win. The decisive moment was the invasion of Panama," he explained to CNN.

Since losing the 1990 election, Ortega has remained an influential leader in the Sandinista movement and Nicaraguan politics, remodeling himself a more democratic leader with the intention of meeting capitalism halfway. The FSLN has remained his personal tool, using strikes and the army to indirectly influence the politics of Nicaragua. However, the FSLN leadership has become more corrupt and undisciplined with time and Ortega's subsequent bids for office have all ended in defeat. His platform remained similar to his old model—defending socialist ideals and fighting for a just and free world—but in line with the new reality. Still, he lost an election bid in 1996, with 39 percent of the vote to Arnoldo Alemán Lacayo's 49 percent.

Ortega faced a personal defeat in 1998 when his adopted stepdaughter Zoilamerica Navaez, a militant Sandinista, accused him of sexually abusing her from 1978, when she was eleven, until her marriage in 1990. Ortega and his wife vehemently dismissed the accusation and supporters branded the incident a CIA plot. The incident threatened to destroy his political career. When he toured the barrios, Ortega required an assembly of guards to divide angry loyalists from protesters brandishing placards that read: "Ortega Violador" or "Ortega Rapist." However, he was never prosecuted and the case was dismissed in 2003, when the Nicaraguan Supreme Court upheld a judge's verdict that Navaez had waited too long to pursue the allegations.

Lost Third Bid for Presidency

Many predicted that the scandal would be his downfall, finally accomplishing what Somoza, Reagan, and the Contras never could. But he bounced back when the corruption of the conservative Alemán government enabled him to take up his cause once again, directing his campaign at the angry and dejected of Nicaragua, the world's poorest Spanish-speaking country. Ortega showed a significant lead the summer before his third election bid in 2001. However, he conceded defeat with 42 percent of the vote to Enrique Bolaños's 56 percent. His third loss could be attributed to a number of factors, including allegations of corruption made against him in relation to the last days of his government in the 1980s, the accusation made by his stepdaughter, and U.S. interference in the election campaign, including critical statements made about him by the State Department which linked him to terrorism and highlighted his ties to both the Libyan leader, Moammar Gaddafi, and Cuban President Fidel Castro.

Ortega's critics have given him his due for supporting the electoral process in his effort to reclaim the presidency. "Although he's obsessed with his quest for power, he's committed to doing it democratically," former FSLN Minister of Housing Miguel Vigil told *National Catholic Report.* "More than any other elected politician we've had in this country, Daniel has a democratic spirit at heart." But after three consecutive losses, it may be time for another leader to take on the cause and for the FSLN to democratize internally

and overhaul its image and agenda. However, they believe that Ortega's support will be essential in facilitating these goals.

Sources

Periodicals

Economist, October 25, 2001.
Houston Chronicle, April 16, 2003.
Monterey County Herald, March 30, 2003.
National Catholic Report, November 16, 2001.
Newsweek, March 23, 1998.
Observer (London), September 2, 2001.
Time Magazine, October 14, 1996; March 23, 1998.
Washington Post, November 6, 2001.
World & I, March 1, 2003.

On-line

"Daniel Ortega interview for *Cold War* documentary series," *CNN,* www.cnn.com/SPECIALS/cold.war/episodes/18/interviews/ortega (June 12, 2003).

—Kelly M. Martinez

Katherine D. Ortega

1934—

Former government official, banker, accountant

In the summer of 1983, Angela Marie Buchanan stepped down from her post as the 38th U.S. Secretary of the Treasury, leaving the post vacant for then president Ronald Reagan to fill. Reagan said to the *New York Times* that he was looking to appoint someone who "reflects the goals and ideals for which the people voted." That person was Katherine D. Ortega, a former member of the Presidential Advisory Committee on Small and Minority Business Ownership as well as an established liaison for the Republican party with the Hispanic community and numerous women's organizations. During her six-year term in office, she properly managed the nation's budget of $220 million, raised $40 million to help restore the Statue of Liberty, and created both a new currency design to prevent counterfeiting as well as the West Point Bullion Depository, the first new mint in the United States since 1862. After her retirement from the Treasury in 1989, Ortega has gone on to become a top consultant in the world of banking and has also served on the board of directors for numerous corporations.

Katherine Davalos Ortega was born on July 16, 1934, in Tularosa, New Mexico, the daughter of Donaciano Ortega and Catarina Davalos Ortega. The town of Tularosa was small—populated by no more then three thousand people—but it was a tight knit community that remembered heavily its Mexican and Spanish roots. Ortega credited much of her success to this community saying to the *New York Times*, "I am the product of a heritage that teaches strong family devotion, a commitment to earning a livelihood by hard work, patience, determination and perseverance." Before Ortega began formal schooling, she only spoke Spanish, the language that most of the inhabitants of Tularosa spoke, but she quickly picked up English once she began attending classes at the public school.

Found Strengths in Banking and Accounting

Along with English skills, Ortega showed an advanced proficiency in mathematics and problem solving. Starting in elementary school, she was far ahead of her classmates, so far ahead that her family began having her run the cash register in the family owned restaurant when she was only ten years old. As she moved along the business, mathematics, and economics classes on her way to a bachelor's degree in business and economics in 1957. With this degree, Ortega felt that many doors were open to her, and she focused on giving back to the institute of education by becoming a high-school teacher. When she began to look for a job, she found many openings on the eastern side of New Mexico, but as she began to apply for them, she found that she was rejected often without even an interview. She eventually consulted the chairman of the Eastern New Mexico State University business school about this problem and was told, according to an interview she did with the *Boston Globe*, that she "need not apply in the eastern part of New Mexico, where such a job was open, because of my Hispanic background." Appalled at the level of discrimination in the world of education, Ortega swore off the idea of becoming a teacher, and decided instead to forgo the whole job hunt altogether.

Since New Mexico, and much of the rest of the United States, was still very much prone to discrimination against Hispanics as well as women, Ortega and one of her sisters decided it would be easier for them to go into business for themselves. As Ortega told the *New York Times*, "My father taught me we were as good as anybody else, that we could accomplish anything we wanted.... He encouraged all three of his daughters to make a living for themselves so we would never have to be dependant on anybody." Taking their father's advice, they started a small accounting firm in Alamogordo, New Mexico, with Ortega's sister, who was a certified public accountant, as the main handler of many of the clients, and Ortega handling more of the day to day business. Ortega floated in the 1960s between the self-started accounting business with her sister and other various accounting jobs throughout the state. In 1967 Ortega felt that she might have more opportunities in another state and headed out to California. This did prove to be a good move for Ortega as she quickly secured work in the accounting field in Los Angeles, and by 1969 was a tax supervisor for Peat, Marwick, Mitchell & Company.

Moved From Accounting to Politics

Ortega would stay at Peat, Marwick, Mitchell & Company until 1972 when she got her first big break in the banking world, becoming the vice president at the Pan American National Bank in Los Angeles. This was definitely a step up for Ortega, although the bank was still small enough that she found herself often working as a cashier at times when employment was down. Ortega worked hard over the next three years to make Pan American National a reputable and trustworthy bank throughout Los Angeles and her effort did not go unnoticed. In 1975 she was approached by the Santa Ana State Bank and offered the position of director and president. Ortega quickly accepted and became the first woman bank president in California. Much as she had at Pan American National, Ortega was known at Santa Ana State Bank to be a hard worker who was not afraid

to junior high and high school, she continued to amass mathematical knowledge and also showed interest and skill in the area of accounting. By the time she was in her senior year of high school, she had graduated from working the register at the family restaurant to being a part-time bank teller at the Ortero County State Bank. She would take on a full time position as a teller when she graduated, spending two and a half years learning the ins and outs of banking while earning enough money to put herself through college.

In the mid 1950s Ortega attended Eastern New Mexico State University at Portales, where she aced many of to pitch in with the more menial tasks to keep the business running smoothly.

Back in New Mexico, the Ortega family accounting firm had grown and changed its name to the Ortero Savings & Loan Association. The family requested in 1979 that Ortega return to New Mexico to help the business succeed as she had the banks she had worked at in California, and Ortega readily did so, becoming a consultant to the firm from 1979 to 1982. During this time period, Ortega also decided to throw herself into the field of accounting more fully and became a certified public accountant in California as well as New Mexico.

In the early 1980s Ortega began to show an interest in politics, claiming to the *New York Times* that she was "born a Republican." She offered her services to the New Mexican Republican party and was soon used as a liaison for both local and state officials to communicate with Hispanic and women's organizations. She became known as a major supporter of the Republicans in New Mexico, not only for her help with the Hispanic community, but also for her activeness in election campaigns. She was a major supporter and rallier for Republican Senator Pete V. Domenici, who once he was elected brought Ortega to the attention of the national Republican party. When President Ronald Reagan needed someone to fill a position on the Presidential Advisory Committee on Small and Minority Business Ownership, Domenici suggested Ortega, and after looking at her credentials, Reagan agreed that she was the right person for the job. She served on the committee for eight months in 1982, and worked to foster a good relationship between the federal government and minority-owned businesses. She did such a good job on the committee that she was appointed to another federal panel, the Copyright Royalty Tribunal, which monitored and determined the amount that cable companies were required to pay in copyright fees to use certain television shows and music.

Became U.S. Secretary of the Treasury

In 1983 the U.S. Secretary of the Treasury was Angela Marie Buchanan. During the summer of that year, Buchanan decided that she had served her term and told Reagan that she would step down as soon as he could find a replacement. Reagan began to solicit suggestions from numerous members of his cabinet and his party, and once again Domenici, who was now a chairman of the Senate Budget Committee, suggested Ortega for the position. Reagan agreed that the country would benefit from someone of Ortega's skills. Reagan officially nominated Ortega on September 12, 1983, surprising many members of the Reagan Administration who assumed that the position would be offered to more long time notable Republicans such as

Nancy Kassebaum or Elizabeth Dole. Yet as Reagan said in his nomination speech, according to the *New York Times*, Ortega was "symbolic of the values the Hispanic community represents" and added that "nothing is a better influence on America than the strength and decency of the Hispanic family." With this type of support behind her, Ortega was quickly put before the Senate for confirmation, and on September 23, 1983, Ortega began her term as the 39th U. S. Secretary of the Treasury.

Ortega found herself part of the long legacy of women that had held the position of U. S. treasurer, but was only the second Hispanic woman to serve in this position; the first being Romana Acosta Bañuelos in 1974. As the U. S. treasurer, Ortega was in charge of the United States Mint along with the Bureau of Engraving and Printing and the United States Savings Bond Division. Her yearly duties included the mammoth job of maintaining an account of government spending, handling the nation's $220 million budget, sorting through and rectifying claims for lost, stolen, or counterfeit government checks, and burning unusable U. S. currency. She was also responsible for overseeing the jobs of 5,000 people employed by her divisions. Even more importantly to the Republican party, she was a high-profile ranking official who often was responsible for attending and representing the party at numerous ceremonial functions.

Ortega spent her time as the U. S. Treasurer split between monitoring and budgeting the nation's spending habits and promoting the role of Hispanics in the U. S. government. In 1984 she was given the honor of delivering the keynote address at the Republican National Convention, where she pushed for the Republican party to strongly look at the Hispanic communities in the country as a source of support. In her address, reprinted in *Vital Speeches of the Day*, she called out to the Hispanic community to embrace the Republican party saying, "To the millions of Democrats abandoned by their national leadership ... we Republicans in Dallas say: we welcome you to our home. Nuestra casa es su casa. Our home is your home." She was also a strong advocate for women to take a closer look at the Republican party. Ortega knew that many women felt that the Republican party, specifically the Reagan administration, were not supportive of women and did not give many positions in the party to women, but as Ortega pointed out to the *New York Times*, "There is a perception that Ronald Reagan has not named women to his Administration. When I'm out there, I talk about all the subcabinet appointments. I want to set the record straight." Besides drawing new members to the Republican party, Ortega also looked to do some good for the country as the U. S. secretary, starting a program in 1985 to sell Liberty Coins that were designed to raise money to restore the State of Liberty. The program raised close to $40 million.

Honored and Sought After Leaving Treasury

Ortega served as the U. S. secretary of the Treasury for six years, stepping down in 1989. For a time she returned to Ortero Savings & Loan as a consultant and has continued to work for the family owned business throughout the 1990s and into the 2000s. She has also served on the board of directors for many well-known corporations starting in 1992, including the grocery chain Kroger Company and the food and animal feed firm Ralston Purina. Ortega continued to promote diversity in government after her retirement from the Treasury as well, serving as an alternative representative to the United Nations as well as on the board of advisors for Leadership American, the National Park Service, Executive Women in Government, and the American Association of Women Accountants.

Before and after her time as the U. S. treasurer, Ortega was recognized by the Hispanic community and others as a trailblazer and a role model. She has received numerous honorary degrees from universities such as Eastern New Mexico University, Kean College of New Jersey, and Villanova University. She has also been honored with the Outstanding Woman of the Year Award from the Damas de Comercio as well as the California Businesswoman's Achievement Award. Ortega felt that many of these awards show what sort of example she has been able to set for other people in her community. As she told the *Boston Globe*, "I think of myself as a role model for my people.... I hope they see me and say: 'Hey, there's hope. We can accomplish.'"

Sources

Books

The Complete Marquis Who's Who, Marquis Who's Who, 2001.
Dictionary of Hispanic Americans, Gale Research, 1996.
Notable Hispanic American Women, Book 1, Gale Research, 1993.

Periodicals

Boston Globe, November, 24, 1985, p. B25
New York Times, September 13, 1983, p. B14; October 4, 1983, p. A19.
PR Newswire, April 22, 1992.
Vital Speeches of the Day, September 15, 1984, pp. 712-13.
U.S. News & Report, September 3, 1984, pp. 65-7.

On-line

"Katherine D. Ortega," *Biography Resource Center,* www.galenet.com/servlet/BioRC (June 16, 2003).

—Adam R. Hazlett

Adolfo Pérez Esquivel

1931—

Artist, activist

Though recognized as a sculptor, Adolfo Pérez Esquivel wanted to bring about peace and prosperity for the poor. He was honored with the 1980 Nobel Prize for Peace for his work to ease human-rights abuses in South America. Pérez Esquivel has devoted much of his adult life to championing fair conditions for the continent's *campesinos,* or landless peasant farmers, and he gained some measure of notoriety in his country for criticizing a brutal military regime that kidnapped, tortured, and killed thousands during the 1970s.

Pérez Esquivel was born on November 26, 1931, in Buenos Aires, Argentina, where his father had emigrated from Spain. His mother died when he was young, and because of his father's travel schedule as a coffee sales agent, he was sent to boarding schools run by Roman Catholic religious orders. He was a devout Roman Catholic from an early age, and as a teenager began to read the teachings of Mohandas K. Gandhi, an Indian political leader whose passive-resistance campaigns against harsh British rule helped bring independence for India and Pakistan. Yet Pérez Esquivel was also a talented artist, and attended the National School of Fine Arts of Buenos Aires and La Plata. When he finished in 1956, he worked as a sculptor and began to gain increasing recognition for his work. He also taught

architecture at his alma mater, and began a family with wife Amanda Pérez, a musician, pianist, and composer.

Argentina, during Pérez Esquivel's lifetime to date, had suffered from great political instability. A popular army colonel, Juan Perón, championed the working class but was ousted in 1955, and Argentina remained an economically depressed country. In the late 1960s Pérez Esquivel was drawn into the left-wing opposition, but unlike some of his fellow activists, espoused the use of Gandhi's non-violent tactics to effect change. To prove his point, he went on a hunger strike in 1970 that lasted nearly two months. He became a co-founder of Servicio Paz y Justicia (Service for Peace and Justice), an umbrella organization of activists who aided South America's poorest. Giving up his career as an artist, he worked to form craft collectives in communities to foster economic self-sufficiency, and published a magazine called *Paz y Justicia.* He was named general coordinator of the Servicio Paz y Justicia in 1974, and gave up his post as a professor of architecture at his alma mater at that point.

Pérez Esquivel traveled to many countries in South America and spoke publicly against military juntas and human-rights abuses. In 1975 he was arrested in

Brazil, and the following year jailed in Ecuador. Back in Argentina, the political climate had destabilized considerably since the brief return to power of Perón in 1973 and his death a year later. The Argentinean military junta came to power in 1976, and instituted a repressive regime. Those opposed to it began disappearing overnight, with no records of their arrest; many were jailed without trial, and their families had no idea of their whereabouts. In some cases entire families disappeared, and many died. It was a dangerous time to be working for justice in the country, but Pérez Esquivel became co-founder of two groups, the Permanent Assembly for Human Rights and the Ecumenical Movement for Human Rights. He worked to link them with other human-rights groups across Latin America that helped workers and peasants, and in 1976 began an international campaign to establish a human-rights commission at the United Nations.

In April of 1977 Pérez Esquivel was arrested by Argentine police and held without trial for 13 months. He was beaten and water was withheld for him for a week. Sometimes, he recalled, his guards would open the door to his cell, which would briefly illuminate the dark room. "I would see things written on the wall," *Rocky Mountain News* writer Dick Foster quoted him as saying. "But one thing I noticed was a big splotch of blood on the wall from somebody who had been tortured. In that blood was an act of faith. That prisoner had written in his own blood, 'God does not kill.' It has stayed engraved in my heart."

Pérez Esquivel's release was called for by a number of human-rights groups, including Amnesty International, and even officials in the administration of U.S. President Jimmy Carter attempted to urge the Argentine government to free him. Finally, in May of 1978, Pérez Esquivel was released, but placed under house arrest for the next several months. By 1980 he was working full-time at the offices of the Servicio Paz y Justicia, which had begun working with the mothers of the 10,000 to 20,000 missing Argentines. These Argentine women became known as the mothers of Plaza de Mayo, after the Buenos Aires square in front of the presidential palace where they held regular vigils.

Despite his work, Pérez Esquivel was not well-known in Argentina—except to its internal security organization—and many in the country were tacitly supportive of the military regime, for it had ended much of the sectionary violence that plagued the country during the early 1970s. He had already been nominated twice before for the Nobel Peace Prize for his work, but was informed by telegram one October day in 1980 that he was that year's recipient. The Prize committee, in the official announcement, lauded Pérez Esquivel, asserting he "represents in his struggle for human rights the struggle for Argentina's image and reputation in the world," according to the *New York Times*. Representatives of news organizations around the world descended on his humble Buenos Aires office to photograph him. "I accept this prize in the name of Latin America and its workers, in the name of its campesinos and its priests who are working diligently for the peace and rights of all," he was quoted as saying by *New York Times* writer Edward Schumacher.

Pérez Esquivel's honor caused some controversy in Argentina. "For Argentines, a strongly nationalistic people, the award and publicity have caused a national debate over what many see as the maligning of their country," explained *New York Times* writer Edward Schumacher. He accepted the award's prize purse of $212,000, but donated it to charities that aided the poor across South America. Authorities continued to harass him, despite his international stature as a recipient of what is considered one of the world's top honors. Interviewed again by Schumacher months later, he recounted telephone death threats, bombs found in his office, and an incident where he and his adult son, who worked with him, were accosted by men with guns as they pulled up to the Servicio Paz y Justicia offices. "Here we always live in uncertainty," he told Schumacher resignedly. "But I cannot let myself be paralyzed by it or I would not do anything."

Still, Schumacher wrote in the *New York Times*, Pérez Esquivel's Nobel Prize win "legitimized the small human-rights movement in Argentina, which had been condemned by the Government and largely ignored by news organizations and the public, partly out of fear." Within a few years, Argentina's political situation deteriorated further and the military junta was ousted. Pérez Esquivel continued to speak out on behalf of the poor and oppressed across Latin America, and was still active twenty years later. He was a regular guest of honor at the annual PeaceJam Youth Conference in the United States, launched in the mid-1990s to bring attention to social-justice causes. "I think part of the goal here is to help young people sense a need to take an interest in the policies of their government," a *Denver Post* report by Ryan Morgan quoted Pérez Esquivel as saying in 2001. "As part of that process, they need to get involved, to participate. They need to be demanding of those who govern."

Sources

Books

Dictionary of Hispanic Biography, Gale, 1996.

Periodicals

Denver Post, February 25, 2001, p. B2.
New York Times, October 14, 1980, pp. 1, A14; November 11, 1980; November 16, 1980, p. 18; July 28, 1981; February 26, 1985, p. A7.
Rocky Mountain News, February 25, 2001, p. 4A.
Star Tribune (Minneapolis, MN), March 8, 2000, p. 4B.

On-line

"Adolfo Perez Esquivel," *Biography Resource Center,* www.galenet.com/servlet/BioRC (March 24, 2003).

—Carol Brennan

John Quiñones

1952—

Broadcast journalist

A familiar face to American television viewers, John Quiñones is one of the most prominent Hispanics in broadcast journalism. An ABC News network correspondent since 1982 and anchor of *20/20 Downtown* since 1999, Quiñones' award-wining reporting has appeared on ABC's *World News Tonight,* and ABC's television news-magazines *PrimeTime Live, Primetime Thursday,* and *20/20.* In addition to national and international events, Quiñones has reported extensively on Latin America and on the Hispanic-American community.

Came From the Barrio

John Manuel Quiñones was born on May 23, 1952, in San Antonio, Texas, the son of Bruno and Maria Quiñones. Although a fifth-generation San Antonian, Quiñones did not learn English until he started school at age six. His tough, Spanish-speaking neighborhood was rife with gangs and drugs. For many years his father worked as a janitor at the high school that he attended and school counselors tried to steer Quiñones and his fellow Hispanics toward lives of manual labor. However, in "My Own Experience: The Latino Expe-

rience Through My Eyes," Quiñones quoted his father as saying: "I asked you, do you think it's good for you to be working hard like I do. And you said, 'No, I'm going to school.'" It was during high school that Quiñones resolved to overcome Hispanic stereotyping and pursue a career in journalism. An Upward Bound program at St. Mary's University in San Antonio helped prepare him for college-level work.

While attending St. Mary's University in 1973, Quiñones began working as a reporter and announcer at KTSA-Radio. He continued on there after graduating in 1974 with a bachelor's degree in speech communications. Between 1975 and 1978 Quiñones was a reporter and news editor at KTRH-Radio in Houston, as well as a reporter and anchor at KPRC-TV. In 1979 he earned his master's degree from the Columbia University School of Journalism.

Quiñones began his rise to prominence as a reporter at WBBM-TV, the CBS affiliate in Chicago. Beginning in 1979 he covered neighborhood and local news, as well as stories of national and international significance. His 1980 documentary series about the plight of undocumented immigrants crossing into the United States from Mexico won two local Emmy awards. Other major

At a Glance . . .

Born John Manuel Quiñones on May 23, 1952, in San Antonio, TX; son of Maria and Bruno Quiñones. *Education:* St. Mary's University, BA, 1974; Columbia School of Journalism, MS, 1979.

Career: KTSA-Radio, San Antonio, reporter, announcer, 1973-75; KTRH-Radio, Houston, reporter, news editor, 1975-78; KPRC-TV, Houston, anchor-reporter, 1975-78; WBBM-TV, Chicago, reporter, 1979-82; ABC News, network correspondent, 1982–; *Discovery News,* reporter, 1997; *20/20 Downtown,* host, 1999–.

Memberships: National Hispanic Journalists Association.

Awards: Two local Emmy Awards, Chicago; six national Emmy Awards; citation, first place international category, Robert F. Kennedy Journalism Awards, 1991; World Hunger Media Award; two Gabriel Awards; Overseas Press Club of America, Eric and Amy Burger Award for Best Reporting from Abroad; Ark Trust Wildlife Award; ALMA Award, National Council of La Raza , 2000.

Address: *Office*—ABC News, 147 Columbus Ave., 10th Floor, New York, NY 10023.

Quiñones reports included the Cuban boat lift of 1980 and the Haitian boat people of 1982.

Moved to ABC

In 1982 Quiñones joined the ABC network news division as a general assignment correspondent for *World News Tonight* and other ABC News programs. His base in Miami, Florida, enabled him to cover Latin American stories that were unavailable to other journalists. Throughout the 1980s he produced analyses of the civil war in El Salvador and the economic crises and political scandals in Argentina. In 1986 Quiñones covered the space shuttle *Challenger* disaster from Cape Canaveral, Florida. During 1988 he filed more than 50 reports from Panama City, Panama, where the U.S. government was attempting to overthrow General Manuel Noriega. Quiñones was one of very few American journalists who was allowed to cover the U.S. invasion of Panama in December of 1989.

Other Quiñones news stories of the 1980s included the explosion aboard the USS *Iowa,* the execution of convicted serial killer Ted Bundy, and the Florida gun control debates for *World News Tonight With Peter Jennings.* He was a correspondent for the 1988 ABC special *America's Kids: Why They Flunk.* Quiñones won his first national Emmy Award in April of 1990 for his anchoring of the ABC News special documentary *Burning Questions, The Poisoning of America,* broadcast in September of 1988. He won another national Emmy Award in 1990 for his story on Venezuela's threatened Yanomamo Indians, "Window in the Past."

In 1990 Quiñones followed the "throwaway" street children of Bogotá, Colombia, into the sewers beneath that city. His report entitled "To Save the Children" garnered him a World Hunger Media Award, a Gabriel Award, and a citation from the Robert F. Kennedy Journalism Awards in 1991. Later that season Quiñones followed up with a report on the violent treatment of thousands of homeless children by police in Guatemala.

Reported for PrimeTime Live

Quiñones became a correspondent for ABC's weekly news program, *PrimeTime Live,* in 1991. During his first season, his report on the exploitation of Haitian children laboring in the cane fields of the Dominican Republic, "Bitter Harvest," earned him the Overseas Press Club's Eric and Amy Burger Award for Best Reporting from Abroad. The program also won a 1992 Emmy and first place in the international category of the Robert F. Kennedy Journalism Awards in 1991.

For another Emmy award-winning documentary, Quiñones and his crew smuggled cameras into Tibet to report on the 40-year Chinese occupation. Quiñones also went undercover to investigate the meat-packing industry. The resulting exposé of the distribution of contaminated meat in the United States led to an investigation by the U.S. Department of Agriculture. Quiñones investigated the cause of an epidemic of brain defects among newborns in Brownsville, Texas; reported on the problems of homeless veterans; traveled to India to investigate the poverty-driven trade in human kidneys for organ transplants; and reported from a Florida research center on the interactions between dolphins and disabled children.

Over the following years, Quiñones conducted wide-ranging investigations and interviews from all corners of the world. He used hidden cameras to investigate the safety and quality of America's seafood and a Peruvian black market that supplied babies for adoption. Quiñones went diving off the coast of Bimini to profile a marine biologist dedicated to preserving sharks and reported on the ancient, endangered Penan Indians of

Sarawak, Malaysia. Quiñones' investigation of U.S. military involvement in Filipino prostitution over a 40-year period revealed the plight of some 9,000 Amerasian children who had been abandoned by their American fathers.

Quiñones continued to report on Latin American issues. He interviewed "tunnel rats," gangs of young Mexicans who rove through tunnels, beating and robbing immigrants trying to enter the United States illegally. He investigated the murder of American Michael Devine by Guatemalan soldiers, and the connections between the Guatemalan military and drug traffickers. Quiñones reported on the Latin singer Selena and her murder by the president of her fan club. A broadcast in March of 1997, in which Quiñones profiled undocumented Mexican boys being preyed upon by men in San Diego's Balboa Park, outraged many Americans. Quiñones also investigated the mistreatment of other ethnicities as well. Police profiling of blacks became a national issue after a 1996 *Prime-Time Live* report, in which Quiñones and his colleagues used hidden cameras to show blacks being routinely stopped for minor traffic violations and then searched without cause. A lawsuit brought by police against ABC, Quiñones, and others involved in the broadcast was dismissed in 2002.

Became News Show Host

In recent years correspondents for ABC and other network news teams have been assigned stories to be used on a variety of news programs. During the 1997-98 television season, Quiñones was a member of the ABC News team assembled to report on the Albanian refugee crisis in Kosovo, for a one-hour *20/20* special and other ABC News programs. The following season ABC ran four editions of *20/20* each week, emphasizing investigative journalism and medical and consumer news. Although his reporting on *20/20* was nominated for a 1999 ALMA award as Outstanding Correspondent in a Primetime News Magazine, Quiñones told *USA Today:* "There was a lot of sameness, whether it was *Dateline* or *20/20.* We had fallen into that trap." So in October of 1999, ABC introduced *20/20 Downtown,* hosted by Quiñones and featuring more emotionally-charged first-person "stories with attitude," as Quiñones called them.

In November of 2000 *20/20 Downtown* broadcast Quiñones' "Childhood of Shame," an exposé of violence and abuse in boarding schools run by the Hare Krishna religious group in the United States and India during the 1970s and 1980s. In his *20/20 Downtown* program "DanceSafe or Sorry?," Quiñones reported on the widespread use of the drug ecstasy, particularly among teenagers, and on DanceSafe, an organization that tested drugs at raves or underground dance parties and then returned the drugs to the patron. In 2001 Quiñones anchored a *20/20 Downtown* program, "Law and Disorder: U.S. Disagrees with Holland's Solution to Illegal Drugs." The season premiere of *20/20 Downtown* in January of 2002 featured Quiñones' investigation, "Vanished: The Mystery of the Missing Girls," about the disappearances of young girls from suburban San Francisco East Bay neighborhoods over a period of 30 years.

Quiñones was also a correspondent for ABC News's 24-hour, live, global millennium broadcast. It won the George Foster Peabody Award for 1999 and an Emmy in 2000 in the Special Classification for Outstanding News and Documentary Program Achievement. In January of 2001, *Primetime Thursday* aired Quiñones' undercover investigation that exposed insurance fraud by rings of doctors, chiropractors, lawyers, and medical centers, causing insurance rates to soar. For the opening Quiñones returned home, to the San Antonio Police Department, where women in the main lobby sorted through the day's accident reports and faxed them to telephone solicitors who contacted victims.

Reported and Anchored Latino Specials

Recognizing the growing influence of Hispanic culture on American life, Quiñones was named reporter and anchor for a 1999 ABC News special called *The Latin Beat.* Having been based in Miami for 15 years, Quiñones was uniquely qualified to present a program that focused on positive aspects of America's Hispanic communities. The program looked at the growing political and economic influence of Hispanics and examined how they are changing America. For example, it showed viewers that although Hispanics are the fastest-growing ethnicity in the United States, they are underrepresented in broadcast media. During 1997 Quiñones was one of only five Latino correspondents on the evening television news. It also featured Latin stars who are gaining popularity across the United States and examined the roots of the Latino "crossover" movement—the music Quiñones had grown up with—including salsa, meringue, and "Tejano," meaning Texan. Quiñones wrote on the ABC website, "*The Latin Beat* has been the most fun I've had professionally in a long time." The program earned critical acclaim and won Quiñones a 2000 ALMA Award from the National Council of La Raza in the category of Outstanding Correspondent, Anchor and/or Host of a National News Program or Special.

In 1999 Quiñones narrated *The Border* for the Public Broadcasting System (PBS), a two-hour program about the culture and issues facing the border regions of Mexico and the United States. He also contributed to the three-part ABC-Time report, "The New Frontier," which looked at the effects of the North American Free Trade Agreement on U.S.-Mexican relations. Quiñones reported from the village of Tulcingo in southern Mexico, from which so many men had emigrated to the United States that only old people and children remained. However the town's standard of living had improved greatly due to millions of dollars sent home from America. In 1999, as a member of the ABC News Crime and Justice team, Quiñones and fellow correspondent Cynthia McFadden reported on "Street Life: Inside America's Gangs." Quiñones provided an inside look at the Latin Kings and their leader King Tone, who was attempting to redirect the gang away from violence.

On January 21, 2000, *World News Tonight with Peter Jennings* focused on Latinos in America. It was the first evening news broadcast devoted to the Latino community. The program also was available live nationwide on the secondary audio program system. In his report, "My Latino Experience," Quiñones used the story of his own family to examine issues of Latino pride and assimilation. He emphasized the pride Latinos feel in the culture, language, and customs of their countries of origin, and the profound effects of the Latino community on American culture. Quiñones returned to his old high school in San Antonio to observe the changes since the 1960s. He found a Latino generation that was much better adapted to America than his own generation had been. Likewise the rest of America had become more accustomed to Latinos. One student told him: "It makes me proud to see my culture overcome all the oppression that we were put through back in the early sixties and seventies." Others told him that they were of two cultures, "Mexican-American" or "Latina/Mexican-American. It's both, equal." Another said: "All we want is success, to be successful in life and still be true to our culture."

In all, Quiñones has won six national Emmy awards for his work on ABC News programs and specials. His report on the Congo's virgin rainforest won both an Emmy and the Ark Trust Wildlife Award. His report *Diamonds and Blood* was a finalist for the 2000 network/syndicated television award of the Investigative Reporters and Editors, Inc., a grassroots, nonprofit organization that seeks to improve the quality of investigative journalism. For this report on the rebel-controlled Central-African diamond trade, Quiñones was a member of the first American newsmagazine crew to enter Sierra Leone since civil war erupted there. In 2002 Quiñones was nominated for an ALMA award in the category of Outstanding Correspondent or Anchor of a National News Program. Quiñones was scheduled to co-host the 2002 Hispanic Media 100 Awards ceremony. However true to his principles, he withdrew after learning that the ceremony would honor an anti-gay activist.

Selected works

Broadcasts

America's Kids: Why They Flunk, ABC, 1988.
Burning Questions, The Poisoning of America, ABC, 1988.
The World is Watching, ABC, 1988.
Only the News That Fits, ABC, 1989.
"Bitter Harvest," *PrimeTime Live,* ABC, 1991.
The Border, PBS, 1999.
The Latin Beat, ABC, 1999.
"Childhood of Shame," *20/20 Downtown,* ABC, 2000.
(With David Fitzpatrick, Thomas E. Goldstone, David Ward, and Jane Hartney) *Diamonds and Blood,* ABC, 2000.
"My Latino Experience," *World News Tonight with Peter Jennings,* ABC, 2000.
"Vanished: The Mystery of the Missing Girls," *20/20 Downtown,* ABC, 2002.

On-line

"The Latin Beat," *ABCNEWS.com,* http://abcnews.go.com/onair/dailynews/sp990907_latinbeat.html (March 30, 2003).
"My Own Experience: The Latino Experience Through My Eyes," *ABCNEWS.com,* http://abcnews.go.com/onair/WorldNewsTonight/wnt_00012111_Quiñones_features.html (April 20, 2003).

Sources

Books

Machamer, Gene, *Hispanic American Profiles,* Ballantine Books, 1996, p. 78.

Periodicals

USA Today, October 4, 1999, p. D3.

On-line

"John Quiñones: ABCNEWS Correspondent, *Downtown* Anchor," *ABCNEWS.com,* http://abcnews.go.com/sections/wnt/2020/Quiñones_john_bio2020downtown.html (April 23, 2003).
"My Own Experience: The Latino Experience Through My Eyes," *ABCNEWS.com,* http://abcnews.go.com/onair/WorldNewsTonight/wnt_00012111_Quiñones_features.html (April 20, 2003).

—Margaret Alic

Tina Ramirez

19(?)(?)—

Dancer, choreographer, educator

Tina Ramirez has managed to bring Hispanic culture to the forefront of mainstream dance through the creation of Ballet Hispanico, a renowned Hispanic-American dance company and school. After years of training as a dancer, choreographer, and teacher, Ramirez realized her dream of blending contemporary American dance and Hispanic culture to create an outlet for arts education and cultural unity. The result has been a phenomenally successful organization that has allowed her to represent the Hispanic community through dance.

Tina Ramirez, whose birth year is unknown, was born on November 7 in Caracas, Venezuela, to José, a prominent Mexican bullfighter, and Cestero, a Puerto Rican who came from a family of educators. They had two other daughters: Katty and Coco. Ramirez's parents divorced when she was five years old and her mother sent the girls to stay with relatives in Puerto Rico and then on to New York City with their grandmother. Ramirez's mother would soon follow—laboring jobs were plentiful in New York and she needed to find work to support her three daughters. Ramirez moved in with a great aunt in the Bronx when she first arrived at age six because her grandmother could not take care of all the girls, but once her mother arrived, the family moved into an apartment at 114th Street and 3rd Avenue in Manhattan, an area commonly known as El Barrio or Spanish Harlem.

Dreamed of Becoming a Performer

Ramirez was educated in the New York Public School system and attended Julia Richman High School, an all-girls school at the time. Although her mother dreamed that she would become a teacher, following in the footsteps of her relatives in Puerto Rico, Ramirez had different plans. "Ever since I was little I always wanted to be in the theater," she said to *Contemporary Hispanic Biography (CHB)*. In fact, it was her mother, who was enamored by the arts, who introduced her to the theater. Ramirez recalled one of the first productions her mother brought her to see as a young girl, a performance of *The Corn is Green* with Ethel Barrymore. She also liked to attend popular films of the day, and remembered admiring Eleanor Powell, a Hollywood musical star who was known for her tap-dance numbers. "Whatever I would see, I would come home and do. And I had very strong feet so I

At a Glance . . .

Born on November 7, (birth year unknown), in Caracas, Venezuela; daughter of José and Cestero. *Education:* Studied with Lola Bravo.

Career: Frederico Rey Dance Company, principal dancer, 1940s; toured Spain with a Gypsy group, 1940s; teamed with her sister Coco to perform in supper clubs in New York City and around the United States and Cuba, 1940s; toured the United States with Xavier Cugat, 1950s; appeared in Spoleto Festival of Two Worlds with John Butler, 1950s; appeared in Broadway productions of *Copper and Brass, Kismet,* and *Lute Song,* 1950s; Lola Bravo's dance studio, owner and educator, 1963-70; Operation High Hopes, founder and educator, 1967; Ballet Hispanico, founder and artistic director, 1970–.

Memberships: The New 42nd Street; Dance USA.

Awards: New York City Mayor's Award of Honor for Arts and Culture, 1983; Mayor's Ethnic New Yorker Award, 1986; New York Governor's Arts Award, 1987; Manhattan Borough President Award, 1988; Citation of Honor, Capezio Dance Awards, 1992; Citation of Honor, New York Dance and Performance Awards, 1995; GEMS Woman of the Year Award, 1997; Hispanic Heritage Award, 1999; Dance Magazine Award, 2002.

Address: *Office*—Ballet Hispanico, 167 West 89th Street, New York, NY 10024.

could walk on my toes without toe shoes," she told *CHB.*

She was also inspired by her father's performances in the bullfighting ring, which she recalled seeing from the age of two. "Bullfighting is like ballet," she told Scott Iwasaki of Salt Lake City's *Deseret News.* "Although it is more turned in; you have to move with elegance and strike the poses." Still, as she approached her adolescence Ramirez had not yet discovered the art form. Her sister Coco was very sickly as a child and was prescribed exercise by her doctor, so her mother decided to enroll her in dance lessons. It became Ramirez's responsibility to take her, and when she saw the dancers in action she knew that this was what she wanted to do. Her mother, however, was still adamant that she was to be the teacher of the family. But after a

year she gave in and let Ramirez take lessons along with her sister.

Unlike most dancers who begin their studies at a very young age, Ramirez started her first lessons at around age 12. Her dance education was of high quality, however, having received instruction from Lola Bravo, New York's grande dame of Spanish dance. She started in the base class, but Bravo quickly moved her to the next levels. "I just took whatever I could learn, but she moved me fast from one class to the other," Ramirez told *CHB.* "She also believed in taking ballet because that's the way she was trained in Spain, so she always pushed ballet. So that's how I also became interested in ballet." Ramirez also studied other styles of Spanish dance, including Spanish folklore, flamenco, semi-classical Spanish, Mexican folklore, and Peruvian dance, getting a little taste of everything very early on. After studying with Bravo for a few years, Ramirez, still a teenager, moved on to professional work.

Joined a Professional Company

Ramirez's dream to make a career out of performing became a reality when she took on her first professional experience with the Federico Rey Dance Company. World War II was raging and there were not many Spanish dancers available at the time, so Rey toured the studios looking for talent. He saw Ramirez perform and liked her, so he asked her to join his concert group, which included three dancers, a guitarist, and a pianist. Ramirez spent two years with the group, touring the United States, Canada, and Cuba, and quickly established her reputation as a Spanish dancer.

She went on to study with Luisa Pericet in Spain, staying with a friend's family in Madrid. She also spent much of her time there touring the country with a gypsy group. Upon her return to the United States, after two years in Spain, her professional contacts had virtually forgotten her, so she had to effectively start over again performing at supper clubs. She teamed with her sister, Coco, doing an act at El Chico, a very exclusive supper club in New York's Greenwich Village, where she was discovered by Xavier Cugat. A very famous Spanish bandleader, Cugat went there to check out another dance team, but he liked the Ramirez sisters and invited them to audition. They joined Cugat and toured the United States for about two years. He invited them to accompany him on tour in Asia, but they were establishing a name for themselves by that point and Ramirez wasn't ready to leave that behind. So they started working on their own as "Tina and Coco" at supper clubs all over the United States and Cuba.

Around this time Ramirez also made an appearance in the Spoleto Festival of Two Worlds with John Butler. On Broadway, she performed in the short-lived 1957 production of *Copper and Brass,* and productions of *Kismet* and *Lute Song.* She also appeared in the first television adaptation of *Man of La Mancha.*

Moved Into Dance Education

Ramirez stopped touring and returned to New York for good in 1963 to take over Lola Bravo's studio. Her former teacher and mentor was retiring and remembered that Ramirez had mentioned a desire to teach dance when she was 13, so she called her out of the blue and asked her to take over the studio. Ramirez agreed and promised to teach for a year because she didn't know if she would like it. Conservative by nature, Ramirez hated waste—especially human talent—so a passion for teaching came naturally to her. She told *CHB,* "I believe in discipline and a stick-to-itiveness … I taught (my students) that a profession has laws. If you wanted to be a dancer this is what you do. Not in so many words I would say 'I've never heard of such a thing. How can you be talking before you go on stage? It's never done!' So that's the way I taught the kids."

Ramirez also recognized the power of praising children and the positive benefits that talented kids brought to their families. It was this that inspired her to start Operation High Hopes, a professional dance and performance training program for underprivileged children from all five boroughs of New York City. The local Office of Economic Opportunity gave her $18,000 to start the program in the summer of 1967, and though it received high ratings from the OEO, Operation High Hopes was cut the following September. Some of the kids from the program continued to work with Ramirez in her studio, and because they wanted to be professional dancers and she wanted to stress professionalism by giving them employment, Ramirez decided to start a professional company.

In 1970 Ramirez founded Ballet Hispanico of New York to provide employment for Hispanics in the arts and to inspire understanding of the diversity of Hispanic culture through a blend of classical ballet, modern dance, and traditional Spanish dance with Hispanic music and literary themes. "I wanted people to know who Hispanics were, how we look, how we felt about music," she said to *CHB.* "I didn't want to be 'the other' because if people don't know you as a human being they treat you as 'the other.'" Ballet Hispanico encompasses three components, including the professional company; a school with more than 600 students; and Primeros Pasos (First Steps), an educational program that serves over 25,000 students and teachers in New York City and across the United States. The company tours both nationally and internationally, allowing people to see through the arts what Hispanics look like in a dramatic and abstract context. Ramirez, who has been managing Ballet Hispanico as founder and artistic director for thirty-plus years, doesn't plan to slow down anytime soon. Arts education will always be in the forefront of her agenda, but she also has dreams of bigger productions. "Every year we raise the bar on ourselves," she said to Iwasaki of the *Deseret News.* "I like challenges, if, of course, they help us become better."

Sources

Periodicals

Dance Magazine, April 1995; March 1997; March 2002.
Deseret News (Salt Lake City), February 23, 2003.

On-line

"Tina Ramirez Biography" *Ballet Hispanico,* http://ballethispanico.org/general_information/about_tina.html (May 30, 2003).

Other

Additional information for this profile was obtained through a personal interview with *Contemporary Hispanic Biography* on May 20, 2003.

—Kelly M. Martinez

Bill Richardson

1947—

Politician

Bill Richardson was installed as the governor of New Mexico on January 12, 2003. His political career began 21 years earlier when he was elected to the U.S. House of Representatives as the representative of New Mexico's third district in 1982. After 14 years in Congress, Richardson served as the U.S. ambassador to the United Nations (UN) and as the secretary of the Department of Energy. Known for his diplomatic skills, Richardson has worked for years as an unofficial ambassador for U.S. interests around the world.

Gave Up Baseball for Political Science

Richardson was born on November 15, 1947, in Pasadena, California. His mother, Maria Luisa Zubiran, a homemaker, was from an upper class family from the southern Mexican state of Oaxaca. His father, William, was an American citizen and a high-ranking executive with Citibank in Mexico City, where Richardson grew up with his younger sister Vesta. Richardson returned to the United States as a teenager to attend Middlesex, a prep school located nearly his father's hometown of Boston. Later, as a politician seeking the working-class vote, he would downplay his socially and economically privileged upbringing.

During his high school years, Richardson was an exceptional baseball pitcher and was drafted in 1967 by the Kansas City (now Oakland) Athletics. However, to his disappointment, his father successfully convinced him that college was a better choice than a career in baseball. The following year Richardson blew out his

elbow, ending any baseball prospects and making his father seem all the wiser.

Richardson majored in political science at Tufts University in Medford, Massachusetts, his father's alma mater. After graduating in 1970 with his bachelor's degree, Richardson enrolled in Tuft's Fletcher School of Law and Diplomacy. A field trip to the U.S. Senate set the course of his future career. He later told the *New Republic,* "I went to the Senate, and Hubert Humphrey gave us one of his orations. He turned me on, talking about Africa. I can still hear him bellowing, and I said, 'I want to be part of that.'"

Began Career in Politics

After receiving his master's degree in international affairs in 1971, Richardson moved to Washington, D.C., and secured a position as a staff member for the U.S. House of Representatives. During 1972 Richardson married Barbara Flavin, an antiques restorer he had known since his teenage years. In 1973 he took a job as a staffer in the Congressional Affairs Office of the U.S. State Department. Three years later he joined the staff of the foreign relations subcommittee of the U.S. Senate, which was under the leadership of Sen. Humphrey.

By 1978 Richardson was eyeing his own political future. His problem, however, was that, although he was born in the United States, he had been raised in Mexico and had no real home base from which to establish himself. To remedy this, Richardson moved to

At a Glance . . .

Born on November 15, 1947, in Pasadena, CA; son of William and Maria Luisa Zubiran Richardson; married Barbara Flavin, 1972. *Education:* Tufts University, BA, 1970; Fletcher School of Law and Diplomacy, Tufts University, MA, 1971. *Religion:* Roman Catholic. *Politics:* Democrat.

Career: U.S. House of Representatives, staff member, 1971-73; Congressional Relations Office, U.S. State Department, staff member, 1973-76; Senate Foreign Relations Committee, U.S. Senate, staff member, 1976-78; New Mexico Democratic Committee, executive, 1978-82; U.S. House of Representatives, representative from New Mexico, 1982-96. U.S. Ambassador to the United Nations, 1997-99; secretary of the U.S. Department of Energy, 1999-00; Harvard University, Kennedy School of Government, instructor, 2001-02; United World College, Montezuma, New Mexico, instructor, 2001-02; business consultant, 2001-02; governor of New Mexico, 2003–.

Awards: Distinguished Public Service Medal, Center for the Study of the Presidency, 1997; Visionary Award, Institute of American Indian Arts Foundation, 1997; International Leadership Award, Institute of American Indian Arts Foundation, 1997.

Address: *Office*—Office of the Governor, State Capitol, Room 400, Santa Fe, NM 87501.

New Mexico in 1978, where he worked for a time as a trade consultant and quickly got involved in local Democratic politics. He became a member of the Bernalillo County Democratic Commission and, before long, was asked by the Arizona governor to assume the duties as executive director of the New Mexico State Democratic Commission.

Richardson's first foray into elective politics was his unsuccessful bid for the second congressional district seat in 1980. On the announcement of his candidacy, Richardson was pelted with charges of carpetbagging. However, he responded that his dual heritage made him a perfect fit for New Mexico's diverse culture, which includes large populations of Anglos, Hispanics, and Native Americans. Richardson won the primary, but faced stiff competition from Rep. Manuel Lujan, Jr., a well-established Republican incumbent, in the general election.

Won Congressional Seat

During the 1980 campaign Richardson worked tirelessly and quickly became known for his campaigning energy. His goal was to not let a day pass without shaking at least 1,000 hands, and he briefly held a spot in the *Guinness Book of Record* for shaking 8,871 hands in a single day. Richardson spent more than $200,000 on his campaign—much more than Lujan. Nonetheless, Lujan held on to win the election by just 5,000 votes (out of 250,000 votes cast). Despite the loss, Richardson's good showing made him the darling of the Democratic party in New Mexico.

When a new district was created in northern New Mexico the following year, Richardson moved to Santa Fe and was quickly pegged as the favorite to win the Democratic nomination. The new third congressional district covered a vast amount of territory and was one of the most ethnically diverse populations in the nation—40 percent Hispanic, 40 percent Anglo, and 20 percent Native American. There were 28 sovereign Native American nations within the district's borders. Richardson traveled throughout the district, visiting every small town and pueblo, speaking both English and Spanish along way.

Richardson struggled through the primary in 1982. He received negative media attention after being forced to retract a statement in his campaign literature that claimed he spent three years working as Humphrey's top foreign affairs aide during his time on the Senate Foreign Relations Committee staff. In fact, Richardson had served on a subcommittee rather than the full committee and never held a leadership position. More bad press was generated when the Federal Election Commission looked into the source of a $100,000 campaign loan. The investigation revealed that Richardson's mother, still living in Mexico City, had helped Richardson obtain a certificate of deposit. Although cleared of any wrongdoing, the incident brought to light Richardson's privileged background. Despite his missteps, Richardson won the primary with 36 percent of the vote, and his continuous glad-handing earned him a relatively easy victory over Republican Marjorie Bell Chambers. Richardson remained in Congress for the next 14 years, winning every bid for reelection by more than 60 percent of the vote.

Had Long Career in Congress

As a member of Congress, Richardson served on numerous committees. In 1983 he was appointed to a coveted seat on the House Energy and Commerce Committee, where he worked as a strong proponent of increased natural gas use and had a significant role in 1990 of strengthening the environmental regulations outlined in the Clean Air Act. Other committee assignments included the Resource Committee on National Parks, Forests, and Lands, the Select Committee on

Intelligence, and the Helsinki Committee. In 1985 Richardson was elected as the chairman of the Congressional Hispanic Caucus, but controversy ensued after he supported immigration legislation that was opposed by most of the House's Hispanic members, leading to Richardson's resignation of the chairmanship. In 1993 he was named chairman of the Native American Affairs Committee, where he introduced some two dozen bills to improve health care and job training services to the Native American population.

During the 1988 presidential election, Richardson traveled widely to campaign for Democratic nominee Michael Dukakis. Although Dukakis' bid was unsuccessful, Richardson was given credit for a higher-than-average Hispanic turnout in the areas where he campaigned. In 1992 there was talk that Democratic presidential nominee Bill Clinton, a friend of Richardson, might tag the Congressman for the vice presidential spot. Although the rumors did not play out, Richardson earned a leadership role in Congress as one of four chief deputy Democratic whips following Clinton's election to the presidency.

During his years in Congress, Richardson pushed consistently for a trade agreement with Mexico. In 1992 debate began regarding the passage of the North American Free Trade Agreement (NAFTA), and Richardson quickly emerged as one of the agreement's most vocal proponents. Debate was heated, and Richardson proved instrumental in working with President Clinton to drum up sufficient support to ensure its passage. When NAFTA was passed in 1994, it created the world's largest tariff-free zone that spanned Mexico, the United States, and Canada.

Became Unofficial U.S. Ambassador

As a member of the House Intelligence Committee, Richardson traveled around the world on international fact-finding missions, and he soon earned a reputation for his abilities as an unofficial emissary for U.S. interests in unfriendly territories. In 1994 he traveled to Burma to work for the release of the Burmese opposition leader, Nobel-prize winner Aung San Suu Kyi, who had been under house arrest since 1989. Leading a United Nations (UN) delegation, Richardson and a *New York Times* reporter were able to arrange to meet with Suu Kyi for over five hours. Although nothing came directly from the meeting, the encounter did instigate further diplomatic activity that led to Suu Kyi's release the following year. Following his trip to Burma, Richardson's innate desire to appease all sides—a trait that some considered a strength and others, weakness—was also receiving attention. Calling for sanction against the government in front of human rights groups, Richardson would speak of the need to remain open when talking with leaders of the Burmese junta.

Following his trip to Burma in February of 1994, Richardson undertook a mission to North Korea in December of 1994. At issue was the North Korean government's sincerity in abiding by the pact it had made with the United States to freeze its nuclear weapons program. By coincidence, while Richardson was in North Korea, a U.S. military helicopter crashed north of the demilitarized zone. One crewman died, and the other was being held in Pyongyang. Richardson immediately informed the North Korean government that he would discuss nothing but the release of the U.S. pilot and the return of the remains of the crewman. The North Koreans continued to push talks on the arms agreement, but Richardson stubbornly refused, until tensions grew to the point that he was asked to leave the country. Holding his ground, Richardson refused to leave. Running up a $10,000 telephone bill with the U.S. State Department, Richardson worked tirelessly to secure the pilot's release. Three days, with negotiations in place, Richardson returned to the United States with the crewman's body. Several days later the pilot was released.

One of Richardson's most high profile diplomatic trips came in July of 1995 when he met with Iraqi president Saddam Hussein. Richardson arrived to discuss the release of two U.S. engineers, who had been imprisoned four months earlier after becoming lost and accidentally crossing the border from Kuwait into Iraq. Richardson's meeting with Hussein did not begin smoothly when Richardson unknowingly insulted Hussein by crossing his legs and showing the Iraq leader the soles of his feet. Hussein left the room but eventually returned. After a 90-minute discussion, Hussein agreed to release the engineers, successfully placing another feather in Richardson's cap.

Richardson was in flight again in December of 1996, this time traveling to the Sudan to negotiate the release of three Red Cross workers who had been taken hostage by rebel leader Kerubino Kwanyin Bol after their plane crashed. Later he was praised for his success in securing the release of the Red Cross workers, as well as five Sudanese who had also been on the plane. Richardson also received criticism for his friendly demeanor toward rebels known for committing crimes and atrocities, and for conceding to give the rebels jeeps, radios, and rice in exchange for the prisoners. Yet Richardson defended his negotiating style by noting that a good negotiator who does whatever gets results. He told *Fortune:* "You have to respect the other side's point of view. You have to know what makes your adversary tick. Certainly you want to have a goal. You want to come out of a meeting with something, even if it's only a second meeting. And basically you have to use every single negotiating technique you know—bluster, reverence, humor."

Path to Governorship

In 1992 Richardson was under consideration for the Interior Secretary's position, but the job went to Bruce Babbitt after environmental groups voiced fears that

Richardson would be too sympathetic to ranching interests. Four years later Clinton appointed Richardson as the new U.S. ambassador to the UN, replacing Madeleine Albright. Later, Richardson became embroiled in Clinton's Monica Lewinsky scandal after it was revealed that he had offered to create a job for the intern at the UN.

In 1999 Clinton convinced Richardson to accept an appointment as secretary of the Department of Energy. As energy secretary, Richardson came into the national spotlight when classified information turned up missing at the Los Alamos nuclear laboratory. Richardson and the administration did their best to blame security lapses on previous administrations, but when it was discovered in July of 2000 that two hard drives containing nuclear secrets mysteriously disappeared for a month, Richardson returned to the hot seat. Once widely rumored as Al Gore's probable choice as a running mate in the 2000, the upheaval in the Department of Energy pushed Richardson back down the list of vice-presidential hopefuls.

In 2000 Richardson resigned his position as secretary of the Department of Energy and returned to New Mexico. He spent 2001 teaching classes at Harvard University's Kennedy School of Government as well as at the United World College in Montezuma, New Mexico. He also worked as a business consultant in Santa Fe and served on the boards of several organizations, including Freedom House (a private organization that promotes democracy worldwide), the Natural Resources Defense Council, and the United Way International. On January 12, 2002, he announced his candidacy for governor of New Mexico.

During the 2002 gubernatorial race, Richardson once again undertook a nonstop press to meet the people and get out the vote. He shattered the world hand-shaking record by glad-handing 13,392 in an eight-hour period. Running on the platform of improved education, tax cuts, higher wages, and a comprehensive statewide water plan, Richardson won the election by the largest margin of victory since 1964. He was inaugurated as the governor of New Mexico on January 1, 2003. According to *Fox News,* when asked if he would accept a nomination to be the Democratic vice presidential candidate in 2004 if asked, Richardson said no, responding, "I love being governor. I love being in New Mexico."

Sources

Books

Contemporary Heroes and Heroines, Book IV, Farmington Hills, MI: Gale Group, 2000.
Ehrenhalt, Alan, ed. *Politics in America,* Washington, DC: CQ Press, 1983.

Periodicals

Economist, December 13, 1997.
Fortune, May 27, 1996.
Insight on the News, October 23, 1995.
National Review, August 30, 1999; July 3, 2000.
New Republican, November 27, 1997.
PR Newswire, July 25, 2000.

On-line

"Richardon: I Don't Want VP Slot," *Fox News,* www.foxnews.com/story/0,2933,85341,00.html (June 19, 2003).
Office of the Governor, State of New Mexico, www.governor.state.nm.us (June 19, 2003).

—Kari Bethel

Carlos Manuel Rodriguez

1918-1963

Religious educator

When he was beatified and thus placed on the road to sainthood by Pope John Paul II in 2001, Carlos Manuel Rodriguez became the first Caribbean-born—and only the second Latin American—lay individual (not a priest or a member of a religious order) to achieve that rank in the hierarchy of Catholic historical figures. Rodriguez, a Puerto Rican religious educator and writer active in the middle of the twentieth century, left a deep imprint on the island's dominant Catholic religion through his teachings and his exemplary life. Forty years after his death, as he approached beatification, Rodriguez became a focus of Puerto Rican protests against the United States Navy's use of the island of Vieques as a practice bombing range.

Carlos Manuel Rodriguez Santiago, known as Chali or Charlie, was born in the town of Caguas, Puerto Rico, on November 22, 1918. Now a suburb of San Juan, Caguas was then a small town whose residents were mostly poor. The Rodriguez family's house burned down when Rodriguez was six, and he and his four siblings had to move in with a grandmother. The religious impulse ran strong in the family. Rodriguez's brother became a priest in the Benedictine order and its first Puerto Rican-born abbot, and one of his three sisters grew up to be a Carmelite nun. When Rodriguez himself was four, his mother found him lying on his back in the courtyard of the family house, looking skyward and praying to God to come and get him.

Deeply Committed to Spirituality and Learning

Rodriguez entered the Catholic School of Caguas when he was six, by which time he could already read and write in Spanish and to some degree in English. He maintained a lifelong friendship with the Sisters of Notre Dame who operated the school, and he began to think of devoting his life to a religious calling. When he graduated from the school in 1932 he received the Medal of Religion award. His characteristic courage had also shown itself in the secular sphere, however: he stepped in when his one-year-old cousin was attacked by a police dog and stopped the attack.

Some of Rodriguez's family members blamed the shock of that incident for the beginnings of his lifelong stomach problems, which developed in his second

At a Glance . . .

Born Carlos Manuel Rodriguez Santiago on November 22, 1918, in Caguas, Puerto Rico; died on July 13, 1963; son of Manuel Baudilio Rodriguez and Herminia Santiago Rodriguez. *Education:* University of Puerto Rico, 1946-1947. *Religion:* Roman Catholic.

Career: Office clerk, early 1940s; University of Puerto Rico Agricultural Research Station, clerk, late 1940s-1950s; offered Catholic instruction and organized student clubs and discussion groups at numerous institutions in Puerto Rico, 1950s-1963; University of Puerto Rico Catholic Center, San Juan, instructor, late 1950s-1963; campaign for posthumous beatification carried on by religious followers, 1981-2001; Vatican posthumous investigation of miracles, early 1990s–; Vatican certified one miracle, 1999; beatified posthumously by the Vatican, 2001; Vatican examined Rodriguez case for sainthood, 2002–.

semester at Gautier Benítez High School in Caguas. His schooling was interrupted several times before he finally graduated in 1939. His ailment was diagnosed as ulcerative colitis, a serious illness that left him prey to high fevers and other incapacitating symptoms. Rodriguez worked as an office clerk during World War II and in 1946 enrolled at the University of Puerto Rico. Unable to cope with the rigors of university study because of his illness, he had to drop out after a year. But it was at this time that Rodriguez's friends began to notice the depth of his commitment to a life of spirituality and learning.

Studying on his own, Rodriguez read about literature, science, and philosophy in addition to religion. He learned, on his own, to play the piano and organ, and he became an avid naturalist and lover of the outdoors. Taking a job as a clerk at the university's agricultural research station, Rodriguez became more and more involved in Catholic lay activities at the school. He began translating religious writings from Latin, French, and English into Spanish, which he favored as a language of worship that could reach ordinary Puerto Ricans (at this time, the Catholic reforms mandating the use of vernacular languages in place of Latin were still years in the future). These efforts coalesced into a magazine, *Cultura Cristiana*, copies of which Rodriguez ran off on a mimeograph machine at first. He lived simply: over his entire adult life he is said to have owned only one pair of shoes.

Inspired Many in Life and Death

Most of Rodriguez's small office-worker's salary went to finance his religious activities, especially after he began organizing student religious clubs like the Circulo del Liturgía and teaching catechism classes. Rodriguez believed that Puerto Rican Catholic faith was being weakened by the rapid urbanization and industrialization, and he worked tirelessly to start student groups at schools and colleges all over the island. As a result, it was a rare member of the next generation of Puerto Rico's Catholic leadership who had not had contact with Rodriguez personally and been inspired by him. "To me, Charlie was a lay person committed to his faith, who lived his life so convinced of what he believed, and who was a living testimony of what an authentic Christian should be," Mother Rosa María Estrema told the *Orlando Sentinel* in an interview quoted on the *Puerto Rico Herald* website.

In the late 1950s Rodriguez was hired to teach full time at the University of Puerto Rico's Catholic Center in San Juan. His message, which stressed that every Catholic had the capacity to do Christ's work and emphasized the importance of direct communication of the faith in terms that ordinary worshippers could comprehend, anticipated in some respects the reforms of church's Vatican II conclave of the 1960s. Before Rodriguez could attend or witness those events, however, his stomach problems worsened into colon cancer. After living and working calmly in the face of severe pain for a time, he died at age 44 on July 13, 1963. "The 13th will be a good day," he had said several days before (according to his biography on the *Santaboricua* website).

Soon some of Rodriguez's friends and students had formed a group with the aim of carrying forward his work. In 1981 the group's treasurer, chemistry professor Carmen Santana, revealed to other members that she had traveled to Boston to be treated for advanced lymphatic cancer—but that when she arrived, doctors found the cancer had mysteriously disappeared. Santana's husband, she recounted, had said a prayer to Rodriguez for her recovery, which was deemed a miracle Rodriguez had accomplished—one of the preconditions for Catholic sainthood. The group drew inspiration from the designation by Pope John Paul II of 1987 as the Year of the Laity, and in the early 1990s began campaigning in earnest for Rodriguez's beatification.

Beatified by Pope John Paul II

The process, usually measured in decades, occurred with unprecedented speed. After an ecclesiastical investigation involving 38 witnesses to Carmen Santana's recovery, the Vatican agreed that a miracle had occurred. Bits of Rodriguez's exhumed bones and articles of his clothing were designated as relics and flown to Rome, and on April 29, 2001, Rodriguez was beatified (and thus given the title of "Blessed") by the Pope. Upwards of 2,500 Puerto Rican devotees attended the ceremony in Rome, and thousands turned out for subsequent observations in Puerto Rico itself; at one of those, Rodriguez's remains were moved from Humacao back to his hometown of Caguas.

Since he was not a martyr, evidence of two other miracles was required before Rodriguez could be elevated to sainthood. That seemed likely after the Vatican began investigating three more miracles credited to Rodriguez, including the case of a paralyzed woman who visited his home, put on his shoes, and shortly afterward began walking unaided. Another measure of Rodriguez's lasting impact was the role he played in Puerto Rico's ultimately successful efforts to put an end to the Navy bombing practice on Vieques, which was blamed for health problems among the island's poverty-stricken residents.

Demonstrators carried Rodriguez's picture, and San Juan Archbishop Roberto O. González called on Puerto Rican worshippers to pray to Rodriguez for a resolution of the situation. "The sanctity of Blessed Carlos is more powerful than the entire military might of the United States," he was quoted as saying by the *Catholic New York* website. The Navy suspended the bombing for several days at the time of the beatification ceremonies, an act attributed by many Puerto Ricans to Rodriguez's direct intervention. Strengthening the Catholic Church in Puerto Rico during his lifetime, he had, it seemed, strengthened the society of the island from beyond the grave.

Sources

Periodicals

Associated Press Worldstream, April 12, 2001; April 28, 2002.
Daily News (New York), May 3, 2001, p. Suburban-4.
Orlando Sentinel, April 30, 2001; May 1, 2002, El Sentinel ed.

On-line

"Beato Carlos M. Rodriguez: Apostol Laico de Puerto Rico," *Santoboricua,* www.santoboricua.com (May 23, 2003).
"San Juan archbishop urges prayers to beatified Puerto Rican in Vieques Strife," *Catholic New York,* http://cny.org/archive/ld/ld060701.htm (May 28, 2003).
"Thousands of Puerto Ricans Receive Blessed Charlie in His Home Town," *Catholic World News,* www.cwnews.com/Browse/2001/05/15618.htm (May 28, 2003).

—James M. Manheim

Phil Roman

1930—

Animator, producer, director

From the time he was eleven, Phil Roman always knew he would be an animator. Beginning as an usher in a theater that screened cartoons, he worked his way through the animation ranks to become one of the most successful and talented animators and animation producers America has seen. A six-time Emmy winner and founder of two film companies, Roman has directed, produced, and animated a number of television series, movies, and commercials.

Disney Movie Sparked Interest

Phil Roman was born on December 21, 1930, to Pedro and Ceceña Roman. The son of immigrant grape workers, Roman's first few memories were, according to *Latino Success*, "going to the vineyards and picking grapes in the hot summer." Although no stranger to hard work, he was always told that he would succeed beyond picking grapes in the vineyard. He remembered his mother constantly stating to Roman and his siblings "You guys are going to get ahead!" That would not be the last time his mother played a pivotal role in the journey that became Roman's life.

In 1942, when Roman was 12 years old, his mother took him to see the animated feature film, *Bambi*. It was from this moment, that Roman knew what his life's calling would be. Sitting in the dark theater, Roman found himself hypnotized by the characters on the screen. He had seen animation before *Bambi* but he had never seen characters come to life like Bambi, Thumper, and Flower. He was hooked. From that moment on, animation was Roman's driving force.

After the spark created by *Bambi*, Roman began drawing. He would copy Bambi onto scraps of paper. His love of drawing continued on through high school, where Roman gained the courage to ask a nun running the school newspaper if he could draw for the paper. She agreed. Roman stated this instance as one of the influences in his life as an animator. Such events, he stated in an interview with *Contemporary Hispanic Biography (CHB),* gave him "more impetus and belief" in himself.

During high school, Roman also took correspondence art courses. This was one of the few ways young people, growing up in small towns like Fresno, could gain an arts education. One of his courses was taught by a gifted artist everyone called Sparky. Sparky's real

At a Glance . . .

Born Philip Roman on December 21, 1930, in Fresno, CA; married Anita in 1970. *Education:* Hollywood Art Center School. *Military Service:* US Air Force.

Career: Animator, 1955–; director, 1970s–; producer, 1984–; Film Roman Inc., founder, 1984–, CEO, 1984-97, creative director, 1997-99; Phil Roman Entertainment, founder/CEO, 1999– .

Awards: Emmy Award, for *Garfield in the Rough,* 1984; Emmy Award, for *Garfield's Halloween Adventure,* 1985; Emmy Award, for *Garfield Babes & Bullets,* 1989; Movieguide Award, for *Tom and Jerry: The Movie,* 1993; Entrepreneur of the Year, Entertainment Category, 1995; Film Roman company named one of the 500 Most Successful Hispanic-owned Businesses, 1996; International TV Programming Award, 1996; Three Emmy Awards, for *The Simpsons;* Children's Advocacy Award, 1997; Hispanic Public Relations Association Permio Award, 1997; Trailblazer Award, 1999; Lifetime Achievement Award, given by Imagen Foundation, 1999; Lifetime Achievement Award, Entertainment Graphics Organization, 2001; Lifetime Achievement Award, Nosotros Foundation, 2001; Media Aztec Award, Mexican American Opportunity Foundation, 2002; Latino Legacy in Hollywood Award, Screen Actor's Guild, 2003.

Address: *Office*—Phil Roman Entertainment, 4040 Vineland Ave. Suite 205, Studio City, CA 91604.

name was Charles Schulz. In an interview with *CHB,* Roman stated that this was one of "those strange twists of life," as he would later go on to work with Schulz on the *Charlie Brown* cartoons. After graduation, Roman knew that he had to go to Los Angeles if he was to make it in the animation business. Having only $60 to his name, he boarded a bus to Los Angeles with a letter of introduction from the manager of the Fresno theater in which he worked.

Dissatisfied At Disney

Phil Roman arrived in Los Angeles at the Hollywood Art Center School. The kind and rather savvy head of the school noticed something in him and he was admitted as a work study student. Roman paid $30

down and $15 thereafter for tuition. Working two hours of manual labor after school allowed Roman to pay off the remaining debt. It was a reasonable arrangement and all was well until the outbreak of the Korean War. Roman left the Hollywood Art Center School for a three-year stint in the Air Force. He worked as a radio mechanic and was mainly stationed in France. He served his country well and upon returning stateside, continued his training at the Art Center. This time, the G.I. Bill helped pay for tuition. Soon, Roman completed his training and was off to find a job in his dream field.

In 1955 the dream that began by a Disney film came full circle as Roman began working at Disney Studios in California. He was hired as an assistant animator and was paid 99 cents per hour. His first assignment was animating cells for *Sleeping Beauty.* It seemed as if all was exactly how Roman had first dreamt it, but there was no room for growth in the booming Disney empire. Roman could continue to work at Disney, but he would have had to stay with the company for nearly a decade before he would become a full animator.

This was too slow for Roman, so in 1957 he left Disney for Imagination, Inc. in San Francisco. He recalled being told by his Disney colleagues that he was making a mistake and would wind up not being successful if he left the Disney studios. However, years later, those same people were laid off from Disney in a downsizing period and Roman had used the skills he'd learned at Imagination, Inc. along with his natural talent to become a success.

Animated Commercials and Cartoons

Imagination, Inc. was mainly a studio that specialized in television commercials. At the San Francisco firm, Roman was exposed to all aspects of the animation world. Roman gained more knowledge in animated production including contacting clients, sound design, camera work, storyboards and budgeting. This education would come in handy in the future as Roman built his own animation empire.

At Imagination, Inc., Roman's portfolio grew. He directed well-known animated commercials like Star-Kist Tuna's "Sorry Charlie" ad and the Western Airlines bird who sipped champagne and knew "The only way to fly!" He learned every step of the process and gained valuable experience. He was now armed with education, knowledge, and experience. After two years at Imagination, Inc., Roman was ready to take on Hollywood again.

Returning to Hollywood in 1959, Roman began working for several top studios including Warner Bros. Cartoons, MGM Animation and UPA Film. Throughout the 1960s, Roman honed his craft and gained more and more experience in the animation industry.

He worked on many projects in this period including the 1965 MGM Oscar-winning *The Dot And The Line*. In 1966 Roman worked as an animator on the CBS Christmas special, *How the Grinch Stole Christmas,* animating the Grinch and Cindy Lou Who. Roman also had the chance to work with such talents at Jay Ward and Chuck Jones. For MGM, Roman worked on shorts of a cat and mouse team named Tom and Jerry. He would come back to the famous duo in the early 1990s in a movie.

The 1970s saw continued success for Roman. This was not only a time of professional success, but personal success as well. In 1970 Roman married his wife Anita. They met 15 years earlier at the wedding of his brother. Roman was the best man and his future wife was the maid of honor. They dated whenever he would make it back to Fresno, but he did not make the final commitment until things began to move along in his career.

In 1970 Roman also began his association with Bill Melendez, of Bill Melendez Productions. This relationship lasted until 1983, and allowed Roman to rise from the title of animator to co-director alongside Melendez. While working with Melendez, Roman directed sixteen animated specials including *He's Your Dog, Charlie Brown!, Bon Voyage, Charlie Brown!,* and *Race for Your Life, Charlie Brown!.* Out of Roman's 16 specials, 15 programs received Emmy nominations. Three of the specials won Emmy awards. Along with Melendez, Roman associated with Ralph Bakshi, who also had his own production studio. Roman worked as an animator for Bakshi's 1978 *Lord of the Rings*.

Founded Own Company

In 1984 Roman founded Film Roman, Inc., with a contract to produce animated specials based on popular comic-strip character, Garfield, created by Jim Davis. The first two Garfield specials, *Here Comes Garfield,* and *Garfield on the Town*, were directed by Roman while he was still working for Melendez Productions. The first special produced under Roman's new company was *Garfield in the Rough*. The special was awarded an Emmy. Film Roman went on to produce nine more Garfield specials. In 1986 two of Roman's Garfield specials were the only animated specials to receive Emmy nominations. He was assured an Emmy that year, winning it for *Garfield's Halloween Adventure*. The final Garfield Emmy came in 1989 with *Garfield's Babes & Bullets*.

In 1992 Film Roman began a relationship with a yellow family created by Matt Groening. *The Simpsons*, the longest-running animated series, became one of Film Roman's most successful ventures. Between the years of 1992 and 1999, Film Roman was responsible for seeing that the popular family made it to the television screen weekly. This responsibility paid off as the show garnered Film Roman three Emmys. Film Roman also produced the popular Butterfinger commercials that featured the Simpson characters.

In 1990 Roman brought his animation success to the former Soviet Union by co-founding ASK/Roman Animation Studios, one of the first full-service animation facilities in the former communist country. Known since the 1920s for their animation talent, the Russian animators welcomed the venture and the joint company went on to produce a five-minute animated short, "Lucky Start." This relationship continued in 1993 when Film Roman acquired old Russian cartoons from the 1920s. His company took the old cartoons and restored the prints plus added music. The result was the *Animated Classic Showcase* which featured these old cartoons refurbished for new viewers.

Stateside, Roman continued to take on more projects including such popular series as *The Mask, Bobby's World,* and *The Critic*. In 1996 Film Roman had exclusive animation rights to Izzy, the Olympic Games mascot, and Film Roman produced a prime time special featuring the character. Roman's company also created and produced Fox Network's hugely successful *King of the Hill* cartoon.

The late 1990s saw trouble brewing for Roman and his company. Since its start, Film Roman grew from freelancers to a staff of more than 300. Profits rose to approximately $50 million. The company went public to garner funds for more big budget projects. The UPN Network backed out of a deal that cost Film Roman $2 million. With investors shaky, Roman was demoted from CEO to creative director. With most animation being done by computer, many thought he would jump on the bandwagon. Instead, Roman tendered his resignation and started another animation production company, Phil Roman Entertainment. This company would focus on keeping the cell tradition alive. However, Roman remained a major shareholder in Film Roman. Under his new company, Roman continued to produce animated specials including, *Grandma Got Run Over by a Reindeer*. He rejoined Film Roman's board of directors in 2001. In 2002 his two companies combined focusing on both computer-generated and cell animation.

Gave Back to the Community

Roman has not forgotten his experience and the mentors that helped him get where he is today. In honor of his experience, Roman established an internship program that allows high school students and other young animators to work in the animation studio. This gives them the chance that Roman received when he began his journey at the Hollywood Art Center School.

In addition to assisting youth in their careers, Roman is also involved in the enrichment of the Hispanic-American community. Roman serves on the U.S. Republican Conference Task Force on Hispanic Affairs and frequently travels to Washington, D.C., to attend meetings with political and industrial players. Roman also serves as a member of the board of trustees for the Hispanic College Fund. He has received the Trailblazer Award from *Hispanic Magazine* as well as a Lifetime Achievement Award from the Imagen Foundation.

Roman saw his heritage as a contributing factor in his creativity and imagination, but also gave credit to his diligence as a factor in his success. He stated in *Latino Success,* "The great thing about this business is that you're judged only on what you do, not who you are.... Your product should speak for you, nothing else. Absolutely."

Selected works

Films

Lord of the Rings, 1978.
Tom and Jerry: The Movie, 1992.

Shorts

The Dot and the Line, 1965.

Television series

Bobby's World, 1990-98.
Garfield & Friends, 1988-95.
The Simpsons, 1992-99.
The Critic, 1993-95.
The Mask, 1995-97.
King of the Hill, 1997-99.

Television specials

How the Grinch Stole Christmas, 1965.
He's Your Dog, Charlie Brown!, 1968.

Race for Your Life, Charlie Brown!, 1977.
Bon Voyage, Charlie Brown!, 1980.
Here Comes Garfield, 1982.
Garfield on the Town, 1983.
Garfield in the Rough, 1984.
Garfield's Halloween Adventure, 1985.
Garfield's Babes & Bullets, 1989.
Grandma Got Run Over by a Reindeer, 2000.

Sources

Books

Latino Success, Simon & Schuster, 1996.

Periodicals

Business Wire, February 20, 2002.
Frenso Bee, September 4, 1999, p. E2.
Los Angeles Times, March 2, 1999, p. 2.
PR Newswire, February 5, 1990.
SHOOT, August 20, 1999, p. 16.

On-line

"Phil Roman," *Internet Movie Database,* http://us.imdb.com/Name?Roman,+Phil (June 14, 2003).
Phil Roman Entertainment, www.philromanent.com, (May 1, 2003).

Other

Additional information for this profile was obtained through an interview with *Contemporary Hispanic Biography* on May 20, 2003.

—Adam R. Hazlett

Ileana Ros-Lehtinen

1952—

U.S. Congressional representative

The first Cuban American and the first Hispanic woman elected to the United States Congress, Ileana Ros-Lehtinen has become, in the words of the *Boston Globe,* "a living symbol of Cuban-American achievement." Ros-Lehtinen is a staunch conservative and an implacable foe of the communist regime of Cuba's Fidel Castro, but she has diverged from the usual positions of the Republican Party to which she belongs on issues relating to the treatment of immigrants. An outspoken woman often in the headlines for her sharp advocacy of positions she believes in, Ros-Lehtinen is a fixture of south Florida's colorful political scene.

Quickly Adapted to New Country

The daughter of accountant Enrique Ros and his wife Amanda Adato Ros, Ileana Ros-Lehtinen was born in Havana, Cuba, on July 15, 1952. She was raised Catholic like most other Cubans, but her mother's father was Jewish. The family left Cuba in 1960, a year after Castro seized power, and supported the U.S.-backed Bay of Pigs invasion aimed at toppling the Castro government in 1961. After that effort failed, however, the Ros children were raised as Americans.

Ileana spoke no English at all when she arrived in Miami, but she adapted quickly to her new homeland. "She was such a normal person to grow up with," her childhood friend Maria St. George told the *Globe.* "When I first met her she was a very American Cuban, not very Latin."

That quick adaptation, however, masked much hard work. Growing up in the 1960s, Ros-Lehtinen did not have the benefit of bilingual education classes, and she would resist Republican-inspired English-only legislation when she became a political leader. "I was lost during the first year I was in the United States because we did not have those bilingual programs," she told *Insight on the News.* "In my second year it was better, and in my third year I was ready for my English classroom." Ros-Lehtinen's father stressed the importance of education, living away from his family for a time in order to improve his English and eventually earning an American college degree through night courses in Miami.

Ros-Lehtinen chose an educational career for herself, earning an associate's degree at Miami-Dade Community College in 1972 and going on for a bachelor's degree at Florida International University in 1975. In 1986 she earned a master's in educational leadership

At a Glance . . .

Born Ileana Ros on July 15, 1952, in Havana, Cuba; daughter of Enrique Emilio Ros and Amanda Adato Ros; married Dexter Lehtinen; children: Amanda, Patricia; stepchildren: Katharine, Douglas. *Education:* Miami-Dade Community College, AA, 1972; Florida International University, BA, 1975, MS, 1986; University of Miami, doctoral studies, 1990s. *Politics:* Republican.

Career: Teacher, mid-1970s; Eastern Academy Elementary School, founder, principal, and teacher, 1978-85; Florida House of Representatives, state representative, 1982-86; Florida Senate, state senator, 1986-89; U.S. House of Representatives, Florida's 18th District representative, 1989–; Committee on International Operations & Human Rights, chair, 2001–.

Addresses: *Office*—2160 Rayburn House Office Bldg., Washington, DC 20515. *Website*—www.house.gov/ros-lehtinen.

from the same school, and she began work on her doctorate in the 1990s. After teaching for several years in the mid-1970s, she opened a private elementary school of her own, the Eastern Academy, teaching and serving as its principal until 1985.

Won First Election

By the time Ros-Lehtinen had retired from the Eastern Academy she already had entered politics. She inherited her interest in politics from her father, who has been described as the mastermind of her political career, but she took naturally to the backslapping world of politics on her own and as of 2003 has never lost an election. Elected to the Florida House of Representatives in 1982, she spent four years there and then won election to the state senate in 1986. There she gained not only political contacts but also a husband: fellow legislator Dexter Lehtinen was a Miami lawyer who served as U.S. attorney for south Florida during the administration of President George H.W. Bush. The couple raised two children of their own as well as two children from Lehtinen's previous marriage, and Ros-Lehtinen's parents, who lived across the street, were there to help out as she juggled motherhood and her rising career trajectory.

Ros-Lehtinen's breakthrough to the national level came in 1989 with the death of longtime Democratic Rep. Claude Pepper. Both the Democratic and Republican

primaries to replace Pepper in an 18th district special election were hotly contested, and Ros-Lehtinen emerged as the opponent of Democratic lawyer Gerald Richman. The ensuing campaign was marked by charges of racism on both sides, as Republicans stressed the importance of electing a Cuban candidate while Richman retorted that the seat in Congress should be regarded as an "American seat" rather than as one belonging to any particular group. Ros-Lehtinen won the election with 53 percent of the vote, gaining an overwhelming majority of the Cuban-American vote but losing heavily among Anglo- and African-American voters. After taking her place in Congress in 1989 she made gestures of reconciliation and was reelected easily in subsequent contests.

During her years in the state legislature, Ros-Lehtinen had moved from a focus on the Cuba issue to the nuts and bolts of constituent service, and in Congress she worked on a mix of national, international, and local issues. She continued to resist any weakening of the U.S. government's anti-Castro policies, emerging as a strong supporter of the Helms-Burton Act (which slapped penalties on companies that traded with the Cuban regime) and leading an ultimately successful drive to block construction of a Cuban nuclear reactor. In 2000 Ros-Lehtinen found herself in the thick of the controversy over six-year-old Cuban Elian Gonzalez, who became the object of a tug-of-war between his Florida relatives and his father in Cuba after a boat carrying him and his mother sank; Elian was rescued after his mother was killed.

Took on More Controversial Issues

"No one talks about Elian's mother, about her sacrifice, so he could reach liberty in this beautiful country," Ros-Lehtinen was quoted as saying by the *New York Times*. The Cuban government (according to the *Times*) called her a "ferocious wolf disguised as a woman," to Ros-Lehtinen's delight. Ros-Lehtinen's already high profile in south Florida was raised further, and her husband contemplated a run for mayor of Miami in the early 2000s. Ros-Lehtinen, as chair of the House Subcommittee on International Operations and Human Rights beginning in 2001, emerged as a strong supporter of Israel and of President George W. Bush's foreign policies, as well as working to scuttle attempts to open up agricultural trade with Cuba. In 2003 she raised eyebrows when she denounced a State Department analyst during administration infighting over how to deal with an Iranian exile group active in Iraq during the Gulf War, calling him a "weasel," and a "gutless bureaucrat who won't come out of his cave," according to *The Hill*.

Ros-Lehtinen's record on domestic issues was mixed and often pragmatic. Conservative in her basic orientation, she was strongly opposed to abortion and in 2000 sponsored a bill (ultimately passed by the House by a 417-0 vote) to ban the execution of pregnant women. She has been active in the area of crime victims' rights and has proposed a constitutional victims' rights amendment. On other issues such as reductions in welfare payments to immigrants, Ros-Lehtinen deserted her Republican colleagues. She refused to sign the Contract with America during the 1994 congressional campaign due to what she considered its anti-immigrant bias, and she urged the party to pay more attention to immigrants' concerns. In 2003 she plunged into the controversial issue of the proposed merger between the giant Spanish-language broadcast firms Univision and HBC, urging government regulators to approve the merger.

"I wish our party would be more aggressive in courting [the] Hispanic vote but because of welfare and immigration reform and English-only issues we are afraid to try and solicit their support," Ros-Lehtinen was quoted as saying by *The Almanac of American Politics*. With the Hispanic vote increasingly up for grabs and Ros-Lehtinen's trademark frosted dark hair an increasingly visible presence at the national level, it seemed likely that Republican policymakers would listen closely to what she had to say. Hers was already an immigrant success story of the first order.

Sources

Books

Barone, Michael, and Richard E. Cohen, with Charles E. Cook Jr., *The Almanac of American Politics 2002*, National Journal, 2001.
Dictionary of Hispanic Biography, Gale, 1996.
Newsmakers 2000, Issue 2, Gale, 2000.

Periodicals

Boston Globe, August 31, 1989, p. 3.
Insight on the News, February 22, 1999, p. 21.
The Hill, April 8, 2003, p. 4.
Jerusalem Post, March 11, 2003, p. 4.
Knight-Ridder/Tribune Business News Service, February 27, 2003.
National Right to Life News, August 2000.
New York Times, January 10, 2000, p. A12.
St. Petersburg Times, August 30, 1989, p. A1.
Time, September 11, 1989, p. 31.

On-line

"Ileana Ros-Lehtinen," *U.S. House of Representatives*, www.house.gov/ros-lehtinen (May 29, 2003).

—James M. Manheim

Paulina Rubio

1971—

Singer, actress

Already one of the brightest stars in the pantheon of Latin American popular music, Paulina Rubio seems poised to become the next big Latin crossover success, following in the footsteps of Shakira, Enrique Iglesias, and Ricky Martin. The daughter of one of Mexico's most successful film stars, Susana Dosamantes, Rubio got into music at an early age, recording her first record at the tender age of three. She made her professional musical debut in 1981 as an original member of the pre-teen singing group Timbiriche, which enjoyed great popularity throughout Latin America. Although she never really left music behind, Rubio in the late 1980s and early 1990s made a detour into acting, appearing in two of Mexico's most popular telenovelas—*Pasión y poder* and *Pobre niña rica*. A member of Timbiriche until 1991, Rubio struck out on her own as a singer with a debut solo album entitled *La chica dorada—The Golden Girl*—a nickname by which she is still known in her native Mexico and elsewhere in Latin America. Only a year after topping the Latin music charts with her hit CD *Paulina,* Rubio crashed the English-language pop market with *Border Girl,* which debuted at number 11 on the U.S. pop music charts in June of 2002.

Joined Teen Singing Group

Paulina Rubio Dosamantes was born on June 17, 1971, in Mexico City, Mexico. Her parents, attorney Enrique Rubio and film actress Susana Dosamantes, divorced three years later. Paulina and her younger brother lived with their mother, with whom they traveled frequently, spending a good deal of their early years not only in Mexico but in Europe and the United States as well. Of her nomadic childhood, Rubio commented on her official website, "My mom was shooting a lot of films in Europe when I was young, so we were traveling with her around the world, with a lot of artists around: writers, architects, singers, filmmakers. It made me very independent, and that is when I started making some of my own decisions, at around seven or eight." A budding singer from the time she was a toddler, Rubio also spent time investigating other artistic pursuits such as painting, ballet, and acting. However, by the time she was eight, Rubio had decided she wanted to focus more on singing and dancing, prompting her mother to enroll her in a performing arts school. The training paid off for Rubio, who two years later was selected to be a founding member of the singing group Timbiriche.

Timbiriche proved an excellent launching pad for Rubio, who became widely known throughout Latin America as a member of the wildly popular teen singing group for nearly a decade. Despite the immense popularity of Timbiriche, Rubio continued to work quietly to hone the skills she knew she'd need to guarantee a lasting career in the music business. She found time to continue her studies, taking private jazz, singing, and phonetics lessons in Los Angeles. Of her years with Timbiriche, Rubio, in a 2002 told an interviewer for the *Orca Sound* website, said, "I joined the group at a young age and stayed with them for about ten years. We were like Menudo, except we were girls. They gave me my first opportunity and because of that I am here today."

While still a member of Timbiriche, Rubio decided to try her hand at acting and at the age of 17 joined the cast of the popular Mexican telenovela *Pasión y poder*. Cast as a villainous seductress, Rubio was an instant hit with fans of the show but later worked hard to shed the somewhat unsavory image she'd picked up as a character on the show. Her success on *Pasión y poder* later led to further television roles on *Baile conmigo* and *Pobre niña rica*, as well as her film debut in 1994 in *Bésame en la boca*. Although well received as an actress, Rubio made clear in an interview on her official website that music remained her first—and most passionate—love. "Acting was like a hobby for me, but music is my priority. I love to perform and to spread my music and my messages." A starring role in *Vaselina*, the Spanish-language version of the popular musical comedy *Grease*, afforded Rubio an opportunity to draw upon both her musical and dramatic talents.

Launched Solo Singing Career

After about a decade with Timbiriche, during which she recorded ten albums with the group, Rubio decided the time had come to try her wings as a solo performer. In 1992 she released her first solo CD, *La chica dorada*, which was a success, going platinum. The album, recorded in Spain, spawned a number of number one singles on the Latin music charts, including "Amor de Mujer" and "Mio." Of Rubio's debut recording, a collection of dance, pop, and rock tunes, *Hispanic* critic Mark Holston wrote, "Much like her role model, Madonna, Rubio is more about style than musical substance. But the album does yield some gems, like the moody 'Sabor a Miel.'" Holston was not the only critic to see a strong connection between Madonna and Rubio, whose music videos oozed the same brand of sensuality long associated with her American counterpart. He was also not the only critic to comment on a lack of substance in Rubio's music.

Rubio's successful solo debut as "The Golden Girl" was quickly followed by her second CD, *24 kilates* in 1993. Not long after its release, Rubio's follow-up album was certified gold. Like its predecessor, the second album spawned a handful of hit singles, including "Nieva, Nieva" and "Asunto de doas." Although the public seemed to have fallen head over heels for Rubio, critics continued to be lukewarm in their appraisal of her talents, suggesting that the singer's popularity had much more to do with her looks than with her singing ability. After being labeled a "sexpot pinup" in a *Los Angeles Times* profile by Agustin Garza, Rubio defended her onstage performances and sexy image. "Well, maybe I'm cheap sometimes. I don't care. Whoever doesn't like it, well, too bad. I'm not going to change because of anyone. On stage, I feel free to do whatever I want to do. I was raised in an environment in which women were always the ones who pulled the family through. The stereotype of the Mexican woman as fragile, full of children, and powerless has completely disappeared. I believe I am a woman with a strong character who knows the value of discipline and decisiveness."

Next up for Rubio, after the success of her first two albums, was *Tiempo es oro*, a CD released in 1995. A year later, she followed up with *Planeta Paulina*. Sales for both her third and fourth CDs were disappointing, prompting Rubio to sever her professional relationship with the Capitol-EMI label not long after the release of *Planeta Paulina*. Of her handling by her former record label, Rubio later told *Billboard*, "I think [EMI] saw me in a way that I didn't fit into. They tried one thing and another and finally I couldn't take it anymore." What followed was a four-year hiatus from recording, during which time Rubio spent a great deal of time pondering the future direction of her musical career. In 2000, recording now for Universal Records, Rubio released her fifth solo CD, titled simply *Paulina*. It proved to be a very successful comeback for Rubio. The new CD sold more than four million copies in the United States alone and was ranked the top-selling album of 2001 on *Billboard*'s Latin album charts. Her successful return to recording was made all the sweeter by the three awards she won at the 2001 El Premio de la Gente Ritmo Latino Music Awards—including Album of the Year, Best Female Artist of the Year, and Best Music Video for "Y yo sigo aqui."

Sought English-Language Project

Although Rubio had long wanted to break into the English-language music market, she had a tough time convincing manager Dario de Leon that the time was right for a crossover attempt. When de Leon continued to resist Rubio's push for the English-language project, arguing that such a move might drive away some of her existing Latino fans, she ended their relationship and hired in his place Angelo Medina and Ricardo Cordero. Medina and Cordero, who had helped guide Puerto Rican singer Ricky Martin to mainstream success, promised to do the same for Rubio.

A little over a month before the June 2002 release of her debut English-language CD, Rubio was once again honored, but this time it was for her beauty and not her music. In May of 2002, *People en Espanol* announced that the Mexican singer had topped its 2002 list of the "25 Most Beautiful Latin Entertainers," besting such other contenders as *The Sopranos* co-star Jamie Lynn Sigler, singer Enrique Iglesias, *NYPD Blue* cast member Esai Morales, and *Rush Hour 2* co-star Rosalyn Sanchez. In announcing the magazine's top pick for 2002, the managing editor of *People en Espanol,* Angelo Figueroa, told the Associated Press, "Paulina is not only beautiful and sexy, but she has that star quality that will certainly put her on the map.... She is destined to be the next breakout performer."

Interviewed by *USA Today* in May of 2002, shortly before the release of her first English-language CD, Rubio spoke fondly of her relationship with Latin singer Marc Anthony and some of the other Latino singing stars who had already made the crossover to mainstream music. "Marc and Ricky and Shakira and Enrique and J. Lo are my friends. We all grew together, wanting in our minds to release worldwide albums. And we all know that Julio Iglesias and Gloria Estefan and Carlos Santana worked hard to open that door for us. Now we're family, in a new moment in music's history." She went on to describe the new CD, *Border Girl,* as "a fusion of rhythms and cultures from all over the world. I think my music is a representation of globalization and of the present time. I love techno music—to me, DJs are musicians now. But I also use acoustic rhythms, and I have my roots. When you hear guitars crying in my music, that's Mexico. When you don't live in Mexico, the country lives inside you."

Critics Were Again Unimpressed

Rubio's *Border Girl* debuted on June 18, 2002, and hit number 11 on the U.S. pop album charts. In her native Mexico, Rubio's first English-language CD made its debut in the number-one position. Although the public was as clearly taken with Rubio in English as they had been with her in native Spanish, the critics predictably were less kind. Of the "Golden Girl's" attempt to establish herself as a singer in the United States, Associated Press music writer Nekesa Mumbi Moody observed, "Unfortunately, Rubio hasn't found her identity yet, as she tries to appeal to as many genres as possible over 16 tracks. She's Britney Spears on one song, J. Lo on another, and Faith Hill on the next. That approach might have worked if the songs weren't so mediocre—and Rubio's slight voice so generic." Equally unkind was the reviewer for *E! Online,* who wrote: "This girl knows how to make an impression. The Latin sensation not only made her first appearance on the cover of Spanish *Rolling Stone* buck naked, but she also reveals a good deal of flesh on her debut disc's cover. Too bad this *Border Girl*'s crossover attempt lands somewhere between Ricky Martin-lame and absolutely annoying."

Never one to be unduly discouraged by bad reviews, Rubio toured during the fall of 2002 in support of *Border Girl.* She also put out another album in 2003 called *Canta Como.* Away from the concert stage and recording studio, the singer maintains homes in Los Angeles, Mexico City, and Miami. She also owns a Miami Beach restaurant called L'Entrecote de Paris. Unmarried, Rubio has had a long-running romance with Spanish-born architect Ricardo Bofill Maggiora. As to what the future holds, Rubio leaves little doubt. She said on her official website, "I grew up doing concerts and I'm going to die doing concerts all over the world. That's what I'm here for and what I believe in."

Selected works

Albums

La Chica Dorada, Capitol, 1992.
24 Kilates, Capitol/EMI, 1993.
Tiempo Es Oro, EMI, 1995.
Planeta Paulina, EMI, 1996.
Paulina, Universal, 2000.
Border Girl, Universal, 2002.
Canta Como, Miami, 2003.

Films

Bésame en la boca, 1994.

Television

Pasión y poder, 1988.
Baila conmigo, 1992.
Pobre niña rica, 1995.

Sources

Books

Contemporary Musicians, Volume 39, Gale Group, 2003.

Periodicals

AP Wire, May 5, 2002.
AP Worldstream, June 21, 2002.
Hispanic, March 1993.
Los Angeles Times, June 9, 2002.
People, July 22, 2002.
USA Today, June 10, 2002.

On-line

"Border Girl Visits Montreal: Meet Paulina Rubio," *Orca Sound Website,* www.orcasound.com/re views/paulina_rubio_interview2002.html (July 23, 2003).

Official Paulina Rubio Website, www.paulinaru bio.com/relaunch.html (June 20, 2003).

"Paulina Rubio," *AskMen,* www.askmen.com/women /singer_100/131_paulina_rubio.html (June 20, 2003).

"Paulina Rubio," *Biography Resource Center Online,* www.galenet/servlet/BioRC (June 20, 2003).

"Paulina Rubio," *Sing365,* www.sing365.com/music/ lyric.nsf/singerUnid/9AA0C520C4B5B98F48256 BE200186D50 (June 20, 2003).

"Paulina Rubio: Biography," *100% Paulina Rubio,* www.100percent-online.com/paulina_rubio/biogra phy.asp (June 20, 2003).

"Paulina Rubio *Border Girl,*" *E! Online,* www.e online.com/Reviews/Facts/Music/RevID/ 0,1107,2718,00.html (June 20, 2003).

—Don Amerman

Gabriela Sabatini

1970—

Tennis player, fragrance designer

Over her 12-year pro career, tennis player Gabriela Sabatini won 27 career singles titles, including the 1990 U.S. Open and two season-ending Virginia Slims Championships. She came close to winning Wimbledon in 1991, and from age 15 to 26, spent most of those years in the top ten ranking of tennis. She retired from tennis in 1996 to devote her time to a career in the perfume industry.

Showed Natural Talent

Sabatini was born on May 16, 1970, in Buenos Aires, Argentina. She grew up watching her father and older brother play tennis at a country club in their home town, and she began playing when she was six years old, quickly showing a natural talent for the game. Her brother, Osvaldo, later told Ron Arias in *People,* "She begged me to let her play. So I gave her an old racket and sent her off to go hit against a wall. All day she'd pound the ball. She was only six but right away we could see she could hit." Sabatini's father soon signed her up for a local clay court program.

By the time she was ten, Sabatini was ranked number one in the country's 12-and-under division, and she continued to hold the number one spot as she moved up through the age group levels. Her brother told Arias, "She hated to lose. In those days she'd fight me all the way—on and off the court. Tennis, Ping-Pong, it didn't matter. She'd fight me, yelling and crying." At the age of 14, Sabatini was number one in the junior world rankings. After a year of junior high school, having beaten all the local competition, she decided to take her game farther. She signed with coach Patricio Apey, a former Chilean Davis Cup player, and moved to Key Biscayne, Florida, to train with him and the other players he coached.

Apey was impressed with Sabatini's ability, and so were her fellow Argentineans, who quickly turned her into a tennis idol. Apey told Bruce Newman in *Sports Illustrated,* "Suddenly in the middle of all the depression and bad news, when everything seemed to be wrong in Argentina, there comes this little angel who makes only good news. I think that is what made her an idol." At the time, Argentina was recovering from the Falklands war as well as the aftereffects of a long-lived dictatorship.

Intensity Won Tournaments

Sabatini's rapid rise to success at such a tender age caused concern among other observers. Dick Dell, who became her agent when she was 14, told Newman that Sabatini was focusing too much of her energy on tennis at a very young age and was thus losing her only chance to have a normal childhood. "I am for anything that would give her an outlet outside tennis," he said. "Instead of being in school every day with girls her own age, she was thrown into an adult world." Sabatini dropped out of school after moving to the United States, and she did not learn to speak English for three more years.

Sabatini's inability to speak English, combined with an innate shyness, led some to believe she was cold and aloof. However, this quality appealed to other observers. Tim Tinling, a tennis official, told Newman, "I think that aloofness is part of her charisma. There's a great arrogance about Sabatini, and it all shows in the carriage of her head. She looks almost goddesslike. Taken together, her beauty and her arrogance form a contradiction. And I don't think one should try to solve a contradiction in a beautiful woman. One has simply to accept her as she is."

Sabatini began making a mark on the international tennis world in 1984, when she won seven of the eight junior tournaments she entered. In that same year she became the youngest player ever to win a round at the U.S. Open, and when she won a second Open round,

the press and other players began calling her "The Great Sabatini." She turned professional shortly afterward, and in June of 1985, she beat two top-ten-ranked players in one morning at the Family Circle Magazine Cup Tournament. Two months later, she reached the semifinals of the French Open, the youngest player ever to do so, and was ranked number 15 in the world. In July of 1985 she competed at Wimbledon, and in August she beat the top seed, Pam Shriver, in the quarterfinals of the United Jersey Bank Classic. In that same year, she was named *Tennis* magazine's Rookie of the Year.

In 1987 Sabatini changed coaches, hiring Angel Gimenez, a former Davis Cup player from Spain. She and Gimenez both worked on increasing her stamina and conditioning. Her training included running for up to an hour each day and practicing for longer hours on the court. By 1988 this training led to results: Sabatini was ranked fifth in the world. And at the end of the 1988 Virginia Slims tournament in Boca Raton, Florida, Sabatini won the final two sets against Steffi Graf, a player whom she had never been able to beat before. Ironically, although she had often been intimidated when it came to the task of beating Graf, she often played successfully with Graf in doubles tournaments.

Reached Peak of Tennis Career

Despite her improvement, Sabatini lost both the U.S. Open and the Summer Olympics finals to Graf in 1988. However, she still won $1 million during that year. In 1989 she continued to win money and tournaments, but failed to gain any major titles. After losing at the 1990 French Open, Sabatini decided to change coaches again. She hired Carlos Kimayr, a top-ranked Brazilian player. Under his guidance, she stopped lifting weights—they had added muscle, but what she really needed was speed—and began seeing a sports psychologist. Kimayr suggested this because he believed she was spending too much time thinking about tennis. He told Alison Muscatine in the *Washington Post*, "She was thinking about her job all the time. It is impossible to act and work like a professional when you live your job twenty-four hours a day." Kimayr and the psychologist encouraged Sabatini to pursue other interests, such as photography, studying French, and sightseeing. In addition, they convinced her to end her doubles partnership with Graf. Kimayr told Muscatine that Sabatini "was not benefiting from that relationship. Steffi was mentally stronger. I didn't think that was a good thing."

The changes in her coaching and lifestyle paid off in 1990, when Sabatini won her first Grand Slam title, the 1990 U.S. Open, beating Graf in the process. Sabatini was now ranked number one in the world, but a new rival soon appeared on the scene: Monica Seles. Seles beat Sabatini at the Virginia Slims Championships, in a five-set final that lasted almost four hours.

By April of 1991, Sabatini had earned $4 million, the fifth-highest amount on the women's tour. Like other players, she made a great deal of money from product endorsements; unlike other players, she had had a perfume named after her. She endorsed the fragrance at the 1991 U.S. Open; it cost $50 for a quarter-ounce.

Retired From Tennis

In early 1992 Sabatini won five tournaments, but she was losing her enthusiasm for the game. By 1994, she had gone two years without winning a tournament, and she was further disgraced at the French Open, when Silvia Farini, who was ranked 108 in the world, beat the number-eight ranked Sabatini. It was only the second time in her pro career that Sabatini had failed to make it past the first round in a Grand Slam event. Of this apparent slump, she told Sally Jenkins in *Sports Illustrated*, "People keep asking me [if I'm burned out]. They want to know if I'm tired, do I need more time off? No. I doubt the solution is in a vacation." She said she would keep playing. "I love this sport. I'm happy to be out there. I like to keep trying and I like to work hard. I just don't like to lose."

However, she did continue to lose, and in 1996, she suffered a pulled stomach muscle that kept her out of the French Open and Wimbledon; her ranking had already dropped to 31. On October 15 Sabatini played what would be her last match, against Jennifer Capriati at the European Indoor in Zurich, Switzerland, and lost 6-3, 6-4. In the locker room after the match, she wept. According to Josh Young in the *Washington Times*, "She said she wasn't crying out of sadness, but out of relief, giving us a glimpse of the real Sabatini." At a news conference announcing her retirement, Sabatini said, "This is what I want to do for my life, this is what makes me happy, and this was the right time to do it," according to Young. Her coach at the time, Juan Nunez, said, "She lost the fire to compete because of the pressure she's put on herself over the years to make

other people—her fans, her family, her coaches— happy, and in doing that I think she left aside a big part of herself. It broke my heart to see her suffering out there. I felt like I was pushing her to do things she didn't want to do anymore."

During the press conference where she announced her retirement from tennis, Sabatini said that she wanted to devote her attention to her perfume business. She has lived quietly and has remained out of the public eye since then. Her perfumes are marketed by Cosmopolitan Cosmetics, which also sells other celebrity fragrances.

Sources

Books

Contemporary Newsmakers 1985, Issue Cumulation, Gale Research, 1986.
Dictionary of Hispanic Biography, Gale Research, 1996.
Great Women in Sports, Visible Ink Press, 1996.

Periodicals

Maclean's, November 4, 1996, p. 15.
People, September 7, 1987, p. 127.
Sports Illustrated, May 2, 1988, p. 52; September 17, 1990, p. 22; March 18, 1991, p. 66; June 6, 1994, p. 60.
Washington Post, July 6, 1991.
Washington Times, October 30, 1996, p. 5.

On-line

"Gabriela Sabatini," *Biography Resource Center*, www.galenet.com/servlet/BioRC (May 7, 2003).
Gabriela Sabatini Official Website, www.gabriela-sabatini.com (June 12, 2003).

—Kelly Winters

Irma Vidal Santaella

1924—

Justice, lawyer

Irma Vidal Santaella championed Puerto Rican and other minority rights in New York for over thirty years. In 1961 she became the first Puerto Rican woman admitted to the New York State Bar, and in 1983 she became the first Puerto Rican woman to be elected to the New York Supreme Court. She helped found the Hispanic Community Chest of America, the National Federation of Puerto Rican Women, and the National Association for Puerto Rico Civil Rights, and served on numerous commissions including the New York City Advisory Council on Minority Affairs. During her 11 years on the bench, she remained committed to social activism, and earned a reputation as a hard working and thorough jurist.

Santaella was born in New York City on October 4, 1924, but was raised by her mother and aunts in Puerto Rico. She graduated from Modern Business College in Ponce, Puerto Rico, in 1942, and enrolled in pre-med classes at Inter-American University in San German, Puerto Rico, where she remained for two years. In New York, she earned a bachelor of arts degree from Hunter College in 1959 and worked as an accountant while attending Brooklyn Law School. After graduating in 1961, she practiced civil law in the South Bronx for two years.

In the early-to-mid 1960s, Santaella contributed to a number of causes supporting Puerto Rican rights in New York. She founded the Legion of Voters, Inc. in 1962 and served as the organization's president until 1968. In this position, she worked with Senator Jacob Javits and the late Robert F. Kennedy on the Voting Rights Act of 1965, helping to draft an amendment

eliminating the English literacy test requirement for non-English speaking citizens. Between 1962 and 1966, Santaella served as the chair of the Puerto Rican Day Parade in New York City. In 1966 she was defeated in her bid for a Congressional seat, and, although she ran again in 1968, her campaign lost momentum after her friend Robert F. Kennedy was assassinated. Despite these setbacks, Santaella remained active in politics. In 1969, she joined the Puerto Rican Committee for the Election of Mario Procaccino and openly criticized Mayor John V. Lindsey for "separating and dividing New Yorkers," quoted the *New York Times*.

Santaella also remained involved in a number of organizations. In 1971 she was named chairman of the Ladies' National Committee of the Coalition of Hispanic American Peoples, Inc., and in 1975 was appointed to the position of chairperson to the state's Human Rights Appeal Board by New York Governor Hugh L. Carey. The following year she served—for the third time—as a delegate to the Democratic National Convention, and also helped found the National Association for Puerto Rican Civil Rights. Between 1975 and 1977, Santaella served on the New York City Commission on the Status of Women.

In 1983 Santaella became the first Puerto Rican to win a seat on the New York Supreme Court, and she continued to champion minority rights from the bench. In 1987 she refused to allow a Park Avenue landlord to evict Dr. Geoffrey Richstone, who operated his practice from the building. The landlord claimed that Richstone had made renovations without permission, but San-

At a Glance . . .

Born Irma Vidal Santaella on October 4, 1924, in New York, NY; divorced; children: Anthony, Ivette. *Education:* Modern Business College, accounting degree, 1942; Hunter College, New York, BA, 1959; Brooklyn Law School, LLB, 1961, JD, 1967.

Career: Public accountant, late 1950s, early 1960s; practiced civil law, 1961-63, 1966-68; NY State Human Rights Appeal Board, 1968-83, chairman, 1975-83; NY State Supreme Court, justice, 1983-94.

Awards: Honorary doctorate, Sacred Heart University, 1990; National Puerto Rican Coalition Life Achievement Award, 1990; Governor Mario M. Cuomo's Recognition Award.

Address: *Home*—853 7th Avenue, New York, NY 10019-5215.

taella discovered that the renovations had been made openly. She also found out that other tenants had complained about the poor, minority clientele that attended Richstone's office, and had requested that they enter by the backdoor of the building. She refused the eviction request, stating that the landlord only seemed to be attempting to block black senior citizens from receiving the medical care they needed.

Santaella also supported First Amendment rights from the bench. In 1990 she was asked by the Catholic Church to stop a production of "The Cardinal Dextoxes" by the RAPP theater company. The Church had rented space to the company, but objected to the content of the 35-minute monologue. "I'm not a censor," the *Buffalo News* quoted Santaella, "and I'm not going to engage in any act of censorship." Although the company was later evicted under a lease clause prohibiting activity "detrimental to the reputation" of the landlord, "the judge said RAPP had a First Amendment right to perform the play in the meantime," noted Samuel Maull in AP News.

In 1991 Santaella stepped in when members of the New York State Board of Elections (NYSBE) stalled on implementing a program to register poor people and minorities. The program offered a chance for individuals in these groups to sign up as voters from any government office or when registering for a driver's license, but Democrats and Republicans on the NYSBE had disagreed on how much information state employees could provide for applicants. "In a stinging ruling," wrote Tom Precious in the *Times Union,* "a judge [Santaella] has ordered the state Board of Elections to stop its internal partisan squabbling and begin a voter registration push to be conducted by state agencies." The program, Santaella noted, was designed to give citizens the opportunity to elect officials of their own choosing. "For too long the public interest has been injuriously violated and raped by the arrogance of partisan politics at (the) board ... to the detriment of the voting rights of thousands of New Yorkers," Santaella was quoted as saying in the *Buffalo News.*

In 1994 Santaella ruled against Mayor Rudolf Giuliani when his administration attempted to delay the expansion of New York City's recycling program. In rejecting the bid for delay, she gave the administration three months to raise the collection of recyclable material from 15% to 25%.

Throughout the 1980s and 1990s, Santaella received several awards for her achievements on and off the bench. In 1989 the New York Assembly recognized her high disposition rate in the Manhattan Supreme Court. Between 1983 and 1990 she completed 21,000 cases, and between 1983 and 1989, the higher courts reversed her decisions only 24 times. In 1990 Santaella received an honorary law degree from Sacred Heart University in Connecticut and in 1991 won the National Council of Hispanic Women's Life Achievement award. Santaella retired from the New York State Supreme Court in 1994.

Sources

Periodicals

AP News, October 12, 1990.
Buffalo News, October 12, 1990, p. A10; March 3, 1991, p. H10.
New York Times, August 20, 1969, p. 30.
Times Union, February 26, 1991, p. B5.

On-line

"Irma Vidal Santaella," *Biography Resource Center,* www.galenet.com/servlet/BioRC (June 9, 2003).

—Ronnie D. Lankford, Jr.

Eligio Sardiñas

1910-1988

Boxer

Cuban boxer Eligio "Kid Chocolate" Sardiñas was the first Cuban world champion in the history of boxing. From the late 1920s to the late 1930s, he was one of the most popular fighters in New York. He was noted for his speed and his fast punches.

Sardiñas was born in Havana, Cuba, on January 6, 1910, and first began fighting as a boy, when he worked as a newspaper seller and had to defend his sales turf from other boys. After winning an amateur boxing tournament that was sponsored by the newspaper *La Noche,* the newspaper's sports editor, Luis Gutierrez, became his manager. Gutierrez was not well-versed in boxing, so he and Sardiñas studied the sport by watching films of famous fighters. In the *Encyclopedia of World Boxing Champions,* Gutierrez commented, "When the Keed first came to me, neither he nor myself knew anything much about boxing. We figured the best thing to do was study the methods of the masters."

The first fight they studied was the Gans-Nelson fight; while the film was playing in Havana movie houses, they viewed it every day, noting how Gans used his left hand. After watching it, they went to the gym, where Sardiñas practiced left-handed techniques. For the next

eight years, Sardiñas continued to study films, learning from the masters.

As an amateur featherweight, Sardiñas won 100 consecutive fights in the Cuban Leagues; among these were 86 knockouts. He became a professional in 1928, winning another 28 consecutive knockouts. In August of that year, he moved to the United States. There Sardiñas extended his winning streak by 13, including eight knockouts, giving him a total of 141 consecutive wins and 122 knockouts. His fights moved from small clubs to huge venues, including Madison Square Garden. By 1929, he was ranked the top featherweight fighter by *The Ring,* a boxing publication.

In 1930 Sardiñas fought hall-of-fame boxer Jackie "Kid" Berg at the Polo Grounds, in front of a crowd of 40,000. Although Berg weighed almost ten pounds more than Sardiñas, Sardiñas kept pounding, slamming uppercuts into Berg's head. Eventually Sardiñas tired, and Berg won by a narrow margin. It was Sardiñas's first defeat.

On July 15, 1931, in Philadelphia, Sardiñas fought Benny Bass, knocking out Bass in the seventh round to win the junior lightweight title. At the time, he weighed

At a Glance . . .

Born Sergio Eligio Sardiñas (also spelled Sardinas and Sardinias) Montalvo on January 6, 1910, in Cerro, Havana, Cuba; died on August 8, 1988, in Cuba.

Career: Boxer, 1928-38; gym owner in Cuba after retired from boxing.

Awards: Junior lightweight champion, 1931; world featherweight champion, 1932.

126 pounds and was five feet, six inches tall. In 1932 Sardiñas lost a rematch with Berg, but came back to challenge Fidel LaBarba for the world featherweight title.

Sardiñas and LaBarba fought three times; Sardiñas won two of these fights. Of the two wins, the most important occurred in New York City on December 9, 1932. Because Sardiñas had beaten the standing champion, on that date he was crowned world featherweight champion by the New York Boxing Commission. He thus became the first Cuban in boxing history to hold the world championship title. Sardiñas kept the title for a year and 17 days, beating seven challengers and ultimately losing to Frankie Klick. On December 26, 1933, Klick knocked him out in the seventh round in Philadelphia, taking the title. Klick remained the champion until 1949.

Although Sardiñas never took the championship title again, he continued fighting, mostly against second-rate competitors, until he retired in 1938. In his decade-long career in the United States, he won 145 of 161 fights with 64 knockouts, one of the best records in featherweight history. He was counted out only twice in 161 fights.

Sardiñas was famous in his day, but like many boxers of that era, he was cheated by dishonest managers, and he also spent a great deal of his money on night life and good times. After retiring, he moved to Cuba, where he ran a gym. As he grew older and his money ran out, he suffered from poverty and alcoholism, troubles common to out-of-work boxers of his time. In the *New York Times*, Ira Berkow reported that he lived quietly, out of the public view, and subsisted on a pension provided by the Cuban government. Berkow quoted boxing expert Nat Fleischer, who said, "He was sickly, bent over and he walked with a cane. It's like he disappeared when [Cuban dictator Fidel] Castro came."

As a Cuban, Sardiñas was revered by the New York Hispanic community, and he also won the admiration of boxing fans throughout the United States. In *A*

Pictorial History of Boxing, Nat Fleischer wrote, "Kid Chocolate, the Cuban bonbon, was a truly finished ringman. He was an excellent boxer, with an abundance of ring skill and a good puncher."

Sardiñas's career also provided inspiration for boxers who came after him, including famed fighter Joe Louis. Before he became a boxer, Louis was considering a musical career as a violinist, but when a friend told him how much Sardiñas made from one fight, he put his violin aside and took up boxing. Sugar Ray Robinson was also a fan of Sardiñas. On the *International Boxing Hall of Fame* website, Robert Cassidy quoted Cuban journalist Fausto Miranda, who said, "Sugar Ray Robinson was a great admirer of Kid Chocolate. No other man, no other Cuban, did in the ring what Chocolate did. For style, he was the best. Fancy, fancy, fancy."

Boxer Archie Moore, like Louis, was inspired by the amount of money Sardiñas made by fighting. Dave Kindred reported in the *Sporting News* that Moore once said, "I suppose I liked him because his name sounded so sweet. Most of all, the money intrigued me." Moore also noted that Sardiñas once made $2,500 for one fight, a very large amount for the time.

Sardiñas died in Cuba in 1988. According to Berkow, his death was announced on Cuban state radio, but no details were provided regarding the cause of his death or whether or not he had any survivors. He was buried in a cemetery designated for significant Cubans, and a boxing stadium in Havana was named in his honor. In 1994, in recognition of his achievements, Sardiñas was inducted into the International Boxing Hall of Fame.

Sources

Books

Dictionary of Hispanic Biography, Gale Research, 1996.
Fleischer, Nat, *A Pictorial History of Boxing,* rev. by Sam Andre and Nat Loubet, Citadel Press, 1975.
McCallum, John D., *The Encyclopedia of World Boxing Champions,* Chilton, 1975.

Periodicals

New York Times, August 21, 1988, p. S5.
Sporting News, December 21, 1998.

On-line

"Enshrinees," *International Boxing Hall of Fame,* www.ibhof.com/chocolate.htm (May 7, 2003).
"The Last Generation of Pro Fighters," *International Boxing Hall of Fame,* www.ibhof.com/ibhfcuba 1.htm (May 7, 2003).

—Kelly Winters

Lupe Serrano

1930—

Ballerina

In a career that has spanned more than half a century, ballerina Lupe Serrano has enjoyed a life studded with moments worthy of red rose-showered standing ovations. By the sheer power of her will, she rose from a second-rate dance school in Chile to become the first Hispanic principal dancer at the prestigious American Ballet Theatre. She has toured with Cuban ballet legend Alicia Alonso and danced with superstar Rudolf Nureyev. On stages worldwide—Europe, the Soviet Union, South America—she moved audiences to near-frenzies with her glowing stage presence and flawless technique. Mexico's *Noticias del día* recalled how at one performance at London's Covent Gardens, Serrano's interpretation of *Combat* melted the audience's usually restrained composure into a chorus of "foot stamping, applause, and shouts." When Serrano retired from performing to teach, she lost none of her passion for ballet. She told *Noticias del día* that her happiest moments are when she is sharing her knowledge of dance with students. "I continue to be in love with this art and still haven't lost my pleasure for the dance."

Born With Desire to Dance

Lupe Serrano was born on December 7, 1930, in Santiago, Chile. At the time her father, Luis Martinez Serrano—a Spanish-born, Argentine-raised musician—was leading an orchestra on a tour through South America. With him was his French-Mexican wife, Luciana Desfassiaux, whom he had met during an earlier tour through Mexico. Following Serrano's birth, her father fell ill and the young family decided to remain in Chile during his recovery. Nearly from the time she could walk Serrano wanted to dance. She recalled in an interview with the *Dictionary of Hispanic Biography* that at her third birthday party she insisted on dancing for all the guests. Not long after that impromptu performance, her parents decided to channel their daughter's incessant house-twirling into formal training by enrolling her in a dance school. However, the Chilean educational system was quite poor in the 1930s and it took a while to find a school. The one they finally settled on was not ideal but it offered the four year-old her first structured training in ballet.

At a Glance . . .

Born on December 7, 1930 in Santiago, Chile; daughter of Luis Martinez Serrano and Luciana Desfassiaux; married Kenneth Schermehorn, 1957, (divorced early 1970s); children: Erica and Veronica. *Education:* Studied with the Mexico City Ballet, mid-1940s; also trained in New York, NY and Santiago, Chile.

Career: American Ballet Theater, principal dancer, prima ballerina, 1953-71; National Academy of Arts in Illinois, assistant director, 1971-74; Pennsylvania Ballet School, director and teacher, 1974-88; Washington (DC) Ballet, artistic associate, 1988–; Juilliard School, New York, NY, teacher, 1997–; also danced with: Ballet Russe de Monte Carlo, New York, NY; Ballet Folklorico de Mexico; the Mexico City Ballet; has also taught at American Ballet Theatre, San Francisco Ballet, Minnesota Dance Theatre, Cleveland Ballet, Washington Ballet, Cincinnati Ballet, Rome Opera Ballet, and Ballet Nacional de Mexico.

Address: *Office*—Public Relations, American Ballet Theatre, 890 Broadway, New York, NY, 10003. Phone: (212) 477-3030.

In 1943 Serrano and her family moved back to her mother's native Mexico City. The move was instrumental for Serrano's dance education. She immediately began training with the Mexico City Ballet. It was difficult at first. "I had terrible habits by then," she told the *Dictionary of Hispanic Biography.* "But I had been in so many recitals that I had a sense of how to fill the stage." She was also completely in love with dancing and had a burning desire to be the best. Her commitment earned her a place in the company's ballet corps within a year and at 14 she debuted in the company's production of *Les Sylphides.* She continued dancing with the company while maintaining a heavy schedule of dance lessons and high school classes. Undaunted, she doubled her load at high school in order to finish a year early and thus be free to tour. Meanwhile, her rank in the Mexico City Ballet continued to rise and according to her official biography from the American Ballet Theatre, she eventually "established herself as Mexico's leading ballerina."

At the age of eighteen, Serrano embarked upon a Central American tour with Alicia Alonso, a Cuban prima ballerina and founder of the Ballet Nacional de Cuba. Alonso is widely considered one of the greatest dancers of the twentieth century and it was a great honor for Serrano to tour with her. When she returned to Mexico City, she joined a brand new ballet company founded by one of her teachers. However, the company was forced by bankruptcy to hang up its pointe shoes and close shop. It upset Serrano but also taught her the realities of dance beyond the bright lights of the stage. "Ballet is not a self-supporting art anywhere in the world," she told the *Dictionary of Hispanic Biography.* "It has to be sponsored. A person like my ballet teacher, who was devoted to the art of ballet, of course would not have the ability to raise funds."

Leapt from Mexico to New York

Serrano soon joined the Ballet Folklorico de Mexico, a Mexican-government sponsored troupe that celebrated the varied cultures of Mexico through their ethnic dances. With this company her fame in Mexico continued to rise. However, by 1950, 20-year-old Serrano yearned for more. Just like the little girl who couldn't help dancing through the rooms of her childhood home, the young woman that Serrano had become longed to dance across the stages of the world. She also wanted to return to ballet. The most natural jumping off point for her was New York City and in 1951 she moved there. The Mexican choreographer Sylvia Ramirez recalled Serrano's departure for New York to *Noticias del día,* "She went full of enthusiasm, fervor, and love for dance. She had no contract, nor the security that she'd be accepted in a ballet company, but she had talent and faith in herself, as well as solid technical training. These qualities opened the doors to the Metropolitan Opera House and the American Ballet Theatre where she soon became one of the most famous principal ballerinas of her era."

Upon her arrival in New York, Serrano auditioned for the Ballet Russe de Monte Carlo and landed a position with the company. With the troupe she traveled throughout North and South America and made her solo debut. However, the company soon folded under financial strain and Serrano dejectedly returned to Mexico City. She promptly landed a starring role on a television show dedicated to the classical arts and danced regularly on the program. It required some changes in her performance technique. "We had to rearrange the way we covered space on the floor, because the cameras were not very mobile," she told the *Dictionary of Hispanic Biography.* "And you had to be much more subtle in expression, because the camera brings you much closer to the audience. On the stage, you have to think of projecting yourself a block away. Television is much more intimate."

Not long after returning to Mexico City, she was summoned back to New York by the former road manager of the Ballet Russe de Monte Carlo. He was now working for the American Ballet Theatre and suggested that Serrano audition. There was no question about it; Serrano had immense respect for the company and longed to dance with it. She left for New York where she immediately enrolled in dance classes and prepared her audition. In 1953 she was accepted into the American Ballet Theatre as a principal dancer, one of the highest ranks within a ballet company. It was the culmination of a lifetime of dreams and dancing. She recalled to the *Dictionary of Hispanic Biography* her feelings the first time she led the company in a grand finale. "[I thought] 'Well, look at you now, leading this group of wonderful dancers.' I felt a great sense of pride." She wasn't the only one filled with pride. By joining the American Ballet Theatre, she became the company's first Hispanic principal dancer and a role model for young Hispanic dancers worldwide.

Danced With Nureyev

Serrano went on to perform with the American Ballet Theatre for almost two decades, eventually rising to the top position of prima ballerina. She danced more than 50 different roles including ballet classics such as *Swan Lake, Giselle, La Fille Mal Gardée,* and *Aurora's Wedding.* She also performed contemporary ballets by famed choreographers such as George Balanchine, William Dollar, Antony Tudor, and Jerome Robbins. With the company she embarked on several worldwide tours, dazzling audiences from the Soviet Union to Greece, England to Venezuela. At one memorable performance in Leningrad, the audience was so moved by her solo performance that they insisted she repeat it when she returned to the stage for the customary bow. In 1962 Serrano's experience dancing for television was called upon when she was asked to perform a duet from *Le Corsaire* with Rudolf Nureyev. The performance was telecast as part of the *Bell Telephone Hour,* a television program that brought the classical arts to the public. At the time Nureyev was already a legend in the dance world and had become the first true ballet superstar. To dance with him in such a high-profile performance was a great achievement for Serrano. A few years later Serrano gave another high-profile performance for President Lyndon Johnson at the White House. She also continued performing with the American Ballet Theatre, both in the United States and abroad and becoming, according to the *Rocky Mountain News,* "one of its main attractions."

In 1957 Serrano married Kenneth Schermerhorn, then conductor for the American Ballet Theatre. When Schermerhorn took a position with the New Jersey Symphony, Serrano began a busy schedule of commuting to New York for rehearsals and classes. In 1963 they had their first daughter, Erica and in 1967, their second, Veronica. Under her mother's tutelage, Veronica would go on to become a principal dancer with the American Ballet Theatre as well. Soon after the birth of her second child, Serrano took a year-long

sabbatical from dance. When she returned to the American Ballet Theatre it was as a permanent guest artist, meaning she would have the freedom to choose her own performances and could devote more time to her family. Eventually Serrano moved to Wisconsin where Schermerhorn had been hired as a conductor with the Milwaukee Orchestra. There she began to teach dance at the Conservatory of Milwaukee and the University of Milwaukee. She proved a natural at teaching and enjoyed sharing her love of ballet with young dancers.

Turned Talent Toward Teaching

In 1971, after nearly three decades onstage, Serrano decided to take her final bow and retire as a dancer. She was 40. At about the same time Serrano and Schermerhorn divorced. Though her family in Mexico begged her to return home, Serrano remained in the United States where she turned her formidable talents to teaching full time. Her first position was with the National Academy of Arts in Illinois. When the company closed in 1974, she joined the faculty of the Pennsylvania Ballet School where she also oversaw the apprenticeship program. From 1974 to 1983 Serrano also served as director of the school. Meanwhile she kept up a busy schedule of master classes for dance companies across the world including the San Francisco Ballet, the Minnesota Dance Theatre, the Cleveland Ballet, the Washington Ballet, the Cincinnati Ballet, the Rome Opera Ballet, and the National Ballet of Mexico. She also became a sought-after judge on the international ballet competition circuit. In 1988 Serrano became the artistic associate for the Washington Ballet. Her duties included coaching the company, the apprentices, and the advanced students. In 1997 she began to give classes at Juilliard, the famed New York City school for the arts. By 2003, inching into her seventies, she was still giving classes worldwide, including a series of studio workshops with her beloved American Ballet Theatre.

Serrano's fifty-year love affair with ballet has left an unforgettable mark on the art—from the hundreds of dancers who have learned to jump higher, twirl more gracefully, and dance better under her watchful eye to the thousands of fans who have swooned to her own graceful moves across the stage. As Linda Urdapilleta, a Mexican ballerina told *Noticias del día,* "Only a person like Serrano could scale the steps she's had to face and arrive at a company like the American Ballet Theater. Those that had the privilege of seeing her dance will never forget it. We will always be proud of her."

Sources

Books

Dictionary of Hispanic Biography, Gale Research, 1996.

Periodicals

*Rocky Mountain News,*Denver, CO, September 20, 1997, p. 65A.

On-line

"Clase Magistral con Lupe Serrano en el Teatro de la Danza," *Noticias del día,* www.conaculta.gob.mx/saladeprensa/2002/19mar/serrano.htm (May 23, 2003).

"Los Bailarines de Hoy Mantienen una Técnica Más Depurada," *Noticias del día,* www.conaculta.gob.mx/saladeprensa/2002/25mar/serrano.htm (May 23, 2003).

"Lupe Serrano," *Biography Resource Center,* www.galenet.com/servlet/BioRC (July 7, 2003).

—Candace LaBalle

Charlie Sheen

1965—

Actor

Charlie Sheen has been a prolific entertainer ever since he began acting as a child alongside his famous father, Martin Sheen. Although at first he thought he might be a baseball player—he was the star pitcher on his high school team—he eventually ended up following in the footsteps of his family. His first big break came when he got a part in Oliver Stone's *Platoon,* and since then, despite a period of wild behavior that effected his entire life, he has worked steadily in Hollywood and is known and loved by moviegoers everywhere.

First Introduced to Acting

Born Carlos Irwin Estevez to Ramon (Martin Sheen) and Janet Estevez on September 3, 1965, in New York City, the ability to entertain was something that all the Estevez clan seemed to inherit. Sheen's siblings also became entertainers—Emilio Estevez and Renee Estevez were also actors and Ramon Estevez was a songwriter. The family moved to Malibu, California, when Sheen was two because Sheen's father had begun to make a movie career for himself and needed to be closer to Hollywood. Sheen became friends as a

youth with such later-known actors as Sean and Christopher Penn, and Rob and Chad Lowe, and the boys were often found making home movies rather than the other things young boys are wont to do. He made his screen debut at age nine in 1974 in *The Execution of Private Slovik,* a movie which starred his father, Martin Sheen. He was also seen as an extra in Martin Scorcese's *Apocalypse Now,* a movie his father also starred in. The movie made a lasting impression on Sheen because the whole family moved to the Philippines during filming. They had to suffer through typhoons and other natural problems, and then his father, Martin, suffered a near-fatal heart attack while filming the movie. Even with all these issues the experience left him with a positive view of the moviemaking business.

Growing up Sheen was involved in various drama clubs, but it was baseball in which he really excelled. He went to baseball camp for four summers in a row and by the time he was a senior in high school he had become the lead pitcher. He was even offered a baseball scholarship by the University of Kansas, but he started skipping school and by the time his senior year ended, it was estimated that he missed two-thirds of the

At a Glance . . .

Born Carlos Irwin Estevez on September 3, 1965, in New York, NY; son of Martin Sheen and Janet Estevez; married Donna Peele, September 3, 1995 (divorced); married Denise Richards, June 15, 2002; children: Cassandra (with Paula Profitt).

Career: Actor 1974–; screenwriter, 1989–; film producer, 1989–.

Memberships: Screen Actors Guild.

Awards: Golden Globe, best performance in a TV Series, Musical or Comedy, for *Spin City,* 2002.

Address: *Agent*—ICM, 8942 Wilshire Blvd., Beverly Hills, CA 90211. Phone: (310) 550-4000.

year. According to *Hollywood.com,* "The bad boy side of him also surfaced early with arrests for marijuana possession and credit card forgery coming prior to his unceremonious failure to graduate from high school." His parents were not happy with Sheen's failure to graduate—something that happened not because he wasn't good at school but because of his missed classes—and were worried when Sheen decided, rather than going back to school to get his degree, that he wanted to attempt a career as an actor. He only managed to pacify his parents with the promise that if he failed to launch a successful career soon he would return home, get his high school degree, and go on to college.

He started out making a few small movies that didn't do much to bring him to the attention of the public, but did get Sheen his Screen Actor's Guild card and some recognition by the industry. In 1985 Sheen had a daughter named Cassandra with Paula Profitt, his childhood sweetheart. They chose not to marry. In 1986, however, he played a small part in *Ferris Bueller's Day Off,* as a rebellious boy who gave advice to Ferris Bueller's sister in jail. The part was endearing and won Sheen a lot of attention, even though it was small. It was this appearance that Oliver Stone saw that made him think that Sheen had something special and he cast him in his movie *Platoon.*

Career Took Off After Platoon

Platoon is considered the movie that launched Sheen's career. In the movie he played a young man going to war in Vietnam, a difficult part, but one that won Sheen critical acclaim, especially after the movie won an

Academy Award for Best Picture in 1987. It was also this movie that led to Sheen being listed as one of twelve promising new actors of 1986 in John Willis' *Screen World.* Stone so admired Sheen's portrayal of Private Chris Taylor in *Platoon* that he decided while the film was still in production that he'd like to work with Sheen again. There was later a debate about what movie to do next, a sequel to the then popular *Platoon* or a movie set in the fast-paced world of Wall Street. The next year Sheen was seen in the movie *Wall Street* alongside Michael Douglas, with his own father playing a small part as his character's father.

He was next seen in the 1989 comedy *Major League,* where he was able to put his old baseball skills to use, playing a near-blind pitcher. With his success at comedy proven, he was next seen in *Hot Shots!* which spoofed action flicks like *Top Gun* and then *Hot Shots! Part Deux* which spoofed the Rambo movies. In 1993 Sheen was seen in the remake of *The Three Musketeers,* in which he played a dreamy and romantic Aramis. The following year, while Sheen was seen onscreen in *Major League II,* he was awarded a star on the illustrious Hollywood Walk of Fame.

It was at this time that Sheen's profligate behavior began to come to the public's notice as he was sent to court for a few infractions. He married Donna Peele in 1995, saying that she was the angel he needed to help him recover. They divorced six months later. Sheen gave the reason, according to *The Buffalo News,* that "I couldn't breathe. I like breathing too much. I had to come up for air." Just before his divorce in 1996, Sheen had his name come to light in connection with infamous Hollywood Madam, Heidi Fleiss.

Returned to Healthy Living

Even though his life was in turmoil, however, Sheen was still seen in movie after movie, including *All Dogs Go to Heaven 2* and *Loose Women* in 1996, and *Money Talks* and *Mission to Mars* in 1997. In 1998 Sheen's substance abuse problem came to a head when he overdosed on drugs. When he was released from the hospital, he checked himself into Promises, a rehab center. He stayed there, however, for only one day before he was out on the street drinking and taking drugs again. The police ordered him to return to Promises. According to the *Herald Sun,* this happened after "his father ... reported his son's drug overdose to a Los Angeles judge and demanded he be 'locked away.'" This seemed to do the trick, because Sheen began cleaning up his act. In 1999 he was seen playing a funny cameo of himself in the movie *Being John Malkovich,* and he told cast members at the time that he had been sober and clean for a year. About his return from his downward spiral, Sheen told *ET Online,* "I'm just excited to be back in the game. I don't just mean the entertainment game; I mean the game of life. I'm excited to have been given a second shot ... I've never had more fun."

In 2000 Sheen co-starred in the movie *Rated X*, alongside his brother Emilio Estevez. In the movie they played the real Mitchell brothers, Jim and Artie, who were famous for producing the porn movie *Behind the Green Door*, a movie that took porn movies into mainstream consciousness. Sheen and his brother had barely spoken in the past ten years while Sheen was ensconced in his rather questionable world of drugs and sex, but now things between the brothers seemed to be improving. Estevez told *The Fresno Bee*, "The experience of making this picture together probably brought us closer together than we had been in the last 10 years. And we went from sporadically conversing to really talking every day. So I feel like, if nothing else, this movie really brought us closer together and I'm thankful for that." There were some fears that people would compare the lives of the Mitchell brothers with Sheen and Estevez, or that the act of pretending to take drugs would increase Sheen's desire to return to his wilder lifestyle. Sheen told *Entertainment Weekly*, however, that this was not the case, "I was reminded why I didn't want to live that lifestyle anymore."

In 2000 Sheen was given the opportunity of his newly cleaned up life—he took over as lead on the sitcom *Spin City* after Michael J. Fox was forced to quit because of his battle with Parkinson's disease. Producers approached him about playing a rather colorful character on the show, and Sheen jumped at the opportunity to, as he told the *Herald Sun*, "deal with my notoriety head-on." According to *Hollywood.com*, "While there were naysayers who weren't sure that the intense actor could pull off working in a weekly comedy series, he more than proved them wrong, developing a nice rapport with the cast. Not only did he reinvigorate his own career, but he also rejuvenated the flagging series." He told *ET Online* about working on the show, "There's such a good camaraderie. It is such a warm and groovy place to work, a lot of laughs, a lot of fun, a lot of freedom.... It's the best working environment I've ever encountered in my 18 years in the business." In 2002 Sheen won a Golden Globe for best actor in a Television Series, Musical or Comedy.

In 2001 Sheen was seen in the movie *Good Advice* alongside Angie Harmon and Denise Richards. Richards also appeared on *Spin City*, guest starring as Sheen's girlfriend. Sheen and Richards had met years before, but it was the *Spin City* spot that brought them together. In 2002 the two were married. Sheen's future projects include a new CBS sitcom, *Two and a Half Men*, with Jon Cryer and Blythe Danner, scheduled to begin airing in the fall of 2003. Sheen has returned to Hollywood like the prodigal son and has managed to retain his bank of supporters and fans. Sheen told the *Sunday Herald Sun* that he had always kept faith that Hollywood would forgive him, despite his temporary ban from the A-list. "It's a hard place, but it's a company town. If you work hard and get the ratings (on TV) they will forgive you almost anything." And things are only looking up from here, with a new wife, a refurbished career, and a Golden Globe under his belt, Sheen should be an exciting person to watch in Hollywood.

Selected works

Film

The Execution of Private Slovik, 1974.
Ferris Bueller's Day Off, 1986.
Platoon, 1986.
Wallstreet, 1987.
Eight Men Out, 1988.
Major League, 1989.
Navy Seals, 1990.
Men at Work, 1990.
Hot Shots!, 1991.
Hot Shots! Part Deux, 1993.
The Three Musketeers, 1993.
The Chase, 1994.
Major League II, 1994.
The Arrival, 1996.
Loose Women, 1996.
Money Talks, 1997.
Mission To Mars, 1997.
Being John Malkovich, 1999.
Rated X, 2000.
Good Advice, 2001.

Film production

Comicitis, 1989.
The Chase, 1994.
No Code of Conduct, 1998.

Screenwriting

Tale of Two Sisters,, 1989.
Mission to Mars, 1997.
No Code of Conduct, 1998.

Television

Spin City, 2000-2002.
Two and a Half Men, 2003.

Sources

Books

Almanac of Famous People, 7th edition, Gale Group, 2000.
Contemporary Theatre, Film, and Television, Volume 17, Gale Research, 1997; Volume 40, Gale Group, 2002.
Dictionary of Hispanic Biography, Gale Research, 1996.

Newsmakers, Issue 2, Gale Group, 2001.
U*X*L Biographies, U*X*L, 1999.

Periodicals

Buffalo News (Buffalo, NY), February 21, 1996, p. C4.
Dayton Daily News (Dayton, OH), July 20, 2000, p. 1C.
Entertainment Weekly, September 5, 1997, p. 25; October 10, 1997, p. 9; June 19, 1998, p. 79; May 12, 2000, p. 60.
Fresno Bee (Fresno, CA), May 11, 2000, p. E3.
Houston Chronicle, May 15, 2003, p. 4.
In Style, February 1, 2003, p. 268.
Lansing State Journal (Lansing, MI), October 18, 2000, p. D5.
National Review, January 22, 1988, p. 65.
Mirror (London, England), June 21, 2002, p. 9; January 19, 2003, p. 36.
New Republic, January 4, 1988, p. 24.
Newsweek, May 15, 2000, p. 72.
People Weekly, September 18, 1995, p. 208; June 15, 1998, p. 11.

Seattle Post-Intelligencer (Seattle, WA), June 18, 2002, p. C2.
Sunday Herald Sun (Melbourne, Australia), October 31, 2001, p. H07; May 4, 2003, p. 115.
Tampa Tribune (Tampa, FL), August 12, 1998, p. 4.
Variety, June 4, 2001, p. 21.
Virginian Pilot, February 6, 1997, p. E3; August 23, 1997, p. E1.

On-line

"Charlie Sheen," *Hollywood.com,* www.hollywood.com/celebs/bio/celeb/1676679 (June 9, 2003).
"Charlie Sheen," *Internet Movie Database,* www.imdb.com/Name?Sheen,+Charlie (June 9, 2003).
"Sheen and Fox on *Spin City,*" *ET Online,* www.etonline.com/television/a6719.htm (June 9, 2003.)
"The Sheens on *Spin City!,*" *ET Online,* www.etonline.com/television/a8716.htm (June 9, 2003).
"The Ultra Lean Charlie Sheen!," *ET Online,* www.etonline.com/celebrity/a2811.htm (June 9, 2003).

—Catherine Victoria Donaldson

Gary Soto

1952—

Children's author, novelist, poet

Hailed as one of the top Mexican-American writers in the United States, Gary Soto is also one of the most versatile. Winning awards and acclaim for his poetry in the years after he completed his education, Soto has also written short stories and autobiographical sketches. Almost single-handedly, he has striven to create a literature for young Mexican-American readers; as he turned to writing full time in the 1990s, he devoted his energies increasingly often to poetry, stories, and picture books for children and intermediate students. Much of Soto's writing is drawn on his recollections of growing up poor in California's agricultural Central Valley; many of his readers have the impression that he has an almost unbroken photographic memory of his entire childhood.

Soto is an extremely prolific writer, having created well over 60 books, plus numerous contributions to periodicals and several films, by the early 2000s. But literature was not even present in his childhood home. Soto was born on April 12, 1952, and grew up in Fresno, California, next to a junkyard and across the street from a pickle factory. His parents were Mexican-American laborers, and his father was killed in an industrial accident when Soto was five. His father's death had a long-lasting emotional impact on Soto, who in an interview with *NEA Today* attributed the detail of his childhood memories to his years of brooding over the accident. "I kept going over those events in my mind until I was in my 30s—thinking if we'd done this instead of that, everything would have been different."

Weak Student in High School

The impact was also economic, forcing Soto along with the rest of his family into whatever jobs they could get. Sometimes this meant migrant farm labor and its hazardous exposure to toxic chemicals. Soto was an indifferent student in high school, with a D grade average and a preference for spending his time as a *novio*—a lover boy—on the school playground. His family had little interaction with the world of education. "We had our own culture which was more like the culture of poverty," Soto said in an interview with the *Dictionary of Literary Biography*.

"I was a marginal kid," he told *NEA Today*. "I could have gone from the playground to prison or to college." One reason he enrolled in Fresno City College

At a Glance . . .

Born on April 12, 1952, in Fresno, CA; son of Manuel Soto and Angie Oftedal Soto; married Carolyn Sadako Oda, May 24, 1975; children: Mariko Heidi. *Education:* Fresno City College, two year degree; California State University at Fresno, BA, English, 1974; University of California at Irvine, MFA, 1976.

Career: Author, 1977–; University of California at Berkeley, lecturer in Chicano studies, 1977-81, assistant professor of English and Chicano studies, 1981-85, associate professor of English and Chicano studies, 1985-95.

Selected awards: American Academy of Poets prize, 1975; U.S. International Poetry Forum award, for *The Elements of San Joaquin,* 1977; Guggenheim fellowship, 1980; National Endowment for the Arts fellowship, 1981; Levinson award, *Poetry* magazine, 1984; Literature Award, Hispanic Heritage Foundation, 1999; Author-Illustrator Civil Rights Award, National Educational Association; PEN Center West Book Award, 1999.

Addresses: *Home*—43 The Crescent, Berkeley, CA 94708; *Website*—www.garysoto.com.

was that he was worried about being drafted and sent to fight in the Vietnam War; another was that he had begun to enjoy reading after coming across *To Sir, with Love,* a British story of an inspiring inner-city teacher who earns the devotion of troubled students. Soto moved on from community college to California State University at Fresno, intending at first to study geography but switching to creative writing after he read a poem about alienation called "Unwanted," by Edward Field.

Soto also encountered the works of California's stream-of-consciousness "Beat" poets such as Allen Ginsberg in college, but his most important influence was his teacher Philip Levine, a native of Detroit known for his poetry about working-class Americans. After receiving his bachelor's degree with high honors, Soto went on for a master of fine arts degree at the University of California's Irvine campus. He married Carolyn Oda, a Japanese American, in 1975 (the couple has one daughter), and finished his degree a year later. Soto taught at San Diego State University and in 1977 was hired as an assistant professor at the

University of California's flagship campus in Berkeley, where he remained until 1993.

Depicted Central Valley in Poems

While still a student, Soto had begun publishing poetry in magazines and journals, and he started winning literary prizes as early as 1975. From the beginning, although he grew up in a Spanish-speaking household, he wrote mostly in English. Soto's first book of poetry, *The Elements of San Joaquin,* was published in 1977 and immediately attracted critical attention and praise; it differed in several respects from the bulk of Chicano poetry that had appeared up to that point. Soto presented poems depicting scenes and figures from the Central Valley of his youth. Although he did not shy away from representing the life of Mexican Americans as hard and hostile—his description of "men whose arms were bracelets of burns" was widely quoted— Soto avoided an explicitly political tone. His poetry was both personal and universal; some reviewers compared his imagery of the dusty, bleak Central Valley to the feeling conveyed by a classic poem of modern alienation, T. S. Eliot's "The Waste Land."

By 1985 Soto had published four books of poetry and contributed to several other volumes, and he ascended to the rank of associate professor in Berkeley's English and Chicano Studies departments that year. His poetry had always had a strong storytelling quality, and in the mid-1980s, he began writing prose stories and autobiographical vignettes. Two books of autobiographical writings, 1983's *Small Faces* and 1988's *Lesser Evils,* were collected in the 2000 volume *The Effects of Knut Hamsun on a Fresno Boy,* along with new material. Soto wrote evocatively about such painful incidents of childhood as schoolyard ridicule over an article of clothing, and from these recollections it was a short step to writing material for readers in the child and young adult age groups.

Soto, according to *Booklist,* hoped "to start Chicanos reading," and indeed when he started out, the selection of books set among Mexican Americans and aimed at young readers was very sparse. One of his first efforts was *Baseball in April and Other Stories,* set among teenagers in neighborhoods much like those where Soto himself had grown up. "His stories are moving, yet humorous and entertaining," noted the *New York Times.* "The best are also quite subtle. Unsentimental yet bittersweet, they chronicle the responses of young people to the difficulties they encounter."

Wrote Picture Books for Children

Over the course of the 1990s and early 2000s, Soto added to his body of literature for children, writing books of poetry, novels, and picture books in addition to short stories. One of his most popular picture books, *Too Many Tamales,* was the story of a girl named Maria who loses her mother's ring while helping to cook a family meal at Christmas time and tries to keep eating tamales until she finds it; others dealt with a cat named Chato. Though his material for young people was naturally lighter in tone than his writing for adults, it often touched on the sadness that comes with poverty. Soto continued to write poetry and prose for adults as well; his literary production, already high, only accelerated after he gave up teaching to write full time in the mid-1990s.

Far from relying on what he was already familiar with, Soto branched out into new forms and media. He wrote a biography of a California union organizer, *Jessie de la Cruz: Profile of a United Farm Worker,* scripted several short films, and wrote the libretto for an opera, *Nerd-landia,* that was staged by the Los Angeles Opera company. Numerous honors came Soto's way; his volume of *New and Selected Poems,* was named a finalist for both the National Book Award and the Los Angeles Times book award, and he became one of the youngest poets included in the prestigious *Norton Anthology of Modern Poetry.*

Soto did not slow down in the early 2000s, releasing the picture book *If the Shoe Fits* in 2002 as well as several other books. An inspiration to younger Mexican-American writers through the sheer quantity and range of his work, Soto held writers' meetings at his home in the Berkeley hills and often appeared at school assemblies. His young readers often asked him where he got the ideas for his stories. "I always tell them, 'From you,'" Soto told *NEA Today.* "You tell me a story, and I'll make it bigger." The Mexican-American experience, indeed, loomed larger in American literature as a result of his efforts.

Selected works

The Elements of San Joaquin (poems), University of Pittsburgh Press, 1977.
The Tale of Sunlight (poems), University of Pittsburgh Press, 1978.
Living Up the Street: Narrative Recollections, Strawberry Hill Publishers, 1985.
Small Faces (prose memoirs), Arte Público, 1986.
Lesser Evils (memoirs and essays), Arte Público, 1988.

A Summer Life (autobiography), University Press of New England, 1990.
Baseball in April and Other Stories (short stories for young readers), Harcourt, 1990.
Too Many Tamales (picture book), Putnam, 1992.
The Cat's Meow (picture book), Scholastic, 1995.
New and Selected Poems, Chronicle Books, 1995.
Novio Boy (play), Harcourt, 1997.
Nerd-landia (play and opera libretto), 1999.
Jessie de la Cruz: Profile of a United Farm Worker (biography), Persea, 2000.
The Effects of Knut Hamson on a Fresno Boy: Recollections and Short Essays, Persea, 2000.
If the Shoe Fits (story for young readers), Putnam, 2002.
Shadow of the Plum: Poems, Cedar Hill Publications, 2002.

Sources

Books

Authors and Artists for Young Adults, volume 37, Gale, 2000.
Dictionary of Hispanic Biography, Gale, 1996.
Dictionary of Literary Biography, Volume 82: Chicano Writers, First Series, Gale, 1989.

Periodicals

Booklist, November 1, 2000, p. 512.
Horn Book Magazine, July-August 2002, p. 451.
NEA Today, November 1992, p. 9.
New York Times, May 20, 1990, Section 7, p. 45.
San Diego Union-Tribune, April 21, 2002, p. E1.
San Francisco Chronicle, April 27, 2003.

On-line

"Gary Soto," *Contemporary Authors Online,* Gale, 2003; reproduced in *Biography Resource Center,* www.galenet.com/servlet/BioRC (May 23, 2003).
Gary Soto Official Website, www.garysoto.com (May 23, 2003).

—James M. Manheim

Antoni Tàpies

1923—

Artist

Art critics hail Spanish painter Antoni Tàpies as his country's greatest living artist. Since the 1950s Tàpies has been creating large, emotionally resonant abstract works that owe much to the cultural heritage of his native Catalonia. "Tàpies is one of a number of post World War II European artists who, in their attempt at breaking through the constraints of cubism and geometric abstraction, came out with revolutionary seminal styles that roughly paralleled the development of Abstract Expressionism in the United States," noted an essay in *Contemporary Artists.*

The painter and sculptor was born Antoni Tàpies Puig on December 13, 1923, in Barcelona. A military dictatorship rose to power in Spain that year, but when he was eight, its royal family fled and a republic was established. Barcelona became the capital city when Catalonia won autonomy for a brief period thereafter. Tàpies's father, a lawyer, was a committed Republican and served in the Catalonian government, and there was some conflict in the home between his father's atheism and his mother's devout Roman Catholicism. When civil war erupted in Spain in 1936, forces led by the fascist Generalissimo Francisco Franco harassed the Republicans, and Tàpies's father was interrogated but released unharmed.

Joined Avant-Garde Group

Tàpies's father was determined that his son follow in his professional footsteps, and he dutifully studied law for five years. In an interview for the *UNESCO Courier* with Serafin García Ibañez, he confessed that art had always been his first passion. "When I was a child I loved drawing," Tàpies recalled. "I lacked the basic skills, but as time went by I became consumed by a desire to do better than all my classmates." Before he turned twenty, Tàpies was diagnosed with tuberculosis after a surprise heart attack. He spent two years recuperating between 1942 and 1943, and used much of the time to draw, read, and listen to the classical operas of nineteenth-century German composer Richard Wagner.

Tàpies recovered from his illness and re-emerged on Barcelona's cultural scene. By the end of World War II, Spain was firmly a dictatorship, and the Franco regime took harsh measures against Catalonia and its proud spirit, including repression of its Catalan language. Around 1948 Tàpies became involved in a group of artists and poets in Barcelona who were drawn to the Dada and Surrealist movements. They included poet Joan Brossa, philosopher Arnau Puig, and three other painters, Modest Cuixart, Joan Ponç, and Joan-Josep

At a Glance . . .

Born Antoni Tàpies Puig on December 13, 1923, in Barcelona, Spain; married Teresa Barbara, 1954; children: Antoni, Miguel, Clara. *Education:* Studied law at the University of Barcelona, 1943, 1945-46; studied drawing at the Academia Valls, Barcelona, 1944.

Career: Artist, 1948–. Held first group exhibition in Barcelona, 1948; first U.S. exhibition, Marshall Field Art Gallery, Chicago, 1953; showed at the Spanish Pavilion of the 1958 Venice Biennale; the Museo de Arte of Bilbao, Spain, hosted his first museum show, 1960; retrospectives held in his honor include the Guggenheim Museum, New York, 1962; Museum des 20 Jahrhunderts, Vienna, 1968; Musee d'Art Modern, Paris, 1973; Museum of Contemporary Art, Chicago, 1977; Museo Espanol de Arte Contemporano, Madrid, 1980; Tàpies Foundation established in Barcelona, 1984.

Awards: Academia Breve prize, Madrid, 1950, 1951; First Prize, Carnegie International, Pittsburgh 1958; Guggenheim Foundation Award, 1964; Stephan-Locher Medal, Cologne, West Germany, 1974; Plastic Arts Prize, City of Barcelona, 1979; Gold Medal for Fine Arts, Ministry of Culture, Madrid, 1981; Wolf Foundation Prize, with Marc Chagall, Israel, 1982.

Addresses: *Office*—Saragossa 57, Barcelona-6, Spain. *Agent*—Galeria Maeght, Calle Montcada 25, Barcelona-3, Spain.

Tharrats. Calling themselves *Dau al Set,* or "Die at Seven," the group put out a daring avant-garde magazine of the same name, and began showing their work in the city. Tàpies's first exhibition with them, in 1948, included his painting "Collage of the Crosses," which provoked controversy among the more conservative elements in Barcelona; Catholic leaders even attempted to have the show shut down by authorities. The crucifix would continue to appear in many works of Tàpies's throughout his career, giving them a ghostly religious mood. He explained his fascination with the form many years later in an interview with the *New York Times*'s Alan Riding. "At the time, Spain was truly a cemetery," Tàpies said, after so many years of civil war and the political repression. "The presence of the cross was very intense and I used it as a symbol of primitive Christianity as well as to criticize what we called National Catholicism."

In 1951 Tàpies won a scholarship from the French Institute that enabled him to live modestly and study in Paris. During this period he was able to meet Spain's greatest living Spanish painter at the time, Pablo Picasso. Returning to Barcelona, his creativity flourished during this decade, and his reputation as an artist accrued accordingly. In 1953 he was invited to show his works in Chicago at the Marshall Field Art Gallery, and the following year he had a show in New York City at its Martha Jackson Gallery. That show was also the occasion of Tàpies's first visit to the United States, and he found the New York art world captivated by the Abstract Expressionist style, in which painters strove to convey emotional content through reducing color and form to its simplest elements. They included the painters Jackson Pollock and Willem de Kooning, and as Tàpies recalled in the interview with Riding, "they were wrestling with canvases, using violent colors and huge brush strokes. I arrived with gray, silent, sober, oppressed paintings. One critic said they were paintings that thought."

Career Languished Briefly

Tàpies gained international attention in 1958, when he and sculptor Eduardo Chillida were invited to represent Spain at the prestigious Venice Biennale. His paintings began to incorporate unusual elements that gave them the "mixed media" tag, as he affixed the thick impasto paint with rags, dirt, sand, straw, cardboard, and even x-ray film. There was often graffiti-type writing, or the letters "A" and "T," as well. In 1962 he was honored with a solo show at the Guggenheim Museum in New York, but then minimalist and pop art began to gain currency on the international art scene, and expressionist works such as his fell out of favor.

Fortunately, his career was revived after the death of Franco in 1975 and the renewal of interest in Catalan culture. Barcelona became one of Europe's most dynamic cities, and Tàpies's works were suddenly viewed in an entirely new light. *New York Times* journalist Edward Schumacher noted that Tàpies became "a father figure and cultural hero" in the province, which was granted autonomy again in 1980, and asserted that "it is from Catalonia's extraordinarily rich Romanesque heritage that the artist draws the simplicity, powerful spirituality and frescolike techniques that for nearly 40 years have remained the basis of much of his painting."

Later in his career, Tàpies began incorporating even larger objects onto his canvases, such as buckets and mirrors. Aside from these, he explained in the *UNESCO Courier* interview with Ibañez, "my equipment is extremely modest—it amounts to a brush whose bristles are rather worn. That's all I need. The simplest tools can express the deepest feelings." He also spoke about the unusual materials he uses. "Gold leaf will make a totally different impression on you from that made by a piece of torn cardboard," he reflected in the same interview. "And the piece of cardboard will have different connotations, and will arouse different feelings from those produced by a piece of polished marble." He remained firm in his belief, he told the *UNESCO Courier,* that "there is profound wisdom in the humblest objects. The Japanese say that the whole universe is contained in a grain of sand. These objects, which seem to be nothing but rubbish, can deliver an authentic human message."

Became Elder Statesman of Spanish Art

In his later years Tàpies became increasingly interested in Eastern philosophies, particularly Zen Buddhism. He viewed his art as an extension of his personal beliefs, describing himself in the interview with Ibañez as "an anxious person. I worry about everything. I need to know everything. I tend to live in a state of anxiety with the feeling that life is some kind of great catastrophe." This attitude compels him, he told the *UNESCO Courier* writer, "to do something useful for society, and that is what stimulates me." He elaborated further in the *New York Times* profile, telling Schumacher, "My illusion is to have something to transmit. If I can't change the world, at least I want to change the way people look at it. There is a crisis of values today. In the spread of modernity, we have made great technological advances, but man at the same time has become more cruel than ever, destroys more than ever."

In 1984 the artist established the Tàpies Foundation in Barcelona, which formally opened with a museum and library in 1990. It holds some 2,000 works of his—though the actual career output is well above 7,000—as well as art from such masters as Louise Bourgeois, Brassaï, and Diego Rivera. The building has a tangled-wire sculpture atop it, designed by Tàpies. He has won several prestigious commissions from the government of Barcelona or its cultural institutions.

Tàpies married Teresa Barbara in 1954, and they have three grown children. He lives in a Barcelona home that has a work studio for him, and he also retreats each summer to a country house in Campins and paints there. In March of 2003 he was honored at New York City's Pace-Wildenstein Gallery in an 80th birthday retrospective.

Selected writings

El pa a la Braca, with poems by J. Brossa, Sala Gaspar (Barcelona, Spain), 1963.
La practica de l'art, Barcelona, 1970.
Suite Catalana: Poems from de Catalan, with poems by J. Brossa, introductory text by Arthur Terry and Roland Penrose, Polígrafa (Barcelona, Spain), 1973.
L'art contre L'estetica, Barcelona, 1974.
Dialogo sobre arte, cultura y sociedad, with Imma Julian, Barcelona, 1977.
Memorial personal, autobiography, Barcelona, 1978.
Conversaciones con Tàpies, with Miguel Fernandez-Brasso, Madrid, 1981.

Sources

Books

Contemporary Artists, fourth edition, St. James Press, 1996.
Dictionary of Hispanic Biography, Gale Research, 1996.

Periodicals

New York Times, January 29, 1990, p. C1725; January 26, 1995, p. C13; January 27, 1995, p. C25; March 14, 2003, p. E41.
Progressive Architecture, May 1993, p. 78.
Publishers Weekly, April 27, 1992, p. 243.
UNESCO Courier, June 1994, p. 4.

—Carol Brennan

Alfred A. Valenzuela

1948(?)—

Major general, army officer

Hispanic Magazine said of Alfred A. Valenzuela, "The nation's highest-ranking active-duty Hispanic military officer loves God, his family, the U.S. Army, sports, and birds. He is a walking recruitment center, a loving husband and dad, a church-going Catholic, live-by-the-rules guy, a perfectionist, and a funny man." Major General Alfred A. Valenzuela has served in posts around the world including Panama, Germany, Korea, El Salvador, and Turkey. He has been decorated many times for his service to his country and although known as being a tough disciplinarian, the people who work with him speak highly of him and his way of doing things.

Valenzuela was born in San Antonio, Texas, around 1948. He went to Catholic School, and was in the Cub and Boy Scouts, where he earned the prestigious rank of Eagle Scout. He was interested in the military early in life and joined the JROTC in high school, and the ROTC at St. Mary's University in San Antonio, where he received both a bachelor of arts degree in government and a master of arts in political science with an emphasis on Latin American studies and national security affairs. He was commissioned there as a distinguished military graduate. He continued his education in the military at the Field Artillery Basic and Advanced Courses, the Defense Strategy Course, the Army War College, the National Security Management Course, and the Airborne Course. He also graduated from the U.S. Army Command and the General Staff College, the Armed Forces Staff College, the Air War College, and the Inter-American Defense College.

After serving in many positions around the globe and working his way up through the ranks of officers, Valenzuela served as the deputy commanding general and deputy joint task force Panama commander at the U.S. Army South. After that he served as assistant division commander (Support) of the 3rd Infantry Division (Mechanized) at Fort Stewart/Hunter Army Airfield, Georgia, from October of 1996 until June of 1998. In 1997, he became a one-star general.

He received his second star in 1998 and in June of that year was made deputy commander in chief of the U.S. Southern Command, based in Miami, Florida, which had relocated from Panama in 1997. The Southern Command oversaw military operations in Latin America and the Caribbean, except Mexico, working, in recent years, on anti-drug efforts, disaster relief, preserving stability, and countering threats to vital U.S. national interests, as well as assisting friendly nations within its area of responsibility. According to the *Southern Command* website, "[U.S. Southern Command] is engaged in promoting democracy and stability while fostering collective approaches to regional threats, and providing the vitality, integrity and strength to our military allies and their support for democracy and their institutions. Furthermore, when required, it responds unilaterally or multilaterally to crises that threaten regional stability or national interests and constantly prepares to meet future challenges in the region." It is one of five regional commands found around the world. About Valenzuela's work with the Southern Command, Secretary of the Army Louis Caldera called Valenzuela "One of our most impressive

At a Glance . . .

Born Alfred A. Valenzuela, ca. 1948 in San Antonio, TX; married Esther Trevino, 1970; children: Lori, Freddie. *Education:* St. Mary's University, San Antonio, TX, BA, government, MA, political science; attended Field Artillery Basic and Advanced Courses, Defense Strategy Course, Army War College, National Security Management Course, Airborne Course; graduated from U.S. Army Command and General Staff College, Armed Forces Staff College, Air War College, Inter-American Defense College. *Military:* U.S. Army, 1970–. *Religion:* Christian.

Career: U.S. Army South, deputy commanding general and deputy joint task force Panama commander; 3rd Infantry Division (Mechanized), Fort Stewart/Hunter Army Airfield, Georgia, assistant division commander (support), 1996-98; U.S. Southern Command, deputy commander in chief, 1998-00; U.S. Army South, commander, 2000–.

Memberships: Board of directors: Eagle Scout Association; Torres Rivera Institute for Policy; Saint Mary's University; TX Chapter of the Boy Scouts of America. Board of trustees, Tomas Rivera Policy Institute; board of advisors, Uniformed Services Benefit Association, Inc.

Awards: Defense Distinguished Service Medal; Defense Superior Service Medal; Legion of Merit (with three Oak Leaf Clusters); Soldier's Medal (for heroism); Bronze Star for Valor; Defense Meritorious Service Medal; Meritorious Service Medal (with two Oak Leaf Clusters); Joint Service Commendation Medal; Army Commendation Medal (with Oak Leaf Cluster); Joint Service Achievement Medal; Army Achievement Medal; Armed Forces Expeditionary Medal; Humanitarian Service Medal; Joint Meritorious Unit Award. Inducted into Boys & Girls Clubs of America's Alumni Hall of Fame, 2001; honorary inductee into the Beta Nu Chapter of Phi Sigma Iota, United States Military Academy, 2001; named one of the "100 Most Influential Hispanics" by *Hispanic Business* magazine.

Address: *Office*—US Army South, Ft. Buchanan, Fort Buchanan Building 1314, Fort Buchanan, PR 00934-3400. Phone: (787) 707-2857.

officers." Valenzuela's one-time executive officer U.S. Air Force Major Elizabeth Almeida told *Hispanic Magazine* that he was "people-oriented, approachable, a people's general, a wonderful role model, and not only for Hispanics, but for all in the military. You don't have to be important to see him or for him to make time for you. He makes everyone who comes to see him feel important."

In July of 2000 Valenzuela assumed command of the U.S. Army South, at Fort Buchanan, Puerto Rico. The U.S. Army South is the Southern Command's Army component, one of the five components of the Command that work together to fulfill the U.S. Southern Command's missions. According to the *U.S. Army South's* website, "[U.S. Army South] is in charge of all Army operations within USSOUTHCOM's twelve million square mile [area of responsibility]." As part of U.S. Army's duties, in 2002 Valenzuela met with Dominican Republic Major General Carlos Diaz Morfa concerning the illegal migrations of Haitians into their country and eventually into the United States. They have begun to work on stopping the flow. At the same time Valenzuela was looking to move U.S. Army South out of Puerto Rico. They considered many locations, but after careful deliberation chose San Antonio as their new home. They were to move there in 2003.

About his life in the military Valenzuela once told *Hispanic Magazine,* "I've had an American Dream since I was young and that was to be the best I could be. It just so happens that it was to be in the professional military. I knew if I could get up there (in the ranks) then I could turn around, come back, and give back to society, give back to the Hispanic youth who really doesn't understand the opportunity before him." And he has certainly taken that attitude and made an inspiring career for himself, while fulfilling his promise to help Hispanic youths. While in the line of duty, Valenzuela won not only respect and promotion, but also many awards. He has received several decorations, including the Defense Distinguished Service Medal, the Defense Superior Service Medal, the Legion of Merit (with three Oak Leaf Clusters), the Soldier's Medal (for heroism), the Bronze Star for Valor, the Defense Meritorious Service Medal, the Meritorious Service Medal (with two Oak Leaf Clusters), the Joint Service Commendation Medal, the Army Commendation Medal (with Oak Leaf Cluster), the Joint Service Achievement Medal, the Army Achievement Medal, the Armed Forces Expeditionary Medal, the Humanitarian Service Medal, and the Joint Meritorious Unit Award.

Amidst his very hectic and awarded Army schedule, Valenzuela has also managed to live a balanced and healthy personal life. He married Esther Trevino on February 1, 1970, when he was about to enter the Army. They have two children, Lori and Freddie, both of whom are very proud of their father's successes. Fred told *Hispanic Magazine,* "It's so weird, everybody says, 'Oh look who your dad is.' We just see him as Dad. Yes, we are proud of him, but at the same time, we don't treat him as a celebrity."

Valenzuela was also a prominent figure in a wider military and also civilian society. In 1999 he spoke at a conference about the Armed Forces' ongoing efforts to provide outreach to the Hispanic community. He was inducted, in 2001, into the Boys & Girls Clubs of America's Alumni Hall of Fame. The Boys & Girls Club was close to his heart because, as *Hispanic PR Wire* said, Valenzuela "learned about direction and discipline, two words that capture the essence of military service, at the Boys & Girls Club of San Antonio." In 2002 he was the honorary inductee into the Beta Nu Chapter of Phi Sigma Iota, an international foreign-language honor society at the United States Military Academy. He gave the keynote address for the ceremony. He has served on the board of directors for the Eagle Scout Association, the Torres Rivera Institute for Policy, Saint Mary's University, and the Texas Chapter of the Boy Scouts of America. He was also on the board of trustees of the Tomas Rivera Policy Institute and the board of advisors for the Uniformed Services Benefit Association, Inc. He was named one of the "100 Most Influential Hispanics" by *Hispanic Business* magazine. In 2003 the Texas House of Representatives honored Valenzuela for his exemplary dedication to the Armed Services and his country. And seeing as Major General Alfred A. Valenzuela has not finished his career yet, there are sure to be many more awards in the future.

Sources

Periodicals

Business Wire, April 16, 2002.
Houston Chronicle, December 30, 2001, p. 41.

On-line

"2001 Scout Jamboree," *First Army Web Site,* http://jambo.forscom.army.mil/army_eagles_1.htm (June 5, 2003).
"About 500 pay tribute to Jasper," *Savannah Now,* www.savannahnow.com/stories/031698/LOCjas pertribute.html (June 5, 2003).
"AmericasUnidas to become Bi-Annual Trade Summit," *Port of Corpus Christi,* www.americasunidas.com/news/PortNews5-30-02.html (June 5, 2003).

"Army reaching out to Hispanic youth," *United States Army Public Affairs,* www.dtic.mil/armylink/news/Dec1999/a19991215hispaniciii.html (June 5, 2003).
"Army South might move? Why? Says who?," *U.S. Army South,* www.usarso.army.mil/news/who.htm (June 5, 2003.)
"Army's highest Hispanic joins Hall of Fame," *United States Army Public Affairs,* www.dtic.mil/army link/news/Apr2001/a20010411valenzuela.html (June 5, 2003).
"Biography," *U.S. Southern Command,* www.south com.mil/PA/Bios/bioUSARSO.htm (June 5, 2003).
"Board of Trustees," *Tomas Rivera Policy Institute,* www.trpi.org/mid_trustees.htm (June 5, 2003).
"Boys & Girls Clubs of America Inducts Outstanding Alumni into Hall of Fame," *Hispanic PR Wire,* www.hispanicprwire.com/release_Boys%20and%20Girls%20Clubs_ENG.htm (June 5, 2003).
"Cadets inducted into honor society," *United States Military Academy,* www.usma.edu/PublicAffairs/PVArchives/000512/Cadet-Honor.htm (June 5, 2003).
"The Challenges For the Foreign Area Officer in Army XXI," *Foreign Area Officer Association,* www.faoa.org/journal/armyxxi.html (June 5, 2003).
"Dominican army tightens watch," *Miami Herald,* www.miami.com/mld/miamiherald/news/world/americas/4598472.htm (June 5, 2003).
"General 'V'," *Hispanic Magazine,* www.hispanic magazine.com/2000/apr/Features/
"Key Players," *Citizens' Educational Foundation—US,* www.cefus.net/background/keyplayers. html (June 5, 2003).
"Puerto Rico Chapter Ups Its Numbers," *The Retired Officer Magazine,* www.troa.org/magazine/Aug ust2002/chapter_activities.asp
"Resolution," *State of Texas Web Site,* www.cap itol.state.tx.us/tlo/75R/billtext/HR00972F.HTM (June 5, 2003).
"Soldier's remains taken home," *My San Antonio,* http://news.mysanantonio.com/story.cfm?xla=saen &xlb=180&xlc=962036 (June 5, 2003).
"Top Guns," *St. Mary's University,* www.stmarytx.edu/sesqui/publication/index.php?go=guns&show-history (June 5, 2003).
U.S. Army Web Site, www.army.mil (June 5, 2003).

—Catherine Victoria Donaldson

Mary Rose Garrido Wilcox

1949—

County official

A fourth-generation member of a pioneering Mexican-American family, Mary Rose Garrido Wilcox in 2000 was re-elected to her third four-year term as a member of the Maricopa County Board of Supervisors in Arizona. It is just the latest chapter in Wilcox's long career of public service, a career which began with nine years on the Phoenix City Council. Wilcox's contributions as a public servant have been matched by her zealous efforts on behalf of the Hispanic community. She was the first Hispanic woman to serve on the Phoenix council and has worked tirelessly to advance the cause of her fellow Hispanic Americans since her childhood days in the predominantly Latino community of Superior, Arizona. As a girl, Wilcox was deeply influenced by the political activism of her parents, John and Betty Nunez Garrido, who were among the first generation of Hispanics unwilling to accept the discrimination that had so cruelly constrained the lives of those who came before them. With her husband, Earl V. Wilcox, who was raised in the heavily Hispanic barrios of southeast Phoenix, Wilcox owns and operates the *New El Sol,* an English-language weekly newspaper serving the Hispanic community.

Faced Discrimination in Arizona

She was born Mary Rose Garrido on November 21, 1949, in Superior, Arizona, a rural mining town of about 5,000, more than 80 percent of whom were Hispanic. Her father, John Garrido, was a copper miner, while her mother, Betty Nunez Garrido, was a homemaker active in the local school system and the Roman Catholic church. After fighting for his country in the Korean War, John Garrido returned to Superior a new man, no longer willing to settle for treatment as a second-class citizen in the town of his birth. He spearheaded a campaign among his fellow miners to form a union. As her parents fought for a better life in Superior, Wilcox experienced changes in her world as well. After years of attending a segregated school in Superior, she found herself in a newly integrated classroom. Mirroring her parents' activism in the community, she took an active role in her local high school, serving on the student council and playing clarinet in the school band. The growing role played by Hispanics in community affairs and in the schools instilled in Wilcox a growing pride in the accomplishments of her people.

Although Hispanics had begun to establish themselves as first-class citizens in her hometown, Wilcox soon discovered that discrimination was still alive and well elsewhere in Arizona. Enrolling at Arizona State University (ASU) in Tempe to study social work, Wilcox was cruelly reminded that not everyone regarded her as an equal. She and three other minority women found themselves relegated to a single room in the ASU dormitory. Striking back against this sort of bias at a state institution, Wilcox threw herself into campus activism, participating in a strike to improve working conditions for ASU's laundry workers, most of whom were Hispanic. Recalling how unionization had improved the quality of life for Superior's copper miners, Wilcox hoped that solidarity among ASU's laundry workers might bring similar benefits.

It was at ASU that Mary Rose met fellow student Earl V. Wilcox, who had grown up in the heavily Hispanic

neighborhoods of southeast Phoenix, an area ravaged by poverty and crime. His background had inspired him to look for ways to help make life better for those with whom he'd grown up. When the two met, Earl Wilcox was working as a youth project director. Mary Rose and Earl married in 1971, and she dropped out of school to go to work in support of her husband's quest for a master's degree in education. He would later become a state representative and a justice of the peace.

Wilcox worked as a job developer for the Manpower program in Maricopa County, helping to find employment opportunities in the private sector. She worked closely with members of the Yaqui Native American tribe who had been displaced from their homes in northern Arizona by a flood control project. She found that the Yaquis, a group with strong Hispanic influences, needed help not only in finding jobs but in locating housing and other forms of support.

Hired by DeConcini

Impressed by Wilcox's work on behalf of the Yaqui, Dennis DeConcini, a Democrat newly elected to the U.S. Senate from Arizona, in 1977 invited Wilcox to join his staff as a caseworker. She eventually was promoted to special assistant and also served as DeConcini's liaison with the Small Business Administration and the Immigration and Naturalization Service. Her work for the senator got Wilcox involved with Friendly House, a nonprofit organization formed in 1920 and dedicated to helping immigrants. She helped the organization develop an educational program targeting at-risk children during after-school hours. Long a supporter of Friendly House, Wilcox was elected a board member in 1992. During the years of Wilcox's involvement, Friendly House has grown significantly, expanding from an annual working budget of $100,000 to one that now exceeds $4 million.

Working for DeConcini gave Wilcox valuable access to the local community. She was eventually elected to the Human Resources Commission of Phoenix, and in that job she successfully campaigned for a restructuring of the city council from at-large representation to districts. In the process, the Phoenix City Council was expanded from six to eight members. Wilcox herself was one of the first beneficiaries of the restructuring, winning election to the council from the heavily Hispanic seventh district in 1982. She became the first Hispanic woman ever elected to serve on the Phoenix council. In an interview with *Dictionary of Hispanic Biography's* Peg MacNichol, she said her campaign was "the most satisfying in my life." Projects championed by Wilcox included a campaign to pass a $37 million bond issue to finance affordable housing in Phoenix. She was eventually selected to chair the council's housing commission. Working with liberal reform Mayor Terry Goddard and fellow councilman Calvin Goode, Wilcox managed to get the bond issue passed, further buttressing her reputation as a housing advocate. She also worked with Goode to win approval for establishment of a $1 million fund for an anti-crime program called Neighborhood Fightback. Monies from the fund were disbursed to strong community associations willing to upgrade their neighborhoods. Neighborhoods in which the program was implemented experienced significant declines in crime, and the program was eventually adopted statewide.

Despite her growing involvement in local politics, Wilcox remained an enthusiastic campaigner for Hispanic rights. In 1983 she joined with five other Hispanic women to found the Hispanic Women's Corporation (HWC), a group that offers annual seminars to help Hispanic women find new ways in which to upgrade their education and careers. Each year the HWC sponsors a national conference, the largest conference of its kind in Arizona. The conference, which draws up to 2,000 attendees yearly, is privately funded by corporations that use the event as a recruiting opportunity. Wilcox in 1983 also helped created IMAGE, a coalition of Hispanic government employees at the federal, state, and local level. She served as IMAGE's first president from 1983 until 1986.

Selected to Serve as Vice Mayor

Wilcox's visibility in Phoenix increased significantly in 1988 when she was elected by her fellow councilmen to serve a two-year term as vice mayor. Encouraged by Mayor Goddard to push the envelope during her time as vice mayor, Wilcox spearheaded a campaign to ban semiautomatic weapons, including the AK-47 assault rifle popular with gangs in Phoenix. She also supported a proposal to build a baseball stadium in her district, convinced that it would draw new jobs and money into the area. In 1989 she was re-elected to the council, largely on the strength of her appeal as a grassroots candidate. In campaign speeches, Wilcox frequently compared herself to typical members of her constituency. The strategy worked. Although there were rumors that Wilcox might seek the mayor's job after Goddard left to seek a state office, in the end she set her sights on the Maricopa County Board of Supervisors, hoping to win election as a replacement for fifth district Supervisor Ed Pastor. In November of 1992, she realized her goal, becoming the first Hispanic woman to serve as a supervisor.

Covering more than 9,200 square miles, Maricopa County, Arizona, is the fourteenth largest county in the nation in terms of area. As the home to nearly 2.3 million, it is the seventh most populous American county. Wilcox's election to the ruling board of the county put her and her fellow supervisors in charge of an annual budget of more than $1.2 billion and a county work force of some 14,000 employees. Now working at the county level, Wilcox continued to push for programs to revitalize downtown Phoenix. Her

support in 1994 of a quarter-cent sales tax to help pay for the $350 million Bank One Ballpark stadium in Phoenix was to prove especially costly for Wilcox.

Leaving a meeting of the supervisors on August 13, 1997, Wilcox was accosted by a gun-toting man who had attended the meeting and followed her from the auditorium. "I saw him out of the corner of my eye and became very alarmed, because he just didn't look right," Wilcox later told reporters. "The next thing I knew, I felt a gun in my back." A split second later, her assailant fired a 38-caliber round into Wilcox's pelvis. The gunman, Larry Marvin Naman, a 49-year-old transient with a history of mental illness, told police he was angry about the supervisor's support of the stadium sales tax. Hospitalized for four days, Wilcox was left with bullet fragments in her hip and thigh. She later blamed what she called "hate radio" for refusing to let the issue of the stadium sales tax die. "I attribute [the shooting] directly to the venom that radio talk shows put out every day," Wilcox told the *Arizona Republic*. "Many of them are just hate-baiting. Because I am the only remaining board member who voted on the stadium I was the target." The gunman was eventually convicted on charges of attempted first-degree murder and sentenced to 15 years in prison.

Shooting Failed to Sideline Wilcox

In the long run, the shooting did little to slow Wilcox down. She continued to work as a supervisor and in 2000 was elected to her third four-year term on the Maricopa County board. Interestingly, earlier that same year Wilcox made election history when she cast the first ballot in Arizona's first Internet presidential primary. It was the nation's first such ballot cast in a binding election for public office. Wilcox recorded her vote with a simple click of the computer mouse.

Apart from her responsibilities as county supervisor, Wilcox stays busy at home and through her involvement in a wide variety of civic affairs. She and her husband bought *El Sol,* a Spanish-language weekly serving the Hispanic community of Greater Phoenix. The newspaper has since been repackaged as the *New El Sol* and is printed in English, although it continues to target Phoenix's growing Hispanic population. The couple also own and operate El Portal, a Mexican restaurant located near Grant Park in downtown Phoenix.

Sources

Books

Carroll's County Directory, Carroll Publishing, 2001.
Complete Marquis Who's Who, Marquis Who's Who, 2001.
Dictionary of Hispanic Biography, Gale Research, 1996.

Periodicals

Access Control & Security Systems, October 1, 1997.
Arizona Republic, August 17, 1997.
Atlanta Constitution, March 8, 2000.
Phoenix New Times, 1997.

On-line

"Mary Rose Garrido Wilcox, Supervisor, District 5," *Maricopa.gov,* www.Maricopa.gov/dist5/bio.asp (June 20, 2003).
"Mary Rose Wilcox - Biography," *Greater Phoenix Economic Council,* www.gpec.org/AnnualReport 2001/intro/Bios-Board/wilcoxbio.html (June 20, 2003).

—Don Amerman

Cumulative Nationality Index

Volume and page numbers appear in **bold**.

American

Aguilera, Christina, **2:1–3**
Alvarado, Linda, **3:5–8**
Alvarez, Luis W., **2:7–10**
Anaya, Rudolfo, **2:11–14**
Anthony, Marc, **3:12–14**
Arrarás, María Celeste, **4:12–14**
Baca, Judith F., **2:21–24**
Baca Zinn, Maxine, **2:25–28**
Baca-Barragán, Polly, **4:15–17**
Baez, Joan, **2:29–33**
Baird, Lourdes G., **4:18–20**
Barretto, Ray, **2:34–36**
Big Punisher, **4:23–25**
Blaine, David, **3:30–32**
Bratt, Benjamin, **3:44–46**
Bustamante, Cruz M., **4:29–32**
Caldera, Louis, **3:47–49**
Carmona, Richard, **3:61–63**
Carter, Lynda, **4:36–39**
Castillo, Ana, **1:33–35**
Castro, Ida, **1:40–42**
Cavazos, Richard E., **4:40–42**
Chávez, César, **2:66–69**
Chávez, Denise, **2:70–73**
Chavez, Dennis, **3:71–79**
Chavez, Linda, **4:48–52**
Chávez, Nick, **4:53–55**
Chavez-Thompson, Linda, **1:47–49**
Cisneros, Evelyn, **3:74–77**
Cisneros, Henry, **1:50–52**
Cisneros, Marc, **4:56–58**
Cisneros, Sandra, **1:53–56**
Coca, Imogene, **2:77–80**
Colón, Willie, **3:78–80**
Corona, Bert, **1:57–59**
De La Hoya, Oscar, **1:66–69**
De Varona, Donna, **4:59–61**
De Vega, Sonia de Léon, **2:93–94**
Diaz, Cameron, **1:73–75**
Díaz-Oliver, Remedios, **4:62–64**
Dunbar, Huey, **4:65–67**
E., Sheila, **3:88–90**
Estés, Clarissa Pinkola, **4:68–72**
Estrada, Erik, **4:73–76**
Fernandez, Joseph A., **2:108–110**
Flores, Patrick, **1:86–88**
Galindo, Rudy, **3:98–101**
Garcia, Jerry, **3:102–105**
Garciaparra, Anthony Nomar, **3:106–108**
Gomez, Scott, **2:119–120**

Gonzales, Richard, **3:116–119**
González, Henry B., **2:125–128**
Gurulé, Jimmy, **4:98–101**
Gutierrez, Carlos M., **4:102–105**
Haubegger, Christy, **1:98–101**
Hayworth, Rita, **1:102–104**
Hidalgo, Edward, **4:109–114**
Hijuelos, Oscar, **1:105–107**
Huerta, Dolores, **2:138–140**
Kanellos, Nicolás, **2:141–144**
Leal, Luis, **4:125–128**
Lobo, Rebecca, **3:144–146**
Lopez, Jennifer, **1:116–119**
Lopez, Nancy, **1:120–122**
Lucero-Schayes, Wendy, **4:129–131**
Mares, Michael A., **4:132–134**
Marin, Cheech, **4:135–138**
Martinez, Arthur C., **4:143–146**
McLish, Rachel, **3:151–153**
Mendoza, Lydia, **3:158–160**
Mohr, Nicholasa, **2:158–160**
Montoya, José, **4:150–153**
Munoz, Anthony, **2:161–163**
Napolitano, Grace, **1:138–141**
O'Brien, Soledad, **1:146–148**
Ocampo, Adriana C., **4:154–157**
Ochoa, Ellen, **1:149–151**
Olmos, Edward James, **1:155–159**
Orlando, Tony, **4:158–161**
Ortega, Katherine D., **4:166–169**
Paredes, Américo, **3:175–177**
Parra, Derek, **1:160–162**
Prinze, Freddie Jr., **3:184–186**
Puente, Tito, **1:172–175**
Quiñones, John, **4:173–176**
Ramirez, Tina, **4:177–179**
Reyes, Sylvestre, **2:181–183**
Richardson, Bill, **4:180–183**
Rodriguez, Alex, **1:183–185**
Rodríguez, Daniel, **3:195–197**
Rodriguez, Jennifer, **2:188–190**
Rodríguez, Narciso, **3:198–200**
Rodríguez, Robert, **3:201–203**
Roman, Phil, **4:187–191**
Romero, Cesar, **3:204–207**
Ronstadt, Linda, **3:208–211**
Ros-Lehtinen, Ileana, **4:191–193**
Roybal-Allard, Lucille, **3:212–214**
Sanchez, Loretta, **1:186–188**
Sánchez, Poncho, **2:194–197**
Selena, **2:205–207**
Sheen, Charlie, **4:209–212**

Sheen, Martin, **1:195–198**
Smits, Jimmy, **3:221–224**
Soto, Gary, **4:213–215**
Tapia, Luis, **1:203–205**
Torres, Dara, **1:206–209**
Treviño, Jesus Salvador, **2:212–214**
Valdez, Luis, **1:210–212**
Valens, Ritchie, **2:218–220**
Valenzuela, Alfred A., **4:219–221**
Velasquez, Jaci, **2:221–223**
Vilar, Alberto, **2:224–227**
Welch, Raquel, **1:219–221**
Wilcox, Mary Rose Garrido, **4:222–225**

Argentinean

Bocca, Julio, **3:33–36**
de la Rúa, Fernando, **1:70–72**
Favaloro, Rene, **4:77–79**
Ginastera, Alberto, **3:109–111**
Guevara, Che, **2:129–133**
Lamarque, Libertad, **4:122–124**
Maradona, Diego, **1:123–122**
Menem, Carlos Saul, **1:131–133**
Pelli, César, **2:167–169**
Pérez Esquivel, Adolfo, **4:170–172**
Perón, Eva "Evita," **1:169–171**
Perón, Juan, **2:170–173**
Sabatini, Gabriela, **4:198–200**

Bolivian

Bánzer Suárez, Hugo, **1:25–28**
Escalante, Jaime, **2:104–107**

Brazilian

Amado, Jorge, **3:9–11**
Arcain, Janeth, **1:19–21**
Boff, Leonardo, **3:37–40**
Braga, Sonia, **3:41–43**
Bundchen, Gisele, **2:47–49**
Cardoso, Fernando, **1:29–32**
de Moraes, Vinícius, **2:90–92**
Gilberto, João, **2:116–118**
Jobim, Antonio Carlos "Tom", **3:134–136**
Mendes, Sérgio, **2:155–157**
Senna, Ayrton, **3:218–220**

Chilean

Allende, Isabel, **1:4–6**
Francisco, Don, **4:83–85**
Lagos, Ricardo, **4:118–121**

Neruda, Pablo, **2:164–166**
Serrano, Lupe, **4:205–208**

Colombian
Betancourt, Ingrid, **2:40–42**
Botero, Fernando, **2:43–46**
García Márquez, Gabriel, **2:111–115**
Leguizamo, John, **3:141–143**
Montoya, Juan Pablo, **3:164–166**
Ocampo, Adriana C., **4:154–157**
Restrepo, Laura, **3:187–190**
Shakira, **1:192–194**

Costa Rican
Arias Sánchez, Oscar, **3:15–18**
Bermúdez, Carmen, **2:37–39**
Chang-Díaz, Franklin, **2:62–65**

Cuban
Acosta, Carlos, **4:1–3**
Alonso, Alicia, **1:11–14**
Arenas, Reinaldo, **4:8–11**
Arnaz, Desi, **2:18–20**
Brito, Maria, **4:26–28**
Canseco, José, **3:54–56**
Carbonell, Josefina, **2:58–61**
Carpentier, Alejo, **3:64–67**
Castro, Fidel, **1:36–39**
Cruz, Celia, **1:60–62**
Díaz-Oliver, Remedios, **4:62–64**
Dominguez, Cari, **2:101–103**
Estefan, Gloria, **1:82–85**
Goizueta, Roberto Crispulo, **3:112–115**
Guillén, Nicolás, **3:120–123**
Gutierrez, Carlos, **4:102–105**
Machado, Eduardo, **2:145–148**
Martínez, Mel **1:127–130**
O'Farrill, Arturo "Chico," **1:152–154**
Pérez, Tony, **1:166–168**
Prida, Dolores, **3:181–183**
Ros-Lehtinen, Ileana, **4:191–193**
Sandoval, Arturo, **2:198–200**
Saralegui, Cristina, **2:201–204**
Sardiñas, Eligio, **4:203–204**
Valdés, Jesus "Chucho," **2:215–217**

Dominican
Alvarez, Julia, **1:15–18**
de la Renta, Oscar, **2:87–89**
Fernández, Mary Joe, **3:94–97**
Gaviño, Juan Bosch, **4:90–94**
Sosa, Sammy, **1:199–202**
Tejada, Miguel, **3:225–227**

Ecuadoran
Baird, Lourdes G., **4:18–20**
Mahaud, Jamil, **2:149–151**

Guatemalan
Asturias, Miguel Angel, **3:19–21**
Menchú, Rigoberta, **3:154–157**

Mexican
Benitez, Elsa, **4:21–22**
Cantinflas, **4:33–35**
Corpi, Lucha, **2:81–83**
Derbéz Bautista, Luis Ernesto, **2:98–100**
Echeverría Álvarez, Luis, **3:91–93**
Esquivel, Laura, **1:79–81**
Fernández, Emilio "El Indio," **4:80–82**
Fox, Vincente, **1:89–91**
Fuentes, Carlos, **1:92–94**
García, Héctor Pérez, **4:86–89**
Gómez-Pompa, Arturo, **2:121–124**
Guzmán, Alejandra, **4:106–108**
Hayek, Salma, **2:134–137**
Hidalgo, Edward, **4:109–111**
Hinojosa, María (de Lourdes), **3:128–130**
Infante, Pedro, **4:112–114**
Kahlo, Frida, **1:113–115**
Leal, Luis, **4:125–128**
Marin, Rosario, **2:152–154**
Quinn, Anthony, **1:176–179**
Ramos, Jorge, **2:178–180**
Rivera, Diego, **2:184–187**
Romero, Alejandro, **2:191–193**
Rubio, Paulina, **4:194–197**
Santana, Carlos, **1:189–191**
Thalía, **2:208–211**

Nicaraguan
Alegría, Claribel Joy, **3:1–4**
Alemán, Arnoldo, **1:1–3**
Cardenal, Ernesto, **3:57–60**
Ortega, Daniel, **4:162–165**

Panamanian
Blades, Rubén, **3:26–29**

Paraguayan
González Macchi, Luis, **1:95–97**

Peruvian
Arana, Marie, **2:15–17**
Vargas Llosa, Mario, **1:213–215**

Puerto Rican
Arrarás, María Celeste, **4:12–14**
Calderón, Sila Marí, **2:50–53**
Camacho, Hector, **3:50–53**
Cepeda, Orlando, **4:43–47**
Clemente, Roberto, **2:74–76**
Cruz, Victor Hernández, **3:81–83**
Del Toro, Benicio, **2:95–97**
Juliá, Raúl, **3:137–140**
Martin, Ricky, **3:147–150**
Moreno, Rita, **1:134–137**
Munoz Marin, Luis, **3:167–170**
Novello, Antonia, **1:142–145**
Ortiz Cofer, Judith, **3:171–174**
Pérez, Eddie, **1:163–165**
Piñero, Miguel, **2:174–177**
Quiñones August, Denise, **1:180–182**
Rodriguez, Carlos Manuel, **4:184–186**
Rodríguez, Chi Chi, **3:191–194**
Santaella, Irma Vidal, **4:201–202**
Velázquez, Nydia, **1:216–218**

Salvadoran
Calderón Sol, Armando **2:54–57**
Mármol, Miguel, **4:139–142**

Spanish
Almendros, Nestor, **2:4–6**
Almodóvar, Pedro, **1:7–10**
Alvariño, Angeles, **4:4–7**
Aznar, José Maria, **1:22–24**
Banderas, Antonio, **3:22–25**
Carreras, José, **3:68–70**
Cugat, Xavier, **2:84–86**
Dalí, Salvador, **1:63–65**
Domingo, Plácido, **1:76–78**
González Márquez, Felipe, **4:95–97**
Iglesias, Enrique, **1:108–112**
Iglesias, Julio, **3:131–133**
Juan Carlos de Borbón y Borbón, **4:115–117**
Moneo, Rafael, **4:147–149**
Montoya, Carlos García, **3:161–163**
Picasso, Pablo, **3:178–180**
Santayana, George, **3:215–217**
Tápies, Antoni, **4:216–218**

Venezuelan
Chávez, Hugo, **1:43–46**
Dallmeier, Francisco, **3:84–87**
Herrera, Carolina, **3:124–127**
Ramirez, Tina, **4:177–179**

Cumulative Occupation Index

Volume and page numbers appear in **bold**.

Accountants
Arenas, Reinaldo, **4:8–11**
Ortega, Katherine D., **4:166–169**
Roybal-Allard, Lucille, **3:212–214**
Santaella, Irma Vidal, **4:201–202**

Actors
Anthony, Marc, **3:12–14**
Arnaz, Desi, **2:18–20**
Banderas, Antonio, **3:22–25**
Blades, Rubén, **3:26–29**
Braga, Sonia, **3:41–43**
Bratt, Benjamin, **3:44–46**
Cantinflas, **4:33–35**
Carter, Lynda, **4:36–39**
Coca, Imogene, **2:77–80**
Del Toro, Benicio, **2:90–92**
Diaz, Cameron, **1:73–75**
Estrada, Erik, **4:73–76**
Fernández, Emilio "El Indio," **4:80–82**
Hayek, Salma, **2:134–137**
Hayworth, Rita, **1:102–104**
Infante, Pedro, **4:112–114**
Juliá, Raúl, **3:137–140**
Lamarque, Libertad, **4:122–124**
Leguizamo, John, **3:141–143**
Lopez, Jennifer, **1:116–119**
Machado, Eduardo, **2:145–148**
Marin, Cheech, **4:135–138**
Martin, Ricky, **3:147–150**
McLish, Rachel, **3:151–153**
Moreno, Rita, **1:134–137**
Olmos, Edward James, **1:155–159**
Piñero, Miguel, **2:174–177**
Prinze, Freddie, Jr., **3:184–186**
Quinn, Anthony, **1:176–179**
Romero, Cesar, **3:204–207**
Rubio, Paulina, **4:194–197**
Sheen, Charlie, **4:209–212**
Sheen, Martin, **1:195–198**
Smits, Jimmy, **3:221–224**
Thalía, **2:208–211**
Valdez, Luis, **1:210–212**
Welch, Raquel, **1:219–221**

Ambassadors
Lagos, Richard, **4:118–121**
Richardson, Bill, **4:180–183**

Animators
Roman, Phil, **4:187–190**

Architects
Moneo, Rafael, **4:147–149**
Pelli, César, **2:167–169**

Artists
Baca, Judith F., **2:21–24**
Botero, Fernando, **2:43–46**
Brito, Maria, **4:26–28**
Dalí, Salvador, **1:63–65**
Kahlo, Frida, **1:113–115**
Montoya, José, **4:150–153**
Pérez Esquivel, Adolfo, **4:170–172**
Picasso, Pablo, **3:178–180**
Rivera, Diego, **2:184–187**
Romero, Alejandro, **2:191–193**
Tàpies, Antonio, **4:216–218**
See also Sculptors

Astronauts
Chang-Díaz, Franklin R., **2:62–65**
Ochoa, Ellen, **1:149–151**

Athletes. See Olympic athletes; specific sports occupations

Attorneys. See Lawyers

Authors. See Essayists; Novelists; Playwrights; Poets; Writers

Ballet dancers
Acosta, Carlos, **4:1–3**
Alonso, Alicia, **1:11–14**
Bocca, Julio, **3:33–36**
Cisneros, Evelyn, **3:74–77**
Serrano, Lupe, **4:205–208**

Bandleaders
Arnaz, Desi, **2:18–20**
Colón, Willie, **3:78–80**
Cugat, Xavier, **2:84–86**
Puente, Tito, **1:172–175**
See also Conductors

Bankers
Ortega, Katherine D., **4:166–169**

Baseball players and managers
Canseco, José, **3:54–56**
Cepeda, Orlando, **4:43–47**

Clemente, Roberto, **2:74–76**
Garciaparra, Anthony Nomar, **3:106–108**
Pérez, Tony, **1:166–168**
Rodriquez, Alex, **1:183–185**
Sosa, Sammy, **1:199–202**
Tejada, Miguel, **3:225–227**

Baseball team owners
Alvarado, Linda, **3:5–8**

Basketball players
Arcain, Janeth, **1:19–21**
Lobo, Rebecca, **3:144–146**

Biologists
Alvariño, Angeles, **4:4–7**
Dallmeier, Francisco, **3:84–87**
Mares, Michael A., **4:132–134**

Bodybuilders
McLish, Rachel, **3:151–153**

Botanists
Gómez-Pompa, Arturo, **2:121–124**

Boxers
Camacho, Hector, **3:50–53**
De La Hoya, Oscar, **1:66–69**
Sardiñas, Eligio, **4:203–204**

Businesspersons
Alvarado, Linda, **3:5–8**
Bermúdez, Carmen, **2:37–39**
Chávez, Nick, **4:53–55**
Díaz-Oliver, Remedios, **4:62–64**
Fox, Vincente, **1:89–91**
Goizueta, Roberto Crispulo, **3:112–115**
Gutierrez, Carlos M., **4:102–105**
Martinez, Arthur C., **4:143–146**
Napolitano, Grace, **1:138–141**

Cabinet officials, U.S.
Cisneros, Henry, **1:50–52**
Martínez, Mel, **1:127–130**
Ortega, Katherine D., **4:166–169**
Richardson, Bill, **4:180–183**

Caddies
Rodríguez, Chi Chi, **3:191–194**

Chief executive officers (CEOs)
Cisneros, Marc, **4**:56–58
Gutierrez, Carlos M., **4**:102–105
Martinez, Arthur C., **4**:143–146

Children's authors
Soto, Gary, **4**:213–215

Choreographers
Alonso, Alicia, **1**:11–14
Ramirez, Tina, **4**:177–179

Cinematographer
Almendros, Nestor, **2**:4–6

Clergy
Boff, Leonardo, **3**:37–40
Cardenal, Ernesto, **3**:57–60
Flores, Patrick, **1**:86–88

Comedians
Cantinflas, **4**:33–35
Leguizamo, John, **3**:141–143
Marin, Cheech, **4**:135–138

Composers
Colón, Willie, **3**:78–80
E., Sheila, **3**:88–90
Ginastera, Alberto, **3**:109–111
Jobim, Antonio Carlos "Tom,"
    3:134–136
O'Farrill, Arturo "Chico," **1**:152–154
See also Songwriters

Conductors
de Vega, Sonia de León, **2**:99–100
Domingo, Plácido, **1**:76–78
See also Bandleaders

Congressmen, congresswomen
González, Henry B., **2**:125–128
Reyes, Silvestre, **2**:181–183
Richardson, Bill, **4**:180–183
Ros-Lehtinen, Ileana, **4**:191–193
Roybal-Allard, Lucille, **3**:212–214

Construction
Alvarado, Linda, **3**:5–8

Dancers
Acosta, Carlos, **4**:1–3
Alonso, Alicia, **1**:11–14
Bocca, Julio, **3**:33–36
Cisneros, Evelyn, **3**:74–77
Coca, Imogene, **2**:77–80
Hayworth, Rita, **1**:102–104
Lopez, Jennifer, **1**:116–119
Moreno, Rita, **1**:134–137
Ramirez, Tina, **4**:177–179
Romero, Cesar, **3**:204–207

Daredevils
Blaine, David, **3**:30–32

Diplomats
Asturias, Miguel Angel, **3**:19–21
de Moraes, Vinícius, **2**:93–95
Munoz Marin, Luis, **3**:167–170

Divers
Lucero-Schayes, Wendy, **4**:129–131

Doctors. See Physicians

Economists
Derbéz Bautista, Luis Ernesto, **2**:96–98
Lagos, Richard, **4**:118–121

Editors
Arana, Marie, **2**:15–17
Chavez, Linda, **4**:48–52
Cruz, Victor Hernández, **3**:81–83
Kanellos, Nicholás, **2**:141–144
Paredes, Américo, **3**:175–177
Prida, Delores, **3**:181–183
Restrepo, Laura, **3**:187–190

Educators
Alvarez, Luis Walter, **2**:7–10
Alvariño, Angeles, **4**:4–7
Anaya, Rudolfo, **2**:11–14
Baca, Judith F., **2**:21–24
Baca Zinn, Maxine, **2**:25–28
Boff, Leonardo, **3**:37–40
Caldera, Louis, **3**:47–49
Chávez, Denise, **2**:70–73
Corpi, Lucha, **2**:81–83
Cruz, Victor Hernández, **3**:81–83
Derbéz Bautista, Luis Ernesto, **2**:96–98
Escalante, Jaime, **2**:104–107
Fernandez, Joseph A., **2**:108–110
Gómez-Pompa, Arturo, **2**:121–124
Gurulé, Jimmy, **4**:98–101
Lagos, Richard, **4**:118–121
Leal, Luis, **4**:125–128
Mares, Michael A., **4**:132–134
Moneo, Rafael, **4**:147–149
Montoya, José, **4**:150–153
Ortiz Cofer, Judith, **3**:171–174
Paredes, Américo, **3**:175–177
Ramirez, Tina, **4**:177–179
Restrepo, Laura, **3**:187–190
Ros-Lehtinen, Ileana, **4**:191–193
Santayana, George, **3**:215–217
Soto, Gary, **4**:213–215

Engineers
Goizueta, Roberto Crispulo, **3**:112–115

Entrepreneurs. See businesspersons

Essayists
Carpentier, Alejo, **3**:64–67
Cruz, Victor Hernández, **3**:81–83
Gaviño, Juan Bosch, **4**:90–94
Guillén, Nicolás, **3**:120–123

Fashion designers
de la Renta, Oscar, **2**:87–89
Herrera, Carolina, **3**:124–127
McLish, Rachel, **3**:151–153
Rodríguez, Narciso, **3**:198–200

Figure skaters
Galindo, Rudy, **3**:98–101

Filmmakers. See Movie directors; Producers

Folklorists
Paredes, Américo, **3**:175–177

Football players
Munoz, Anthony, **2**:161–163

Fragrance designers
Sabatini, Gabriela, **4**:198–200

Golfers
Lopez, Nancy, **1**:120–122
Rodríguez, Chi Chi, **3**:191–194

Government officials, international
Derbéz Bautista, Luis Ernesto, **2**:96–98

Government officials, U.S.
Baca-Barragán, Polly, **4**:15–17
Baird, Lourdes G., **4**:18–20
Bustamante, Cruz M., **4**:29–32
Carbonell, Josefina G., **2**:58–61
Castro, Ida, **1**:40–42
Dominguez, Cari, **2**:101–103
Marin, Rosario, **2**:152–154
Ortega, Katherine D., **4**:166–169
Ros-Lehtinen, Ileana, **4**:191–193
Wilcox, Mary Rose Garrido, **4**:222–225
See also Politicians, U.S.

Governors, states and commonwealths
Calderón, Sila María, **2**:50–53
Munoz Marin, Luis, **3**:167–170
Richardson, Bill, **4**:180–183

Guitarists
Montoya, Carlos García, **3**:161–163

Hair designers
Chávez, Nick, **4**:53–55

Heart surgeons
Favaloro, Rene, **4**:77–79

Hockey players
Gomez, Scott, **2**:119–120

Ice skaters
Galindo, Rudy, **3**:98–101
Gomez, Scott, **2**:119–120
Parra, Derek, **1**:160–162
Rodriguez, Jennifer, **2**:188–190

Inventors
Alvarez, Luis Walter, **2**:7–10

Journalists
Arrarás, María Celeste, **4**:12–14
Carpentier, Alejo, **3**:64–67
Chavez, Linda, **4**:48–52
García Márquez, Gabriel Jose,
    2:111–115
Gaviño, Juan Bosch, **4**:90–94
Guillén, Nicolás, **3**:120–123
Hinojosa, María de Lourdes, **3**:128–130
O'Brien, Soledad, **1**:146–148
Prida, Delores, **3**:181–183
Quiñones, John, **4**:173–176
Ramos, Jorge, **2**:178–180
Restrepo, Laura, **3**:187–190
Saralegui, Cristina, **2**:201–204
Torres, Dara, **1**:206–209

Judges
Baird, Lourdes G., **4**:18–20
Santaella, Irma Vidal, **4**:201–202

Kings
Juan Carlos de Borbón y Borbón,
    4:115–117

Labor activists
Chávez, César, **2:66–69**
Chavez-Thompson, Linda, **1:47–49**
Corona, Bert, **1:57–59**
Huerta, Dolores, **2:138–140**
Mármol, Miguel, **4:139–142**

Law enforcement officers
Rodríguez, Daniel, **3:195–197**

Law professors
Gurulé, Jimmy, **4:98–101**

Lawyers
Baird, Lourdes G., **4:18–20**
Blades, Rubén, **3:26–29**
Caldera, Louis, **3:47–49**
Castro, Ida, **1:40–42**
Chavez, Dennis, **3:71–73**
de la Rúa, Fernando, **1:70–72**
Echeverría Álvarez, Luis, **3:91–93**
Gurulé, Jimmy, **4:98–101**
Hidalgo, Edward, **4:109–111**
Santaella, Irma Vidal, **4:201–202**

Literary critics
Leal, Luis, **4:125–128**

Magicians
Blaine, David, **3:30–32**

Mammologists
Mares, Michael A., **4:132–134**

Marine biologists
Alvariño, Angeles, **4:4–7**

Mayors, U.S.
Cisneros, Henry, **1:50–52**
Pérez, Eddie Alberto, **1:163–165**

Media relations specialists
Baca-Barragán, Polly, **4:15–17**

Ministers. See Clergy

Models
Benitez, Elsa, **4:21–22**
Bundchen, Gisele, **2:47–49**
Chávez, Nick, **4:53–55**
Díaz, Cameron, **1:73–75**
McLish, Rachel, **3:151–153**
Torres, Dara, **1:206–209**

Movie directors
Almodóvar, Pedro, **1:7–10**
Banderas, Antonio, **3:22–25**
Del Toro, Benicio, **2:90–92**
Fernández, Emilio "El Indio," **4:80–82**
Leguizamo, John, **3:141–143**
Rodriguez, Robert, **3:201–203**
Roman, Phil, **4:187–190**
Treviño, Jesus Salvador, **2:212–214**
Valdez, Luis, **1:210–212**

Muralists
Baca, Judith F., **2:21–24**
Rivera, Diego, **2:184–187**
Romero, Alejandro, **2:191–193**

Musicians
Barretto, Ray, **2:34–36**
Colón, Willie, **3:78–80**

Cugat, Xavier, **2:84–86**
E., Sheila, **3:88–90**
Garcia, Jerry, **3:102–105**
Gilberto, João, **2:116–118**
Jobim, Antonio Carlos "Tom,"
3:134–136
Mendes, Sérgio, **2:155–157**
Mendoza, Lydia, **3:158–160**
Montoya, Carlos García, **3:161–163**
O'Farrill, Arturo "Chico," **1:152–154**
Puente, Tito, **1:172–175**
Sánchez, Poncho, **2:194–197**
Sandoval, Arturo, **2:198–200**
Santana, Carlos, **1:189–191**
Valdés, Jésus "Chucho," **2:215–217**
Valens, Richie, **2:218–220**

Nonprofit organization administration
Roybal-Allard, Lucille, **3:212–214**

Novelists
Alegría, Claribel Joy, **3:1–4**
Allende, Isabel, **1:4–6**
Amado, Jorge, **3:9–11**
Anaya, Rudolfo, **2:11–14**
Arenas, Reinaldo, **4:8–11**
Asturias, Miguel Angel, **3:19–21**
Carpentier, Alejo, **3:64–67**
Castillo, Ana, **1:33–35**
Chávez, Denise, **2:70–73**
Corpi, Lucha, **2:81–83**
Esquivel, Laura, **1:79–81**
Fuentes, Carlos, **1:92–94**
García Márquez, Gabriel Jose,
2:111–115
Gaviño, Juan Bosch, **4:90–94**
Hijuelos, Oscar, **1:105–107**
Mohr, Nicholasa, **2:158–160**
Restrepo, Laura, **3:187–190**
Soto, Gary, **4:213–215**

Oceanographers
Alvariño, Angeles, **4:4–7**

Olympic athletes
Arcain, Janeth, **1:19–21**
De La Hoya, Oscar, **1:66–69**
de Varona, Donna, **4:59–61**
Fernández, Mary Joe, **3:94–97**
Garciaparra, Anthony Nomar,
3:106–108
Lobo, Rebecca, **3:144–146**
Lucero-Schayes, Wendy, **4:129–131**
Parra, Derek, **1:160–162**
Rodriguez, Jennifer, **2:188–190**
Sabatini, Gabriela, **4:198–200**
Torres, Dara, **1:206–209**

Opera singers
Carreras, José, **3:68–70**
Domingo, Plácido, **1:76–78**

Pageant contestants
Quiñones August, Denise, **1:180–182**

Painters. See Artists

Percussionists
E., Sheila, **3:88–90**

Philanthropists
Cantinflas, **4:33–35**
Vilar, Alberto, **2:223–227**

Philosophers
Santayana, George, **3:215–217**

Physicians
Carmona, Richard, **3:61–63**
Favaloro, Rene, **4:77–79**
García, Héctor Pérez, **4:86–89**
Guevara, Ché (Ernesto), **2:129–133**
Novello, Antonia, **1:142–145**

Physicists
Alvarez, Luis Walter, **2:7–10**
Chang-Díaz, Franklin R., **2:62–65**

Planetary geologists
Ocampo, Adriana C., **4:154–157**

Playwrights
Chávez, Denise, **2:70–73**
de Moraes, Vinícius, **2:93–95**
Machado, Eduardo, **2:145–148**
Mohr, Nicholasa, **2:158–160**
Piñero, Miguel, **2:174–177**
Prida, Delores, **3:181–183**
Valdez, Luis, **1:210–212**

Poets
Alegría, Claribel Joy, **3:1–4**
Anaya, Rudolfo, **2:11–14**
Asturias, Miguel Angel, **3:19–21**
Cardenal, Ernesto, **3:57–60**
Carpentier, Alejo, **3:64–67**
Castillo, Ana, **1:33–35**
Corpi, Lucha, **2:81–83**
Cruz, Victor Hernández, **3:81–83**
de Moraes, Vinícius, **2:93–95**
Guillén, Nicolás, **3:120–123**
Montoya, José, **4:150–153**
Neruda, Pablo, **2:164–166**
Ortiz Cofer, Judith, **3:171–174**
Piñero, Miguel, **2:174–177**
Prida, Delores, **3:181–183**
Soto, Gary, **4:213–215**

Political activists
Arias Sánchez, Oscar, **3:15–18**
Baez, Joan, **2:29–33**
Blades, Rubén, **3:26–29**
Carpentier, Alejo, **3:64–67**
Chavez, Linda, **4:48–52**
Colón, Willie, **3:78–80**
de Varona, Donna, **4:59–62**
García, Héctor Pérez, **4:86–89**
Mármol, Miguel, **4:139–142**
Menchú, Rigoberta, **3:154–157**
Pérez Esquivel, Adolfo, **4:170–172**
Restrepo, Laura, **3:187–190**
Wilcox, Mary Rose Garrido, **4:222–225**

Politicians, international
Arias Sánchez, Oscar, **3:15–18**
Aznar, José Maria, **1:22–24**
Bánzer Suárez, Hugo, **1:25–28**
Betancourt, Ingrid, **2:40–42**
Blades, Rubén, **3:26–29**
Calderón Sol, Armando, **2:54–57**
Cardenal, Ernesto, **3:57–60**
Echeverría Álvarez, Luis, **3:91–93**
Gaviño, Juan Bosch, **4:90–94**
González Márquez, Felipe, **4:95–97**
Juan Carlos de Borbón y Borbón,
4:115–117
Lagos, Richard, **4:118–121**
Ortega, Daniel, **4:162–165**

Perón, Eva "Evita," **1:169–171**
See also Presidents and heads of state

Politicians, U.S.
Baca-Barragán, Polly, **4:15–17**
Bustamante, Cruz M., **4:29–32**
Caldera, Louis, **3:47–49**
Calderón, Sila María, **2:50–53**
Chavez, Dennis, **3:71–73**
Chavez, Linda, **4:48–52**
Munoz Marin, Luis, **3:167–170**
Napolitano, Grace, **1:138–141**
Pérez, Eddie Alberto, **1:163–165**
Richardson, Bill, **4:180–183**
Ros-Lehtinen, Ileana, **4:191–193**
Roybal-Allard, Lucille, **3:212–214**
Sanchez, Loretta, **1:186–188**
Velázquez, Nydia, **1:216–218**

Presidents and heads of state
Alemán, Arnoldo, **1:1–3**
Arias Sánchez, Oscar, **3:15–18**
Aznar, José Maria, **1:22–24**
Bánzer Suárez, Hugo, **1:25–28**
Cardoso, Fernando, **1:29–32**
Castro, Fidel, **1:36–39**
Chávez, Hugo, **1:43–46**
de la Rúa, Fernando, **1:70–72**
Echeverría Álvarez, Luis, **3:91–93**
Fox, Vincente, **1:89–91**
Gaviño, Juan Bosch, **4:90–94**
González, Macchi, Luis, **1:95–97**
González Márquez, Felipe, **4:95–97**
Juan Carlos de Borbón y Borbón, **4:115–117**
Lagos, Richard, **4:118–121**
Mahaud, Jamil, **2:149–151**
Menem, Carlos Saul, **1:131–133**
Ortega, Daniel, **4:162–165**
Perón, Juan, **2:170–173**

Priests. See Clergy

Prime ministers. See Presidents and heads of state

Producers
Arnaz, Desi, **2:18–20**
Colón, Willie, **3:78–80**
E., Sheila, **3:88–90**
Roman, Phil, **4:187–190**
Sheen, Charlie, **4:209–212**
Treviño, Jesus Salvador, **2:212–214**

Prosecutors
Gurulé, Jimmy, **4:98–101**

Psychologists
Estés, Clarissa Pinkola, **4:68–72**

Publishers
Haubegger, Christy, **1:98–101**
Kanellos, Nicholás, **2:141–144**
Saralegui, Cristina, **2:201–204**

Race car drivers
Montoya, Juan Pablo, **3:164–166**
Senna, Ayrton, **3:218–220**

Rappers
Big Punisher, **4:23–25**

Religious educators
Rodriguez, Carlos Manuel, **4:184–186**

Reporters. See Journalists

Revolutionary leaders
Guevara, Ché (Ernesto), **2:129–133**
Ortega, Daniel, **4:162–165**

Scholars
Leal, Luis, **4:125–128**

Scientists
Alvarez, Luis Walter, **2:7–10**
Alvariño, Angeles, **4:4–7**
Chang-Díaz, Franklin R., **2:62–65**
Dallmeier, Francisco, **3:84–87**
Gómez-Pompa, Arturo, **2:121–124**
Mares, Michael A., **4:132–134**
Ocampo, Adriana C., **4:154–157**

Screenwriters
Fernández, Emilio "El Indio," **4:80–82**
Rodriguez, Robert, **3:201–203**
Sheen, Charlie, **4:209–212**

Sculptors
Botero, Fernando, **2:43–46**
Brito, Maria, **4:26–28**
Pérez Esquivel, Adolfo, **4:170–172**
Tapia, Luis, **1:203–205**
Tàpies, Antonio, **4:216–218**

Senators, U.S.
Chavez, Dennis, **3:71–73**

Singers
Aguilera, Christina, **2:1–3**
Anthony, Marc, **3:12–14**
Arnaz, Desi, **2:18–20**
Big Punisher, **4:23–25**
Blades, Rubén, **3:26–29**
Cruz, Celia, **1:60–62**
Dunbar, Huey, **4:65–67**
E., Sheila, **3:88–90**
Estefan, Gloria, **1:82–85**
Gilberto, João, **2:116–118**
Guzmán, Alejandra, **4:106–108**
Iglesias, Enrique, **1:108–112**
Iglesias, Julio, **3:131–133**
Infante, Pedro, **4:112–114**
Lamarque, Libertad, **4:122–124**
Lopez, Jennifer, **1:116–119**
Martin, Ricky, **3:147–150**
Mendoza, Lydia, **3:158–160**
Moreno, Rita, **1:134–137**
Orlando, Tony, **4:158–161**
Rodríguez, Daniel, **3:195–197**
Ronstadt, Linda, **3:208–211**
Rubio, Paulina, **4:194–197**
Sánchez, Poncho, **2:194–197**
Selena, **2:205–207**
Shakira, **1:192–194**
Thalía, **2:208–211**
Valens, Richie, **2:218–220**
Velasquez, Jaci, **2:221–223**
See also Opera singers

Soccer players
Maradona, Diego, **1:123–126**

Sociologists
Baca Zinn, Maxine, **2:25–28**
Cardoso, Fernando, **1:29–32**

Songwriters
Anthony, Marc, **3:12–14**
Baez, Joan, **2:29–33**
de Moraes, Vinícius, **2:93–95**
Estefan, Gloria, **1:82–85**
Guzmán, Alejandra, **4:106–108**
Iglesias, Enrique, **1:105–109**
Iglesias, Julio, **3:131–133**
Jobim, Antonio Carlos "Tom," **3:134–136**
Shakira, **1:192–194**
See also Composers

Speedskaters
Parra, Derek, **1:160–162**
Rodriguez, Jennifer, **2:188–190**

Storytellers
Estés, Clarissa Pinkola, **4:68–72**

Swimmers
de Varona, Donna, **4:59–61**

Talk show hosts
Hinojosa, María de Lourdes, **3:128–130**
Saralegui, Cristina, **2:201–204**

Television news anchors
Arrarás, María Celeste, **4:12–14**
Quiñones, John, **4:173–176**

Television show hosts
Francisco, Don, **4:83–85**

Television sports analysts
de Varona, Donna, **4:59–61**
Fernández, Mary Joe, **3:94–97**
Lucero-Schayes, Wendy, **4:129–131**

Tennis players
Fernández, Mary Joe, **3:94–97**
Gonzales, Richard "Pancho," **3:116–119**
Sabatini, Gabriela, **4:198–200**

Theologians
Boff, Leonardo, **3:37–40**

Trombonists
Colón, Willie, **3:78–80**

U.S. Army generals
Cavazos, Richard E., **4:40–42**
Cisneros, Marc, **4:56–58**
Valenzuela, Alfred A., **4:219–221**

U.S. Attorneys
Baird, Lourdes G., **4:18–20**

U.S. Secretary of the Army
Caldera, Louis, **3:47–49**

U.S. Secretary of the Navy
Hidalgo, Edward, **4:109–111**

U.S. Surgeon General
Carmona, Richard, **3:61–63**

University presidents
Cisneros, Marc, **4:56–58**

Writers
Alegría, Claribel Joy, **3:1–4**
Allende, Isabel, **1:4–6**
Alvarez, Julia, **1:15–18**
Amado, Jorge, **3:9–11**
Anaya, Rudolfo, **2:11–14**
Arana, Marie, **2:15–17**
Arenas, Reinaldo, **4:8–11**
Arias Sánchez, Oscar, **3:15–18**
Asturias, Miguel Angel, **3:19–21**
Boff, Leonardo, **3:37–40**
Carpentier, Alejo, **3:64–67**
Chávez, Denise, **2:70–73**
Cisneros, Sandra, **1:53–56**
Corpi, Lucha, **2:81–83**

Del Toro, Benicio, **2:90–92**
Estés, Clarissa Pinkola, **4:68–72**
García Márquez, Gabriel Jose, **2:111–115**
Gaviño, Juan Bosch, **4:90–94**
Guillén, Nicolás, **3:120–123**
Hinojosa, María de Lourdes, **3:128–130**
Leal, Luis, **4:125–128**
Leguizamo, John, **3:141–143**
Machado, Eduardo, **2:145–148**
Mares, Michael A., **4:132–134**
McLish, Rachel, **3:151–153**
Menchú, Rigoberta, **3:154–157**
Mohr, Nicholasa, **2:158–160**
Montoya, José, **4:150–153**

Ortiz Cofer, Judith, **3:171–174**
Paredes, Américo, **3:175–177**
Ramos, Jorge, **2:178–180**
Restrepo, Laura, **3:187–190**
Rodriguez, Carlos Manuel, **4:184–186**
Rodriguez, Robert, **3:201–203**
Santayana, George, **3:215–217**
Saralegui, Cristina, **2:201–204**
Soto, Gary, **4:213–215**
Treviño, Jesus Salvador, **2:212–214**
Vargas Llosa, Mario, **1:213–215**
See also Essayists; Novelists; Playwrights; Poets

Cumulative Subject Index

Volume and page numbers appear in **bold**.

ABC News
de Varona, Donna, **4:60–61**
Quiñones, John, **4:173–176**

Academy Awards
Almendros, Nestor, **2:5**
Almodóvar, Pedro, **1:9–10**
de Moraes, Vinícius, **2:94**
Del Toro, Benicio, **2:90–92**
Moreno, Rita, **1:134, 135**
Quinn, Anthony, **1:178**

Academy of Country Music Awards
Ronstadt, Linda, **3:209**

Accounting
Ortega, Katherine D., **4:166–169**
Roybal-Allard, Lucille, **3:212–214**
Santaella, Irma Vidal, **4:201–202**

Acting
Anthony, Marc, **3:12–14**
Banderas, Antonio, **3:22–25**
Blades, Rubén, **3:26–29**
Braga, Sonia, **3:41–43**
Bratt, Benjamin, **3:44–46**
Cantinflas, **4:33–35**
Carter, Lynda, **4:36–39**
Coca, Imogene, **2:77–80**
Cugat, Xavier, **2:85**
Del Toro, Benicio, **2:90–92**
Diaz, Cameron, **1:73–75**
Estrada, Erik, **4:73–76**
Fernández, Emilio "El Indio," **4:80–82**
Hayek, Salma, **2:134–137**
Hayworth, Rita, **1:102–104**
Infante, Pedro, **4:112–114**
Juliá, Raúl, **3:137–140**
Lamarque, Libertad, **4:122–124**
Leguizamo, John, **3:141–143**
Lopez, Jennifer, **1:116–119**
Machado, Eduardo, **2:146**
Marin, Cheech, **4:135–138**
Martin, Ricky, **3:147–150**
Moreno, Rita, **1:134–137**
Olmos, Edward James, **1:156–159**
Perón, Eva "Evita," **1:169–170**
Piñero, Miguel, **2:174–175**
Prinze, Freddie, Jr., **3:184–186**
Quinn, Anthony, **1:176, 177–179**
Romero, Cesar, **3:204–207**

Ronstadt, Linda, **3:208–211**
Rubio, Paulina, **4:194–197**
Sheen, Charlie, **4:209–212**
Sheen, Martin, **1:195–198**
Smits, Jimmy, **3:221–224**
Thalía, **2:208–209**
Valdez, Luis, **1:210–211**
Welch, Raquel, **1:219–221**

Activism. See Civil rights; Environmental activism; Labor activities; Political activism

AFL-CIO. See American Federation of Labor and Congress Industrial Organizations

AFSCME. See American Federation of State, County and Municipal Employees Union

Alcoholism Council of East Los Angeles
Roybal-Allard, Lucille, **3:212–214**

All American Containers
Díaz-Oliver, Remedios, **4:63**

American Ballet Theater
Alonso, Alicia, **1:12, 13**
Bocca, Julio, **3:33–34**
Serrano, Lupe, **4:205–208**

American Book Awards
Chávez, Denise, **2:71–73**

American Federation of Labor and Congress Industrial Organizations (AFL-CIO)
Chávez, César, **2:66–69**
Chavez-Thompson, Linda, **1:47–49**

American Federation of State, County and Municipal Employees Union (AFSCME)
Chazvez-Thompson, Linda, **1:48**

American League Most Valuable Player Awards
Canseco, José, **3:54–56**
Clemente, Roberto, **2:75**

Tejada, Miguel, **3:226, 227**

American Music Awards
Iglesias, Enrique, **1:111**
Orlando, Tony, **4:159**

Animation
Roman, Phil, **4:187–190**

Annual Havana International Jazz Festival
Valdés, Jésus "Chucho," **2:216**

Architecture
Moneo, Rafael, **4:147–149**
Pelli, César, **2:167–169**

Arias Foundation for Peace and Human Progress
Arias Sánchez, Oscar, **3:15, 17**

Arias Peace Plan
Arias Sánchez, Oscar, **3:15, 17**

Army University Access Online
Caldera, Louis, **3:49**

Association of Naval Service Officers (ANSO)
Hidalgo, Edward, **4:110**

Ballet
Acosta, Carlos, **4:1–3**
Alonso, Alicia, **1:12–13**
Bocca, Julio, **3:33–36**
Cisneros, Evelyn, **3:74–77**
Ginastera, Alberto, **3:109–111**
Serrano, Lupe, **4:205–208**

Ballet Nacional de Cuba
Alonso, Alicia, **1:13**

Banking
Ortega, Katherine D., **4:166–169**

Baseball
Alvarado, Linda, **3:5–8**
Canseco, José, **3:54–56**
Cepeda, Orlando, **4:43–47**
Clemente, Roberto, **2:74–76**

Garciaparra, Anthony Nomar,
3:106–108
Pérez, Tony, 1:166–167
Rodrigues, Alex, 1:183–184
Sosa, Sammy, 1:199–201
Tejada, Miguel, 3:225–227

Baseball Hall of Fame
Cepeda, Orlando, 4:43–46
Clemente, Roberto, 2:74, 76

Basketball
Arcain, Janeth, 1:19–20
Lobo, Rebecca, 3:144–146

Beatification
Rodriguez, Carlos Manuel, 4:184–186

Billboard Awards
Anthony, Marc, 3:13
Dunbar, Huey, 4:66
Iglesias, Enrique, 1:109
Martin, Ricky, 3:148

Biology
Alvariño, Angeles, 4:4–7
Dallmeier, Francisco, 3:84–87
Mares, Michael A., 4:132–134

Bodybuilding
McLish, Rachel, 3:151–153

Book-of-the-Month Club
Chávez, Denise, 2:72

Bossa nova music
de Moraes, Vinícius, 2:93–95
Gilberto, João, 2:116–118
Jobim, Antonio Carlos "Tom,"
3:134–136
Mendes, Sérgio, 2:155–156

Boston Red Sox baseball team
Garciaparra, Anthony Nomar,
3:106–108

Botany
Gómez-Pompa, Arturo, 2:121–124

Boxing
Camacho, Hector, 3:50–53
De La Hoya, Oscar, 1:66–69
González, Henry B., 2:125–128
Sardiñas, Eligio, 4:203–204

Brazilian Analysis and Planning Center
Cardoso, Fernando, 1:30

Broadcasting
Arrarás, María Celeste, 4:12–14
de Varona, Donna, 4:59–61
Fernández, Mary Joe, 3:94–95
Hinojosa, María de Lourdes, 3:128–130
Lucero-Schayes, Wendy, 4:129–131
O'Brien, Soledad, 1:146–148
Quiñones, John, 4:173–176
Ramos, Jorge, 2:178–180
Saralegui, Cristina, 2:201–204

Cable News Network (CNN)
Hinojosa, María de Lourdes, 3:128–129

Cambio magazine
García Márquez, Gabriel Jose, 2:111,
113–114

Caracol Radio
Ramos, Jorge, 2:179

Cartoons
Roman, Phil, 4:187–190

Casa de Los Tres Mundos
Cardenal, Ernesto, 3:60

Cathedral of Our Lady of the Angels
Moneo, Rafael, 4:147–149

Catholicism. See Roman Catholic Church

Center for Equal Opportunity (CEO)
Chavez, Linda, 4:51

**Center for Intercultural Studies of Folk-
lore and Ethnomusicology**
Paredes, Américo, 3:176

Centers for Autonomous Social Actions
Corona, Bert, 1:58

Champions Tour (Senior PGA)
Rodríguez, Chi Chi, 3:191–194

Championship Auto Racing Teams (Cart)
Montoya, Juan Pablo, 3:164–166

Chicago Cubs baseball team
Sosa, Sammy, 1:199, 200–201

Chicano studies and literature
Leal, Luis, 4:125–128
Paredes, Américo, 3:175–177
Soto, Gary, 4:214

Christian Base Communities
Boff, Leonardo, 3:37–40

Christian music
Velasquez, Jaci, 2:221–223

Cincinnati Bengals football team (NFL)
Munoz, Anthony, 2:161–162

Cincinnati Reds baseball team
Pérez, Tony, 1:166–167

Cinematography
Almendros, Nestor, 2:4–6

City government
Calderón, Sila María, 2:50–51
Cisneros, Henry, 1:51
de la Rúa, Fernando, 1:71–72
Marin, Rosario, 2:153
Napolitano, Grace, 1:138
Pérez, Eddie Alberto, 1:163, 164–165
Velázquez, Nydia, 1:217
Wilcox, Mary Rose Garrido, 4:222–225

Civil rights
Baez, Joan, 2:30–31
Chavez, Dennis, 3:71–73
Chavez, Linda, 4:48–52
Corona, Bert, 1:57, 58–59

Corpi, Lucha, 2:81–83
Dominguez, Cari, 2:101–103
García, Héctor Pérez, 4:86–89
González, Henry B., 2:125–128
Guillén, Nicolás, 3:120–123

Classical music
Cugat, Xavier, 2:84
de Vega, Sonia de León, 2:99–100
Ginastera, Alberto, 3:109–111
Sandoval, Arturo, 2:198–199

Cleveland Clinic
Favaloro, Rene, 4:77–78

Coca-Cola Company
Fox, Vincente, 1:89, 90
Goizueta, Roberto Crispulo, 3:112–115

Coffee Growers Association of Managua
Alemán, Arnoldo, 1:2

Colorado Party
González, Macchi, Luis, 1:95–96

Colorado Rockies baseball team
Alvarado, Linda, 3:5–8

Comedy
Cantinflas, 4:33–35
Leguizamo, John, 3:141–143
Marin, Cheech, 4:135–138

Communism. See also Marxism
Amado, Jorge, 3:10
Mármol, Miguel, 4:139–142

Community Service Organization (CSO)
Chávez, César, 2:67–69

Construction
Alvarado, Linda, 3:5–8

Corporate management
Alvarado, Linda, 3:5–8
Díaz-Oliver, Remedios, 4:62–64
Fox, Vincente, 1:89–90
Gutierrez, Carlos M., 4:102–105
Martinez, Arthur C., 4:143–146

Corridos
Paredes, Américo, 3:175–177
Ronstadt, Linda, 3:210

Country music
Ronstadt, Linda, 3:208–211

Cubism
Picasso, Pablo, 3:179
Tàpies, Antonio, 4:216–218

Dancing
Bocca, Julio, 3:33–36
Cisneros, Evelyn, 3:74–77
Coca, Imogene, 2:77–78
Ginastera, Alberto, 3:109–111
Ramirez, Tina, 4:177–179
Romero, Cesar, 3:204–207

Diplomacy and international relations
Arias Sánchez, Oscar, 3:15–17, 17–18
Asturias, Miguel Angel, 3:19–21
de Moraes, Vinícius, 2:93, 95

Fuentes, Carlos, **1:93–94**
Gaviño, Juan Bosch, **4:90–94**
Juan Carlos de Borbón y Borbón,
    4:115–119
Lagos, Richard, **4:118–121**
Neruda, Pablo, **2:165, 166**
Ortega, Daniel, **4:162–165**
Perón, Eva "Evita," **1:170–171**
Richardson, Bill, **4:180–183**

Diving
Lucero-Schayes, Wendy, **4:129–131**

Drama
Chávez, Denise, **2:70–73**
de Moraes, Vinícius, **2:93–95**
Juliá, Raúl, **3:137–140**
Machado, Eduardo, **2:145–148**
Mohr, Nicholasa, **2:158–160**
Piñero, Miguel, **2:174–177**
Romero, Cesar, **3:204–207**
Treviño, Jesus Salvador, **2:212–214**

Ecology
Dallmeier, Francisco, **3:84–87**

Economics
Derbéz Bautista, Luis Ernesto, **2:96–98**
Echeverría Álvarez, Luis, **3:91–93**
Lagos, Richard, **4:118–121**

Editing
Arana, Marie, **2:15–16**
Chavez, Linda, **4:48–52**
Cruz, Victor Hernández, **3:81–83**
Kanellos, Nicholás, **2:141–144**
Paredes, Américo, **3:175–177**
Prida, Delores, **3:181–183**
Restrepo, Laura, **3:187–190**
Saralegui, Cristina, **2:201–204**

Emmy Awards
Arnaz, Desi, **2:19–20**
Blades, Rubén, **3:26–29**
Coca, Imogene, **2:78, 79**
de Varona, Donna, **4:60–61**
Juliá, Raúl, **3:138, 140**
Moreno, Rita, **1:134**
Olmos, Edward James, **1:157**
Quiñones, John, **4:174–175**
Roman, Phil, **4:187–189**
Sandoval, Arturo, **2:199**
Sheen, Martin, **1:197**
Smits, Jimmy, **3:221–224**

Engineering
Goizueta, Roberto Crispulo, **3:112–115**

Environmental activism
Napolitano, Grace, **1:140**

Environmental science
Gómez-Pompa, Arturo, **2:121–124**

Essays
Carpentier, Alejo, **3:64–67**
Estés, Clarissa Pinkola, **4:68–72**
Guillén, Nicolás, **3:120–123**
Leal, Luis, **4:125–128**

European Space Agency
Ocampo, Adriana C., **4:154–157**

F1 World Championship
Senna, Ayrton, **3:218–220**

Fashion designing
de la Renta, Oscar, **2:87–89**
Herrera, Carolina, **3:124–127**
Rodríguez, Narciso, **3:198–200**

Favaloro Foundation
Favaloro, Rene, **4:78–79**

Feminism
Castillo, Ana, **1:34–35**
Haubegger, Christy, **1:99–100**
Huerta, Dolores, **2:138–140**

Fiction
Alegría, Claribel Joy, **3:1–4**
Allende, Isabel, **1:5–6**
Alvarez, Julia, **1:16–18**
Amado, Jorge, **3:10**
Anaya, Rudolfo, **2:11–14**
Arenas, Reinaldo, **4:8–11**
Asturias, Miguel Angel, **3:19–21**
Blades, Rubén, **3:26–29**
Carpentier, Alejo, **3:64–67**
Castillo, Ana, **1:34–35**
Chávez, Denise, **2:71–73**
Cisneros, Sandra, **1:53–56**
Corpi, Lucha, **2:81–83**
Esquivel, Laura, **1:79–81**
Fuentes, Carlos, **1:92–94**
García Márquez, Gabriel Jose,
    2:111–115
Gaviño, Juan Bosch, **4:90–94**
Guillén, Nicolás, **3:120–123**
Hijuelos, Oscar, **1:105–107**
Mohr, Nicholasa, **2:158–160**
Ortiz Cofer, Judith, **3:171–174**
Restrepo, Laura, **3:187–190**
Santayana, George, **3:215–217**
Soto, Gary, **4:213–215**
Treviño, Jesus Salvador, **2:212–214**
Vargas Llosa, Mario, **1:213–215**

Figure skating
Galindo, Rudy, **3:98–101**

Film direction
Almendros, Nestor, **2:5**
Almodóvar, Pedro, **1:8–10**
Banderas, Antonio, **3:22–25**
Del Toro, Benicio, **2:91**
Fernández, Emilio "El Indio," **4:80–82**
Rodriguez, Robert, **3:201–203**
Roman, Phil, **4:187–190**
Treviño, Jesus Salvador, **2:212–214**
Valdez, Luis, **1:211**

Financial services
Bermúdez, Carmen, **2:37–39**

Flamenco guitar music
Montoya, Carlos García, **3:161–163**

Florida Marlins baseball team
Pérez, Tony, **1:167**

Folk art
Rivera, Diego, **2:184–187**
Tapia, Luis, **1:203–205**

Folk music
Baez, Joan, **2:29–33**

Football
Munoz, Anthony, **2:161–163**

Formula One (F1) auto racing
Montoya, Juan Pablo, **3:164–166**
Senna, Ayrton, **3:218–220**

Frente Sandinista Liberación National (FSLN)
Cardenal, Ernesto, **3:57–60**
Ortega, Daniel, **4:162–165**

GED Plus program
Caldera, Louis, **3:48–49**

Geology
Ocampo, Adriana C., **4:154–157**

GI Forum
García, Héctor Pérez, **4:86–88**

Golden Globe Awards
Cantinflas, **4:34–35**
Del Toro, Benicio, **2:91, 91–92**
Juliá, Raúl, **3:138, 140**
Sheen, Charlie, **4:210–211**
Sheen, Martin, **1:197**
Smits, Jimmy, **3:221–224**

Golden Gloves boxing championships
Camacho, Hector, **3:50–53**
González, Henry B., **2:125–128**

Golf
Lopez, Nancy, **1:120–122**
Rodríguez, Chi Chi, **3:191–194**

Grammy Awards
Aguilera, Christina, **2:1–3**
Blades, Rubén, **3:26–29**
Carreras, José, **3:68–70**
Cruz, Celia, **1:61–62**
de Moraes, Vinícius, **2:94**
Estefan, Gloria, **1:84**
Gilberto, João, **2:117**
Iglesias, Enrique, **1:109**
Iglesias, Julio, **3:131–132**
Jobim, Antonio Carlos "Tom," **3:135**
Marin, Cheech, **4:136**
Martin, Ricky, **3:147–150**
Mendes, Sérgio, **2:155, 156, 157**
Moreno, Rita, **1:134, 136**
O'Farrill, Arturo "Chico," **1:153**
Ronstadt, Linda, **3:208–211**
Sánchez, Poncho, **2:195**
Sandoval, Arturo, **2:199**
Santana, Carlos, **1:190**
Selena, **2:206**
Thalía, **2:209**
Valdés, Jésus "Chucho," **2:215–216**

Grateful Dead
Garcia, Jerry, **3:102–105**

Guggenheim fellowships
Soto, Gary, **4:214**

Guitar music
Montoya, Carlos García, **3:161–163**

Hair designing
Chávez, Nick, **4:53–55**

Heart surgery
Favaloro, Rene, **4:77–79**

La Hermandad Mexicana
Corona, Bert, **1:58–59**

Hispanic Officer Recruitment Conference (HORC)
Hidalgo, Edward, **4:110**

HIV/AIDS
Galindo, Rudy, **3:98–101**

Hockey
Gomez, Scott, **2:119–120**

Houston Comets basketball team
Arcain, Janeth, **1:19–20**

Human rights
Bánzer Suárez, Hugo, **1:27**
Menchú, Rigoberta, **3:154–157**
Pérez Esquivel, Adolfo, **4:170–171**

Hunger Project
Juliá, Raúl, **3:137–140**

Ice skating
Galindo, Rudy, **3:98–101**
Gomez, Scott, **2:119–120**
Parra, Derek, **1:160–162**
Rodriguez, Jennifer, **2:188–190**

Immigration Reform and Accountability Act
Reyes, Silvestre, **2:183**

Interfaith relations
Flores, Patrick, **1:87–88**

International Ballet Competition
Bocca, Julio, **3:33–36**

Investments
Vilar, Alberto, **2:224–225**

Jazz
Barretto, Ray, **2:34–36**
de Moraes, Vinícius, **2:93–95**
Gilberto, João, **2:116–118**
Mendes, Sérgio, **2:155–157**
O'Farrill, Arturo "Chico," **1:152–154**
Puente, Tito, **1:172–175**
Sánchez, Poncho, **2:194–197**
Sandoval, Arturo, **2:198–200**
Valdés, Jésus "Chucho," **2:215–217**

John G. and Marie Stella Kenedy Memorial Foundation
Cisneros, Marc, **4:57–58**

Journalism
Allende, Isabel, **1:4**
Arrarás, María Celeste, **4:12–14**
Carpentier, Alejo, **3:64–67**
Chavez, Linda, **4:48–52**
García Márquez, Gabriel Jose, **2:111–115**
Hinojosa, María de Lourdes, **3:128–130**
O'Brien, Soledad, **1:146–148**

Prida, Delores, **3:181–183**
Quiñones, John, **4:173–176**
Ramos, Jorge, **2:178–180**
Restrepo, Laura, **3:187–190**
Saralegui, Cristina, **2:201–204**

Kart racing
Senna, Ayrton, **3:218–220**

Kellogg Company
Gutierrez, Carlos M., **4:102–105**

Kentucky Arts Commission
Alvarez, Julia, **1:16**

Labor activities
Chávez, César, **2:66–69**
Corona, Bert, **1:58–59**
Huerta, Dolores, **2:138–140**
Mármol, Miguel, **4:139–142**

Ladies Professional Golf Association (LPGA)
Lopez, Nancy, **1:120–122**

Latin Grammy Awards
Aguilera, Christina, **2:1–3**
Anthony, Marc, **3:13**
Guzmán, Alejandra, **4:107**
Shakira, **1:193**

Latin music
Arnaz, Desi, **2:18–20**
Barretto, Ray, **2:34–36**
Cruz, Celia, **1:60–62**
Cugat, Xavier, **2:84–86**
de Moraes, Vinícius, **2:93–95**
Dunbar, Huey, **4:65–67**
Ginastera, Alberto, **3:109–111**
Guzmán, Alejandra, **4:106–108**
Iglesias, Julio, **3:131–133**
Infante, Pedro, **4:112–114**
Jobim, Antonio Carlos "Tom," **3:134–136**
Lamarque, Libertad, **4:122–124**
Martin, Ricky, **3:147–150**
Mendes, Sérgio, **2:155–157**
Mendoza, Lydia, **3:158–160**
O'Farrill, Arturo "Chico," **1:152–154**
Puente, Tito, **1:172–175**
Rubio, Paulina, **4:194–197**
Sánchez, Poncho, **2:194–197**
Selena, **2:205–207**
Thalía, **2:208–211**
Velasquez, Jaci, **2:223**

***Latina* Magazine**
Haubegger, Christy, **1:98, 99–100**

Legal system
Baird, Lourdes G., **4:18–20**
Gurulé, Jimmy, **4:98–101**
Santaella, Irma Vidal, **4:201–202**

Liberal Constitutionalist Party
Alemán, Arnoldo, **1:2**

Literary criticism
Leal, Luis, **4:125–128**

Little Havana Activities and Nutrition Centers (LHANC)
Carbonell, Josefina G., **2:58–59**

LPGA. See Ladies Professional Golf Association

Magazine publishing
Saralegui, Cristina, **2:202–204**

Magic tricks
Blaine, David, **3:30–32**

Magical realism
García Márquez, Gabriel Jose, **2:111, 113**

Manhattan Project
Alvarez, Luis Walter, **2:8–9**

Marine biology
Alvariño, Angeles, **4:4–7**

Marxism. See also Communism
Cardenal, Ernesto, **3:57–60**
Guevara, Ché (Ernesto), **2:129–133**

Media relations
Baca-Barragán, Polly, **4:15–17**

Medicine
Carmona, Richard, **3:61–63**
Favaloro, Rene, **4:77–79**
García, Héctor Pérez, **4:86–89**
Guevara, Ché (Ernesto), **2:130**
Novello, Antonia, **1:142, 143–145**

Menudo
Anthony, Marc, **3:41–43**
Matin, Ricky, **3:147-150**

Miss Puerto Rico Pageant
Quiñones August, Denise, **1:181**

Miss Universe Pageant
Quiñones August, Denise, **1:180, 181**

Miss USA Pageant
Carter, Lynda, **4:36–37**

Modeling
Benitez, Elsa, **4:21–22**
Bundchen, Gisele, **2:47–49**
Chávez, Nick, **4:53–55**
Diaz, Cameron, **1:73**

Modern dance
Cisneros, Evelyn, **3:76**

Montreal Expos baseball team
Pérez, Tony, **1:167**

Ms. Olympia (International Federation of Bodybuilding)
McLish, Rachel, **3:151–153**

Murals
Baca, Judith F., **2:21–24**
Rivera, Diego, **2:184, 186–187**
Romero, Alejandro, **2:191–193**

Music. See Bossa nova music; Christian music; Classical music; Folk music; Jazz; Latin Music; Pop music; Rap Music; Rock music; Salsa music; Tejano music

NASA. See National Aeronautics and Space Administration

National Action Party
Fox, Vincente, **1:90–91**

National Aeronautics and Space Administration (NASA)
Chang-Díaz, Franklin R., **2:62–65**
Ocampo, Adriana C., **4:154–157**
Ochoa, Ellen, **1:149–151**

National Association of Hispanic CPAs
Roybal-Allard, Lucille, **3:212–214**

National Broadcasting Company (NBC)
Arrarás, María Celeste, **4:12–14**
O'Brien, Soledad, **1:147–148**

National Democratic Action Party
Bánzer Suárez, Hugo, **1:26–27**

National diving championship
Lucero-Schayes, Wendy, **4:129–131**

National Endowment for the Arts fellowships
Brito, Maria, **4:27**
Cruz, Victor Hernández, **3:82**
Montoya, José, **4:151–152**
Soto, Gary, **4:214**

National Family Caregiver's Support Program (NFCSP)
Carbonell, Josefina G., **2:60**

National Heritage Award
Mendoza, Lydia, **3:159**

National Hispanic Foundation for the Arts
Smits, Jimmy, **3:221–224**

National Hockey League (NHL)
Gomez, Scott, **2:119–120**

National League Most Valuable Player Awards
Cepeda, Orlando, **4:45**

National Public Radio (NPR)
Hinojosa, María de Lourdes, **3:128–130**

Native American issues and culture
Asturias, Miguel Angel, **3:19–21**
Menchú, Rigoberta, **3:154–157**

NBC. See National Broadcasting Company

NCAA diving championship
Lucero-Schayes, Wendy, **4:129–131**

New Jersey Devils hockey team
Gomez, Scott, **2:119–120**

The New Mickey Mouse Club
Aguilera, Christina, **2:1–2**

New York Shakespeare Festival (NYSF)
Juliá, Raúl, **3:137–140**
Smits, Jimmy, **3:221**

New York State Supreme Court
Santaella, Irma Vidal, **4:201–202**

Nobel Prize
Alvarez, Luis Walter, **2:7–9**
Arias Sánchez, Oscar, **3:15, 17**
Asturias, Miguel Angel, **3:19, 21**
García Márquez, Gabriel Jose, **2:112–113**
Menchú, Rigoberta, **3:154–157**
Neruda, Pablo, **2:165, 166**
Pérez Esquivel, Adolfo, **4:170–171**

Nonfiction
Anaya, Rudolfo, **2:13–14**
Arana, Marie, **2:15–17**
Carpentier, Alejo, **3:64–67**
Esquivel, Laura, **1:80–81**
García Márquez, Gabriel Jose, **2:113–114**
Gaviño, Juan Bosch, **4:90–94**
Hinojosa, María de Lourdes, **3:128–130**
Leal, Luis, **4:125–128**
Mares, Michael A., **4:132–134**
Menchú, Rigoberta, **3:154–157**
Paredes, Américo, **3:175–177**
Ramos, Jorge, **2:179**
Santayana, George, **3:215–217**

North Atlantic Free Trade Agreement (NAFTA)
Derbéz Bautista, Luis Ernesto, **2:98**

Noticiero Univisión
Ramos, Jorge, **2:179**

Notre Dame University
Gurulé, Jimmy, **4:99–100**

Oakland Athletics (A's) baseball team
Canseco, José, **3:54–56**
Tejada, Miguel, **3:225–227**

Oceanography
Alvariño, Angeles, **4:4–7**

Olympic Games
Arcain, Janeth, **1:19**
De La Hoya, Oscar, **1:66, 67**
de Varona, Donna, **4:59–61**
Fernández, Mary Joe, **3:94–96**
Garciaparra, Anthony Nomar, **3:106**
Lobo, Rebecca, **3:144–146**
Lucero-Schayes, Wendy, **4:129–131**
Parra, Derek, **1:160, 161**
Rodriguez, Jennifer, **2:188–190**
Sabatini, Gabriela, **4:198–199**
Torres, Dara, **1:206, 207–208**

Opera
Carreras, José, **3:68–70**
Domingo, Plácido, **1:76–78**
Ginastera, Alberto, **3:109–111**
Ronstadt, Linda, **3:208–211**

Orlando Housing Authority
Martínez, Mel, **1:128**

Painting
Baca, Judith F., **2:21–24**
Botero, Fernando, **2:43–46**
Brito, Maria, **4:26–28**
Dalí, Salvador, **1:63–65**
de la Renta, Oscar, **2:87**
Kahlo, Frida, **1:113–115**
Montoya, José, **4:150–153**
Picasso, Pablo, **3:178–180**

Quinn, Anthony, **1:178**
Rivera, Diego, **2:184–187**
Romero, Alejandro, **2:191–193**
Tàpies, Antonio, **4:216–218**

Pan American Games
Arcain, Janeth, **1:19**

Partido de Liberación Nacional (PLN)
Arias Sánchez, Oscar, **3:15–17**

Partido Justicialista
Menem, Carlos Saul, **1:131–133**

Partido Popular
Aznar, José Maria, **1:22, 23**

Partido Revolucionario Institucional (Institutional Revolutionary Party or PRI)
Echeverría Álvarez, Luis, **3:91–93**

Partidos por la Democracia
Lagos, Richard, **4:119–120**

Patriotic music
Rodríguez, Daniel, **3:195–197**

Percussion
E., Sheila, **3:88–90**

Perfumes
Sabatini, Gabriela, **4:198–200**

Philanthropy
Cantinflas, **4:34–35**
Vilar, Alberto, **2:224–227**

Philosophy
Santayana, George, **3:215–217**

Physics
Alvarez, Luis Walter, **2:7–10**
Chang-Díaz, Franklin R., **2:64–65**

Pittsburgh Pirates baseball team
Clemente, Roberto, **2:74–76**

Planetary geology
Ocampo, Adriana C., **4:154–157**

Poetry
Alegría, Claribel Joy, **3:1–4**
Anaya, Rudolfo, **2:13–14**
Chávez, Denise, **2:72**
Cisneros, Sandra, **1:55**
Corpi, Lucha, **2:81–83**
Cruz, Victor Hernández, **3:81–83**
de Moraes, Vinícius, **2:95**
Montoya, José, **4:150–153**
Neruda, Pablo, **2:164–166**
Ortiz Cofer, Judith, **3:171–174**
Paredes, Américo, **3:175–177**
Piñero, Miguel, **2:174–177**
Prida, Delores, **3:181–183**
Soto, Gary, **4:213–215**

Political activism
Amado, Jorge, **3:10**
Baca-Barragán, Polly, **4:15–17**
Baez, Joan, **2:29–33**
Blades, Rubén, **3:26–29**
Carpentier, Alejo, **3:64–67**
Chavez, Linda, **4:48–52**

Colón, Willie, **3:78–80**
de Varona, Donna, **4:60–61**
García, Héctor Pérez, **4:86–89**
Mármol, Miguel, **4:139–142**
Menchú, Rigoberta, **3:154–157**
Ortega, Daniel, **4:162–165**
Pérez Esquivel, Adolfo, **4:170–172**
Restrepo, Laura, **3:187–190**
Wilcox, Mary Rose Garrido, **4:222–225**

Politics, international
Alemán, Arnoldo, **1:2–3**
Arias Sánchez, Oscar, **3:15–18**
Aznar, José Maria, **1:22**
Bánzer Suárez, Hugo, **1:25–28**
Betancourt, Ingrid, **2:40–42**
Blades, Rubén, **3:26–29**
Calderón Sol, Armando, **2:54–57**
Cardoso, Fernando, **1:29–32**
Castro, Fidel, **1:36–39**
Chávez, Hugo, **1:43–46**
de la Rúa, Fernando, **1:70–72**
Echeverría Álvarez, Luis, **3:91–93**
Fox, Vincente, **1:89–91**
Gaviño, Juan Bosch, **4:90–94**
González, Macchi, Luis, **1:95–97**
González Márquez, Felipe, **4:95–97**
Guevara, Ché (Ernesto), **2:129–133**
Juan Carlos de Borbón y Borbón,
  4:115–119
Lagos, Richard, **4:118–121**
Mahaud, Jamil, **2:149–151**
Menem, Carlos Saul, **1:131–133**
Munoz Marin, Luis, **3:167–170**
Ortega, Daniel, **4:162–165**
Perón, Eva "Evita," **1:169, 170–171**
Perón, Juan, **2:170–173**
Richardson, Bill, **4:180–183**

Politics, U.S.
Baca-Barragán, Polly, **4:15–17**
Bustamante, Cruz M., **4:29–32**
Calderón, Sila María, **2:50–53**
Castro, Ida, **1:40–42**
Chavez, Dennis, **3:71–73**
Chavez, Linda, **4:48–52**
González, Henry B., **2:125–128**
Huerta, Dolores, **2:138–139**
Marin, Rosario, **2:152–154**
Munoz Marin, Luis, **3:167–170**
Napolitano, Grace, **1:138–140**
Ortega, Katherine D., **4:166–169**
Richardson, Bill, **4:180–183**
Sanchez, Loretta, **1:187–188**
Wilcox, Mary Rose Garrido, **4:222–225**

Pop music
Anthony, Marc, **3:12–14**
Baez, Joan, **2:29–33**
E., Sheila, **3:88–90**
Estefan, Gloria, **1:82–85**
Guzmán, Alejandra, **4:106–108**
Iglesias, Enrique, **1:108–112**
Iglesias, Julio, **3:131–133**
Lopez, Jennifer, **1:116–119**
Martin, Ricky, **3:147–150**
Orlando, Tony, **4:158–161**
Rodríguez, Daniel, **3:195–197**
Ronstadt, Linda, **3:208–211**
Rubio, Paulina, **4:194–197**

Posters, event-based
Romero, Alejandro, **2:192**

Pritzker Prize
Moneo, Rafael, **4:148–149**

Pro Football Hall of Fame
Munoz, Anthony, **2:162**

Professional Golf Association (PGA)
Rodríguez, Chi Chi, **3:191–194**

Psychology
Estés, Clarissa Pinkola, **4:68–72**

Publishing
Haubegger, Christy, **1:98–100**
Kanellos, Nicholás, **2:141–144**

Puerto Rico, commonwealth status
Munoz Marin, Luis, **3:167–170**

Pulitzer Prize
Hijuelos, Oscar, **1:106**

Race car driving
Montoya, Juan Pablo, **3:164–166**
Senna, Ayrton, **3:218–220**

Rap music
Big Punisher, **4:23–25**

Remote sensing
Ocampo, Adriana C., **4:154–157**

Rock and Roll Hall of Fame
Garcia, Jerry, **3:104**
Valens, Richie, **2:219, 220**

Rock music
Aguilera, Christina, **2:1–3**
Garcia, Jerry, **3:102–105**
Ronstadt, Linda, **3:208–211**
Santana, Carlos, **1:189–191**
Shakira, **1:192, 193–194**
Valens, Richie, **2:218–220**

Roman Catholic Church
Boff, Leonardo, **3:37–40**
Flores, Patrick, **1:86–88**
Perón, Juan, **2:172**
Rodriguez, Carlos Manuel, **4:184–186**

Rookie of the Year (baseball)
Canseco, José, **3:54–56**
Cepeda, Orlando, **4:44**
Garciaparra, Anthony Nomar,
  3:106–107

Royal Ballet of England
Acosta, Carlos, **4:1–3**

Royal Chicano Air Force (RCAF)
Montoya, José, **4:151–152**

Sabado Gigante
Francisco, Don, **4:83–85**

Salsa music
Anthony, Marc, **3:12–14**
Barretto, Ray, **2:34–36**
Blades, Rubén, **3:26–29**
Colón, Willie, **3:78–80**
Cruz, Celia, **1:60–62**
Dunbar, Huey, **4:65–67**

Sánchez, Poncho, **2:194–197**

San Francisco Ballet
Cisneros, Evelyn, **3:74–77**

San Francisco Giants baseball team
Cepeda, Orlando, **4:44**

**Sandanista National Liberation Front
  (FSLN)**
Cardenal, Ernesto, **3:57–60**
Ortega, Daniel, **4:162–165**

Santa Cecelia Orchestra
de Vega, Sonia de León, **2:99–100**

School administration
Caldera, Louis, **3:47–49**
Cisneros, Marc, **4:56–58**
Fernandez, Joseph A., **2:108–110**

School-Based Management
Fernandez, Joseph A., **2:109–110**

School of American Ballet
Alonso, Alicia, **1:11–12**

Science
Alvarez, Luis Walter, **2:7–10**
Alvariño, Angeles, **4:4–7**
Chang-Díaz, Franklin R., **2:62–65**
Dallmeier, Francisco, **3:84–87**
Gómez-Pompa, Arturo, **2:121–124**
Mares, Michael A., **4:132–134**
Ocampo, Adriana C., **4:154–157**

Screen Actors Guild Awards
Juliá, Raúl, **3:138, 140**

Screenplays
Esquivel, Laura, **1:80**

Sculpture
Botero, Fernando, **2:44–45**
Brito, Maria, **4:26–28**
Pérez Esquivel, Adolfo, **4:170–172**
Tapia, Luis, **1:203–205**
Tàpies, Antonio, **4:216–218**

Sears, Roebuck, and Company
Martinez, Arthur C., **4:143–146**

Seattle Mariners baseball team
Rodriquez, Alex, **1:183–184**

**SINA. See Southside Institutions Neigh-
  borhood Association**

**Smithsonian Institution's Monitoring and
  Assessment of Biodiversity Program**
Dallmeier, Francisco, **3:84–87**

Soccer
Maradona, Diego, **1:123–125**

Socialism
González Márquez, Felipe, **4:95–97**

Sociology
Baca Zinn, Maxine, **2:25–28**
Cardoso, Fernando, **1:29–30**

Solentiname Commune
Cardenal, Ernesto, **3:58–59**

Songwriters Hall of Fame
Jobim, Antonio Carlos "Tom," **3:135**

Southside Institutions Neighborhood As-sociation (SINA)
Pérez, Eddie Alberto, **1:164**

Southwest Fisheries Science Center (SWFSC)
Alvariño, Angeles, **4:6**

Space research
Ocampo, Adriana C., **4:154–157**

Space shuttle
Chang-Díaz, Franklin R., **2:63–64**

Spanish dance
Ramirez, Tina, **4:177–179**

Spanish royal family
Juan Carlos de Borbón y Borbón, **4:115–119**

Spanish Socialist Workers Party (PSOE)
González Márquez, Felipe, **4:96–97**

Speedskating
Parra, Derek, **1:160–162**
Rodriguez, Jennifer, **2:188–190**

St. Louis Cardinals baseball team
Cepeda, Orlando, **4:43–45**

Stanley Cup, NHL championship
Gomez, Scott, **2:120**

Storytelling
Estés, Clarissa Pinkola, **4:68–72**

Stunts
Blaine, David, **3:30–32**

Surrealism
Picasso, Pablo, **3:179**

Swimming
de Varona, Donna, **4:59–60**
Torres, Dara, **1:206–207**

Talk shows
Francisco, Don, **4:83–85**
Hinojosa, María de Lourdes, **3:128–130**
Saralegui, Cristina, **2:202–204**

Teaching
Alvarez, Luis Walter, **2:8–9**
Anaya, Rudolfo, **2:11, 12–14**
Baca Zinn, Maxine, **2:27–28**
Chávez, Denise, **2:72**
Corpi, Lucha, **2:82**
Escalante, Jaime, **2:104–107**
Fernandez, Joseph A., **2:108–110**
Huerta, Dolores, **2:138–139**
Kanellos, Nicholás, **2:141–142**

El Teatro Campesino
Valdez, Luis, **1:210–211**

Tejano music
Mendoza, Lydia, **3:158–160**
Selena, **2:205–206**

Telemundo
Arrarás, María Celeste, **4:12–14**

Television news
Arrarás, María Celeste, **4:12–14**
Quiñones, John, **4:173–176**

Television series
Arnaz, Desi, **2:18–20**
Bratt, Benjamin, **3:44–46**
Carter, Lynda, **4:36–39**
Estrada, Erik, **4:73–76**
Lamarque, Libertad, **4:123–124**
Marin, Cheech, **4:136–137**

Television sports broadcasting
de Varona, Donna, **4:59–61**
Fernández, Mary Joe, **3:94–95**

Television variety shows
Francisco, Don, **4:83–85**
Orlando, Tony, **4:156–160**
Rubio, Paulina, **4:194–197**
Smits, Jimmy, **3:221–224**
Thalía, **2:208–209**
Treviño, Jesus Salvador, **2:212–213**

Tennis
Fernández, Mary Joe, **3:94–97**
Gonzales, Richard "Pancho," **3:116–119**
Sabatini, Gabriela, **4:198–200**

Texas A&M University-Kingsville
Cisneros, Marc, **4:57**

Texas Rangers baseball team
Rodriquez, Alex, **1:183, 184**
Sosa, Sammy, **1:200**

Theatre Hall of Fame
Juliá, Raúl, **3:138, 140**

Theology
Boff, Leonardo, **3:37–40**

Three Tenors
Carreras, José, **3:68–69**
Domingo, Placido, **1:76–78**

Timbiriche
Rubio, Paulina, **4:194–197**
Thalía, **2:108–109**

Title IX legislation
de Varona, Donna, **4:59–61**

Tony Awards
Moreno, Rita, **1:134, 136**

Trombone
Colón, Willie, **3:78–80**

Union of Writers and Artists of Cuba
Guillén, Nicolás, **3:122**

United Farm Workers (UFW)
Chávez, César, **2:66, 67–69**
Huerta, Dolores, **2:138–139**

U.S. Administration on Aging
Carbonell, Josefina G., **2:58–61**

U.S. Army
Cavazos, Richard E., **4:40–42**
Cisneros, Marc, **4:56–58**
Valenzuela, Alfred A., **4:219–221**

U.S. Border Patrol
Reyes, Silvestre, **2:181–182**

U.S. Congressional Hispanic Caucus (CHC)
Reyes, Silvestre, **2:183**

U.S. Department of Energy
Richardson, Bill, **4:180–183**

U.S. Department of Health and Human Services
Calderón, Sila María, **2:52**
Carbonell, Josefina G., **2:58**

U.S. Department of Housing and Urban Development
Cisneros, Henry, **1:51–52**
Martínez, Mel, **1:127, 128–130**

U.S. Department of Labor
Castro, Ida, **1:40, 41**

U.S. Equal Employment Opportunity Commission
Castro, Ida, **1:40–41**

U.S. Equal Employment Opportunity Commission (EEOC)
Dominguez, Cari, **2:101–103**

U.S. Figure Skating Association
Galindo, Rudy, **3:98–101**

United States Golf Association (USGA)
Lopez, Nancy, **1:120**

U.S. House of Representatives
Castro, Ida, **1:41**
González, Henry B., **2:125–128**
Napolitano, Grace, **1:138, 139–140**
Reyes, Silvestre, **2:181–183**
Richardson, Bill, **4:180–183**
Ros-Lehtinen, Ileana, **4:191–193**
Roybal-Allard, Lucille, **3:212–214**
Sanchez, Loretta, **1:186, 187–188**
Velázquez, Nydia, **1:217–218**

U.S. Immigration and Naturalization Services (INS)
Reyes, Silvestre, **2:181–182**

U.S. Justice Department
Baird, Lourdes G., **4:18–20**

U.S. Military Academy at West Point
Caldera, Louis, **3:47–49**

U.S. Navy
Calderón, Sila María, **2:50, 51–52**
Hidalgo, Edward, **4:109–111**

U.S. Public Health Service
Novello, Antonia, **1:142, 144–145**

U.S. Senate
Chavez, Dennis, **3:71–73**

U.S. Surgeon General
Carmona, Richard, **3:61–63**

U.S. Treasury
Gurulé, Jimmy, **4:98–101**
Marin, Rosario, **2:152–154**
Ortega, Katherine D., **4:166–169**

University of California
Alvarez, Luis Walter, **2:7–9**

University of New Mexico
Anaya, Rudolfo, **2:13–14**
Baca Zinn, Maxine, **2:26–27**

Univision
Arrarás, María Celeste, **4:12–13**
Francisco, Don, **4:83-85**

USGA. See United States Golf Association

Volunteers in Service to America (VISTA)
Pérez, Eddie Alberto, **1:164**

WNBA. See Women's National Basketball Association

Women's National Basketball Association (WNBA)
Arcain, Janeth, **1:19–20**
Lobo, Rebecca, **3:144–146**

Women's Tennis Association
Fernández, Mary Joe, **3:94–97**

World Bank
Derbéz Bautista, Luis Ernesto, **2:96, 97**

World Cup
Maradona, Diego, **1:124–125**

World featherweight boxing championship
Sardiñas, Eligio, **4:203–204**

World Series Championship (baseball)
Cepeda, Orlando, **4:43–47**

World Team Tennis
Fernández, Mary Joe, **3:94–97**

Writing. See Drama; Essays; Fiction; Journalism; Nonfiction; Poetry

Zooplankton
Alvariño, Angeles, **4:4–7**

Cumulative Name Index

Volume and page numbers appear in **bold**.

A

Acosta, Carlos, **4:1–3**
Aguilera, Christina, **2:1–3**
Alegría, Claribel Joy, **3:1–4**
Alemán, Arnoldo, **1:1–3**
Allende, Isabel, **1:4–6**
Almendros, Nestor, **2:4–6**
Almodóvar, Pedro, **1:7–10**
Alonso, Alicia, **1:11–14**
Alvarado, Linda, **3:5–8**
Alvarez, Julia, **1:15–18**
Alvarez, Luis Walter, **2:7–10**
Alvariño, Angeles, **4:4–7**
Amado, Jorge, **3:9–11**
Anaya, Rudolfo, **2:11–14**
Anthony, Marc, **3:12–14**
Arana, Marie, **2:15–17**
Arcain, Janeth, **1:19–21**
Arenas, Reinaldo, **4:8–11**
Arias Sánchez, Oscar, **3:15–18**
Arnaz, Desi, **2:18–20**
Arrarás, María Celeste, **4:12–14**
Asturias, Miguel Angel, **3:19–21**
Aznar, José Maria, **1:22–24**

B

Baca, Judith F., **2:21–24**
Baca Zinn, Maxine, **2:25–28**
Baca-Barragán, Polly, **4:15–17**
Baez, Joan, **2:29–33**
Baird, Lourdes G., **4:18–20**
Banderas, Antonio, **3:22–25**
Bánzer Suárez, Hugo, **1:25–28**
Barretto, Ray, **2:34–36**
Benitez, Elsa, **4:21–22**
Bermúdez, Carmen, **2:37–39**
Betancourt, Ingrid, **2:40–42**
Big Punisher, **4:23–25**
Blades, Rubén, **3:26–29**
Blaine, David, **3:30–32**
Bocca, Julio, **3:33–36**
Boff, Leonardo, **3:37–40**
Botero, Fernando, **2:43–46**
Braga, Sonia, **3:41–43**
Bratt, Benjamin, **3:44–46**
Brito, Maria, **4:26–28**
Bundchen, Gisele, **2:47–49**
Bustamante, Cruz M., **4:29–32**

C

Caldera, Louis, **3:47–49**
Calderón, Sila María, **2:50–53**
Calderón Sol, Armando, **2:54–57**
Camacho, Hector, **3:50–53**
Canseco, José, **3:54–56**
Cantinflas, **4:33–35**
Carbonell, Josefina G., **2:58–61**
Cardenal, Ernesto, **3:57–60**
Cardoso, Fernando, **1:29–32**
Carmona, Richard, **3:61–63**
Carpentier, Alejo, **3:64–67**
Carreras, José, **3:68–70**
Carter, Lynda, **4:36–39**
Castillo, Ana, **1:33–35**
Castro, Fidel, **1:36–39**
Castro, Ida, **1:40–42**
Cavazos, Richard E., **4:40–42**
Cepeda, Orlando, **4:43–47**
Chang-Díaz, Franklin R., **2:62–65**
Chávez, César, **2:66–69**
Chávez, Denise, **2:70–73**
Chavez, Dennis, **3:71–73**
Chávez, Hugo, **1:43–46**
Chavez, Linda, **4:48–52**
Chávez, Nick, **4:53–55**
Chavez-Thompson, Linda, **1:47–49**
Cisneros, Evelyn, **3:74–77**
Cisneros, Henry, **1:50–52**
Cisneros, Marc, **4:56–58**
Cisneros, Sandra, **1:53–56**
Clemente, Roberto, **2:74–76**
Coca, Imogene, **2:77–80**
Colón, Willie, **3:78–80**
Corona, Bert, **1:57–59**
Corpi, Lucha, **2:81–83**
Cruz, Celia, **1:60–62**
Cruz, Victor Hernández, **3:81–83**
Cugat, Xavier, **84–86**

D

Dalí, Salvador, **1:63–65**
Dallmeier, Francisco, **3:84–87**
De La Hoya, Oscar, **1:66–69**
de la Renta, Oscar, **2:87–89**
de la Rúa, Fernando, **1:70–72**
de Leira, Angeles Alvariño. See Alvariño, Angeles
de Moraes, Vinícius, **2:93–95**
de Varona, Donna, **4:59–61**
de Vega, Sonia de León, **2:99–100**
Del Toro, Benicio, **2:90–92**

Derbéz Bautista, Luis Ernesto, **2:96–98**
Diaz, Cameron, **1:73–75**
Díaz-Oliver, Remedios, **4:62–64**
Domingo, Plácido, **1:76–78**
Dominguez, Cari, **2:101–103**
Dunbar, Huey, **4:65–67**

E

E., Sheila, **3:88–90**
Echeverría Álvarez, Luis, **3:91–93**
Escalante, Jaime, **2:104–107**
Escovedo, Sheila. See E., Sheila
Esquivel, Laura, **1:79–81**
Estefan, Gloria, **1:82–85**
Estés, Clarissa Pinkola, **4:68–72**
Estevez, Ramon. See Sheen, Martin
Estrada, Erik, **4:73–76**

F

Favaloro, Rene, **4:77–79**
Fernández, Emilio "El Indio," **4:80–82**
Fernandez, Joseph A., **2:108–110**
Fernández, Mary Joe, **3:94–97**
Flores, Patrick, **1:86–88**
Fox, Vincente, **1:89–91**
Francisco, Don, **4:83–85**
Fuentes, Carlos, **1:92–94**

G

Galindo, Rudy, **3:98–101**
García, Héctor Pérez, **4:86–89**
Garcia, Jerry, **3:102–105**
García Márquez, Gabriel Jose, **2:111–115**
Garciaparra, Anthony Nomar, **3:106–108**
Gaviño, Juan Bosch, **4:90–94**
Gilberto, João, **2:116–118**
Ginastera, Alberto, **3:109–111**
Goizueta, Roberto Crispulo, **3:112–115**
Gomez, Scott, **2:119–120**
Gómez-Pompa, Arturo, **2:121–124**
Gonzales, Richard "Pancho," **3:116–119**
González, Henry B., **2:125–128**
González, Macchi, Luis, **1:95–97**
González Márquez, Felipe, **4:95–97**
Guevara, Ché (Ernesto), **2:129–133**
Guillén, Nicolás, **3:120–123**
Gurulé, Jimmy, **4:98–101**

Gutierrez, Carlos M., **4:102–105**
Guzmán, Alejandra, **4:106–108**

H

Haubegger, Christy, **1:98–101**
Hayek, Salma, **2:134–137**
Hayworth, Rita, **1:102–104**
Herrera, Carolina, **3:124–127**
Hidalgo, Edward, **4:109–111**
Hijuelos, Oscar, **1:105–107**
Hinojosa, María de Lourdes, **3:128–130**
Huerta, Dolores, **2:138–140**

I

Iglesias, Enrique, **1:108–112**
Iglesias, Julio, **3:131–133**
Infante, Pedro, **4:112–114**

J

Jobim, Antonio Carlos "Tom,"
3:134–136
Juan Carlos de Borbón y Borbón,
4:115–117
Juliá, Raúl, **3:137–140**

K

Kahlo, Frida, **1:113–115**
Kanellos, Nicholás, **2:141–144**
Kreutzberger, Mario, See Francisco,
Don

L

Lagos, Richard, **4:118–121**
Lamarque, Libertad, **4:122–124**
Leal, Luis, **4:125–128**
Leguizamo, John, **3:141–143**
Lobo, Rebecca, **3:144–146**
Lopez, Jennifer, **1:116–119**
Lopez, Nancy, **1:120–122**
Lucero-Schayes, Wendy, **4:129–131**

M

Machado, Eduardo, **2:145–148**
Mahaud, Jamil, **2:149–151**
Maradona, Diego, **1:123–126**
Mares, Michael A., **4:132–134**
Marin, Cheech, **4:135–138**
Marin, Rosario, **2:152–154**
Mármol, Miguel, **4:139–142**
Martin, Ricky, **3:147–150**
Martinez, Arthur C., **4:143–146**
Martínez, Mel, **1:127–130**
McLish, Rachel, **3:151–153**
Menchú, Rigoberta, **3:154–157**
Mendes, Sérgio, **2:155–157**
Mendoza, Lydia, **3:158–160**
Menem, Carlos Saul, **1:131–133**
Mohr, Nicholasa, **2:158–160**

Moneo, Rafael, **4:147–149**
Montoya, Carlos García, **3:161–163**
Montoya, José, **4:150–153**
Montoya, Juan Pablo, **3:164–166**
Moraes, Vinícius de. See de Moraes,
Vinícius
Moreno, Rita, **1:134–137**
Muniz, Marco Antonio. See Anthony,
Marc
Munoz, Anthony, **2:161–163**
Munoz Marin, Luis, **3:167–170**

N

Napolitano, Grace, **1:138–141**
Neruda, Pablo, 2:40, **164–166**
Novello, Antonia, **1:142–145**

O

O'Brien, Soledad, **1:146–148**
Ocampo, Adriana C., **4:154–157**
Ochoa, Ellen, **1:149–151**
O'Farrill, Arturo "Chico," **1:152–154**
Olmos, Edward James, **1:155–159**
Orlando, Tony, **4:158–161**
Ortega, Daniel, **4:162–165**
Ortega, Katherine D., **4:166–169**
Ortiz Cofer, Judith, **3:171–174**

P

Paredes, Américo, **3:175–177**
Parra, Derek, **1:160–162**
Pelli, César, **2:167–169**
Pérez, Eddie Alberto, **1:163–165**
Pérez, Tony, **1:166–168**
Pérez Esquivel, Adolfo, **4:170–172**
Perón, Eva "Evita," **1:169–171**
Perón, Juan, **2:170–173**
Picasso, Pablo, **3:178–180**
Piñero, Miguel, **2:174–177**
Prida, Delores, **3:181–183**
Prinze, Freddie, Jr., **3:184–186**
Puente, Tito, **1:172–175**

Q

Quinn, Anthony, **1:176–179**
Quiñones, John, **4:173–176**
Quiñones August, Denise, **1:180–182**
Quintanilla, Selena. See Selena

R

Ramirez, Tina, **4:177–179**
Ramos, Jorge, **2:178–180**
Restrepo, Laura, **3:187–190**
Reyes, Mario Moreno. See Cantinflas
Reyes, Silvestre, **2:181–183**
Richardson, Bill, **4:180–183**
Rios, Christopher. See Big Punisher
Rivera, Diego, **2:184–187**

Rodriguez, Alex, **1:183–185**
Rodriguez, Carlos Manuel, **4:184–186**
Rodríguez, Chi Chi, **3:191–194**
Rodríguez, Daniel, **3:195–197**
Rodriguez, Jennifer, **2:188–190**
Rodríguez, Narciso, **3:198–200**
Rodriguez, Robert, **3:201–203**
Roman, Phil, **4:187–190**
Romero, Alejandro, **2:191–193**
Romero, Cesar, **3:204–207**
Ronstadt, Linda, **3:208–211**
Ros-Lehtinen, Ileana, **4:191–193**
Roybal-Allard, Lucille, **3:212–214**
Rubio, Paulina, **4:194–197**

S

Sabatini, Gabriela, **4:198–200**
Sanchez, Loretta, **1:186–188**
Sánchez, Poncho, **2:194–197**
Sandoval, Arturo, **2:198–200**
Santaella, Irma Vidal, **4:201–202**
Santana, Carlos, **1:189–191**
Santayana, George, **3:215–217**
Saralegui, Cristina, **2:201–204**
Sardiñas, Eligio, **4:203–204**
Selena, **2:205–207**
Senna, Ayrton, **3:218–220**
Serrano, Lupe, **4:205–208**
Shakira, **1:192–194**
Sheen, Charlie, **4:209–212**
Sheen, Martin, **1:195–198**
Smits, Jimmy, **3:221–224**
Sodi y Miranda, Ariadne Thalía. See
Thalía
Sosa, Sammy, **1:199–202**
Soto, Gary, **4:213–215**

T

Tapia, Luis, **1:203–205**
Tàpies, Antonio, **4:216–218**
Tejada, Miguel, **3:225–227**
Thalía, **2:208–211**
Torres, Dara, **1:206–209**
Treviño, Jesus Salvador, **2:212–214**

V

Valdés, Jésus "Chucho," **2:215–217**
Valdez, Luis, **1:210–212**
Valens, Richie, **2:218–220**
Valenzuela, Alfred A., **4:219–221**
Valenzuela, Richard Steven. See Valens,
Richie
Vargas Llosa, Mario, **1:213–215**
Velasquez, Jaci, **2:221–223**
Velázquez, Nydia, **1:216–218**
Vilar, Alberto, **2:223–227**

W

Welch, Raquel, **1:219–221**
Wilcox, Mary Rose Garrido, **4:222–225**